Cross-Border Enforcement in Europe: National and International Perspectives

This publication has been produced with the financial support of the Justice Programme of the European Union. The contents of this publication are the sole responsibility of authors and can in no way be taken to reflect the views of the European Commission.

With the support of
the Civil Justice Programme
of the European Union

Editors:
V. Rijavec
K. Drnovšek
C.H. van Rhee

Cross-Border Enforcement in Europe: National and International Perspectives

INTERSENTIA
Cambridge – Antwerp – Portland

Intersentia Ltd
8 Wellington Mews
Wellington Street | Cambridge
CB1 1HW | United Kingdom
Tel: +44 1223 736 170
Email: mail@intersentia.co.uk
www.intersentia.com | www.intersentia.co.uk

Distribution for the UK and Rest of the World (incl. Eastern Europe)
NBN International
1 Deltic Avenue, Rooksley
Milton Keynes MK13 8LD
United Kingdom
Tel: +44 1752 202 301 | Fax: +44 1752 202 331
Email: orders@nbninternational.com

Distribution for Europe
Intersentia Publishing nv
Groenstraat 31
2640 Mortsel
Belgium
Tel: +32 3 680 15 50
Email: mail@intersentia.be

Distribution for the USA and Canada
Independent Publishers Group
Order Department
814 North Franklin Street
Chicago, IL 60610
USA
Tel: +1 800 888 4741 (toll free) | Fax: +1 312 337 5985
Email: orders@ipgbook.com

Cover photo by Steve Johnson from Pexels

ISBN 978-1-78068-777-3
D/2020/7849/82
NUR 828

British Library Cataloguing in Publication Data. A catalogue record for this book is available from the British Library.

ACKNOWLEDGEMENTS

The editors would like to express their gratitude to everyone that participated in the project 'BIARE' (Remedies concerning Enforcement of Foreign Judgements according to Brussels I Recast) and contributed to its results, including this volume.

Special thanks to Randolph Davidson (Novi Liguri) for his efforts in finalizing and double-checking the English, as well as to all authors for their research input and contributions to this volume. It is hoped and expected that the results of the project will be useful to practitioners and stimulate further research into the area of cross-border enforcement in Europe and beyond.

TABLE OF CONTENTS

LIST OF AUTHORS

Denis Baghrizabehi, Research and Teaching Assistant, Faculty of Law, University of Maribor (Slovenia)

Katja Drnovšek, Teaching Assistant, Faculty of Law, University of Maribor (Slovenia)

Fokke Fernhout, Associate Professor of Procedural Law, Faculty of Law, Maastricht University (Netherlands)

Andrea Giussani, Full Professor of Civil Procedure, Director of the post-graduate School for the Legal Professions, University of Urbino (Italy)

Tjaša Ivanc, Associate Professor, Institute for Civil, Comparative and International Private Law, Faculty of Law, University of Maribor (Slovenia)

Wendy Kennett, Senior Lecturer in Law, School of Law and Politics, Cardiff University (Wales)

Tomaž Keresteš, Institute for Civil, Comparative and International Private Law, Faculty of Law, University of Maribor (Slovenia)

Suzana Kraljić, Associate Professor, Head of Center for Medical Law, Faculty of Law, University of Maribor (Slovenia)

Tereza Kyselovská, Assistant Professor, Department of International and European Law, Faculty of Law, Masaryk University (Czech Republic)

Walter H. Rechberger, Professor emeritus at the Institute for Civil Procedure Law, Head of the Research Institute for Legal Development, Faculty of Law, University of Vienna (Austria)

Vesna Rijavec, Full Professor, Institute for Civil, Comparative and International Private Law, Faculty of Law, University of Maribor (Slovenia)

Jiří Valdhans, Assistant Professor, Department of International and European Law, Faculty of Law, Masaryk University (Czech Republic)

C.H. (Remco) van Rhee, Professor of Comparative Civil Procedure, Director of the Program on Foundations and Principles of Civil Procedure, Ius Commune Research School, Faculty of Law, Maastricht University (Netherlands)

Tatjana Zoroska Kamilovska, Professor, Head of the Chair of Civil Procedure Law, Faculty of Law, Ss. Cyril and Methodius University, Skopje (North Macedonia)

LIST OF ABBREVIATIONS

AJA	Administration of Justice Act
BIR	Brussels I Recast Regulation
CA	Courts Act
CCBE	Council of Bars and Law Societies of Europe
CCP	Code of Civil Procedure
CEPEJ	European Commission for the Efficiency of Justice
CJEU	Court of Justice of the European Union
CMR	Convention on the Contract for the International Carriage of Goods by Road
CNUE	Conseil des Notariats de l'Union européenne
COTIF	Convention concerning International Carriage by Rail
CPA	Civil Procedure Act
CSES	Center for Strategy and Evaluation Services
CZK	Czech koruna
DBAOD	Dutch Bulletin of Acts, Orders and Decrees
EA	Enforcement Act
EC	European Community/ies
EC Treaty	Treaty Establishing the European Community
ECHR	European Convention on Human Rights
ECJ	European Court of Justice
ECR	European Court Reports
ECtHR	European Court of Human Rights
EEA	European Economic Area
EEO	European Enforcement Order
EEX	Brussels Convention [1968] on Jurisdiction and the Enforcement of Judgments in Civil and Commercial Matters
EFTA	European Free Trade Agreement
EJN	European Judicial Network
EMU	Economic and Monetary Union
ENP	École Nationale de Procédure
ESCCA	Enforcement and Securing of Civil Claims Act
EU	European Union

FJ(RE)A	Foreign Judgments (Reciprocal Enforcement) Act
FPRY	Federal People's Republic of Yugoslavia
HR	Hoge Raad (Supreme Court of the Netherlands)
IAB IA	Implementation Act EU-Execution Regulation and Lugano Convention
KEI	Kwaliteit en Innovatie (Quality and Innovation)
PILA	Private International Law Act
PILPA	Private International Law and Procedure Act
RaTG	Rechtsanwaltstarifgesetz
Rb	Rechtbank (Dutch Court of First Instance)
RM	Republic of Macedonia
RS	Republic of Slovenia
SFRY	Socialist Federal Republic of Yugoslavia
SPJ	Summary Proceedings Judge
TEU	Treaty on European Union
TFEU	Treaty on the Functioning of the European Union
UIHJ	International Union of Judicial Officers
UK	United Kingdom
US	United States
USC	United States Code
USCA	United States Code Annotated
VAT	value added tax
ZPO	Zivilprozessordnung (German Code of Civil Procedure)

C.H. van Rhee

INTRODUCTION

Timely and effective enforcement of judgments and other enforceable documents is the backbone of any civil justice system. Without timely and effective enforcement, the administration of justice becomes problematic and the rule of law is put under threat. A slow and ineffective enforcement system may induce creditors to take the law into their own hands, while debtors may be encouraged not to pay their debts.

The present volume addresses enforcement from a cross-border perspective (Part 1) and a national perspective (Part 2).

Part 1 focuses on Brussels I Recast (BIR hereafter). It opens with the contribution by Denis Baghrizabehi comparing the abolition of exequatur under BIR with the US experience of enforcement in the context of judicial federalism. In the European Union, cross-border enforcement is based on the mutual recognition and free movement of judgments, whereas interstate enforcement in the United States is based on the constitutional 'Full Faith and Credit Clause' (diversity jurisdiction). This clause obliges the US State courts to treat judgments from another State in the same way as judgments from the State of enforcement, subject to requirements of due process. The author notes that the EU may be heading towards an approach to matters that is similar to that in the US. In order to explain this, in the first part of his contribution Baghrizabehi provides an overview of judicial federalism in the EU and the US (obviously, where it concerns the EU, 'federalism' is only tentatively the suitable term). In the second part of his contribution his attention shifts to the procedural autonomy of the EU Member States and the application of federal law in the US courts, and in the final part he addresses cross-border enforcement in the EU and interstate enforcement in the US. The starting point of the contribution is that in the United States the State courts are presumed to favour State interests, while the federal courts are presumed to give priority to those of the nation. In that context the author asks whether the courts of the EU Member States may also be presumed to be biased. Baghrizabehi is of the opinion that a limited faith and credit clause may be read in BIR and other EU instruments dealing with cross-border enforcement in civil and commercial matters. However, the introduction of a full faith and credit clause in the EU would in his opinion require a properly worded legislative 'clause' that unifies all of the existing EU regulations on topics of civil and commercial matters under one umbrella regulation.

Part I continues with contributions by Katja Drnovšek and Andrea Giussani dealing with specific aspects of the abolition of exequatur and two important grounds for refusal of foreign judgments under BIR – public order and conflicting decisions. The European Commission based its justification of the abolition of exequatur under BIR on political and economic grounds. The political grounds can be summarized under the heading of mutual trust and do not need much explanation (even though mutual trust may be more aspirational in nature than a reality), but the economic grounds do. Drnovšek discusses them in depth, finding that the reliability of statistical data used in economic arguments is fairly unreliable. The financial impact of the abolition of exequatur is in her opinion grossly overstated. Various authors have noted that the savings related to this abolition are not as significant as the Commission estimated. Some commentators have even found that other measures are more significant for reducing costs and shortening delays: new rules on jurisdiction, the promotion of arbitration agreements, abolition of the requirement for the party seeking enforcement to have a postal address or an authorized representative in the Member State of enforcement, as well as the changes relating to the translation of documents. In this context, the author analyses data collected in the EU project 'Remedies concerning Enforcement of Foreign Judgments according to Brussels I Recast' (which gave rise to the present volume): Austria, the Czech Republic, Italy, Lithuania and Sweden.

Andrea Giussani concentrates on the differences that remain in the rules governing the refusal of the recognition of foreign judgments, both judgments originating in other EU Member States governed by BIR and judgments originating elsewhere. He highlights the following grounds for refusal of recognition: (1) procedural public order, (2) substantive public order and (3) conflicting decisions. Where it concerns procedural public order, he notes that differences between the Member States may be limited due to a growing convergence as regards fundamental procedural rights. Substantive public order may be more problematic, but even in that area differences have become less pronounced, for example where it concerns the recognition of punitive damages. However, recognition in the case of conflicting decisions is complex. The author examines various situations in which conflicting decisions may give rise to problems, paying particular attention to (a) the preclusive effects of *lis pendens* and (b) *res judicata*. Giussani concludes that the task of granting decisions identical effects in Europe might require a European federal judiciary, a type of judiciary that within the present context is politically unacceptable for the Member States.

The two concluding contributions in Part 1 deal with the cross-border enforcement of public documents (Walter Rechberger) and BIR's sister regulation Brussels II bis dealing with jurisdiction and the recognition and enforcement of judgments in matrimonial matters and the matters of parental responsibility (Suzana Kraljić). Rechberger introduces Regulation (EU) 2016/1191 of the European Parliament and of the Council of 6 July 2016 on promoting the free movement of citizens by simplifying the requirements for presenting certain public documents in the European Union. The author states that granting foreign authentic documents the same judicial effect abroad as national authentic documents (similar to what happens under BIR with foreign judgments) is not possible since public documents have neither any *res judicata* effect nor a declaratory character. Rechberger asserts that the recognition of public documents abroad can be better defined as an extension of the substantive constitutive effect of the document in the country of origin to the state of enforcement. The public documents regulation provides that public documents cannot give rise to more rights abroad than in the state of origin, nor have more legal effects abroad than public documents of the accepting state.

At the close of Part 1, Suzana Kraljić observes that Brussels II bis on jurisdiction and the recognition and enforcement of judgments in matrimonial matters is the first European Regulation to abolish exequatur, albeit only for decisions concerning access rights and decisions determining the return of the child in cases of parental abduction. She also observes that in this sense Brussels II bis is more extensive and bolder than its predecessor. Moreover, it aims at the abolition of the remaining obstacles to the free movement of judgments in accordance with the principle of mutual recognition of decisions. Kraljić feels that Brussels II bis provides for additional improvement of the protection of the child's best interests by way of simpler procedures and an increase in their effectiveness. Since Brussels II bis impacts family relations between parents and children in fundamental ways, she holds that the influence of the further abolition of exequatur on human rights has to be researched. Procedural safeguards such as the right to a fair trial need to be upheld and common minimum standards will have immense importance. These standards should provide the guarantee of equivalent procedural protection, as well as the protection of fundamental rights, and should build on the further efficiency of judicial cooperation between the EU Member States. If indeed such standards are guaranteed, the Commission proposal for a Brussels II bis Recast should, in Kraljić's view, extend the abolition of exequatur to the other types of decisions mentioned in the present regulation.

Part II of the volume is devoted to the national perspective. The contributions discuss aspects of national rules on (cross-border) enforcement in a selection of European states: Poland, the Czech Republic, the Netherlands, Slovenia and the Republic of North Macedonia. Their focus is on, amongst other issues, the authorities entrusted with enforcement, judicial assistance and national enforcement rules relevant from the perspective of BIR.

In the first contribution to Part II Wendy Kennett introduces a legal transplant, namely the introduction of the judicial officer (bailiff) in Poland and the Czech Republic. The author shows that legal transplants may have an effect entirely different from that originally anticipated and this occurs, in her view, due to the political, legal and social culture surrounding the transplant. As regards judicial officers, the transplant in Poland and the Czech Republic has given rise to a judicial officer model that is very different from the model in the states of origin (especially France, Belgium and the Netherlands) and that can be qualified as truly domestic. It seems that only the concept of the judicial officer has been transplanted, and that features of the pre-existing legal culture have had a particularly strong effect on the creation of the institution. Ideas from the court-based model of enforcement (e.g. the role of the courts in enforcement and the idea that enforcement agents are public civil servants), still seem to play a preponderant role in the two jurisdictions mentioned, and this makes the judicial officer model less effective. In Poland and the Czech Republic, ideas rooted in tradition have a huge impact on questions of competition and the range of competences that are appropriate for judicial officers, and that also make the professional body of judicial officers rather weak in negotiations with the government.

In the second contribution, Jiří Valdhans and Tereza Kyselovská study the basic underlying principles of recognition and enforcement of foreign judgments in the Czech Republic. They give special attention to the recognition and enforcement of judgments coming to the Czech Republic from third, non-member states of the European Union, and they discuss the relevant Czech private international law rules and procedural rules on enforcement. One interesting Czech rule is that creditors are not permitted to use the services of judicial officers in cases of monetary foreign judgments from third countries (in the Czech Republic, a court-based system of enforcement is used next to the judicial officer model). The authors underline that, as elsewhere, the procedure of enforcement is regulated by national rules only and that there are no uniform international legal regulations that address enforcement itself. They also discuss the grounds for refusal of recognition of foreign judgments from non-BIR states in the Czech Republic, and they compare these grounds with those in BIR. Valdhans and Kyselovská note that the main difference between BIR and the Czech rules concerns reciprocity as a ground for recognition and enforcement.

The contribution by Fokke Fernhout concentrates on enforcement in the Netherlands, both under BIR and as regards titles from third countries. The author provides an overview of what can be expected when enforcement of a foreign title regarding a monetary claim is sought in the Netherlands. Since the Netherlands uses the judicial officer model, no court interference is needed to enforce a title as long as this title has been issued by the designated authorities. It is the judicial officer who is authorized to take all necessary steps, and this gives rise to a system of enforcement that is private. Fernhout explains that there are three methods of enforcement of titles regarding monetary claims in the Netherlands: (1) attachment of assets, (2) attachment of ready money, and (3) garnishment of claims of the debtor on a third party. There is an exception to this rule for a specific type of monetary claim (payment of maintenance) where an additional means of enforcement is available, namely civil imprisonment. The Dutch procedure of enforcement is governed by various important underlying principles, such as the principle of efficiency and the protection of the debtor against unwarranted enforcement. To some readers these principles may seem contradictory, but in actual practice in the Netherlands this is not the case. The author comes to the conclusion that the Dutch system is flexible, fast and relatively cheap.

Tjaša Ivanc takes the reader both to Brussels and to Slovenia in her contribution. The author examines the rules on the recognition and enforcement of civil and commercial judgments under BIR and the changes introduced by BIR when compared to the previous regulation. In addition, she discusses the implications of both BIR and the identified changes for Slovenia and the Slovenian enforcement system (ie a court-based system). Specific attention is given to the procedural aspects of refusal of recognition and enforcement and the features of Slovenian law in this respect. The author also examines the rules on suspension of enforceability and the limitations on protective measures as foreseen by BIR. Ivanc concludes that it would be helpful if there were minimum harmonization of enforcement procedures in Europe and if national and international grounds for non-enforcement under BIR could be considered in the same set of (national) proceedings.

In the fifth contribution Vesna Rijavec and Tomaž Keresteš deal with international legal assistance, especially from the perspective of Slovenian law. The authors define this assistance as the cooperation between courts in situations where official acts are carried out for the purpose of civil litigation in the territory of a court of another state. This comprises the enforcement of civil judgments outside the territory of the state where the judgment originates. Topics explored are the legal bases of international legal assistance, the format and content of requests for the assistance, language restrictions, the way the request for assistance is handled by the requested state or court, as well as costs. The types of international cooperation that they focus on include cross-border service, cross-border acquisition of evidence, the cross-border use of public documents, and recognition and enforcement of foreign judgments.

Part II concludes with the contribution by Tatjana Zoroska-Kamilovska who takes the reader to North Macedonia, a state which is currently not a Member State of the European Union and therefore not subject to BIR. The country hopes to join the EU in the foreseeable future, and it is with that aspiration as background that she discusses the North Macedonian law of enforcement, also from the perspective of changes that are needed when BIR becomes applicable. The author explains that North Macedonia introduced judicial officers in 2005 and that these officers are in charge of the enforcement of foreign judgments. Leave from the court to enforce enforceable titles has been abolished in Macedonia, and for foreign judgments the absence of reciprocity is not a ground to refuse enforcement anymore. The current law also states that the merits of the foreign judgment should not be reviewed by the Macedonian court. Zoroska-Kamilovska is of the opinion that extensive changes to Macedonian enforcement proceedings are not needed for the purposes of the introduction of BIR. She believes, however, that efforts are needed in the field of training and the expertise of Macedonian judges and judicial officers, because it seems that at the moment their level of expertise for cross-border enforcement is insufficient.

I. Cross-border Enforcement in Europe

D. Baghrizabehi

UNDERSTANDING CROSS-BORDER ENFORCEMENT AGAINST THE BACKDROP OF JUDICIAL FEDERALISM AND PROCEDURAL AUTONOMY: ANY USEFUL CUES FROM THE UNITED STATES?

1. Introduction

With the coming into effect of the Brussels I Recast Regulation[1] (hereinafter BIR), cross-border enforcement of judgments in civil and commercial matters has shifted from a model providing for exequatur to a model which (nominally)[2] abolishes exequatur. Even though European Union (EU) legislation provided several instruments abolishing exequatur prior to the introduction of BIR, the latter marks a stepping stone in the evolution of the Brussels regime[3] and profoundly strengthens mutual trust in cross-border proceedings overall. At the very least, BIR 'requires' mutual trust to establish and maintain the envisaged system of mutual recognition and enforcement of judgments. The achievement of BIR is nothing shy of remarkable, considering BIR's respect for national law, i.e. the preserved (and in certain cases expanded) scope of procedural (remedial) autonomy.

While the EU's system of cross-border enforcement rests on the principles of mutual recognition and the free movement of judgments,[4] the functioning of interstate enforcement in the United States (US) hinges on constitutional grounds, i.e. the Full Faith and Credit Clause.[5]

1 Regulation (EU) No. 1215/2012 of the European Parliament and of the Council of 12 December 2012 on jurisdiction and the recognition and enforcement of judgments in civil and commercial matters (recast).

2 It can be said to still provide an 'inverse-exequatur'; see Section 4.2 below.

3 The Brussels regime in said context refers to BIR, its predecessor and the Lugano Convention.

4 The principle of the free movement of judgments is independent of the realisation and good functioning of the internal market, however, still not fully independent. Article 81 TFEU provides that EU legislative measures shall be adopted, particularly when necessary for the proper functioning of the internal market. A subsidiary but necessary link thus remains. Cuniberti & Rueda 2016, p. 837.

5 Prior to the adoption of the Articles of Confederation by the colonies, the courts of each colony, in the absence of a statute providing otherwise, regarded the judgments of the courts of the other colonies as foreign judgments, and so only *prima facie* evidence of the matter →

The two legal systems differ in several aspects. However, they also share similarities, which are comparable in quality and worth comparing in value,[6] seeing how the legislative and judicial landscape of EU cross-border enforcement is subject to constant challenges and change. If BIR is any indication of future developments in the field of judicial cooperation in civil matters, then one ought to (at least) expect development geared towards a regulation similar to that of a full faith and credit clause.[7] Taking this into account, a comparison of the two systems ought to be undertaken in a holistic manner, since cross-border enforcement is merely a cog in an overarching mechanism comprising (*inter alia*) judicial federalism and procedural autonomy (the 'enforcement of (federal)[8] law'). A proper comparison thus entails a broadened comparative analysis.

This contribution attempts to provide an understanding of the underlying mechanism of the EU system of cross-border enforcement and its prospects through the prism of a comparable (US) system and through the looking-glass of enforcing 'federal' law. The first part of the contribution provides an overview of judicial federalism in both entities. The second part focuses on the procedural autonomy of EU Member States and the application of federal law in US courts. The last portion concerns itself with cross-border enforcement in the EU and interstate enforcement in the US.

For the purposes of this contribution, concessions must be made due to the sheer scope of the research topic. Some issues of grandeur, pertaining particularly to matters of constitutional law and polity, shall be left aside. Those issues are best left to constitutional lawyers and social scientists. This contribution will attempt to provide a more 'proceduralist' outlook. In that vein, the purpose of the contribution at hand is not to furnish a recommendation for future action or a complete picture of the research topic, but to advance discussion of cross-border enforcement (and intra-EU litigation at large) in the vertical dimensions of EU law (finding its footing in the EU's quasi-federal structures).[9] The interplay of the described factors seems

adjudged. Such judgments could be re-examined on their merits. When the Articles of Confederation were adopted, the framers realised that the judgments of each colony must be allowed greater force in the other colonies, so they inserted a 'full faith and credit clause' that was later facilitated in the US Constitution. See O'Neill 1930, p. 199.

6 Some commentators dispute the idea that EU and US (judicial) federalism are comparable, as the EU example is a *sui generis* one, whereas the US example is unique in that it is not centred solely on the federal power to have control over the states but also on the power to directly address the legal position of all citizens. Accetto, however, points out that the two systems are in fact comparable, since EU measures are not intended solely to address the Member states but also to have effect in them; see Accetto 2007, p. 72-73. In addition, the powers of Congress include (*inter alia*) the power to regulate commerce among the several states, which is comparable to the EU conferred competence on the regulation of the internal market.

7 Haibach 2003, p. 299.

8 For the purposes of this contribution, 'federal' will equate to EU law, meaning those measures that have been drafted by the EU legislator.

9 According to some authors the EU lacks the constitutive elements of a federal state, hence the description of the EU as a 'quasi-federation' is often used; see Vila Maior 2009, p. 14. The EU, however, generally does fall under the standard definition of federalism in constitutional theory; see Young 2018, p. 146.

rather vaguely dealt with in the scholarly and professional literature.[10] Those issues which are – on the other hand – subject to perpetual academic discourse (e.g. harmonisation of civil procedure in the EU) will only be marginally addressed.

2. Judicial federalism in the US and the EU

2.1. *Outline*

To convey a concise description and comparison, as well as for general purposes of brevity, three assumptions shall be made. First, I will assume that the reader is acquainted with the notion of 'federation'. In a nutshell, a federal system is one in which political power is divided between central and subordinate authorities.[11] Second, I will not attempt to define the EU wholly as a federation, confederation or *sui generis* form of political union. Suffice it to say, the EU shares commonalities with those of a federation, and those quasi-federative commonalities can provide an ample *tertium comparationis*. The third and last assumption I make is that the reader is versed in the administration of justice in proceedings falling under the competence of the Court of Justice of the European Union (hereinafter CJEU).

The federalisation of the judiciary is not a moot issue, nor is it a question of mere procedure and effectiveness of judicial administration. It pertains, when considered *largo sensu*, to the delicate balance of federal-state powers. For instance, determining the jurisdiction of the federal judiciary strikes a delineation of powers.[12]

To this end, the Treaty on European Union (TEU) sets out the goal of perpetuating an ever-closer union among the peoples of Europe.[13] The cited goal can be thwarted by a weak EU judicial federalism, since the allocation of judicial power within a polity influences the degree of political integration. State courts tend to favour state interests, while federal courts give priority to those of the nation[14] (or supra-state entity). If such a statement holds true, then it is a fortiori not inconceivable to imagine Member State courts holding bias in cases of cross-border enforcement and acting on said bias; be it by attenuating cumbersome national procedural law or by interpreting the catalogue of grounds for refusal of recognition and enforcement to the interest of that Member State vis-à-vis domiciled debtors.

2.2. *The US federal judiciary*

To begin with, the US Constitution sets up a federal government with a Supreme Court together with the power to establish such inferior courts as the Congress may

10 Most notably, Wells has provided a comparative review of the EU and US federal judiciaries from the American perspective, while Lindholm has given a concise overview of enforcing federal rights in both systems; see Wells 2017; Lindholm 2007.

11 Kramer 1994, p. 1488.

12 Wright, Charles & Kane 2002, p. 2.

13 Article 1(2) TEU.

14 Wells 2017, p. 702-703.

from time to time ordain and establish (hereinafter Federal courts).[15] States, however, remain free to set up their own court systems (hereinafter State courts). Congress acted on these powers and gradually established a three-tier system of Federal courts. There are ninety-four District Courts, competent to hear cases within their respective territories, against whom judgments may be appealed to thirteen Courts of Appeal and finally to the US Supreme Court.[16] Federal courts and State courts form a two-track system of original jurisdiction in a given state. Each track holds power to adjudicate on issues of federal or State law, respectively. In some instances, as will be shown below, Federal courts apply national law and State courts apply federal law.

2.2.1. (Diversity) Jurisdiction of the federal judiciary

Since federal power is an entrusted power and by that virtue a limited power,[17] the same holds true for federal jurisdiction; Federal courts are courts with limited jurisdiction.[18] Federal courts can entertain cases in several distinct situations. They may be seized when: the US is a party to a case; in cases of federal question jurisdiction;[19] in cases of supplemental jurisdiction;[20] and in cases of diversity jurisdiction.[21]

The first three noted jurisdictional bases are rather straightforward, while the last holds greater importance for the discussion at hand. Diversity jurisdiction is given when parties to the case are citizens of different states[22] or citizens of a state

15 US Constitution, Article III, Section 1.

16 The drafters of the US Constitution at first agreed there would be a single Supreme Court and one or more inferior courts, but that decision about inferior courts was soon reversed. Many proposed that the State courts serve as the courts of first instance, or trial courts, in cases raising federal issues. After the delegates rejected a proposal to establish inferior Federal courts, they decided to give Congress authority to establish inferior courts, thus leaving open the option that State courts may serve as trial courts for many questions arising under federal law. See Ragsdale 2013, p. 16-17.

17 As opposed to State courts, which hold general jurisdiction. One consequence of Federal courts' limited jurisdiction is also the presumption that the court lacks jurisdiction in a case until it has been demonstrated that jurisdiction over the subject matter exists. See *Turner v. President, Directors and Co. of the Bank of North America*, 1799, 4 Dall. 8, 1 L.Ed. 718.

18 Wright 1983, p. 27.

19 Federal judicial power extends 'to all Cases, in Law and Equity, arising under this Constitution, the Laws of the United States, and Treaties made, or which shall be made, under their Authority', Article III, Section 2 US Constitution.

20 When a Federal court has acquired subject matter jurisdiction over a claim, it also has jurisdiction over all other claims that form part of the same case or controversy; see 28 U.S.C. § 1367(a).

21 Diversity and federal question jurisdiction are set forth in the explicit text of the US Constitution and by statute. The Constitution is silent on supplemental jurisdiction and it is only constitutional because of a series of US Supreme Court decisions interpreting the phrase 'case or controversy'. There are other bases for subject matter jurisdiction in the Federal courts, including, but not limited to, admiralty cases.

22 Citizenship and domicile are identical for purposes of diversity jurisdiction; see Rowe, Sherry & Tidmarsh 2008, p. 554.

and a foreign nation.[23] Hence, at first glance, one can recognise parallels to cases involving residents domiciled in different Member States of the EU.

Diversity jurisdiction is not inherently linked to a subject matter of federal stature. Rather, its defining feature is the diversity of the litigants (the parties to the case).[24] The rationale of federal jurisdiction is then not adjudication on issues of federal law. It has, to the contrary, been put forth that the reason for establishing diversity jurisdiction lies in diminishing State court bias,[25] in other words, to avoid potential prejudice against citizens of one state in another state's court.[26] Even though this rationale has been found to be questionable by way of historical interpretation, the fact of the matter remains that it finds footing in commentary. Notably, one distinguished author concluded that State courts have not been given reason to be 'hostile' to litigants from other states for the mere sake of it. He has, nonetheless, found that it is legitimate to assume that diversity jurisdiction came to be due to the concern that State courts in states with more favourable laws for debtors would apply the laws in favour of their own residents regardless of the fact that the debt was payable in another state.[27]

2.2.2. Applicable law under diversity jurisdiction

If the purpose of diversity jurisdiction lies in the elimination of State court bias and if the object of litigation is not inherently intertwined with federal law, the question arises then as to which law is deemed applicable. The law alluded to beforehand can differ on matters of substance and procedure. Therefore, both venues need to be explored. Regarding this topic, the year 1938 constitutes a key moment when the modus of judicial choice-of-law was reversed.

Regarding substantive law, prior to 1938 Federal courts were only bound to apply the positive statutes of the state. When sitting under diversity jurisdiction, a federal judge applied the statutory acts of the state in which the court was sitting, the federal procedural code and the federal common law in areas not governed by the first two.[28] However, since there were no federal rules on civil procedure up to that point in time (apart from those pertaining to the US Supreme Court), a Federal court would have to apply the procedural rules of the state wherein it was sitting. Ultimately, an interstate harmonisation of procedural law would be achieved through common praxis. Procedural interstate uniformity was, however, never

23 28 U.S.C. § 1332.

24 There is also a *competentia ratione valoris* condition which needs to be cumulatively adhered to for jurisdiction.

25 There is no clear record of the original rationale for diversity jurisdiction. It may also be that cases involving cross-border parties are more national or federal than local.

26 Mullenix, Redish & Vairo 1998, p. 111.

27 Friendly 1928, p. 496-497.

28 This was the result of the US Supreme Court's reading of the Rules of Decision Act (28 U.S.C. § 1652) in *Swift* (*Swift v. Tyson*, 41 U.S. 1 (1842)). The Rules of Decision Act declares that the laws of the several states, except where the Constitution or Acts of Congress otherwise require or provide, shall be regarded as rules of decision in civil actions in the courts of the United States.

achieved and the described approach complicated litigation rather than simplifying it.[29] Numerous exceptions to the general rule that Federal courts apply State procedural law for certain actions and issues contributed to this fact.[30]

In 1938, the aforementioned reversal took place. On the substantive side of things, the US Supreme Court effectively postulated State law as 'primary' in *Erie*.[31] Federal courts were thenceforth bound to apply the law of the state, including the decisions of State courts, rather than create and fashion federal common law.[32] On the procedural venue, Federal courts went from applying State procedural law to applying the newly enacted Federal Rules of Civil Procedure.[33] The Federal Rules of Civil Procedure have been deemed a great success on both the federal level and the state level, since more than half of the states have been keen on adopting the rules at the state level, with minor modifications.[34]

2.2.3. Differentiating substance and procedure

One issue which accompanied the development just described pertains to the method of identifying what is procedural law and what is substantive law. Since the choice governs judicial choice-of-law for the Federal court, it bears significant importance. Certain institutes of law may possess a hybrid nature, i.e. statutes of limitation, burden of proof, etc. More so, even the Federal Rules of Civil Procedure may include substantive provisions.[35] To resolve this conundrum, a formula known as the 'outcome-determination test' was established.[36] In *Guaranty Trust*[37] the US Supreme Court pointed out that the difference between procedure and substance (for *Erie* purposes) is dependent on the context. According to *Guaranty Trust*, the outcome of the litigation in a Federal court should be substantially the same as the outcome of the same litigation if it had been heard in a State court (as far as issues of law are concerned).[38] Thus, when determining whether a matter is procedural or substantive for purposes of *Erie* doctrine, the federal judge should consider whether replacing the state rule (the law of the forum) with the federal rule would significantly affect the outcome of the litigation. If proved positive, then the Federal court ought to apply the state rule instead. The outcome-determination test was

29 Wright, Charles & Kane 2002, p. 424-426.

30 Lindholm 2007, p. 168.

31 *Erie Railroad Co. v. Tompkins*, 304 U.S. 64 (1938).

32 Wells 2017, p. 721.

33 Fed. R. Civ. P.

34 Lindholm 2007, p. 171; Wright, Charles & Kane 2002, p. 430.

35 Mullenix, Redish & Vairo 1998, p. 529.

36 For a more comprehensive understanding of what is procedure and what substance under *Erie* doctrine, see Sedler 1962, p. 819 *et seq*. Note, however, that the Supreme Court has struggled with providing a decisional rule or decision tree for applying *Erie*. It is still an evolving legal landscape. For more recent developments in case law, see *Shady Grove Orthopedic Associates, P. A. v. Allstate Ins. Co.*, 559 U.S. 393 (2010).

37 *Guaranty Trust Co. v. York*, 326 U.S. 99 (1945), 108-112.

38 *Ibid.*, 101, 109.

subsequently criticised, since both substantive rules and procedural rules may determine an outcome of litigation, depending on the rules *in concreto*.[39]

This was later addressed in *Byrd*[40] and in *Hanna v. Plumer*.[41] In *Byrd*, the issue was - simply put - whether a judge could, in accordance with State law, decide on an issue himself, or whether he should follow federal law and allow a jury to decide. The US Supreme Court was clear in answering that the state rule was only a form and mode of enforcement, not a rule intended to be bound up with the definition of the 'rights and obligations' of the parties.[42] The court found that if the 'outcome' only were determinate to judicial choice-of-law, then State law should apply. The court maintained, however, that a strong federal interest was vested in the right to jury trial. This 'federal' interest ultimately prevailed, striking a balance between the interest of the 'Union' and that of the State.[43] Ambiguities were further dealt with in *Hanna v. Plumer*. There,[44] the Supreme Court enunciated two *Erie* aims which must be respected when determining the nature of a rule. First, the application of law must ensure uniform results in State and Federal courts so that forum shopping between the state and federal systems is discouraged. Second, the application must prevent the party who chooses the forum from obtaining an advantage over the other party, thus avoiding the inequitable administration of law.[45]

Here, it must be emphasised that the issue of the applicable law is not an issue exclusive to precedent. The statutory basis for the determination is provided in the Rules Enabling Act.[46] Under the Act, the US Supreme Court has the power to prescribe general rules of practice and procedure and rules of evidence for cases in the Federal courts.[47] However, such rules must not abridge, enlarge or modify any substantive right. The Act also sanctions conflicting rules, stating that such rules shall be of no further force or effect after such rules have taken effect. One can (grossly simplifying) conclude therefore that when federal and state rules cover the same situation, the federal rule will displace the state rule. It is also worth mentioning that the Supreme Court has virtually never found any federal rule to abridge, enlarge or modify substantive rights.[48]

39 *Hanna v. Plumer*, 380 U.S. 460 (1965).
40 *Byrd v. Blue Ridge Rural Elec. Coop.*, 356 U.S.
41 *Hanna v. Plumer*, 380 U.S. 460 (1965).
42 *Byrd v. Blue Ridge Rural Elec. Coop.*, 356 U.S., 525-528.
43 Mullenix, Redish & Vairo 1998, p. 531.
44 The issue under scrutiny in *Hanna v. Plumber* involved rules on service. The Supreme Court ultimately ruled that the Federal Rules of Civil Procedure govern the manner of service of process in federal diversity jurisdiction suits.
45 *Hanna v. Plumer*, 380 U.S. 460 (1965) 460-465.
46 28 U.S.C. § 2072.
47 It is worth noting that it was not Congress that prepared the Federal Rules of Civil Procedure but the Supreme Court, precisely through the Rules Enabling Act.
48 Mullenix, Redish & Vairo 1998, p. 536-537; 28 U.S.C. § 2072(b).

2.2.4. Federal review of State court decisions

The federal and state judiciaries form part of a two-track system. One track generally cannot exclude or protrude into the other (e.g. situations of *lis pendens*). However, the decisions of State courts may be subject to review by the US Supreme Court. The general authority for US Supreme Court appellate review of State court decisions rests in the US Constitution.[49] More precise regulation is provided in 28 United States Code (U.S.C.) § 1257. To ensure that State court autonomy might remain firm and respected, the appellate jurisdiction of the Supreme Court may be exercised over State courts only where the Constitution or federal treaties or statutes are drawn into question.[50]

2.3. *The EU 'federal judiciary' and comparative outlook*

Setting aside semantics, the EU 'federal judiciary' is composed merely of the dual body of the CJEU.[51] In this sense, the General Court can be understood as a 'lower instance' court of the federal judiciary, due to the appellate function of the Court of Justice. There is no parallel system of a federal judiciary such as that found in the US.[52] Furthermore, individuals are, save for a few exceptions, generally barred from access to the CJEU. They may not initiate litigation in civil matters at the federal level, nor is their dispute appealable to the CJEU. A litigated dispute may appear before the CJEU indirectly, through the preliminary ruling proceedings under Article 267 of the Treaty on the Functioning of the European Union (hereinafter TFEU). These proceedings, however, are not targeted at dispute resolution. The CJEU only has jurisdiction to give preliminary rulings concerning the interpretation of the Treaties and the validity and interpretation of Acts of secondary law. The decisions of the CJEU in this regard concern the interpretation of EU law, not the interpretation of national law[53] or its validity.[54] The national court[55] is bound by the interpretation (as a question of law), but its capacity to issue a ruling remains unscathed. The frustrated party may seek to remedy issues of EU law through the national judiciary, including lodging actions for damages against the state. This mechanism is not something reserved to federations, since some unitary countries

49 More precisely Article III, Sections 1 and 2, which vest the Supreme Court with the judicial power of the United States.

50 Schlueter 1984, p. 1082.

51 Akin to that of the German example (where the Basic Law establishes an array of federal courts holding supreme power in their respective jurisdictions but not also a lower network of federal courts). See Article 95 of the Basic Law for the Federal Republic of Germany in the revised version published in the Federal Law Gazette III, as last amended by Article 1 of the Act of 23 December 2014 (Federal Law Gazette I, p. 2438).

52 Young 2018, p. 174.

53 On the other hand, rulings for preliminary reference are understood, by some, as an effective judicial review of national law; see Carrubba & Murrah 2005, p. 403.

54 Once that opinion is passed back down to the national court, the national court then makes a final ruling. See Carrubba & Murrah 2005, p. 400.

55 This decision nonetheless has *erga omnes* effect; Brkan 2014, p. 102.

also enable preliminary judicial review on interpretations of law.[56] It does, nonetheless, serve the proper usage (and through it, 'approximation') of 'federal' law. The EU judiciary is thus distinct from the US judiciary in that it provides only one-track for the 'federal judiciary' and otherwise relies on the national courts to enforce EU law locally.

To line up the differences noted: first, the EU judiciary lacks a system of federal courts which would adjudicate (hear litigation) on questions of federal law at 'first instance' (such as US Federal District Courts) or in diversity jurisdiction proceedings. Nor do the Treaties provide ample grounds for the creation of such a system. Second, the EU federal judiciary holds no appellate power over the judgments of the national courts, even if issues of EU law are brought to concern. Third, there are no unified EU rules of civil procedure, apart from legislation enacted under the prerogative of Article 81 of TFEU, from which BIR justification stems.[57]

These differences may be striking. However, Wells aptly recognises similarities between the two as well. First, both US law and EU law show restraint, against issues of state law and national law, respectively. Those issues pertain to the original jurisdiction of State courts and national courts. Second, there are topics of law in both the US and the EU which the state vis-à-vis national law does not fully regulate.[58] Cross-border enforcement evidently is one of the topics, since EU regulation on the subject precludes national law.[59] Wells goes on to explain that from the US perspective the EU's judicial federalism seems to give too much weight to Member State interests, both by relying heavily on the national courts and by the preliminary reference procedure in lieu of appellate review by the national courts. This approach better shields Member States from centralisation and safeguards their autonomy and interests, but to the detriment of integration.[60]

Indeed, judicial federalism in the EU can be deemed weak with regard to the authority of the CJEU and strong with regard to the respect for the autonomy of the Member States. However, this can, I believe, be attributed to what Avbelj describes as 'pluralism in the EU'. According to him, the EU is (in normative frames) best conceived in a pluralist form (a pluralist entity, not a federation) and that systemic defiance inside the EU is inherent to it. Plurality in this sense of the word is a normative framework for an ordered plurality. It stands for differences and diversity. It also requires that different entities forming a plurality should be

56 For example, the new Slovenian CPA – Civil Procedure Act (*Zakon o pravdnem postopku*) – enables courts to stay proceedings and address the Supreme Court with questions on law if appellate case law is not in conformity and the Supreme Court has of yet not addressed the issue. See Article 206 CPA.

57 For a thorough grasp of EU procedural law, see Hess 2012, p. 159-174.

58 Wells 2017, p. 722.

59 It has been evidenced already from the Treaty of Amsterdam that the competence to regulate cross-border enforcement is in the domain of the EU when cooperation on matters of the police and administration of justice was transferred from the 'third pillar' (intragovernmental instruments) to the EC Treaty.

60 Wells 2017, p. 723-726.

preserved by mutually recognising this right for each other.[61] Indeed, one needs only to glance at the EU motto 'United in diversity', in contrast to the US pledge of allegiance 'One nation under God …'[62] to find the footing of the aforementioned construct. Even from such a simplified standpoint it seems evident that the EU would feature a weak federal judiciary, owing respect to the diverse national judiciaries and the values they hold meaningful. The EU was not envisaged as a project of 'nation building' and long ago already described by then-president of the Commission Jacques Delors as a legally and politically unidentified project.[63] Even though the EU is almost certainly not intended to be a 'nation-building' project, its ambit of creating an ever-closer union among the peoples of Europe may be hindered by a weak federal judiciary.

It remains questionable therefore, whether there are any cues from the US federal judiciary to adopt. If we first take into consideration setting up a parallel system of (federal) courts, vested with an analogue diversity jurisdiction, do we gain a more effective[64] judicial system overall? This question needs to first address whether courts are in fact biased towards litigants (creditors) domiciled in other Member States, for that was supposedly the reason for introducing diversity jurisdiction in the US.[65] If the answer is in the affirmative, then setting up an EU equivalent might contribute to a more uniform, non-biased[66] approach across the individual jurisdictions of the Member States, strengthening the effectiveness of EU law. On the other hand, it must also be emphasised that the 'bias' the (US) State court judges are purported to be guilty of stems from, to a certain degree, their electability by the voters (the people). For this reason they are supposedly more inclined to produce judgments in favour of their constituents (potential debtors).[67] In the EU, this problem is not as pertinent, since judges are usually elected or nominated by the other branches of power. On the flip side, federal judges would be (at least initially) better versed in EU law. This could be especially important to litigants in newly joined Member States who do not 'trust' the national judges'

61 Avbelj 2017, p. 45-47.

62 Another example is the preamble to the US Constitution, which begins with the passage 'We the people …', constituting the citizens of the US as one 'people', in contrast to the notion of the many 'peoples' as observed in the TEU.

63 Avbelj 2017, p. 47; see Jacques Delors' speech, available at: <https://www.cvce.eu/content/-publication/2001/10/19/423d6913-b4e2-4395-9157-fe70b3ca8521/publishable_en.pdf>, last accessed in April 2019.

64 Effective, pertaining to the effective enforcement of EU law (*effet utile*).

65 Diversity jurisdiction is intended to prevent local bias against an out-of-state litigant by ensuring control of the trial by a federal judge who enjoys life tenure and is free from local pressures. See Sedler 1962, p. 819.

66 It must be emphasised that the past has seen calls for the abolishment of diversity jurisdiction. The historical prejudices judges are presumed to have had are said to have disappeared with the strengthening of the nation and modernisation of society. However, diversity jurisdiction is still praised for its educational function. The Federal Rules of Civil Procedure have been emulated and placed into the states' laws. In addition, a party whose dispute was resolved in the federal track will less likely invoke 'blame on factors of law and prejudice. See Frank 1963, p. 11.

67 Mullenix, Redish & Vairo 1998, p. 112-113.

prowess in EU law or doubt their impartiality (which is a hindrance to the functioning of the internal market).[68] Such a system would also contribute to more efficient cross-border enforcement, because mutual trust would be inherently strengthened. Federal judgments could be taken at face value (especially those provided by appellate federal court review) anywhere in the EU. All of the described is of course a far cry from the current legislative and judicial landscape of the EU. Concrete political action and serious discussion on what the EU is and aims to be must be taken to enable such constructs to become reality. In the end, the issue is that of a cost–benefit analysis: whether systemic integration and promotion of EU law and its values prevail over the diversified values and procedural guarantees of Member States.[69]

3. Procedural autonomy and State court application of federal law

3.1. *The US: Application of federal law in State courts*

In the US, Congress has the power to create exclusive jurisdiction for Federal courts over all matters within the judicial authority of the federal government.[70] However, Federal courts have exclusive jurisdiction only where Congress has labelled it as such or where such jurisdiction has already been provided for by the US Constitution. Thus, where Congress has not vested Federal courts with exclusive jurisdiction, the State courts have concurrent jurisdiction with the Federal courts.[71] Federal law is enforceable in State courts because the Supremacy Clause[72] makes federal law the 'supreme law of the land' and charges State courts with a coordinate responsibility to enforce it.[73] As expressed in *Mondou v. New York*,[74] 'The existence of concurrent jurisdiction of State courts implies a duty to exercise it.' Therefore, refusal by a State court to entertain litigation in federal matters violates the Supremacy Clause.

The duty of the State courts in this regard cannot be alleviated even in those cases where exceptions to the Full Faith and Credit Clause might be considered. This conclusion was elaborated in *Testa*,[75] where the State court refused to entertain a federal claim pertaining to treble damages,[76] which are a form of penal damages and could by that virtue fall outside the Full Faith and Credit Clause, rendering

68 Indeed, diversity jurisdiction was also meant to enhance awareness in the people of the existence of the new and originally weak central government and foster a secure environment for interstate commerce. See Kramer 1990, p. 97.

69 Note, however, that the CJEU case law may be considered a reflection of national legal traditions already. See Nicola 2016, p. 865-889.

70 See Article III of the US Constitution.

71 Friedenthal, Kane & Miller 1999, p. 240.

72 See Article VI, Section 2 of the US Constitution.

73 Mullenix, Redish & Vairo 1998, p. 574.

74 *Mondou v. New York, New Have & Hartford R.R.*, 223 U.S. 1, 58 (1912).

75 *Testa v. Katt*, 330 U.S. 386, 394 (1947).

76 Damages that, by statute, are three times the amount of actual damages that the fact-finder determines is owed. Garner 2009, p. 449.

enforcement in another state ineffective. Still, the Supreme Court upheld the Supremacy Clause notwithstanding the State court's rationale. Another unsuccessful defence of refusal to entertain federal matters is invoking the discordance of federal law with state policy.[77] A State court may, in contrast, refuse jurisdiction over a federal claim if a 'neutral' state law rule regarding court administration provides so.[78]

State jurisdiction over federal matters logically implies the application of federal substantive law to those matters. However, the described construction begs the question of the applicable procedural law. States are permitted to apply their own neutral procedural law, unless federal law pre-empts those rules or because the application of State law would defeat federal substantive rights.[79] The situation is therefore inverse to that of judicial choice-of-law in Federal courts, where federal procedural law governs the proceedings of state substantive rights. For this reason, it has been described as the 'reverse-*Erie*' doctrine by academia.[80]

Importantly, the US Supreme Court stated in *Murdock*[81] that the jurisdiction of Federal courts over State court judgments is limited to the correction of errors relating solely to federal law. Where a State court judgment is based on both federal law and State law, the Supreme Court may not review the judgment if the non-federal ground is independent of the federal ground and adequate to support the judgment.[82] This became known as the 'Adequate and independent State ground' doctrine. It is of particular importance for evaluating whether state procedural rules are adequate and independent. If they are, the federal judiciary cannot review the judgment, and the supposed deficiency of the state procedural law is effectively cured. One way to determine whether or not a state procedural rule may be fashioned 'inadequate' is to consider the question, Does the rule unnecessarily burden the federal right? A two-fold test is proposed to answer this query: firstly, is the procedural rule so burdensome that it violates the litigant's right to due process and, secondly, is the rule, although not unconstitutionally burdensome, nevertheless unnecessarily burdensome such that it must be ignored when State courts enforce federal claims?[83] If answered in the affirmative, federal review may be permitted.

3.2. *Procedural autonomy of Member States and a comparative outlook*

3.2.1. The notion

The enforcement of EU law at the Member State level does not differ greatly from the enforcement of US federal law at the state level, since EU law does not

77 *Mondou v. New York, New Have & Hartford R.R.*, 223 U.S. 1, 55-57 (1912).
78 *Missouri ex rel. Southern Ry. v. Mayfield*, 340 U.S. 1, 2-5 (1950).
79 Friedenthal, Kane & Miller 1999, p. 241.
80 Clermont 2006, p. 2.
81 *Murdock v. City of Memphis*, 87 U.S. 590 (1875).
82 *Fox Film Corp. v. Muller*, 296 U.S. 207, 210 (1935).
83 Lindholm 2007, p. 230.

preconceive a centralised judicial mechanism for its own enforcement. Instead, it is built on the premise of decentralised (private) enforcement through the national courts, generally lacking unified rules of supranational procedure.[84] Accordingly, national procedural law must accommodate EU (substantive) rights (analogous to federal rights in this context).[85] Since EU law is based on the premise of *ubi ius, ibi remedium*,[86] national procedural law must provide a suitable remedy to the EU right, and the national court must, under certain conditions, of its own accord, raise questions of EU law.[87] Nevertheless, the Member State enjoys a certain measure of autonomy. In the absence of EU regulation (which is generally the norm), Member States are free to set up their own system of courts (institutional autonomy) and procedures (procedural autonomy) wherein EU rights are enforced. Since here procedure is usually concerned with the provision of remedies (recourses), it may also be labelled as 'remedial autonomy' (but 'remedies' may also refer to substantive law).[88] National procedural autonomy must at the very least adhere to the principles of effectiveness and equivalence. While the former provides that national procedure must not make the exercise of EU rights excessively difficult or impossible in practice, the latter prescribes that procedures designed or designated to govern the enforcement of EU law must not be less favourable than those relating to similar actions under domestic law (that relate to completely internal situations). This was established in CJEU case law, which can be uniformly addressed as the *Rewe/San Giorgio*[89] doctrine. However, the principle of effectiveness, often used interchangeably with the notion of *effet utile*, has not one single expression in EU law doctrine, but several. The most recognisable are the following: full effectiveness; the *Rewe/San Giorgio* doctrine; the procedural rule of reason; and effective judicial protection.[90] If national procedural law proves to be in discordance with the principles of effectiveness and equivalence, then that law should be sanctioned via consistent interpretation (indirect effect) or disapplication (primacy).[91]

84 A decentralised system must almost entirely rely on the proper adherence to the principles of direct effect and primacy. A vigilant party that invokes an EU right will have it enforced through those principles.

85 It is for the domestic legal system of each Member State to determine the procedural conditions governing actions at law intended to ensure the protection of the rights which [individuals] derive from [EU] law, [in the absence of EU rules on this subject]. See Case 33-76, *Rewe-Zentralfinanz v. Landwirtschaftskammer für das Saarland* [1976].

86 See Kilpatrick 2000, p. 36.

87 Engström 2008, p. 68 *et seq.*

88 See Lenaerts & Gutman 2006.

89 Case C-199/82, *Amministrazione delle Finanze dello Stato v. San Giorgio* [1982].

90 For a concise overview of the development of these doctrines, see Schütze 2012, p. 388-392.

91 Even the most minor piece of technical EU legislation ranks above the most cherished constitutional norm. Weatherill 1995, p. 106. The principle of primacy can thus, in combination with the principle of indirect and direct effect, be of incredible potency for the vigilant party wishing to 'defeat' national law.

3.2.2. Procedural autonomy and BIR

The notion of procedural autonomy is not foreign to cross-border enforcement proceedings under BIR either. More specifically, the principle of effectiveness must be respected when applying national procedural law to enforcement proceedings in the Member State forum. National rules cannot be applied to the extent that they would defeat the effectiveness (render enforcement excessively difficult) of BIR's provisions.[92] As Dickinson explains, the principle was used when the CJEU outlawed the English courts' practice of granting anti-suit injunctions to restrain substantive proceedings in other Member States under particular jurisdiction constraints.[93] Perhaps most profoundly, procedural autonomy finds its footing in Article 47 of BIR, which states that the procedure for refusal of enforcement shall, in so far as it is not covered by BIR, be governed by the law of the Member State. Fitchen aptly points out that there is the clear possibility of Member States' unconsciously or consciously magnifying the existing procedural differences between their civil procedural rules by which the application of BIR is facilitated.[94] The control over this issue will necessarily fall under the above-enumerated doctrines that attempt to determine the scope and limits of Member States' procedural autonomy. In this regard, BIR seems to show strong respect to national procedural autonomy, e.g. it removed the one-month, time-barring restriction for lodging an appeal against the declaration of enforceability pursuant to the service of the declaration; it allows Members States to freely opt for a second appeal (Article 50 BIR); etc.

The problem with such an autonomy-centric approach lies in the aforementioned disparities which arise among Member States' procedural rules on enforcement proceedings in the EU law context. One must be aware that national procedural law governs issues of standing, limitation periods and preclusion of actions, burden of proof, etc., which are all capable of rendering enforcement of BIR (and by extension – the actual enforcement proceedings) excessively difficult. Grashof, who has conducted recent and extensive research into national procedural autonomy (albeit in the field of environmental law), aptly points out the negative effects of such disparities, namely:

- parties are subject to different proceedings, meaning they must approach different litigation (here, enforcement) rules;
- they have to cope with different hurdles, meaning there are different enforcement chances under the same set of EU rules applicable to the situation;
- judges issue different judgments because of different procedural rules.[95]

92 Case 288/82, *Ferdinand M.J.J. Duijnstee v. Lodewijk Goderbauer* [1983].
93 More on this, see Dickinson 2015, p. 42.
94 Fitchen 2015, p. 484.
95 Grashof 2016, p. 231.

From the perspective of the individual, this system cannot be optimal. Parties are treated unequally,[96] even though cross-border enforcement is governed by the same EU regulation, as this is intrinsic to the decentralised system of enforcement. It may then be argued that an optimal solution would provide for as little disparity as possible, while still retaining the fundamentals of Member State procedural law (policy). This way a debtor or creditor could rely on having their rights protected equivalently across the EU, independent of the procedural particularities of the Member State of enforcement.[97]

Usually, the debate on unifying procedural rules is quickly extinguished due to lack of EU competence to regulate matters of procedure. However, the regulation of cross-border enforcement does not face the same lacuna of competence, since Article 81 of TFEU provides ample ground for harmonisation, taking into consideration cross-border implications are a given, and mutual trust is paid due respect.[98] However, if one were to push for the harmonisation of litigation and enforcement proper, the ambit of regulating the national procedure, pertaining to the actual enforcement (not merely the recognition of enforceability) of judgments, would likely escape the confines of Article 81.[99] Even though enforcement procedures *stricto sensu* are conceptualised to be independent of litigation, they are, nevertheless, a means of realising the creditor's substantial right.[100] The EU lacks competence to interfere with said processes, since they lack cross-border implications (these being anterior to execution).[101]

3.2.3. Brief excursion: Is there a 'federal common law' in the EU?

Considering that this contribution has outlined only the utmost fundamental cornerstones of both legal systems under scrutiny, it is thus possible to conclude that they are alike. Akin to what occurs in the US, the enforcement of EU law rests on Member State courts. In a similar fashion, national procedural law can be overridden to accommodate EU rights. Neither system imposes upon the states a set of federal rules of procedure. However, while the US States have been very keen on

96 *Ibid.*, p. 231-232.

97 The principle of equal treatment is enshrined in Articles 2 and 9 TEU, and Article 19 TFEU. *Ibid.*, p. 232.

98 There is no need to defer to 'proceduralisation through the back door' vis-à-vis through incidental proceduralisation under Article 114 TFEU and other grounds of substantive policy. On incidental proceduralisation, see Eliantonio & Muir 2015, p. 4-31.

99 It has been argued that the harmonisation of actual enforcement proceedings has already been ushered in by Regulation (EU) No. 655/2014 of the European Parliament and of the Council of 15 May 2014 establishing a European Account Preservation Order procedure to facilitate cross-border debt recovery in civil and commercial matters. See Wiedemann 2015, p. 178.

100 Rijavec 2003, p. 44.

101 See, however, Van Rhee 2012, p. 54 and Kramer 2012, p. 127, on the potency (and underappreciation) of Article 81(2)(f) as grounds for the harmonisation of civil procedure, not because of cross-border implications per se, but due to the elimination of obstacles to the proper functioning of civil proceedings.

adopting the Federal Rules of Civil Procedure as domestic procedure, the Member States' national procedural law must be manipulated (consistent interpretation) or set aside to avoid obstruction of EU law. The case of Member States modifying their national procedural laws is particularly interesting. Delicostopoulus, for example, raised the logically appealing construct of national procedural law serving two masters – national (substantive) law and EU (substantive) law, whereas procedure will always make way for the latter, thus (possibly) enabling the spillover of regular (substantive) primacy into procedural primacy.[102] If we accept that different (modified) procedural rules apply via the aforementioned effect, can we still consider such national law as 'national' or could we postulate the expression of a 'federal common law'[103] on the basis of the (substantive) right and the requirement of effectiveness it carries? Even in the most extreme examples of denial of procedural autonomy, where *de novo* remedies are sometimes said to have been created,[104] the effect of EU law is pertinent only with regard to the EU right invoked, not to domestic rights. Take for example the well-known case of *Factortame*,[105] where the English court had to set aside a parliamentary Act in order to make a decision on an interim measure regarding a statute that barred the exercise of an EU right. Said right, endowed with the principle of effectiveness and adhering to CJEU case law, brought with it the authority to set aside obstructing national rules, and the national court ought to have considered the limits of procedural autonomy of its own accord. This is somewhat in line with Bobek's work 'denying' the existence of procedural autonomy,[106] due to the omnipresent restraints of effectiveness and equivalence. But if the Member State is not autonomous and its law is denied the very same quality, what purpose does it then serve to call it 'national'? It is correct to say national, since it was enacted by the national legislator and it is the valid law of the Member State, but as soon as it is modified by an EU right (regardless of the modus of this operation; judicial or otherwise), new law (procedural primacy) is generated (even if the substance of this law lies in the setting aside of a national rule). This 'new' law is not a consequence of the national legislator's action, nor is it a consequence of the judge's loyal interpretation. It is the consequential result of the principle of effectiveness and its corollary expression in CJEU case law. Since the effectiveness of EU law is ubiquitous in the temporal dimension (it is birthed together with the adher-

102 Delicostopoulos 2003, p. 606-608.

103 Granted, this term is used extremely loosely here. Perhaps Leanerts and Gutman's definition derivative of the US example is most worked out: European 'federal common law' refers to EU concepts, principles and rules of decision formulated by the CJEU that are not clearly suggested on the face of a provision of primary or secondary EU law; see Lenaerts & Gutman 2006, p. 7.

104 Take note, however, that this is a gross simplification of the matters at stake. The principle of effectiveness, as drawn up by an extensive body of CJEU case law, is sometimes 'finite' and gives way to autonomy, especially when fundamental principles of procedural law are involved (e.g. legal certainty, right to defence, *res judicata*). On these, very broad controversies, see, for instance, Claes 2006, p. 120-135.

105 Case C-221/89, *The Queen v. Secretary of State for Transport, ex parte Factortame Ltd* [1991].

106 Bobek 2012, p. 315-331.

ing right), the consequences it carries must be aprioristic.[107] Even if disparities with EU law do not require the setting aside of a national procedural rule, and if consistent interpretation in line with the principle of sincere cooperation enshrined in Article 4(3) of TEU suffices, this interpretative momentum was still required by EU law from the moment it took effect. However, Galleta avoids such extreme views as described here, by simply constructing the 'functionalisation' of national procedural rules for the purposes of EU law enforcement.[108] In any case, the principle of procedural autonomy remains a *non-liquet* notion.

Regarding the state of the art on cross-border enforcement, the EU 'right' may not necessarily be a 'substantive' right, but a 'procedural' one[109] (if such a concept is capable of construction). Here, the US 'outcome-determination' doctrine (in diversity jurisdiction case law) is not relevant, since it holds little to no value if the EU right is procedural or substantive. Regardless whether the applicable EU right is substantive or procedural, the same consequence occurs for the national provision (consistent interpretation, or – if that proves *contra legem* – setting aside the provision). Granted, procedural autonomy usually implies indirect normative collision[110] (a collision of an EU substantive right with a national procedural rule). What is more troublesome, however, is how to recognise such a collision. The value of the outcome determination doctrine may, nevertheless, be interesting for general academic discourse on the division and definition of substance and procedure[111] or with regard to the limits of *révision au fond* under Article 52 of BIR (substance and procedure in international private law).

107 The CJEU's rulings on referral under Article 276 TFEU also have an *ex tunc* effect. See Joined Cases 66, 127 and 128/79, *Amministrazione delle finanze dello Stato v. Salumi* [1980].

108 Galleta 2010, p. 41-59, 75-79.

109 The notion of a 'right' is barely discussed in academic discourse on procedural autonomy and the same holds true for 'procedural law'. Van Gerven has perhaps provided the most apt definition of rights, remedies and procedures. According to him, the concept of right refers to a legal position which a person (subject) may have and which in its normal state can be enforced by that person against (some or all) others before a court of law by means of one or more remedies, i.e. classes of action or other procedural means (motion, petition), intended to make good infringements of the rights concerned, in accordance with procedures governing the exercise of such means intended to make the remedy concerned operational. See Van Gerven 2000, p. 502.

110 Verhoeven & Ortlep 2012, p. 2-4.

111 The division of substance and procedure is an elusive problem that had to be addressed by the Supreme Court when deciding in *Erie* and developing the outcome deterministic approach. The Supreme Court did not follow a system-formalistic approach (observing the self-description of a statute); it did not opt for an empirical analysis (observing *casus* and making a statement thereon); nor did it opt for an intuitive approach (following the judge's own intuition). See Solum 2004, p. 194-199. The least that can be accomplished in this discourse is to demote procedural law to something only instrumental or ancillary. Bentham, for instance, labelled procedural law as 'adjective', something which was later perpetuated in American doctrine. See Kocourek 1941, p. 157-158.

4. Full faith and credit clause – a reality for the EU?

4.1. *Interstate enforcement and the Full Faith and Credit Clause*

Enforcement of judgments in the US is several fold. It can pertain to interstate, state-to-federal, federal-to-state and intrafederal relations. For the purposes of this contribution, focusing on interstate enforcement suffices. US interstate enforcement is marked by parity between two competing principles. On the one hand, the principle expressive of full faith and credit, on the other, due process.[112]

Article IV, Section 1 of the US Constitution states the content of the Full Faith and Credit Clause as follows: 'Full Faith and Credit shall be given in each State to the public Acts, Records, and judicial Proceedings of every other State. And the Congress may by general Laws prescribe the Manner in which such Acts, Records and Proceedings shall be proved, and the Effect thereof.'

This principle is found and expanded upon in statutory law,[113] where it is stated that the courts of one state must give the judgments of the courts of another state the same faith and credit that they would be given in the judgment-rendering state.[114] In addition, State courts are compelled to give the same faith and credit to Federal court judgments. The clause thus serves as a nationally unifying force.[115] Furthermore, full faith and credit does not require judgments to be final. States must give full faith and credit to all judicial proceedings, including interlocutory holdings.[116] However, enforcement 'proper' is still governed by the respective state's law, without the federal government imposing any requirement for uniformity or abolition of the exequatur system.[117]

For the Full Faith and Credit Clause to be properly exercised, statutory law sets out several requirements. Importantly, the state of origin[118] must provide authentication (the clerk's attestation and the court seal, as well as the judge's certificate that the attestation is in proper form). Additionally, the judgment must be properly filed in the state of enforcement.[119]

Defences against the Full Faith and Credit Clause must be based on due process exceptions. Over the decades, courts (the US Supreme Court being the final arbiter) have identified a (non-exhaustive) catalogue of both successful defences and unsuccessful defences.[120] Examples of successful defences include: the debtor may

112 See Friedenthal, Kane & Miller 1999, p. 710-711.
113 U.S.C.A. § 1738.
114 Friedenthal, Kane & Miller 1999, p. 711.
115 *Magnola Petroleum Co. v. Hunt*, 320 U.S. 439, 439, 64 S.Ct. 208, 214, 88 L.Ed. 149 (1943).
116 George 2009, p. 403.
117 Pretelli 2011, p. 20.
118 The law does not use the terminology 'State of origin/enforcement'. This is only used here for a more effortless understanding.
119 See U.S.C.A. § 1738.
120 The exceptions that next appear in the text are summarised following George 2009, p. 406-412.

raise the non-finality of the judgment;[121] the fact that the judgment was not given on the merits, but on other grounds; the invalidity of the judgment (on issues not litigated in the state of origin,[122] pertaining to lack of personal jurisdiction, fraud); the penal nature of the judgments;[123] *in rem* judgments; judgments interfering with the state of enforcement's exclusive interests (not to be confused with public policy; the latter is not an exception to full faith and credit); stale judgments (where the enforcement time has lapsed); and matters subsequent to the judgment (satisfaction, subsequent reversal of judgments, set-offs, etc.). Examples of unsuccessful defences include: erroneous judgments (judicial errors; judgment irregularities which could have been raised in the state of origin); the non-litigious nature of the dispute in the state of origin; and public policy in the state of enforcement.

To sum up, the Full Faith and Credit Clause is a powerful instrument in US law. It creates the obligation of State courts to treat a judgment from another state as though it had been given in the state of enforcement, subject to expressions of due process.

4.2. *Full faith and credit in the EU: Are we there yet?*

The Treaties do not contain a functional equivalent to that of the constitutional stature of the Full Faith and Credit Clause. However, commentators in the past,[124] and recently,[125] have said that a full faith and credit clause (at least regarding judgments in civil and commercial matters) would be desirable in the EU.[126] Without considering past matters of polity and competences on cross-border enforcement in the EU (with plentiful academic discourse available), it can be observably deduced that (a) limited faith and credit clause(s) is (are) – in effect – already established by BIR and other instruments pertaining to cross-border enforcement in civil and commercial matters. To elaborate, according to Article 39(1) of BIR, a judgment given in a Member State which is enforceable in that Member State shall be enforceable in the other Member States without any declaration of enforceability being required. In contrast to its predecessors, BIR has

121 Even though neither the Constitution nor statutory law requires finality, case law has, in certain cases, established otherwise. See *Williams v. North Carolina*, 325 U.S. 226 (1945); *Barber v. Barber*, 323 U.S. 77 (1944); *Maner v. Maner*, 412 F.2d 449, 451 (5th Cir. 1969).

122 *Adam v. Saenger*, 303 U.S. 59, 62 (1938).

123 *Huntington v. Attrill*, 146 U.S. 657, 686 (1892).

124 Haibach 2003, p. 295.

125 Frackowiak-Adamska 2015, p. 210-218.

126 One American commentator has provided an illustrative description of the potency of the clause for integrative purposes: 'There never was any doubt in the minds of the delegates to the Constitutional Convention that the people whom they represented would cheerfully relinquish the sovereign right of determining as an independent question the effect to be given judgments … of the other states. Whatever opposition might have arisen respecting the surrender of other powers and the relinquishment of rights, there was unanimity on this question. If there was to be established a more perfect union, it was realized that there must exist in the national government power to demand recognition as to judgments …' See Tapley 1943, p. 87.

abolished exequatur and with that contributed to the promotion of the free movement of judgments in the EU.[127] However, the abolition is not absolute. Verification of foreign judgments is now conditional and postponed to the enforcement stage, pending the debtor's action.[128]

This 'reverse-exequatur' does not, however, take away from the acceptance of 'having' faith and 'giving' credit, since defences under the US clause may still be made by the debtor. As seen above (Section 4.1), full faith and credit does not entail automatic and unconditional enforcement. Some European procedures (e.g. small claims procedure,[129] European order for payment procedure,[130] European enforcement order for uncontested claims)[131] thus provide for outcomes which are more stringent on defences than those found under the Full Faith and Credit Clause. Granted, some of these (alternative and 'genuine' EU) procedures regulate portions of the litigation stage, generating an anterior entrusting effect.

Another reason to consider the existence of a limited faith and credit clause is the crossing effects of a foreign judgment into another Member State.[132] In EU law the theory of the extension of effects predominates, as is clear from the case law of the CJEU. The CJEU has, in *Hoffmann v. Krieg*, acknowledged the theory of extension of effects. A judgment recognised in accordance with the Brussels regime has in principle the same legal effect in the Member State of enforcement as it does in the Member State of origin.[133] Even the effects of the judgment that are not known to domestic law are considered by the other Member State if there is no conflict with public policy.[134] The CJEU's approach resembles the US Supreme Court's stance in *McElmoyle v. Cohen*,[135] interpreting the Full Faith and Credit Clause with the following:

> [T]he judgment of a [S]tate Court carries with it into every [S]tate all its original attributes, energies, and incidents; that it goes forth armed with the powers of the Court that pronounced it, and clothed with the authority of the laws under which it was pronounced; that it is at home withersoever it goes, through the whole length and

127 Fitchen 2015, p. 404-405.

128 Cuniberti & Rueda 2016, p. 836.

129 Regulation (EC) No. 861/2007 of the European Parliament and of the Council of 11 July 2007 establishing a European Small Claims Procedure.

130 Regulation (EC) No. 1896/2006 of the European Parliament and of the Council of 12 December 2006 creating a European order for payment procedure.

131 Regulation (EC) No. 805/2004 of the European Parliament and of the Council of 21 April 2004 creating a European Enforcement Order for uncontested claims.

132 Historically, many of the US courts in deciding cases involving the question have held that the clause was merely intended to provide a means of authentication and proof of records and judicial proceedings. Consequently, such judgments were not conclusive but *prima facie* evidence of the matter adjudged. In 1813, the Supreme Court decided (*Mills v. Duryee*, 7 Cranch 481) that the judgment of a State court was to be conclusive in a sister state, provided that the court which rendered the decision had jurisdiction of the person of the defendant and of the subject matter and the judgment was otherwise valid. See O'Neill 1930, p. 200.

133 C-145/86, *Horst Ludwig Martin Hoffmann v. Adelheid Krieg* [1988].

134 Nagel & Gottwald 2007, p. 537.

135 *McElmoyle v. Cohen*, 38 U.S. 312 (1839).

breadth of the Union; that, in relation to judicial proceedings, the states are not foreign to each other.[136]

A judgment must therefore be given the same *res judicata* effect that it enjoys under the law of the state of origin, while the method of enforcing a judgment is determined by the law of the state of enforcement. It is for the latter to determine whether a new action in the nature of debt must be brought on the judgment or whether it can be enforced by means of a registration procedure.[137]

The cross-border enforcement regime of the EU therefore already satisfies the elements of a 'limited' faith and credit principle, because there is no 'general clause'[138] (of constitutional order, but not necessarily)[139] such as the US counterpart. Each instrument on cross-border enforcement can in its own right be considered a particular faith and credit clause for the subject matter it pertains to, not because it is based on a general clause of primary law, but because it is similar in nature and effect (as stated, the level of automation found in EU instruments even exceeds the requirements of the US clause). To establish a full faith and credit clause would require the enactment of a properly worded 'clause'[140] that would unify all the existing EU regulations on topics of civil and commercial matters under an umbrella regulation, while also providing for unified defences.[141]

To summarise, a full faith and credit clause, enshrined in the US Constitution, is capable of being perceived as an expression of mutual trust to the utmost degree. It follows then that mutual trust can be understood as the precondition for mutual recognition.[142] Mutual recognition is required where there is a lack of harmonisation and federal legal structures. Since neither the US nor the EU (fully) regulate interstate vis-à-vis cross-border enforcement, the principle of mutual recognition plays an important role in both entities.[143] Both the Full Faith and Credit Clause and the particular EU regulations on judicial cooperation are thus expressions of the same principle. The difference between the compared systems is that the principle of mutual recognition is curtailed in the EU, where the respect for the autonomy (thereby diversity of legal traditions) of Member States is of a heightened stature.

136 Kühn Baca 2014, p. 465.

137 *Ibid.*

138 The main shortcomings *de lege lata* are found in the plurality of subject matter-specific instruments; the overlapping of regulations, which causes confusion among the parties as to the most suitable (proper) instrument; the different legal status of certificates and their effects, etc. Frackowiak-Adamska 2015, p. 199-202.

139 A codification of 'EU private international law' would be easier to achieve on terms of policy and competence.

140 One of the objections against codification is that it impairs the dynamics of judicial cooperation in civil matters. However, the CJEU cannot be relied on to produce all-encompassing case law on existing incoherences. See Wiedemann 2015, p. 193.

141 The preceding statement is based on the premise of establishing full faith and credit in civil and commercial matters. The US clause, to the contrary, covers public Acts and records as well.

142 See Kühn Baca 2014, p. 450, 459-463.

143 *Ibid.*

5. Conclusion

The US and EU judiciaries have as many similarities as they have differences. The concept of enforcing EU law is rooted in greater respect for Member State autonomy, attested by the lack of a federal judiciary network and the principle of national procedural autonomy. This does not, however, on its own, obstruct the administration of justice in cross-border enforcement proceedings. The lack of a federal judiciary and federal rules of civil procedure contributes to diverging outcomes of concrete cases under the same provisions of EU law and – potentially – to national court bias against foreign creditors. This further translates to cross-border proceedings where the procedural autonomy of Member States allows for different remedial opportunities. The framework of decentralised enforcement does not, however, affect the possibilities of exercising full faith and credit in EU cross-border enforcement proceedings. Establishing such a regime is not conditioned on a pre-existing federal judiciary, nor on federal rules on litigation. Its effectiveness, nevertheless, may be hampered due to these deficits.

As described above, the US Constitution allowed for the option of establishing Federal courts; it did not impose an obligation to do so. Simultaneously, it maintained the Full Faith and Credit Clause. Understandably, the predecessors of the contemporary EU Treaties were not vested with sufficient competence to frame an equivalent clause, prompting a gradual development of mutual trust and the free movement of judgments. These principles have birthed a plethora of subject matter-specific regulations that shows similar effects to that of the Full Faith and Credit Clause. With BIR's transformation (the abolishment of exequatur), the general framework for cross-border enforcement in civil and commercial matters rendered the level of 'mutual trust' to the extent of limited faith and credit. Prospects for the creation of an EU full faith and credit clause are bright, since they do not require alteration of the existing system and underlying principles of the decentralised enforcement of the law. Unifying the complex regulation *de lege ferenda* will, however, require consideration on substantive limitations regarding the debtor's defences. Here the US example might be of comparative value.

References

Accetto 2007
Accetto, M., *Sodni federalizem Evropske unije: primerjava z ameriškim in nekdanjim jugoslovanskim modelom*, Ljubljana: Uradni list Republike Slovenije, 2007.

Avbelj 2017
Avbelj, M., 'Pluralism and Systemic Defiance in the EU', in: A. Jakab & D. Kochenov (eds.), *The Enforcement of EU Law and Values: Ensuring Member States' Compliance*, Oxford: Oxford University Press, 2017.

Bobek 2012
Bobek, M., 'Why there is no Principle of "Procedural Autonomy" of the Member States', in: B. de Witte & H. Micklitz (eds.), *The European Court of Justice and the Autonomy of the Member States*, Leiden: Intersentia, 2012.

Brkan 2014
Brkan, M., *Postopki pred Sodiščem EU*, Ljubljana: GV Založba, 2014.

Carrubba & Murrah 2005
Carrubba, J.C. & Murrah L., 'Legal Integration and Use of the Preliminary Ruling Process in the European Union', *International Organization*, 2005, p. 399-418.

Claes 2006
Claes, M., *The National Courts' Mandate in the European Constitution*, Oxford: Hart Publishing, 2006.

Clermont 2006
Clermont, K., 'Reverse-Erie', *Notre Dame Law Review*, 2006, p. 1-58.

Cuniberti & Rueda 2016
Cuniberti, G. & Rueda, I., 'Article 39', in: U. Magnus & P. Mankowski (eds.), *European Commentaries on Private International Law: ECPIL: Commentary, Brussels Ibis Regulation*, Cologne: O. Schmidt, 2016, p. 836-841.

Delicostopoulos 2003
Delicostopoulos, J., 'Towards European Procedural Primacy in National Legal Systems', *European Law Journal*, 2003, p. 599-613.

Dickinson 2015
Dickinson, A., 'Background and Introduction to the Regulation', in: A. Dickinson & E. Lein (eds.), *The Brussels I Regulation Recast*, Oxford: Oxford University Press, 2015, p. 1-54.

Eliantonio & Muir 2015
Eliantonio, M. & Muir, E., 'Conclusions on the "Proceduralisation" of EU Law Through the Backdoor', *REALaw*, 2015, available at: <https://papers.ssrn.com/-sol3/papers.cfm?abstract_id=2620729##>.

Engström 2008
Engström, J., 'National Courts' Obligation to Apply Community Law Ex Officio – The Court Showing New Respect for Party Autonomy and National Procedural Autonomy?', *Review of European Administrative Law*, 2008, p. 67-89.

Fitchen 2015
Fitchen, J., 'The Recognition and Enforcement of Member State Judgements', in: A. Dickinson & E. Lein (eds.), *The Brussels I Regulation Recast*, Oxford: Oxford University Press, 2015, p. 373-519.

Frackowiak-Adamska 2015
Frackowiak-Adamska, A., 'Time for a European "Full Faith and Credit Clause"', *Common Market Law Review*, 2015, p. 191-218.

Frank 1963
Frank, J.P., 'For Maintaining Diversity Jurisdiction', *Yale Law Journal*, 1963, p. 7-13.

Friedenthal, Kane & Miller 1999
Friedenthal, J.H., Kane, M.K. & Miller, A.R., *Civil Procedure*, St. Paul MN: West Publishing, 1999.

Friendly 1928
Friendly, J.H., 'The Historic Basis of Diversity Jurisdiction', *Harvard Law Review*, 1928, p. 483-510.

Galleta 2010
Galleta, D.U., *Procedural Autonomy of EU Member States: Paradise Lost? A study on the 'Functionalized Procedural Competence' of EU Member States*, Heidelberg: Springer, 2010.

Garner 2009
Garner, B. (ed.), *Black's Law Dictionary*, St. Paul MN: West, 2009.

George 2009
George, J.P., 'Enforcing Judgments Across State and National Boundaries: Inbound Foreign Judgments and Outbound Texas Judgments', *South Texas Law Review*, 2009, p. 399-447.

Grashof 2016
Grashof, F., *National Procedural Autonomy Revisited*, Groningen: Europa Law Publishing, 2016.

Haibach 2003
Haibach, G., 'The Mutual Recognition of Decisions in Civil and Commercial Matters in the European Union in the Light of the Full Faith and Credit Clause of the U.S. Constitution', *Maastricht Journal of European and Comparative Law*, 2003, p. 291-300.

Hess 2012
Hess, B., 'Procedural Harmonisation in a European Context', in: X.E. Kramer & C.H. van Rhee (eds.), *Civil Litigation in a Globalising World*, The Hague: TMC Asser Press, 2012, p. 159-174.

Kilpatrick 2000
Kilpatrick, C., *The Future of Remedies in Europe*, Oxford: Hart Publishing, 2000.

Kocourek 1941
Kocourek, A., 'Substance and Procedure', *Fordham Law Review*, 1941, p. 157-186.

Kramer 1990
Kramer, L., 'Diversity Jurisdiction', *BYU Law Review*, 1990, p. 97-129.

Kramer 1994
Kramer, L., 'Understanding Federalism', *Vanderbilt Law Review*, 1994, p. 1485-1561.

Kramer 2012
Kramer, X.E., 'Harmonisation of Civil Procedure and the Interaction with Private International Law', in: X.E. Kramer & C.H. van Rhee (eds.), *Civil Litigation in a Globalising World*, The Hague: TMC Asser Press, 2012, p. 121-140.

Kühn Baca 2014
Kühn Baca, W.M., 'The Principle of Mutual Recognition of Judicial Decisions in EU Law in the Light of the "Full Faith and Credit" Clause of the US Constitution', *Boletín Mexicano de Derecho Comparado*, 2014, p. 449-484.

Lenaerts & Gutman 2006
Lenaerts, K. & Gutman, K., '"Federal Common Law" in the European Union: A Comparative Perspective from the United States', *The American Journal of Comparative Law*, 2006, p. 1-121.

Lindholm 2007
Lindholm, J., *State Procedure and Union Rights: A Comparison of the European Union and the United States*, Uppsala: Iustus Förlag, 2007.

Mullenix, Redish & Vairo 1998
Mullenix, L., Redish, M. & Vairo, G., *Understanding Federal Courts and Jurisdiction*, New York, San Francisco: Matthew Bender, 1998.

Nagel & Gottwald 2007
Nagel, H. & Gottwald, P., *Internationales Zivilprozessrecht*, Cologne: O. Schmidt, 2007.

Nicola 2016
Nicola, F.G., 'National Legal Traditions at Work in the Jurisprudence of the Court of Justice of the European Union', *The American Journal of Comparative Law*, 2016, p. 865-889.

O'Neil 1930
O'Neil, J.T., 'Full Faith and Credit Clause of the Federal Constitution', *Notre Dame Law Review*, 1930, p. 199-207.

Pretelli 2011
Pretelli, I., 'Proposal for a Regulation of the European Parliament and of the Council on Jurisdiction and the Recognition and Enforcement of Judgments in Civil and Commercial Matters (recast)', 2011, available at: <http://www.europarl.europa.eu/thinktank/en/document.html?reference=IPOL-JURI_NT(2011)453205>.

Ragsdale 2013
Ragsdale, A.B., *Debates on the Federal Judiciary: A Documentary History [1787–1875]*, Washington DC: Federal Judicial Center, 2013.

Rijavec 2003
Rijavec, V., *Civilno izvršilno pravo*, Ljubljana: GV Založba, 2003.

Rowe, Sherry & Tidmarsh 2008
Rowe, D.T., Sherry, S. & Tidmarsh, J., *Civil Procedure*, New York: Thompson/Foundation Press, 2008.

Schlueter 1984
Schlueter, A.D., 'Judicial Federalism and Supreme Court Review of State Court Decisions: A Sensible Balance Emerges', *Notre Dame Law Review*, 1984, p. 1079-1117.

Schütze 2012
Schütze, R., *European Constitutional Law*, Cambridge: Cambridge University Press, 2012.

Sedler 1962
Sedler, R.A, 'The Erie Outcome Test as a Guide to Substance and Procedure in the Conflict of Laws', *NYU Law Review*, 1962, p. 813-880.

Solum 2004
Solum, L.B., 'Procedural Justice', *Southern California Law Review*, 2004, p. 181-322.

Tapley 1943
Tapley, W., 'Is "Full Faith" Divorced from Divorces?', *St. John's Law Review*, 1943, p. 87-97.

Van Gerven 2000
Van Gerven, W., 'Of Rights, Remedies and Procedures', *Common Market Law Review*, 2000, p. 501-533.

Van Rhee 2012
Van Rhee, C.H., 'Harmonisation of Civil Procedure: An Historical and Comparative Perspective', in: X.E. Kramer & C.H. van Rhee (eds.), *Civil Litigation in a Globalising World*, The Hague: TMC Asser Press, 2012, p. 39-64.

Verhoeven & Ortlep 2012
Verhoeven, M. & Ortlep, R., 'The Principle of Primacy versus the Principle of National Procedural Autonomy', *Netherlands Administrative Law Library*, 2012, p. 1-16.

Vila Maior 2009
Vila Maior, P., 'The European Union as a Federal Polity?', Universidade Fernando Pessoa, 2009, available at: <https://bdigital.ufp.pt/bitstream/10284/1420/2/-The%20European%20Union%20as%20a%20Federal%20Polity_%20An%20Input%20to%20an%20Unfinished%20Symphony.pdf>.

Weatherill 1995
Weatherill, S., *Law and Integration in the European Union*, Oxford: Oxford University Press, 1995.

Wells 2017
Wells, M., 'Judicial Federalism in the European Union', *Houston Law Review*, 2017, p. 697-774.

Wiedemann 2015
Wiedemann, D., 'Convergence and Divergence in the EU's Judicial Cooperation in Civil Matters: Pleading for a Consolidation through a Uniform European Conflict's Codification', in: E.V. De Sequeira & G. De Almeida Ribeiro (eds.), *Católica Graduate Legal Research Conference 2014 – Conference Proceedings*, Lisbon, 2015, p. 175-198.

Wright 1983
Wright, C.A., *Law of Federal Courts*, St. Paul MN: West, 1983.

Wright, Charles & Kane 2002
Wright, C.A., Charles, A. & Kane, K.M., *Law of Federal Courts*, St. Paul MN: West, 2002.

Young 2018
Young, E.A., 'A Comparative Perspective', in: R. Schütze & T. Tridimas (eds.), *Oxford Principles of European Union Law: The European Union Legal Order*, Oxford: Oxford University Press, 2018, p. 142-190.

K. Drnovšek

ECONOMIC IMPLICATIONS OF THE ABOLITION OF EXEQUATUR UNDER BRUSSELS I RECAST

1. Introduction

The Brussels I Recast Regulation (BIR hereafter),[1] which replaced the Brussels I Regulation,[2] is arguably one of the most widely discussed - and also criticised - legislative steps that have recently been taken within the European Area of Justice. This is quite unsurprising, considering the scope and implications of the regulation which applies to most civil judgments and is mandatory. One of its most controversial changes, which also represents one of the main objectives behind the recast, as well as the topic of this contribution, is the abolition of exequatur. In its Proposal for BIR,[3] the European Commission emphasised that 'civil judicial cooperation has developed in the context of the creation of an internal market in Europe based on the premise of mutual recognition of judgments' and that, '[T]oday, judicial cooperation and the level of trust among the Member States has reached a degree of maturity which permits the move towards a simpler, less costly, and more automatic system of circulation of judgments, removing the existing formalities among the Member States.'[4] The notion of the principle of mutual

1 Regulation (EU) No. 1215/2012 of the European Parliament and of the Council of 12 December 2012 on jurisdiction and the recognition and enforcement of judgments in civil and commercial matters [2012] OJ L 351.

2 Council Regulation (EC) No. 44/2001 of 22 December 2000 on jurisdiction and the recognition and enforcement of judgments in civil and commercial matters [2001] OJ L 012.

3 European Commission, Proposal for a Regulation of the European Parliament and of the Council on jurisdiction and the recognition and enforcement of judgments in civil and commercial matters (Recast), SEC (2010) 1547 final, SEC (2010) 1548 final, COM (2010) 748 final, Brussels, 14 December 2010, p. 6, available at: <http://eur-lex.europa.eu/legal-content/EN/TXT/PDF/?uri=CELEX:52010PC0748&from=EN>, last accessed 20 June 2019.

4 Free movement of civil judgments means that parties are able to invoke a judgment in a civil case in a Member State other than the state in which it was delivered and is a prerequisite for international trade. Complete free movement would mean that judgments are recognised and can be enforced across borders without the interested parties needing to surmount any procedural obstacles. Hazelhorst 2017, p. 17.

recognition as a cornerstone of judicial cooperation in civil matters is not new and can be traced back to at least 1999, when it was discussed at a special meeting of the Tampere European Council,[5] as well as to Article 81 of the Treaty on the Functioning of the European Union (TFEU), according to which judicial cooperation in civil matters having cross-border implications is based on the principle of mutual recognition. Since then, several European Union (EU) regulations have been adopted that have simplified judicial protection in cross-border cases to various degrees, circumventing, replacing or abolishing exequatur.[6] Encouraged by a generally successful implementation of these instruments, the European Commission undertook the very demanding project of recasting the Brussels I Regulation and abolishing exequatur for all civil and commercial matters that fall within the scope of the regulation. BIR in its final form, which notably differs from the initial proposal,[7] was generally received quite favourably by many shareholders and was, for example, described as possibly the most straightforward model thus far, which meets the desire to abolish formalities that may delay enforcement and that increase costs, while also retaining debtor protection through the well-

5 For more, see Tampere European Council, 'Presidency Conclusions', No. 200/1/99, 15 and 16 October 1999, available at: <http://www.europarl.europa.eu/summits/tam_en.htm>, last accessed 25 June 2019.

6 These regulations are the following:

- Council Regulation (EC) No. 2201/2003 of 27 November 2003 concerning jurisdiction and the recognition and enforcement of judgments in matrimonial matters and matters of parental responsibility, repealing Regulation (EC) No. 1347/2000 [2003] OJ L 338. Under the Brussels IIA Regulation, exequatur is required, with certain exceptions (e.g. judgments relating to the return of a child). See Articles 40-50 of the Brussels IIA Regulation.
- Regulation (EC) No. 805/2004 of the European Parliament and of the Council of 21 April 2004 creating a European Enforcement Order for uncontested claims [2004] OJ L 143. Under this regulation, the court of origin is authorised to certify the judgment as a European Enforcement Order, which is directly enforceable throughout the EU, without exequatur. Traditional grounds of refusal (including public policy) were replaced with particular minimum requirements (e.g. related to the service of documents). See Articles 12-19 of the European Enforcement Order Regulation.
- Regulation (EC) No. 1896/2006 of the European Parliament and of the Council of 12 December 2006 creating a European order for payment procedure [2006] OJ L 399 and Regulation (EC) No. 861/2007 of the European Parliament and of the Council of 11 July 2007 establishing a European Small Claims Procedure [2007] OJ L 199. These two regulations established new European civil procedures that automatically result in a title that is enforceable throughout the EU. See Article 19 of the European Order for Payment Regulation and Article 20 of the European Small Claims Procedure Regulation.
- Council Regulation (EC) No. 4/2009 of 18 December 2008 on jurisdiction, applicable law, recognition and enforcement of decisions and cooperation in matters relating to maintenance obligations [2008] OJ L 7. The Maintenance Regulation abolished exequatur for those Member States that have adopted the Protocol of 23 November 2007 on the Law Applicable to Maintenance Obligations.

7 European Commission, Proposal for Brussels I Recast, *supra* n. 3.

established grounds of refusal in the enforcement stage.[8] However, the abolition of exequatur itself was subject to a heated discussion and greatly divided opinions – including some very heavy criticism, parts of which will be discussed in this contribution.

The European Commission based its justification of the abolition of exequatur on two groups of reasons: political reasons, which refer to the above-mentioned concept of mutual trust and mutual recognition, and economic reasons, which will be discussed in this contribution.

Under the Brussels I Regulation, the exequatur procedure consisted of two stages. In the first stage a foreign judgment was declared enforceable as long as it met the formal requirements listed in Article 53, while in the second stage certain limited grounds of refusal from Articles 34 and 35 (e.g. public policy, irreconcilability of judgments, improper service) were examined if the judgment was being challenged. Under BIR, the declaration of enforceability (i.e. exequatur) was abolished and 'a judgment given in a Member State which is enforceable in that Member State shall be enforceable in the other Member States without any declaration of enforceability being required' (Article 39). The grounds for refusal are again considered only in the case of an appeal. Although the premise that the removal of an additional step in the proceedings may lead to lower costs and shorter delays is reasonable, it is very difficult to estimate, at least somewhat accurately, the amount of the savings. The European Commission's arguments relied on studies that anticipated savings of as much as €48 million in direct costs (court fees, lawyers' fees, translation costs) per year, without even counting the indirect benefits of increased cross-border business relationships. However, the methodology used in these studies and the collected data arguably turned out to be somewhat arbitrary and imprecise, raising many doubts as to the trustworthiness of the European Commission's conclusions and arguments. Not all criticism is justified and some savings resulting from the abolition of exequatur (in addition to some other cost-saving measures, such as new rules on the translation of documents) can doubtlessly be expected, but the first estimates could very well turn out to be overly optimistic. This contribution explains the basis for the economic arguments used to justify the abolition of exequatur, discusses concerns regarding the reliability of the statistical data used in these arguments and presents some examples of what financial impact the abolition of exequatur is expected to have in the different Member States.

2. Economic justification for the abolition of exequatur

The impact and efficiency of the existing regulation of exequatur under the Brussels I Regulation was the subject of extensive theoretical discussions and empirical studies, of which the Center for Strategy and Evaluation Services (CSES) Impact

8 Dickinson & Lein 2015, p. 406.

Analysis[9] and the Heidelberg Report[10] were the most widely cited. In its Impact Assessment accompanying the proposal for a recast of the Brussels I Regulation,[11] the European Commission largely relied on and referred to data presented in exactly these two reports when justifying the recast of a regulation that had been adopted only eight years prior to this proposal.[12] The European Commission followed the overall opinion that the Brussels I Regulation worked successfully and considered it 'a highly successful instrument, which has facilitated cross-border litigation through an efficient system of judicial cooperation based on comprehensive jurisdiction rules, coordination of parallel proceedings, and circulation of judgments.'[13] It nevertheless concluded that these studies also revealed the need and potential for reform, which could make cross-border litigation prompter, cheaper and more efficient.[14]

As the main objective of the revision of the Brussels I Regulation, the European Commission emphasised the abolition of the exequatur procedure in all matters covered by the regulation.[15] In its Green Paper on the review of the Brussels I Regulation,[16] it explained that while the exequatur procedure in the Brussels I Regulation simplified the procedure for recognition and enforcement compared to

9 Centre for Strategy & Evaluation Services [CSES], 'Data Collection and Impact Analysis – Certain Aspects of a Possible Revision of Council Regulation No. 44/2001 on Jurisdiction and the Recognition and Enforcement of Judgments in Civil and Commercial Matters ('Brussels I')', 17 December 2010, available at: <http://ec.europa.eu/justice/civil/files/-study_cses_brussels_i_final_17_12_10_en.pdf>, last accessed 19 June 2019.

10 The Heidelberg Report (Hess, Pfeiffer & Schlosser 2008).

11 European Commission, 'Impact Assessment – Accompanying Document to the Proposal for a Regulation of the European Parliament and of the Council on jurisdiction and the recognition and enforcement of judgments in civil and commercial matters (Recast)', COM (2010) 748 final, SEC (2010) 1548 final, 14 December 2010, available at: <http://ec.europa.eu/-justice/policies/civil/docs/sec_2010_1547_en.pdf>, last accessed 19 June 2019.

12 For the full list of reports, studies and conferences where empirical data was collected, see European Commission, 'Impact Assessment', *supra* n. 11, p. 7 and 50-51.

13 European Commission, 'Report from the Commission to the European Parliament, the Council and the European Economic and Social Committee on the application of Council Regulation (EC) No. 44/2001 on jurisdiction and the recognition and enforcement of judgments in civil and commercial matters', COM (2009) 174 final, Brussels, 21 April 2009, p. 3, available at: <http://ec.europa.eu/civiljustice/news/docs/report_judgments_en.pdf>, last accessed 20 June 2019.

14 See European Commission, 'Impact Assessment', *supra* n. 11, p. 6.

15 See European Commission, 'Report from the Commission', *supra* n. 13, p. 4. Three other shortcomings were listed by the Commission: (1) access to justice in the EU is unsatisfactory in disputes involving defendants from outside the EU and the diversity of national law leads to unequal access to justice for EU companies in transactions with partners from third countries; (2) the efficiency of choice of court agreements needs to be improved; (3) the interface between arbitration and litigation needs to be improved. See European Commission, 'Proposal for Brussels I Recast', *supra* n. 3, p. 3-4.

16 European Commission, 'Green Paper on the review of Council Regulation (EC) No. 44/2001 on jurisdiction and the recognition and enforcement of judgments in civil and commercial matters', COM (2009) 175 final, Brussels, 21 April 2009, p. 2, available at: <http://eur-lex.europa.eu/legal-content/EN/TXT/PDF/?uri=CELEX:52009DC0175&from=en>, last accessed 21 June 2019.

the previous system, '[I]t is difficult to justify, in an internal market without frontiers, that citizens and businesses have to undergo the expenses in terms of costs and time to assert their rights abroad.' Since the collected data demonstrated that recognition and enforcement of foreign judgments are very rarely refused, the abolition of exequatur was considered a sensible next step.

The estimated economic impact of the abolition of exequatur was significant; it would allow European companies engaged in cross-border business to save no less than €48 million each year – the amount that represents the costs of intermediate procedures under the Brussels I Regulation regime. This number is based on the statistical data contained in the CSES Impact Analysis, which collected information on 9,922 cases of exequatur (in 2009).[17] The main costs associated with exequatur applications are the court fees and legal costs (amounting to an average of 48 per cent of all costs), followed by the costs of translation, preparation of documentation, service of documents and other costs (e.g. expert fees),[18] although the costs could vary between individual cases.[19]

CSES calculated the average cost for two types of cases – straightforward cases, in which exequatur is granted without an appeal (with estimated expenses for the translation of a 25-page document, court fees and lawyers' charges for five hours) and more complex or contested cases (with estimated expenses for the translation of a 100-page document and lawyers' charges for five days). The average cost of exequatur proceedings in straightforward cases was thus estimated at €2,208 (with the lowest estimated cost amounting to €1,048 in Spain and the highest estimated cost amounting to €3,955 in the UK) and the average cost of contested cases was estimated at €12,791. The amount of €48 million was calculated for a scenario in which 25 per cent of all cases are complex, i.e. appealed.[20]

These estimated costs seem especially significant when taking into consideration a very high success rate of exequatur applications. Both the CSES Impact Analysis and the Heidelberg Report estimated that over 90 per cent of exequatur cases are successful. According to statistical data obtained by CSES, 93 per cent of exequatur applications across the EU were successful in 2009 (with the lowest success rate in Bulgaria at 56 per cent and the highest in Finland at 100 per cent). The Heidelberg Report similarly found that more than 90 per cent (often 100 per cent) of all applications for a declaration of enforceability were successful and that the percentage of appeals is between 1 per cent and 5 per cent of all decisions.[21]

Further economically beneficial consequences were expected to result from new transactions entered into by an estimated number of 5.8 million small and medium-sized enterprises that were not yet involved in cross-border relationships,

17 For remarks on the accuracy of statistical data, see Section 3 below.

18 CSES Impact Analysis, *supra* n. 9, p. 41-42.

19 It is important to emphasise that the CSES Impact Analysis is attempting to make an estimate of those additional costs that are incurred as a result of exequatur and not the total costs of enforcement; other costs of enforcement will be incurred regardless of whether the case is cross-border or not.

20 CSES Impact Analysis, *supra* n. 9, p. 44-45.

21 The Heidelberg Report (Hess, Pfeiffer & Schlosser 2008).

as well as from cross-border commerce of newly encouraged consumers who were previously discouraged by the risk of costly and time-consuming litigation.[22] In the CSES survey, 39.4 per cent of business and consumer organisations said that they would be a lot more inclined to engage in cross-border commercial activities if a judgment obtained in one Member State was enforceable in another Member State without additional procedures, and a further 26.7 per cent said that they would be slightly more inclined to do so. The calculation based on the number of small and medium-sized enterprises that are currently only doing business in their own Member State (there are an estimated 15 million of such enterprises) has shown that some 2,800 enterprises could benefit from the abolition of exequatur with direct cost savings of between €6.16 million and €33.6 million.[23] These enterprises have been deterred thus far by extra costs, as well as by extra delays in enforcement proceedings that occurred because of exequatur. According to the Heidelberg Report, exequatur proceedings may last from days (or even hours) to more than half a year, with an average duration of two weeks,[24] whereas according to the CSES Impact Analysis, more than one month (over three months in 40 per cent of cases) is the typical duration.[25] According to the CSES Impact Analysis, the abolition of exequatur would therefore not only positively impact businesses and consumers that are already involved in cross-border trade by making court procedures quicker and cheaper, but should also encourage other businesses and consumers to start cross-border trading for the first time, which would have a wider positive effect on the European economy.[26]

However, the implementation of these changes, accompanied by all these benefits, would result in a minimum amount of costs for the EU and its Member States. According to the European Commission's cost assessment, the only expenses related to the reform would be the costs for training and for changes to existing rules. With regard to the non-financial aspects, the abolition of exequatur would improve access to justice (thereby positively affecting the exercise of fundamental rights) and protect weaker parties (e.g. consumers and employees).[27]

Considering all of these factors, it is not surprising that the abolition of exequatur was initially based on an economic justification. Several shareholders joined the discussion and responded to the Green Paper and to the Proposal for BIR with their own input. In this regard, it should be noted that while a large majority of stakeholders and all Member States supported the objective of the free movement of judgments within the EU, with the abolition of exequatur as a means to achieve this objective, a very large majority also insisted that the abolition should be accompanied by safeguards to protect the rights of the party against whom the

22 Other estimated savings were foreseen as a result of the new rules on jurisdiction and more effective regulation of arbitration agreements. See European Commission, 'Impact Assessment', *supra* n. 11, p. 40-41, 59.

23 For more details on methodology, see CSES Impact Analysis, *supra* n. 9, p. 63-65.

24 The Heidelberg Report (Hess, Pfeiffer & Schlosser 2008, p. 226).

25 CSES Impact Analysis, *supra* n. 9, p. 47.

26 *Ibid.*, p. 61.

27 European Commission, 'Impact Assessment', *supra* n. 11, p. 41.

enforcement is sought.[28] The main concern was that the judgment debtor's assets may otherwise be seized and disposed of without any warning, or in other words, that 'facilitating the free movement of judgments across borders by removing a layer of judicial scrutiny may also create a risk of fraudulent activity which is higher than that present in purely domestic cases.'[29] Following a heated discussion, the grounds for refusal remained practically unchanged under BIR.[30]

3. Criticism and doubts regarding the accuracy of statistical data

The methodology used by the above-mentioned studies as well as the conclusions drawn on the basis of the collected data were subject to considerable criticism and reservations. Even authors of the above-discussed research explained that the data might be less than accurate and mainly represent a broad estimation. For example, CSES noted that in many cases, data regarding the number of exequatur applications is not collected at a national level (19 of the 27 Member States), with the exception of the smaller countries and/or those with relatively centralised jurisdictions. In nineteen Member States where no statistics are available at a national level, the numbers on which the conclusions were drawn are therefore an

28 *Ibid.*, p. 48. For example, the Council of Bars and Law Societies of Europe (CCBE) noted that the trust in foreign judgments would be improved if the level of access to justice in all Member States were comparable and that there should be minimum standards of procedural safeguards in cross-border cases to guarantee that the abolition of exequatur would facilitate enforcement but still ensure adequate protection for judgment debtors. They noted that even though the service of judgments and judicial documents is regulated to some extent by EU legislation, the lack of harmonisation leads to difficulties when applying national procedural rules. For a more detailed explanation, see CCBE 'Response to the Green Paper on the review of the Council Regulation (EC) No. 44/2001 on jurisdiction and the recognition and enforcement of judgments in civil and commercial matters', 26 June 2009, available at: <http://www.ccbe.eu/NTCdocument/CCBE_response_to_the1_1246371870.pdf>, last accessed 20 June 2019.

29 Dickinson 2011, p. 7.

30 The original proposal of the European Commission included a system with three different remedies against enforcement of a foreign judgment, submitted to three different authorities. In the Member State of enforcement, the competent authority would be responsible for remedies filed against judgments irreconcilable with another judgment which had been issued in the Member State of enforcement or – provided that certain conditions were fulfilled – in another country. Furthermore, courts in the Member State of enforcement would decide in cases of procedural defects which might have arisen during the proceedings before the court of origin and which might have infringed the debtor's right to a fair trial. In the Member State of origin, the court would review remedies in a situation where the debtor was not properly informed about the proceedings in that Member State (default judgment). These procedural safeguards would ensure that the defendant's right to a fair trial and his rights of defence as guaranteed in Article 47 of the EU Charter on Fundamental Rights are adequately protected. They were intended to remedy primarily procedural errors and thus to replace the grounds for review under the Brussels I Regulation. Furthermore, the European Commission proposed to abolish substantive public policy; a suggestion that was not met favourably by almost any Member State. In this respect, the proposal was not implemented in its suggested form and was greatly criticised as being too complex. See, e.g., Dickinson & Lein 2015, p. 406; Nielsen 2012, p. 585, 591-593; Kramer 2011a, p. 633, 640.

estimate that is based on the data provided by a sample of fifteen courts and on data obtained through interviews. Where no estimate at all could be provided, the researchers scaled up the numbers for the sample of courts using population as a multiplier.[31] The European Commission was aware of this when it stated that 'a major issue with these data is a consequence of the fact that there is no systematic collection of statistical data on the application of the Brussels I Regulation in most Member States. Some data was thus gathered from central databases of the Ministries of Justice, directly from courts and based on interviews, literature and other sources.'[32]

Such divergent methodologies of data collection necessarily result in unreliable and imprecise information. Significantly, many critics have noted that the report is based on arbitrary parameters, on vague and small data samples, that it lacks supportive data, is riddled with inaccurate estimates, etc.[33] It is clear that any estimated average amount related to the cost of any proceedings cannot be anything more than a very broad approximation, considering the fact that each case is unique in its course, duration and therefore in expenses incurred. Because it would take an enormous amount of time and resources (and would probably not even then be possible) to obtain more precise information on the expenditure in each individual exequatur case, CSES decided on two hypothetical scenarios for its calculations (straightforward and complex/contested cases) which may serve as an illustration, but are in no way a true indication of the actual costs that would occur in an actual case. The approximation of the average cost in straightforward exequatur proceedings in the amount of €2,208 does not represent empirical data at all, but is simply based on the calculation that such a case will require twenty-five pages to be translated at an average rate of €30 per page, that the amount of €100 should be added to cover expert fees and administration costs and that a lawyer will need five hours to work on such a case, whereas this last number is then simply multiplied by 'the average legal fees' in the Member State (as have been estimated by the study on the Transparency on Costs of Civil Judicial Proceedings in the European Union).[34] [35] Legal fees turned out to be especially problematic in this regard. While court fees are usually transparent and straightforward, the manner in which legal fees are

31 CSES Impact Analysis, *supra* n. 9, p. 37-38. Timmer 2013, p. 129, 143-144. Timmer somewhat humorously described the methodology in the case of Greece, where no data had been collected and the figures were estimates obtained from a legal expert from Greece in a way that 'they basically simply asked a Greek to make an educated guess and then shook their magic eight-ball for confirmation. The number "500" fell out of the hat and was then placed in the CSES report, while the origin of this number was relegated to an appendix.' Since in as many as 19 of the 27 Member States the data had not been collected on a national level, she finds such approach extremely problematic.

32 See also European Commission, 'Report from the Commission', *supra* n. 13, p. 3.

33 See, e.g., Hovaguimian 2005, p. 212, 241-242; Timmer 2013, p. 143; Pretelli 2011, p. 16. Timmer noted that the word 'estimate' is used in the report no less than 142 times.

34 'Study on the Transparency of Costs of Civil Judicial Proceedings in the European Union, Final Report', JLS/2006/C4/007-30-CE-0097604/00-36.

35 Timmer 2013, p. 143. Timmer noted that even then the CSES Impact Analysis used the maximum of the identified legal fees as a basis for calculation, with added inflation.

determined varies from case to case, from one Member State to another and even from one organisation to another in the same country (fixed sums, fee rates depending on the type of litigation, success-related fees linked to the size of the claim, fees calculated on an hourly basis, charges depending on the amount of the litigation, etc.).[36]

The least precise part of the CSES Impact Analysis is probably the estimation of the impact of the abolition of exequatur on the participation of small and medium-sized enterprises in cross-border transactions, and related economic benefits. The fact that the estimation of direct cost savings ranges from between about €6 million and €33 million demonstrates that any precise calculation is practically impossible in this regard.[37]

Even if we overlook the potentially problematic reliability of the collected data and assume that they are correct, some authors have noted that the savings would not be as significant as the conclusions of the European Commission would lead us to believe. The estimated amount of €48 million per year was based on the assumption that parties would save on average €53 in court fees, €1,250 in lawyer's fees and €850 in translation fees. This assumption was disputed with the argument that the abolition of exequatur would not eliminate this entire amount, but only the exequatur court fees (€53).[38] The translation of the entire judgment would still be required in certain cases[39] and only time will tell how often this will happen in practice.[40] Furthermore, the parties will often still acquire legal representation, considering the fact that many parties do not feel comfortable with participation in proceedings before a foreign court, in a foreign language, using foreign procedural law. At the very least, professional assistance will still be needed when investigating the competent authorities and submitting the appropriate documents, meaning that legal costs will not be entirely eliminated. In the case of the debtor's appeal, the expenses would be practically the same as before the abolition of exequatur,[41] while the delays could even be longer when compared to the previous regime (especially where national procedural rules prohibit enforcement during the time of appeal).[42]

36 CSES Impact Analysis, *supra* n. 9, p. 43.

37 See also Timmer 2013, p. 144-145.

38 See Hovaguimian 2005, p. 243.

39 Pursuant to Articles 37, 42, 47 and 53 BIR.

40 See also Section 5 below.

41 Hovaguimian 2005, p. 243. Hovaguimian estimates that at least half of the costs of exequatur as calculated by CSES will still have to be paid in straightforward cases and that the average costs of complex cases would hardly change at all.

42 An example of changes that could lead to further delays is Recital 32 of BIR, according to which, 'In order to inform the person against whom enforcement is sought of the enforcement of a judgment given in another Member State, the certificate established under this Regulation, if necessary accompanied by the judgment, should be served on that person *in reasonable time* before the first enforcement measure.' Another example is the abolished provision of Article 43 of the Brussels I Regulation, stating that, 'An appeal against the declaration of enforceability is to be lodged within one month of service thereof.' Additionally, the costs charged by enforcement agencies may now be higher, especially if they are to adapt non-monetary measures into a suitable equivalent in the state of enforcement. For more, see Timmer 2013, p. 134, 145.

The actual savings will, therefore, depend on the number of judgment debtors that will actually apply to a court for refusal of enforcement and on the Member States involved.[43]

To contradict the European Commission's proposal, some alternative solutions and measures were presented by legal scholars and professionals that would reduce costs and shorten delays as well, without having to resort to the abolition of exequatur to achieve this aim. Among such measures were, for example, EU-wide exequatur deadlines, harmonised caps on costs, the loser-pays rule, the use of information technology, and others.[44] While the abolition of exequatur is now a fact, these suggestions are worth further attention, as they could indeed further simplify and expedite cross-border enforcement.

4. Expectations and initial experience with BIR in the EU Member States

At the time of the writing of this contribution, no extensive study had yet been conducted that would calculate the actual savings in enforcement proceedings following the implementation of BIR and either confirm or refute the expectations of supporters or opponents of the abolition of exequatur. Considering the fact that BIR only entered into force in 2015, it is very doubtful that it would even be possible to collect enough data for any definitive conclusions at this point. However, some efforts have already been made to make sense of the first encounters with the amended regulation. In the scope of the ongoing research conducted under the EU Project 'Remedies concerning Enforcement of Foreign Judgments according to Brussels I Recast',[45] the national reporters from fifteen EU Member States have

43 Oberhammer 2010, p. 197-284. Oberhammer noted that Germany probably is not among the countries where the abolition of exequatur will shorten delays, since the exequatur is at the same time the first step of enforcement under domestic law (the so-called *Vollstreckungsklausel*), which is required for both domestic and foreign judgments. Kramer 2011b, p. 202, 218. Kramer noted that enforcement measures differ significantly from one Member State to another, and some allow for a review that may even go beyond the grounds of refusal under the Brussels I Regulation, which is why a uniform exequatur procedure could even be replaced by 27 national enforcement regimes. See also Kramer 2011a, p. 641 and Kramer 2013, p. 343, 358; Schramm 2013/2014, p. 143, 172. Schramm expects that the timing of enforcement measures will in many cases not be fundamentally different under the Brussels I Regulation and BIR, at least in Member States that provide for one level of appeal under the Brussels I Regulation. In Member States that provide for two levels of appeal, enforcement measures might even take longer under BIR.

44 For more details, see Hovaguimian 2005, p. 242; Timmer 2013, p. 145; Kramer 2011b, p. 216-217.

45 JUST/2014/JCOO/AG/CIVI/7749, co-financed by the European Commission within the framework of the Civil Justice programme. The project lasted from 1 February 2016 until 1 February 2018 and was implemented by the Faculty of Law, University of Maribor as coordinator, together with the beneficiary partners University of Rijeka, Portucalense University, Masaryk University, Leibniz University of Hannover, University of Graz, University of Maastricht, Mykolas Romeris University, Institute for Comparative Law at Law →

answered questionnaires on the implementation of BIR[46] and have thus provided very valuable data and explanations on its success and possible issues in their Member States (in addition to a highly comparable presentation of national enforcement systems). One of the questions required the authors of the national reports to provide their own opinion regarding the costs that will be incurred when enforcing foreign judgments under BIR and whether they think that the new regulation will be more cost-effective (when compared with the Brussels I Regulation). Based on the analysis of these reports,[47] it can be concluded that the national reporters are generally in agreement that BIR and the abolition of exequatur should result in decreased costs in enforcement proceedings involving their Member State, considering the fact that one procedural step less will be needed which generally gives rise to some costs on its own (e.g. court fees when applying for exequatur). However, they are also convinced that the savings will not exactly be sky-high. The main costs that occurred in the enforcement proceedings under the Brussels I Regulation still remain; most notably various types of other court fees and the cost of legal representation, which usually represent a significant percentage of the total cost in each individual proceeding. In spite of the best intentions behind the use of general forms, creditors and debtors still find it difficult and risky to participate in proceedings before a foreign court without a legal representative who is familiar with the relevant foreign legislation. The national reporters further noted that additional cost reductions should result from the new provisions on translation, according to which it is no longer necessary for the creditor to provide a translation of the entire judgment, as was frequently required by the courts under the Brussels I Regulation. However, even this will not always be the case, as the translation of the whole judgment might still be required if the court is unable to proceed with enforcement without the translation.[48] The French national report even mentioned that the complexity of the new certificate, which will now contain more information, might at first cause some difficulties for the registrars who will issue the certificates and might thus cause additional delays.[49]

Faculty in Ljubljana, Tallinn University of Technology, Law firm Sladič-Zemljak, CEPRIS and Chamber of Notaries of Slovenia.

46 Participating Member States are the following: Austria, Belgium, Croatia, the Czech Republic, Estonia, France, Germany, Greece, Italy, Lithuania, the Netherlands, Portugal, Slovenia, Sweden and the UK.

47 National reports are published on the project website, together with other project results (the questionnaire, conference papers, etc.); for more, see <https://www.pf.um.si/en/acj/projects/pr04/activities/>, last accessed 27 May 2019.

48 E.g. N. Bessa Vilela, 'National Report – Portugal', 2017 <https://www.pf.um.si/site/-assets/files/3539/national_report_portugal.pdf>, last accessed 27 May 2019; M. Poola, 'National Report – Estonia', 2017 <https://www.pf.um.si/site/assets/files/3539/-national_report_estonia.pdf>, last accessed 27 May 2019; J. Valdhans & T. Kyselovská, 'National Report – the Czech Republic', 2017 <https://www.pf.um.si/site/assets/files/-3539/national_report_czech_republic.pdf>, last accessed 27 May 2019. See also Section 5 below.

49 O. Bošković Pillet, 'National Report – France', 2017 <https://www.pf.um.si/site/assets/-files/3539/national_report_france.pdf>, last accessed 27 May 2019.

The following is a sample of the first impressions and expectations expressed by the national reporters from different Member States:

4.1. *Austria*[50]

The Austrian national reporters expect little difference in the costs of the enforcement. If Austria is the Member State of origin, there is generally no difference in costs, since, under both the previous Brussels I regime and BIR, the creditor needs a certificate (Article 54 of the Brussels I Regulation and Article 53 BIR). Court fees that have to be paid in order to receive a copy of any official certificate that shall be issued to a party – including the certificate under the Brussels I Regulation or BIR – amount to €3.57 per page.[51] An additional cost can be the lawyer's tariffs for an application to issue a certificate, which depends on the value in dispute and amounts to between €3.50 and €260.00 (in 2016).[52]

If Austria is the Member State of enforcement, there are slight differences between the old and the new situation. Even under the Brussels I Regulation, no additional court fees needed to be paid for exequatur; instead, the creditor had to cover the fees for a regular enforcement procedure. However, when it came to legal representation, the statutory lawyers' tariffs were higher if the creditor needed to apply for exequatur first: if the application for exequatur was filed separately, the lawyer's tariff was to be determined according to tariff list 2 (*Tarifpost* 2) of the RaTG (*Rechtsanwaltstarifgesetz*), but if it was combined with the application for an enforcement order, it was to be determined according to tariff list 3A (*Tarifpost 3A*) of the RaTG. The actual tariff depends on the value in dispute, but would amount to between €14.90 and €1,298.50 in tariff list 2 (in 2016) and between €29.20 and €17,308.80 in tariff list 3A (in 2016). Under BIR, the additional costs for exequatur will not occur.

4.2. *The Czech Republic*[53]

According to the Czech national report, costs are expected to be slightly lower. Costs of enforcement in the case of judicial enforcement are regulated by Act No. 549/1991 Coll., on court fees, Attachment, Item 21: they amount to a minimum 1.000 CZK and are calculated on the basis of a percentage of the amount at stake. This fee does not need to be paid when the enforcement is executed by an executor; instead, the executor receives a commission as a percentage of the amount according to the Decree of the Ministry of Justice 330/2001 Coll. Under BIR, no fee for the application for exequatur needs to be paid.

50 P. Anzenberger & B. Nunner-Krautgasser, 'National Report – Austria', 2017 <https://www.pf.um.si/site/assets/files/3539/national_report_austria.pdf>, last accessed 27 May 2019.

51 Point 15 lit a, of the tariff list of the Court Fees Act (*Gerichtsgebührengesetz*, GGG).

52 Tariff list 1 (TP 1.I.b.), of the Law on Lawyers' Tariffs (*Rechtsanwaltstarifgesetz*, RaTG).

53 J. Valdhans & T. Kyselovská, *supra* n. 48.

4.3. *Italy*[54]

The Italian national reporter states that BIR will undeniably be more cost-effective for the creditors than the Brussels I Regulation, since there is now one procedural step less required for the enforcement of a foreign judgment, regardless of the fact that the costs were not very high even under the Brussels I Regulation, because only an *ex parte* proceeding was strictly necessary. In the procedure for the enforcement of a foreign judgment before Italian courts, the creditor would not have to cover court fees and the costs of a standard legal representation amounts to between less than €500 to more than €10,000 (or even more, if the debtor challenges the enforcement), depending on the value of the claim.[55]

4.4. *Lithuania*[56]

The Lithuanian reporters expect the procedure under BIR to reduce expenses for the creditor seeking to enforce the judgment in another EU Member State as well. Even though Lithuanian legislation foresees no fee for the application to recognise and to declare enforceable a foreign judgment, it is practically impossible to file an application to the court of another Member State without additional costs (at least for legal representation). However, they do not expect a significant reduction in other expenses related to the enforcement of foreign judgments in the other Member States, as the need for the translation of documents remains, as well as enforcement fees, etc. Under Lithuanian legislation, the creditor shall pay the administration fee in advance when submitting the enforceable document to the judicial officer for enforcement, including a foreign judgment enforceable under BIR. Other enforcement expenses shall be recovered from the debtor if the enforcement is successful.

4.5. *Sweden*[57]

The Swedish national reporters mentioned that in the average case BIR will probably be more cost-effective when compared to the former Brussels I Regulation if no legal representation is needed. However, they also noted that the need for legal representation will most likely still be inevitable (e.g. because of the different official

54 A. Giussani, 'National Report – Italy', 2017 <https://www.pf.um.si/site/assets/files/-3539/national_report_italy.pdf >, last accessed 27 May 2019.

55 Court fees were determined by Decree No. 115 of 30 May 2002 and amended by several decrees of the Ministry of Justice. Lawyers' ordinary fees were determined by Law No. 247 of 31 December 2012 and amended by decrees of the Ministry of Justice on a regular basis (the decree was enacted on 10 March 2014). Any fees exceeding the ordinary amount must be negotiated in advance.

56 D. Bolzanas, L. Kamarauskienė, E. Tamošiūnienė & D. Vasarienė, 'National Report – Lithuania', 2017 <https://www.pf.um.si/site/assets/files/3539/national_report_lithuania_-_part_1.pdf>, last accessed 27 May 2019.

57 M. Linton & E. Bylander, 'National Report – Sweden', 2017 <https://www.pf.um.si/site/-assets/files/3539/national_report_sweden.pdf>, last accessed 27 May 2019.

languages in the EU) and the costs associated with the cross-border enforcement of foreign judgments will be higher compared to the costs of the enforcement of domestic judgments.

5. Concluding remarks

In the absence of a study that provides precise, reliable and comparable statistical data regarding the costs that would be incurred in proceedings for the enforcement of a foreign judgment under both the Brussels I Regulation and BIR,[58] it is impossible to speak of the exact amount of savings resulting from the abolition of exequatur. The existing studies, which were conducted before BIR entered into force and could thus merely represent an educated guess of what was to come, had many shortcomings. In addition to the methodological flaws pointed out by the researchers themselves, other legal scholars and researchers also demonstrated that the calculated amounts were at best based on very broad and imprecise assumptions and at worst practically made up. A major part of the economic justifications for the recast of the Brussels I Regulation, as presented by the European Commission, which was based precisely on this flawed data, therefore seems unreliable. However, while it is true that we probably cannot expect savings amounting to the optimistic numbers included in those reports, it would not be prudent to necessarily conclude just on these grounds that the abolition of exequatur is not economically beneficial for the parties involved in cross-border enforcement.

Even if the numbers on which the European Commission's proposals are based really are as erroneous as presented by the critics of the abolition of exequatur, common sense suggests that at least in some cases (arguably, in the majority of cases) the costs of proceedings should be lower and delays should be shorter. It can hardly be denied that exequatur represents an additional step and therefore unavoidably causes at least some costs and delays. Even the critics of the new regime under BIR noted that some savings (e.g. court fees for the procedure for declaration of enforceability) would result.[59] In addition to the court fees for the exequatur procedure, lawyers' fees and translation costs should at least be lower, if

58 Unfortunately, other regulations that abolished exequatur (most notably Regulation (EC) No. 805/2004 of the European Parliament and of the Council of 21 April 2004 creating a European Enforcement Order for uncontested claims and Council Regulation (EC) No. 4/2009 of 18 December 2008 on jurisdiction, applicable law, recognition and enforcement of decisions and cooperation in matters relating to maintenance obligations) have not yet been evaluated by the European Commission either and no study yet exists that would provide comparable statistical or other numerical data on the economic impact of the abolition of exequatur. Differences between these regulations are significant and the amounts of potentially saved costs could not be directly applied to the case of the Brussels I Regulation and BIR, but any such data would at least provide a useful indication of what could generally be expected. To some extent, the issue of costs in cross-border enforcement in certain selected Member States was addressed by Rijavec, Ivanc & Keresteš 2014.

59 Hovaguimian 2005, p. 243. According to his estimate, the savings could still add up to about €40 million, which is not a negligible amount.

not completely eliminated. If the rate of successful cross-border enforcement proceedings really is over 90 per cent, as is indicated by the collected statistical data, even these smaller-than-estimated amounts should on average exceed the costs that will occur in a few very complex appealed cases that might be higher under BIR than in the previous system.

It is also worth noting that while this contribution dealt with the very narrow issue of the economic impact of the abolishment of exequatur, this is not the only factor that might have a significant impact in this regard. Other changes that could reduce the costs of enforcement proceedings relate to the new rules on jurisdiction, to the promotion of arbitration agreements,[60] to the abolished requirement for the party seeking enforcement to have a postal address or an authorised representative in the Member State of enforcement,[61] as well as to the changes relating to the translation of documents. One of the criticised issues in the regime under the Brussels I Regulation was the provision of the second paragraph of Article 55, which stated that if the court or competent authority so requires, a translation of the documents shall be produced. The translation shall be certified by a person qualified to do so in one of the Member States. The provision itself seems reasonable and the forms introduced by the Brussels I Regulation[62] are indeed an improvement when compared to the older means of communication between the ministries, but in practice the courts very frequently requested the creditor to provide a translation of the entire judgment when requesting enforcement, even if that was not necessary for the enforcement itself, and if they actually understood the language of the foreign judgment in question.[63] That naturally led to increased costs for translation that could be quite exorbitant, as the length of the judgment could reach hundreds of pages in some cases and in some Member States. Furthermore, a great deal of confusion frequently occurred regarding the required qualifications of the translator, since these requirements were determined by national provisions, which vary greatly between the Member States. Under BIR these requirements have changed, and while the court of enforcement may still request a translation or transliteration of a certificate that has to accompany the foreign judgment (issued pursuant to Article 53), it may only require the party to provide a translation of the judgment instead of a translation of the contents of the certificate if it is unable to proceed without such a translation.[64] It is true that the certificate now holds more information, but its translation nevertheless requires less time and expense than the

60 Even though BIR itself does not apply to arbitration; see Recital 12.

61 Article 41 BIR.

62 In BIR, the amended forms are expected to further facilitate the enforcement of the judgment by the competent authorities, in particular where interest and costs have to be calculated. They also reduce the need for a translation of the judgment and ease the application for a review of the judgment by the defendant who has to act in another Member State. European Commission, Proposal for Brussels I Recast, *supra* n. 3, p. 6.

63 According to the Heidelberg Report (Hess, Pfeiffer & Schlosser 2008), the translation of the whole judgment is regularly required in the following Member States: Austria, Belgium, Cyprus, Czech Republic, Estonia, Greece, Hungary, Latvia, Lithuania, Luxembourg, Poland, Scotland, Slovenia and Sweden.

64 See Articles 37, 42, 47 and 53 BIR.

translation of the entire judgment. A further provision regulating translation, which is intended to safeguard the debtor's procedural rights, is contained in the second paragraph of Article 43, which states that where the person against whom enforcement is sought is domiciled in a Member State other than the Member State of origin, one may request a translation of the judgment in order to contest the enforcement if the judgment is not written in or accompanied by a translation into either a language which one understands, or the official language of the Member State in which one is domiciled or, where there are several official languages in that Member State, the official language or one of the official languages of the place where one is domiciled. Until such translation is provided, no measures of enforcement may be taken, except for protective measures. This provision protects the debtor's right to a fair trial, allowing one to get familiar with the contents of the judgment that is being enforced, if it has not already been previously served on him in one of the above-listed languages or accompanied by a translation into one of those languages, in cases where the court assesses that it can proceed without translation of the judgment.[65] On the other hand, it remains to be seen how frequently the courts and debtors will decide that they are unable to proceed without the translation and whether their reasons will truly be justified, or if the general practice will once again be established where courts will require translations of the full judgment in most of the cases. In the latter case, savings on costs would be less significant than expected. Furthermore, considering the contents of Article 57 of BIR,[66] the differences between national legal systems (e.g. required credentials and qualifications of the translator, the price of translation)[67] will once again determine the actual translation-related expenses. Even among the opponents of the abolition of exequatur, a general opinion regarding these other measures seems to be favourable.[68] Nevertheless, further efforts should be made to address the recurring problems resulting from the differences in national legal systems that would help to avoid situations where the costs in one Member State are significantly higher than the costs in another Member State, therefore deterring

65 Cf. Kramer 2013, p. 358.

66 Article 57 states that when a translation or a transliteration is required under this regulation, such translation or transliteration shall be into the official language of the Member State concerned or, where there are several official languages in that Member State, into the official language or one of the official languages of court proceedings of the place where a judgment given in another Member State is invoked or an application is made, in accordance with the law of that Member State. For the purposes of the forms referred to in Articles 53 and 60, translations or transliterations may also be into any other official language or languages of the institutions of the Union that the Member State concerned has indicated it can accept. Any translation made under this regulation shall be done by a person qualified to do translations in one of the Member States.

67 For a comparison of translation requirements and costs in the EU Member States in civil procedure, see Drnovšek 2016.

68 E.g. Timmer 2013, p. 134. Timmer noted that translation and legal costs have been identified as the major culprits behind the costs of the exequatur procedure and that regardless of how one feels about the decision to abolish exequatur altogether, the changes in this regard are a step in the right direction to minimise the costs related to the cross-border enforcement of judgments.

potential creditors from conducting business transactions in Member States with more expensive and complicated enforcement proceedings.[69]

At this point, it has to be emphasised that while this contribution focused solely on economic reasons for the abolition of exequatur, a very important rationale behind this step is political.[70] Political and ideological reasons additionally fuel opposition and frequently even represent the main argument against the abolition of exequatur, with the economic argument of insufficient savings used merely as support for such opinions, i.e. that the promised savings are not significant enough to justify the disadvantages accompanying the abolition of exequatur.[71] Arguably the most important discussion in this regard is the question of whether the abolition of exequatur jeopardises the protection of human rights in accordance with the EU Charter of Fundamental Rights, considering the fact that exequatur may be considered a remedy against violations of human rights, intended to prevent certain violations from producing effects outside the jurisdiction where they were committed.[72] The real question that should be answered - but not in this contribution - in order to assess the value and consequences of the abolition of exequatur is whether the protection of the parties' rights was compromised in order to achieve lower costs and shorter proceedings, and whether economic benefits really outweigh such consequences.

69 Hovaguimian 2005, p. 251. Hovaguimian notes that BIR favours a challenge procedure governed by national law and judicial discretion, discarding the rules that formerly harmonised critical issues such as the debtor's grace period, the time limits to challenge enforcement, the time limits to proceed with protective measures, or the availability of definitive enforcement measures after a failed first-instance challenge.

70 The European Commission considers the exequatur procedure as an obstacle to the free circulation of judgments, which deters companies and citizens from making full use of the internal market. See European Commission, Proposal for Brussels I Recast, *supra* n. 3, p. 3-4.

71 E.g. Timmer 2013, p. 136, 147.

72 Cuniberti 2012, p. 568-576. Cuniberti offers an interesting perspective on the question of whether the abolishment of exequatur is justified by stating that the real question is whether the legal costs incurred by both parties are higher than the costs that the debtor would incur if he had actually suffered a human rights violation in the foreign proceedings and could not avoid enforcement on this ground. He bases his explanation on the presumption that exequatur affords a useful remedy against human rights violation in less than 1 per cent of the cases and poses the question of whether the protection of the sole right to a fair trial should be balanced against the collective interests of society.

References

Cuniberti 2012
Cuniberti, G., 'Some Remarks on the Efficiency of Exequatur', Law Working Paper Series, Paper Number 2012-01, University of Luxembourg, 2012, p. 568-576.

Dickinson 2011
Dickinson, A. (for the European Parliament, Directorate-General for Internal Policies, Policy Department C, 'Citizens' Rights and Constitutional Affairs, Legal Affairs), *Note to the Proposal for a regulation of the European Parliament and of the Council on jurisdiction and the recognition and enforcement of judgments in civil and commercial matters (recast)*, PE 453.200, European Parliament, Brussels, 2011, p. 7 <http://www.europarl.europa.eu/RegData/etudes/STUD/2011/453200/IPOL-JURI_NT(2011)453200_EN.pdf>.

Dickinson & Lein 2015
Dickinson, A. & Lein, E., *The Brussels I Regulation Recast*, Oxford: Oxford University Press, 2015.

Drnovšek 2016
Drnovšek, K., 'Language Obstacles in the Search for Effective and Fair Fact-Finding', in: V. Rijavec, T. Keresteš & T. Ivanc (eds.), *Dimensions of Evidence in European Civil Procedure*, Alphen aan den Rijn: Kluwer Law International, 2016, p. 237-264.

Hazelhorst 2017
Hazelhorst, M., *Free Movement of Civil Judgments in the European Union and the Right to a Fair Trial*, The Hague: TMC Asser Press, 2017.

Hess, Pfeiffer & Schlosser 2008
Hess, B., Pfeiffer, T. & Schlosser, P., *The Brussels I – Regulation (EC) No 44/2001: The Heidelberg Report on the Application of Regulation Brussels I in 25 Member States (Study JLS/C4/2005/03)*, Munich: Verlag C.H. Beck, 2008.

Hovaguimian 2005
Hovaguimian, P., 'The Enforcement of Foreign Judgments under Brussels I bis: False Alarms and Real Concerns', *Journal of Private International Law*, 2005, p. 212-251.

Kramer 2011a
Kramer, X.E., 'Abolition of Exequatur under the Brussels I Regulation: Effecting and Protecting Rights in the European Judicial Area', *Nederlands Internationaal Privaatrecht*, 2011, Vol. 29(4), p. 633-641.

Kramer 2011b
Kramer, X.E., 'Cross-border Enforcement in the EU: Mutual Trust versus Fair Trial? Towards Principles of European Civil Procedure', *International Journal of Procedural Law*, 2011, Vol. 2, p. 202-230.

Kramer 2013
Kramer, X.E., 'Cross-border Enforcement and the Brussels I-bis Regulation: Towards a New Balance between Mutual Trust and National Control over Fundamental Rights', *Netherlands International Law Review*, 2013, Vol. 60(3), p. 343-373.

Nielsen 2012
Nielsen, P.A., 'Current Developments, The State of Play of the Recast of the Brussels I Regulation', *Nordic Journal of International Law*, 2012, Vol. 83(1), p. 585-603.

Oberhammer 2010
Oberhammer, P., 'The Abolition of Exequatur', *Praxis des Internationalen Privat- und Verfahrensrechts*, 2010, p. 197-284.

Pretelli 2011
Pretelli, I. (for the European Parliament, Directorate-General for Internal Policies, Policy Department C: Citizens' Rights and Constitutional Affairs, Legal Affairs), *Note to the Proposal for a regulation of the European Parliament and of the Council on jurisdiction and the recognition and enforcement of judgments in civil and commercial matters (recast)*, PE 453.205, European Parliament, Brussels, 2011, p. 16, available at: <http://www.europarl.europa.eu/RegData/etudes/STUD/2011/453205/IPOL-JURI_NT(2011)453205_EN.pdf>.

Rijavec, Ivanc & Kerestes̆ 2014
Rijavec, V., Ivanc, T. & Kerestes̆, T. (eds.), *Simplification of Debt Collection in the EU*, Alphen aan den Rijn: Kluwer Law International, 2014.

Schramm 2013/2014
Schramm, D., 'Enforcement and the Abolition of Exequatur under the 2012 Brussels I Regulation', *Yearbook of Private International Law*, 2013/2014, Vol. 15, p. 143-174.

Timmer 2013
Timmer, L.J.E., 'Abolition of Exequatur under the Brussels I Regulation: Ill Conceived and Premature?', *Journal of Private International Law*, 2013, p. 129-147.

A. Giussani

GROUNDS FOR REFUSAL OF RECOGNITION OF FOREIGN JUDGMENTS: DEVELOPMENTS AND PERSPECTIVES IN EU MEMBER STATES REGARDING PUBLIC ORDER AND CONFLICTING DECISIONS

Regulation (EU) No. 1215/2012 of the European Parliament and of the Council of 12 December 2012 on jurisdiction and the recognition and enforcement of judgments in civil and commercial matters supports extension of the effects of EU decisions as a means to grant them identical scope within the whole European judicial space. Complete fulfilment of such a task, however, is hindered by residual margins of sovereignty.

Notwithstanding growing convergence between the legal systems of European Union (EU) Member States and corresponding public order issues, in fact, conflicts may nevertheless survive due to the limits of preventive procedural devices nested in rules governing *lis pendens* and related actions, differences in the operation of *res judicata*, variations of systems of recognition of non-EU judgments and even hidden equitable considerations.

A European federal judiciary with jurisdiction on the merits would be needed to significantly enhance achievement of the aim of granting the winning party the same benefits throughout the Union.

1. Converging notions of procedural public order

This contribution aims at developing a comparative analysis of the rules governing the refusal of recognition of foreign judgments; it is fundamentally based on the national reports delivered within the research project Remedies Concerning Enforcement of Foreign Titles According to Brussels I Recast.[1]

Despite the fact that Member States provide for different procedural devices, when it comes to recognition and enforcement of non-EU foreign judgments (e.g.

1 Reports came from the following countries: Austria, Belgium, the Czech Republic, Estonia, France, Greece, Italy, Lithuania, Portugal, Sweden, the Netherlands and England & Wales.

automatic recognition in Italy,[2] the exequatur system in Slovenia,[3] a new trial in Sweden),[4] and even if only some of them require reciprocity,[5] they all significantly converge with respect to the reasons that justify refusal to give effect.

This convergence is determined mainly by the general clause of public order, and the growing consensus over the idea that the clause applies in cases of violation of fundamental procedural rules: hence, despite several variations in the wording of the rules concerning specific procedural violations, such as lack of jurisdiction, violation of the rights of the defence or fraud, it is quite unlikely that a judgment whose recognition is refused in a Member State for this kind of procedural considerations would nevertheless be recognised and enforced in a different Member State.[6]

The same reasoning obviously applies to the recognition of EU judgments, since the grounds for refusal provided by Regulation (EU) No. 1215/2012 substantially correspond, in these respects, to those provided by Member States' national rules for recognition and enforcement of non-EU ones (albeit violation of public order must also be manifest when it comes to Regulation (EU) No.

2 Pursuant to Article 64 of Law No. 218 of 31 May 1998; recognition is also automatic in Belgium, pursuant to Article 22 of the *Code de droit international privé*, in Greece, pursuant to Article 323 of the Code of Civil Procedure, and in Estonia, pursuant to Article 620 of the Code of Civil Procedure; England & Wales allow automatic recognition in actions *in rem* after the case *Carl Zeiss Stiftung v. Rayner & Keeler Ltd* [1967] 1 AC 853; according to the Austrian report, the same holds for § 415 of the *Exekutionsordnung* and § 236 of the *Zivilprozessordnung;* according to the pertinent reports, recognition is also deemed automatic in the Czech Republic and in France, albeit with some unclear limits in the latter (on the topic, compare also, e.g., Cuniberti, Normand & Cornette 2010, p. 30-31, 40, 62).

3 Pursuant to Articles 94-111 of the *Zakon o mednarodnem zasebnem pravu in postopku;* exequatur is also required in Lithuania, pursuant to Article 809 of the code of civil procedure, and in Portugal, pursuant to Article 978 of the *Código de Processo Civil* (*Novo*).

4 Pursuant to Ch. 3, § 2 of the *Kronofogdemyndigheten;* a new trial is also required in the Netherlands, pursuant to Article 431(1) of the code of civil procedure, and in England & Wales for actions *in personam* after the case *Adams v. Cape Industries plc* [1990] Ch. 433.

5 Although no mention of reciprocity can be found in the reports from Italy, France, Belgium, Greece, Portugal, Lithuania, Estonia and England & Wales, this requirement appears in Article 101(3) of the Slovenian *Zakon o mednarodnem zasebnem pravu in postopku*, and in § 406 of the Austrian *Exekutionsordnung*, and according to pertinent reports is also applied in Sweden and the Czech Republic.

6 Correspondingly, comparatively restrictive interpretations of the notion of public order may also be countered by broad interpretations of, e.g., the notion of lack of jurisdiction (see, e.g., for a refusal to recognise, on the ground of lack of territorial jurisdiction, a judgment disregarding foreign states' immunity for *acta iure imperii*, after the holding by the Italian Constitutional Court No. 238 of 22 October 2014, in *Giurisprudenza italiana*, 2015, 339, that denied the latter defence in cases of violation of human rights, and the judgment of the Italian Court of Cassation No. 21946 of 28 October 2015 in *Giurisprudenza italiana*, 2016, 859); on European procedural public order, European Court of Justice leading cases are Case C-7/98, *Dieter Krombach v. André Bamberski* [2000] ECR I-1935 and Case C-38/98, *Régie nationale des usines Renault SA v. Maxicar SpA and Orazio Formento* [2000] ECR I-2973.

1215/2012),[7] but for the obvious general curtailment of challenges concerning jurisdiction and *lis pendens*.

2. Development of notions of substantive public order

With respect to violations of substantive public order, two relevant fields of general interest deserve mention: antisuit injunctions and punitive damages (instances of violation of a specific Member State's substantive public order will not be considered here, because exposition of such details is not necessary for the analysis of the procedural problems involved).

English antisuit injunctions have been held incompatible with the system of reciprocal trust between Member States,[8] but after 'Brexit' (with the UK leaving the EU) interested parties might try to plead that they should be recognised as non-EU foreign judgments. However, antisuit injunctions are not only a form of unfair jurisdictional competition within the system of reciprocal trust, but they also infringe the fundamental principle of *Kompetenz-Kompetenz*[9] and, most importantly, the fundamental right of action of their addressee;[10] hence, the public order clause contemplated in every Member State should preclude their recognition even as non-EU foreign judgments.

Traditional European hostility towards US punitive damages awards, by contrast, seems to be fading. Case law admitting their enforcement is emerging in several Member States, at least when they are not exceedingly disproportionate to the actual damages, especially because many European legal systems actually contemplate instances of civil damages discretionally awarded by the court to a tort victim, regardless of the proof of prejudice, as a punishment for reckless wrongdoing.[11]

7 In this respect it is worth noting that public order precluding recognition of foreign judgments according to national rules is anyway often more limited in scope than public order governing implementation of national law (see, e.g., in Italy the judgment of the Court of Cassation No. 17349 of 6 December 2002, in *Archivio civile*, 2003, 1081; cf., on the scope of public order in the field of recognition of EFTA decisions, the judgment of the Court of Cassation No. 4392 of 24 February 2014).

8 The European Court of Justice reaffirmed this principle beyond any reasonable doubt in Case C-185/07, *Allianz SpA v. West Tankers Inc* [2009] ECR I-663, para 30.

9 See again *Allianz SpA v. West Tankers Inc, supra* n. 8, para 29.

10 *Ibid.*, para 31.

11 Paralleling the rejection of proposals for a mandatory exclusion of punitive damages in Regulation (EC) 864/2007 of the European Parliament and of the Council of 11 July 2007 on the law applicable to non-contractual obligations (Rome II) [2007] OJ L 199 (see Consideration 32 thereof), in Germany, the notorious halt to punitive damages in the judgment of the *Bundesgerichtshof*, 4 June 1992, in *ZZP*, 1993, 79, has been tempered by a decision of the *Bundesverfassungsgericht*, 24 January 2007, in *JZ* 2007, 1046; in France, a general preclusion to recognition was denied by judgments of the Cour de cassation, 1 December 2010, in *Bull.* 2010, I, No. 248, and 7 November 2012, in *Bull.* 2012, I, No. 228; in Spain, treble damages were already recognised by a decision of the *Tribunal Supremo*, 13 November 2001, ECLI:ES:TS:2001:1803A; in Greece, a punitive damages award was recognised in judgment →

3. Conflicting decisions

The most complex difficulties in this field stem from the problem of the recognition of conflicting judgments: case law specifically on the topic is limited, but the issue is very often intensely litigated in the context of the issues of *lis pendens* and parallel litigation, both with respect to cases pending in a different Member State and with respect to cases pending outside the EU (albeit in such circumstances there is not yet an actual conflict, but only a prediction of risk of conflict: hence, *lis pendens* precludes also decisions that in the end might have turned out coherent, and not conflicting, if the case had not been stayed).

A realistic evaluation of the dynamics of the resolution of conflicts of decisions, however, should warn from the start that rules governing preclusive effects are actually applied with a much less analytical approach than what the supporting opinions would directly tell.

In fact, especially when it comes to the determination of the scope of the preclusive effects of a judgment with respect to issues explicitly or implicitly resolved, or with respect to third parties, governing principles have incoherencies that allow courts to exercise hidden discretionary powers, in order to take account of the possible errors of the judgment they should conform to: *res judicata* is enforced according to several balancing factors, including symptoms of the reliability of the holdings whose implementation is asked, allowing the court to disregard effects that would determine a gross injustice; when this happens, however, reference to such factors remains implicit in the court's supporting opinion, where the refusal to enforce the previous judgment is generally explicitly justified by way of an arbitrary selection of one of the principles governing operation of preclusive effects fit to reach the desired outcome.[12]

Public interest in the transparency of the administration of justice indicates that courts should be more candid in their exercise of such inevitable discretionary powers, although such transparency may be more discomforting for civil law judges than for their common law colleagues (since their legitimacy is based more on

17/1999 of the plenary session of the *Areios Pagos*, (see) D'Alessandro 2016, p. 91; in Slovenia, a punitive damages award was enforced by a decision of the *Vrhovno sodišče*, 29 May 2013, in *DR* 2014, 18; an opposite trend appeared, e.g., in Poland after the judgment of the *Trybunał Konstytucyjny* of 23 June 2015, but the European Court of Justice seemingly put an end to it in Case C-367/15, *Stowarzyszenie Oławska Telewizja Kablowa v. Stowarzyszenie Filmowców Polskich*, 25 January 2017, EU:C:2017:36; in Italy, recognition was denied by the judgments of the Court of Cassation No. 1183 of 19 January 2007, in *Giurisprudenza italiana*, 2008, 395, and No. 1781 of 8 February 2012, in *Giurisprudenza italiana*, 2013, 126, but the issue has been deferred anew to the plenary session of the Court of Cassation for reconsideration by Decision No. 9978 of 16 May 2016 in *Giurisprudenza italiana*, 2016, 1854, and the following Decision by the plenary session No. 16601 of 5 July 2017 finally allowed recognition; cf. the analysis developed in Giussani 2008, p. 396-397.

12 This phenomenon is explored, in the Italian context, e.g. in Giussani 2014, p. 1193-1198; Giussani 2015, p. 1564-1568; Giussani 2017, p. 260-267; cf., for an overview in English of the set of general principles governing preclusive effects of judgments in Italian case law, Giussani 2010, p. 123-160.

technical rather than political grounds, due to differences in the respective recruiting systems).[13]

In the current state of opacity, however, the consequent difficulties in decoding the nuances of foreign judgments' preclusive effects in the field of recognition are not the only factors putting at risk the identity of the effects of an EU decision within the whole European judicial space. In fact, several other factors, depending on the relative timing and force of conflicting decisions, concur with them, according to the following analysis.

3.1. *Conflicts with local decisions*

The first set of problems to consider concerns conflicts with local decisions. European Court of Justice (ECJ) case law provides a very broad notion of conflict when Regulation (EU) No. 1215/2012 rules on *lis pendens* and related actions apply,[14] and Member States tend to follow a similar approach with respect to national rules governing the effects of non-EU foreign judgments.[15]

With respect to the latter, despite the fact that *lis pendens* might preclude recognition only if the proceedings in the state of destination began before the foreign proceedings, local *res judicata* can be preclusive even if both the action and the judgment came after the foreign proceedings, even though there might have been a violation of the *lis pendens* rule in the local proceedings: in fact, such violation cannot be pleaded any more after *res judicata*.[16] This also reflects the idea, prevailing in the Member States, that a subsequent *res judicata* prevails over a preceding one, because the effects of the latter could have been raised in the proceedings that led to the former, and therefore were (at least implicitly) conclusively denied: the second *res judicata* might be illegal, but its violation of the law cannot be challenged any more (with the exception of some Member States' providing for a special extraordinary remedy for violation of *res judicata*).[17]

13 This aspect is analysed in the classic contribution of Damaška 1986, p. 67-69.

14 Notorious European Court of Justice leading cases in the field are Case C-144/86, *Gubisch Maschinenfabrik KG v. Giulio Palumbo* [1987] ECR 4861; Case C-406/92, *The owners of the cargo lately laden on board the ship 'Tatry' v. the owners of the ship 'Maciej Rataj'* [1994] ECR I-5439; Case C-351/96, *Drouot assurances SA v. Consolidated metallurgical industries (CMI industrial sites), Protea assurance and Groupement d'intérêt économique (GIE) Réunion européenne* [1998] ECR I-3091.

15 See, e.g., in Italy the judgment of the Italian Court of Cassation No. 11185 of 15 May 2007 (in *Rivista di diritto internazionale privato e processuale*, 2008, 224).

16 For this solution see, e.g., in Italy Article 64(e) and (f) of Law No. 218 of 31 May 1998; cf. also, e.g., Article 99 of the Slovenian *Zakon o mednarodnem zasebnem pravu in postopku*, and Article 25 of the Belgian *Code de droit international privé*.

17 Within Italian scholarly analysis, the prevalence of the subsequent internal *res judicata* is justified according to the general rule for resolution of conflicts favouring the last-in-time, pursuant to Article 15 of the preliminary rules of the Italian Civil Code (see, e.g., the order of the Italian Constitutional Court No. 77 of 24 February 2006, in *Giusto processo civile*, 2006, 143), e.g., in Civinini 2001, p. 50, note 54; Merlin 2004, p. 50-55; D'Alessandro 2007, p. 311-313; this also means that subsequent internal *res judicata* erroneously recognising foreign *res judicata* whose recognition should have been precluded by former internal *res judicata* also prevails, →

With respect to EU decisions, whenever rules on *lis pendens* and related actions fail to prevent a conflict, a similar rule applies: recognition is precluded by a local conflicting decision, even if issued after the foreign one, and even if foreign proceedings started before the local ones. In such cases the purpose of granting a judgment the same effects within the whole European judicial space, according to the principle of 'extension of effects', which is a pillar of the European system further implemented by the new wording of Article 54 of Regulation (EU) No. 1215/2012, can be frustrated. However, since EU decisions are recognised regardless of *res judicata*, and even if they are merely provisional remedies, and preclusive effects are also granted, correspondingly, to decisions still subject to ordinary appeal, or even to merely provisional remedies, this rule must be

see again Merlin 2004, p. 55-57; cf., for an implicit statement in the same direction, the judgment of the European Court of Justice Case C-145/86, *Horst Ludwig Martin Hoffmann v. Adelheid Krieg* [1988] ECR 645; see also Subsection 3.4 and following below; in France, the traditional preference for the last-in-time *res judicata* has been superseded by Decree No. 79-941 of 7 November 1979 providing for discretionary resolution of conflicts by the Cour de cassation, pursuant to Article 618 of the French Code of Civil Procedure, according to the transparency needs expressed above in the text, but this means that the remedy is not aimed at protecting the effects of previous *res judicata*, and that later *res judicata* therefore generally prevails, if any, because a later judgment is generally more accurate (for a recent implementation of the rule in favour of the later decision, see, e.g., the judgment of the plenary session of the Cour de cassation No. 621 of 3 July 2015, ECLI:FR:CCASS:2015:AP00621); an extraordinary remedy for violation of *res judicata*, and consequently, the prevalence of the first-in-time, by contrast, seems to be the rule, e.g., in Germany, pursuant to § 580, n. 7, of the *Zivilprozessordnung*, such remedy being extraordinary especially because according to some doctrinal analyses the priority rule should allow the interested party to plead violation of previous *res judicata* at any time (that is, even after expiry of the five-year deadline set by § 586 of the same *Zivilprozessordnung*), the main reference being the seminal work of Gaul 1956, p. 94; in Italy, general theory suggested that remedies should be deemed ordinary, that is to say, automatically postponing the effects of *res judicata*, whenever their ground can be detected from the judgment, while grounds for extraordinary remedies (such as fraud) do not postpone such effects because they can be detected at any time, so that the deadline to file them runs from the moment of the detection, and only in an exceptional case does a ground detectable from the judgment give an extraordinary remedy, which is the case introduced by Law No. 353 of 26 November 1990 of Article 391-*bis* of the Italian Code of Civil Procedure, qualifying the special remedy against manifest error in the reading of the fact-finding in the proceedings at the Court of Cassation, introduced by a holding of the Italian Constitutional Court No. 17 of 30 January 1986, in *Giurisprudenza italiana*, 1986, I, 1, 1440, as an extraordinary one, see, e.g., on the reasons of this choice, Consolo 1989, p. 185-235; it was argued that a special remedy against violations of European law, implementing holdings of the European Court of Justice such as Case C-119/05, *Ministero dell'Industria, del Commercio e dell'Artigianato v. Lucchini SpA* [ECR] I-6199, should also be extraordinary, see, e.g., Consolo 2008, p. 225-238, 237-238, but see also, *contra*, Caponi 2011, p. 239-390, esp. p. 363; revocation of a judgment for violation of *res judicata* in Italy, however, is always an ordinary remedy, and is not available against judgments of the Court of Cassation, see the holding of its plenary session No. 10867 of 30 April 2008, in *Giurisprudenza italiana*, 2008, 2776, and, e.g., the subsequent judgments No. 29580 of 29 December 2011, and again from the plenary session No. 17557 of 18 July 2013 (a contrary view was endorsed in an *obiter dictum* of judgment No. 18234 of 22 August 2006 in *Giurisprudenza italiana*, 2007, 1722).

reconciled with the principles governing conflicts between decisions of different force.

3.2. *Conflicts between local provisional remedies and EU judgments*

In this regard, it is worth remembering from the start that whenever different Member States have concurring jurisdiction on a case, pendency of proceedings for provisional remedies in one of them does not prevent the action on the merits in the other one.[18] This necessarily implies that a subsequent judgment on the merits conflicting with a prior provisional remedy in a different Member State is not even in violation of the *lis pendens* rule: hence, such a judgment must prevail over the provisional remedy not only in the Member State that issued it (where a conflicting decision prevails even if it was issued in violation of the *lis pendens* rule or of the foreign *res judicata*), but also in the Member State that issued the provisional remedy.

In fact, a different solution would introduce an incentive to another form of unfair competition between Member States' jurisdictions: if a Member State's provisional remedy could be superseded only by a judgment on the merits in the same jurisdiction, a Member State could become a magnet jurisdiction simply by being very generous with provisional remedies; moreover, proceedings on the merits in the Member State that issued the provisional remedy might be precluded altogether by *lis pendens* on the merits in a different Member State. Hence, the correspondence between conflicts relevant for *lis pendens* and related actions and conflicts relevant for recognition within Regulation (EU) No. 1215/2012 must be preserved: rules on refusal of recognition apply only to conflicts that could have been prevented; conflicts between decisions of different force are not prevented because they are resolved according to their difference of force, without undermining the production of the same effects within the whole European space by the (prevailing) judgment on the merits.

18 This can be seen as a necessary implication of Article 35 of Regulation (EU) No. 1215/2012. See also European Court of Justice Case C-321/95, *Van Uden Maritime BV, trading as Van Uden Africa Line v. Kommanditgesellschaft in Firma Deco-Line and Another* [1998] ECR I-7091, para 29 ('The mere fact that proceedings have been, or may be, commenced on the substance of the case before a court of a Contracting State does not deprive a court of another Contracting State of its jurisdiction under Article 24 of the Convention'); cf. also European Court of Justice Case C-29/16, *Hanse Yachts AG v. Port D'Hiver Yachting SARL and Others*, 4 May 2017, para 35 ('Having regard to that independence and the very clear distinction between the proceedings for the taking of evidence, on the one hand, and any substantive procedure, on the other, the concept of an "equivalent document" to a document instituting legal proceedings, set out in Article 30 of Regulation No. 44/2001, must be interpreted as meaning that a document instituting proceedings for the taking of evidence cannot be regarded, for the purposes of assessing a situation of *lis pendens* and of determining which court is the court first seized within the meaning of Article 27(1) of that regulation, as also being the document instituting the substantive proceedings'); Italian case law already reached this conclusion with the holding of the plenary session of Court of Cassation No. 1821 of 13 February 1993.

The inevitable conclusion is that local decisions prevent recognition of foreign decisions only if they have the same force: a provisional remedy precludes recognition of a conflicting EU provisional remedy, regardless of violation of the *lis pendens* rule by the former or by the latter, and regardless of violation of the first-in-time decision by the second decision, but not of a conflicting EU judgment on the merits.[19] Likewise, a local judgment on the merits precludes recognition of a conflicting EU judgment on the merits, but does not necessarily preclude recognition of EU, and non-EU, conflicting *res judicata*.

3.3. *Conflicts between local appealable judgments and foreign res judicata*

With respect to non-EU judgments, the above is made quite clear in rules, such as those in Italy, providing that local pendency is preclusive only if it precedes pendency abroad, and that local conflicting judgments preclude recognition only if they are *res judicata*: a foreign *res judicata* subsequent to a local judgment still subject to an ordinary remedy prevails over it, if the proceedings abroad started before the local proceedings.[20] However, the same should hold with respect to EU *res judicata*, according to the rationales shown above: a Member State's jurisdiction should not be allowed to compete unfairly, and become a magnet jurisdiction, by granting expeditious, generous first-instance judgments still subject to appellate review; rules on refusal of recognition should govern only conflicts that could have been prevented by rules on *lis pendens* and related actions; *res judicata* implies that the losing party lost every further opportunity to plead the effects of a previous conflicting decision in a different Member State.

Hence, a local conflicting decision, still subject to ordinary remedy, should not preclude recognition of a conflicting *res judicata* from a different Member State, nor hinder the purpose of granting a judgment the same effects within the whole European judicial space, even if rules on *lis pendens* or related actions were also violated in the foreign proceedings: in fact, when it comes to Regulation (EU) No.

19 Preclusion of recognition of conflicting provisional remedies was upheld in European Court of Justice *Italian Leather SpA v. WECO Polstermöbel GmbH & Co.*, C-80/00, 6 June 2002; the prevalence of a foreign judgment on the merits, even if still subject to ordinary remedies, was so obvious in Italian law (Article 669-*novies*, c. 4, of the Italian Code of Civil Procedure expressly provides it), that even minor case law has applied it straightforwardly since the last century (see, e.g., the holding of the Tribunal of Rome of 25 March 1993, in *Giustizia civile*, 1996, I, 1479); according to the pertinent report, the same was held in the Netherlands by a decision of the Court of The Hague of 25 August 2011; for the same conclusion, see also the judgment of the French Cour de cassation of 14 May 1996, in *Bull.* 1996, I, No. 201, 140; the holding to the contrary of the same Cour de cassation of 20 June 2006, in *Bull.* 2006, I, No. 315, 272, seems therefore a violation of European law (see, e.g., for a deeper analysis of the latter decision, the critical considerations developed by D'Alessandro 2006, p. 134-139; cf., however, for the solution adopted in 1996, and with no mention of the odd 2006 precedent, Gaudemet-Tallon 2010, p. 441).

20 According to Italian doctrinal analysis, the effects of such recognition lapse when the local conflicting judgment also becomes *res judicata* (cf., e.g., also for further references, Merlin 2004, p. 53-55; D'Alessandro 2007, p. 311-312; cf. *supra* n. 16).

1215/2012 (as opposed to Member States' national legislation on recognition of non-EU judgments), violation of rules governing *lis pendens* or related actions is no ground for refusal, and recognition should not be precluded by a conflicting local decision still subject to ordinary appeal, because *res judicata* has a greater force.[21] However, it is important to stress that in such circumstances the interested party has the right, and therefore the burden, of pleading the foreign, automatically recognised *res judicata* in the appellate proceedings concerning the local decision: the proceedings concerning recognition should be stayed until exhaustion, or waiver, of all ordinary remedies against the local judgment.[22]

3.4. *Conflicts between local res judicata and foreign res judicata*

Therefore, the preclusion of recognition of a conflicting EU foreign *res judicata* operates only when the local judgment is also *res judicata*: in such a case the judicial determination is final and conclusive within the local jurisdiction, and conflicting foreign *res judicata* cannot overcome it, regardless of the relative timing of the judgment or the start of the litigation. However, even this holds only if the later foreign *res judicata* deals with the effects of a wider set of facts, including subsequent ones producing effects overcoming the effects previously ascertained: in fact, in

21 The irrelevance of violation of *lis pendens* in the foreign proceedings for the purposes of recognition of an EU judgment derives directly from the wording of Article 45 of Regulation (EU) No. 1215/2012 and its predecessors (see, e.g., the judgments of the Italian Court of Cassation No. 12181 of 15 September 2000, and No. 9554 of 12 November 1994 in *Giurisprudenza italiana*, 1995, I, 1, 2093; the irrelevance of such a violation in local proceedings is the necessary premise of the European Court of Justice case law cited in *supra* n. 14); according to some doctrine, enforceability should also grant a judgment a greater force, see, e.g., Kropholler 1998, p. 364, but see, *contra*, for the sound reply that enforceability has no inherent relation with the degree of finality of a decision, e.g., Merlin 2004, p. 93-94; the judgment of the Italian Court of Cassation No. 9554 of 12 November 1994 granted enforcement to a German *res judicata* notwithstanding a contrary local appealable judgment on the merits (albeit with an unclear supporting opinion); the prevalence of a foreign *res judicata* over a local appealable judgment was also granted by a decision of the *Tribunal de grande instance de Paris* of 31 May 1989, in *Revue critique de droit international privé*, 1990, 550 (before the odd judgment of the Cour de cassation cited in *supra* n. 19); it is worth repeating that relevant finality derives from the exhaustion of the waiver of all remedies whose deadline starts to run from the judgment (cf. *supra* n. 17), so that a French judgment subject to appeal to the Cour de cassation, despite being a *chose jugée*, is not yet *res judicata* within the meaning of the analysis developed here, and has a lesser force than an Italian judgment not subject to an ordinary remedy, see again Merlin 2004, p. 95, 99-101.

22 The stay of proceedings may be justified by way of an analogical application of Article 51.1 of Regulation (EU) No. 1215/2012 (see the considerations developed by Merlin 2004, p. 95-103); since such stay does not prejudice recognition, but rather helps it, allowing the local jurisdiction to implement the foreign judgment, and does not allow resisting recognition on grounds that should have been alleged in the Member State of origin, it would not defy the rationales that supported the ruling for a restrictive interpretation of the power of staying the proceedings in the Member State of destination held by the European Court of Justice Case C-183/90, *B.J. van Dalfsen and others v. B. van Loon and T. Berendsen* [1991] ECR I-04743.

such circumstances the second judgment is not actually conflicting, because *res judicata* operates always, as it were, *rebus sic stantibus*.[23]

It is worth noting that this last reasoning might lead one to think that subsequent foreign *res judicata* might also prevail whenever in the foreign proceedings the effects of the previous local *res judicata* were denied, explicitly or even implicitly: in fact, in such a case the subsequent foreign *res judicata* might be deemed to cover a wider set of facts and effects exactly because it dealt also with the new fact consisting in the previous local *res judicata* and its effects. The idea that the foreign judgment should never be recognised in such cases prevails in doctrinal analysis, but on quite weak grounds: with respect to non-EU judgments, it can be justified by a sovereign nationalistic choice,[24] but in the context of Regulation (EU) No. 1215/2012 general principles of mutual trust indicate that a later *res judicata*, having a greater force than a previous one, should prevail even over local *res judicata*.

In fact, the relationship between rule and exception in the field of recognition is entirely the other way around: a strict interpretation is required for the grounds of refusal;[25] hence, if extension of effects is the rule, the superseding effects of later *res judicata* should be recognised as well, unless the procedural public order exception may apply, but no procedural public order can preclude recognition of such effects if violation of previous *res judicata* is not subject to an extraordinary remedy. Since such extraordinary remedy is contemplated only in some Member States, there seems to be no ground for refusal at least in Member States that do not have it.

For this reason, the purpose of granting a judgment the same effects within the whole European judicial space should not be generally hindered when local *res judicata* precedes a foreign one: since later *res judicata* has a greater force, rules on refusal of recognition should generally not apply. Therefore, refusal to recognise in such cases, especially in Member States that do not grant extraordinary remedies for violation of *res judicata*, looks rather like a breach of mutual trust between Member States, in defence of local jurisdiction, unauthorised by Regulation (EU) No. 1215/2012, and certainly should not operate for the resolution of conflicts between decisions both coming from different jurisdictions, which will be discussed in the

23 Obviously, new facts are relevant only insofar as they change the previous course of business between the parties (see, for an analysis of the meaning of the *rebus sic stantibus* clause, Caponi 1991, p. 103-106); the relevance of a wider set of facts may explain, e.g. the elusive judgment of the European Court of Justice Case C-145/86, *Horst Ludwig Martin Hoffmann v. Adelheid Krieg* [1988] ECR 645 (cf. *supra* n. 17), and the predicable frequency of such development in family matters explains why the need to give prevalence to the later judgment was more easily acknowledged in Article 15.2(f) of Council Regulation (EC) 1347/2000 of 29 May 2000 on jurisdiction and the recognition and enforcement of judgments in matrimonial matters and in matters of parental responsibility for children of both spouses [2000] OJ L 160 (cf. again Merlin 2004, p. 106-107).

24 A concurring rationale might consist in the aim of simplifying the court's task (see again Merlin 2004, p. 42-45).

25 See, *ex multis*, the judgment of the European Court of Justice Case C-414/92, *Solo Kleinmotoren GmbH v. Emilio Boch* [1994] ECR I-2237, para 20.

following sections: it is only with respect to non-EU foreign judgments that local *res judicata* might result in full preclusion.

3.5. *Conflicts between foreign non-EU decisions*

Whenever a conflict ensues between foreign decisions, both Regulation (EU) No. 1215/2012 and some national rules[26] governing the effects of non-EU foreign judgments provide that, in principle, priority should determine its resolution. It is worth noting at the outset of this analysis, however, that the identification of priority between different judgments must be carried out by making reference to the last moment available for the parties to plead the effects of the foreign judgment: if *res judicata* depends on the losing party's neglect of an ordinary remedy that allowed such pleading, the deadline to file such a remedy is the relevant moment; otherwise, it coincides with the deadline for the last procedural step that allowed it.[27]

This consideration leads one to underscore, with respect to conflicts between different non-EU foreign judgments, whose resolution is not governed by Regulation (EU) No. 1215/2012, that the priority rules explicitly provided by some Member States may find a rationale in at least one of the following factors: (*i*) in the Member State violation of *res judicata* is a ground for an extraordinary remedy and is deemed contrary to public order; (*ii*) in the Member State, recognition of foreign judgments has constitutive effects; (*iii*) in a Member State, recognition does not follow the theory of extension of effects.[28] In contrast, whenever in the state of destination automatic recognition in respect of foreign judgments with the same effects they have in the state of origin applies, and violation of *res judicata* allows ordinary remedies only, systematic reasons dictate a preference for the later *res judicata* that cannot be overcome by any parochial bias: in fact, in such a case there is no purpose to defending the local jurisdiction that can justify the denial of recognition, utterly regardless of the relative timing of the start of the respective proceedings.

3.6. *Conflicts between foreign EU decisions*

The analysis of the rules provided by Regulation (EU) No. 1215/2012 for resolution of conflicts between different EU decisions seems to require from the start to emphasise that the differences in wording with respect to the identification of conflicts should not be overestimated: despite the fact that only conflicting decisions

26 See, e.g., Article 99(1) of the Slovenian *Zakon o mednarodnem zasebnem pravu in postopku;* Article 25 of the Belgian *Code de droit international privé;* Article 620 of the Estonian Code of Civil Procedure, § 15 of the Czech Private International Law Act (this might also be the French rule).

27 On these classic problems, see again, for a thorough analysis and details of nuances and exceptions that need not be dealt with here, Caponi 1991, p. 113-172.

28 The third factor can be identified, e.g., in Article 94(1) of the Slovenian *Zakon o mednarodnem zasebnem pravu in postopku,* and in the Czech Republic.

specifically concerning the same cause of action and the same parties are considered, the scope of the rule tends anyway to coincide with the scope of the rules aimed at preventing conflicts, given the broad notion of *lis pendens* adopted by European case law. Hence, reversed claims and third parties subject to the effects of the judgment might well be involved in conflicts to be resolved pursuant to Article 45.1(d) of Regulation (EU) No. 1215/2012.

However, this rule refers to conflicting decisions: hence, just like Article 45.1(c), it applies only to decisions having the same force, for several reasons already seen above. Since recognition of EU decisions is automatic under the theory of extension of effects, this means, for example, that: (*i*) a subsequent conflicting judgment on the merits prevails over a provisional remedy; (*ii*) a later *res judicata* prevails over a judgment on the merits, having a higher force (even when the proceedings leading to *res judicata* started after the other proceedings, because the state of destination would have no interest in defending local *lis pendens*); (*iii*) a later *res judicata* prevails over a previous one, having a higher force, at least when the state of destination does not provide for an extraordinary remedy for violation of *res judicata*, and the former *res judicata* could have been pleaded in the state of origin.

3.7. *Conflicts between foreign EU and non-EU decisions*

Some further observations may be devoted to the conflict between an EU decision and a non-EU recognisable decision, also governed by the priority rule pursuant to Article 45.1(d) of Regulation (EU) No. 1215/2012. In this field, the choice of the state of destination between automatic or constitutive recognition of non-EU judgments is obviously dispositive: in fact, in the latter case only prior recognition of the non-EU judgment might preclude recognition of a conflicting subsequent EU decision of the same or even of a lesser force.

If, on the contrary, automatic recognition of non-EU decisions applies, the same set of conclusions as seen above would hold. However, Member States may provide for automatic recognition of non-EU decisions only when they have acquired force of *res judicata*:[29] in such states, the wording of Article 45.1(d) of Regulation (EU) No. 1215/2012 might then imply that enforcement of a subsequent EU provisional remedy would not be prevented by a non-EU appealable conflicting judgment on the merits, notwithstanding the greater force of the latter.

Moreover, the preclusive effects of recognised non-EU judgments may be influenced by a Member State's choice to assimilate instead of extend the scope of such judgments: whenever a conflict ensues, its resolution may be accordingly different.[30] All these variations, however, do not seem to foster significant unfair competition between Member States' jurisdictions, and do not undermine the

29 For this solution, see, e.g., in Italy Article 64(d) of Law No. 218 of 31 May 1998, in Greece Article 323 of the code of civil procedure, in the Czech Republic § 15 of the Private International Law Act; the same rule might also apply in France.

30 Italy should apply the extension system also with respect to recognition of non-EU judgments, according to the analysis developed by D'Alessandro 2007, esp. p. 64-76, but other Member States may not (cf. *supra* n. 28).

operation of rules aimed at preventing conflicts between EU decisions: the purpose of granting an EU decision the same effects in the whole European judicial space may be sometimes frustrated by differences between the Member States in their degree of openness to non-EU legal systems, but these differences remain within the realm of their own sovereignty; hence, they may be deemed compatible with the reciprocal trust between Member States in the field of recognition of foreign judgments.

A more comprehensive fulfilment of the task of granting a decision identical effects within the whole European judicial space, in fact, probably requires that a European federal judiciary provide it.

References

Caponi 1991
Caponi, R., *L'efficacia del giudicato civile nel tempo*, Milan: Giuffrè, 1991.

Caponi 2011
Caponi, R., 'Corti europee e giudicati nazionali', in: Associazione italiana fra gli studiosi del processo civile (ed.), *Corti europee e giudicati nazionali*, Bologna: Bologna University Press, 2011, p. 239-390.

Civinini 2001
Civinini, M.G., *Il riconoscimento delle sentenze straniere*, Milan: Giuffrè, 2001.

Consolo 1989
Consolo, C., *La revocazione delle decisioni della Cassazione e la formazione del giudicato*, Padua: Cedam, 1989.

Consolo 2008
Consolo, C., 'La sentenza Lucchini della Corte di Giustizia: quale possibile adattamento degli ordinamenti processuali interni e in specie del nostro?', *Rivista di diritto processuale*, 2008, p. 225-238.

Cuniberti, Normand & Cornette 2010
Cuniberti, G., Normand, C. & Cornette, F., *Droit international de l'exécution*, Paris: LGDJ, 2010.

D'Alessandro 2006
D'Alessandro, E., 'Il diniego di riconoscimento per contrasto tra provvedimenti nell'interpretazione della Corte di cassazione francese: il caso dell'*ordonnance de référé* in conflitto con una sentenza di condanna straniera', *Int'l Lis*, 2006, p. 134-139.

D'Alessandro 2007
D'Alessandro, E., *Il riconoscimento delle sentenze straniere*, Turin: Giappichelli, 2007.

D'Alessandro 2016
D'Alessandro, E., 'Riconoscimento di *punitive damages*: in attesa delle Sezioni Unite', *Int'l Lis*, 2016, p. 90-96.

Damaška 1986
Damaška, M., *The Faces of Justice and State Authority*, New Haven/London: Yale University Press, 1986.

Gaudemet-Tallon 2010
Gaudemet-Tallon, H., *Compétence et exécution des jugements en Europe*, Paris: LGDJ, 2010.

Gaul 1956
Gaul, H.-F., *Die Grundlagen des Wiederaufnahmerechts und die Ausdehnung der Wiederaufnahmegründe*, Bielefeld: Deutscher Heimat, 1956.

Giussani 2008
Giussani, A., 'Resistenze al riconoscimento delle condanne al pagamento di *punitive damages*: antichi dogmi e nuove realtà', *Giurisprudenza italiana*, 2008, p. 396-397.

Giussani 2010
Giussani, A., 'Effects of judgments - res judicata', in: M. De Cristofaro & N. Trocker (eds.), *Civil Justice in Italy*, Tokyo: Jigakusha, 2010, p. 123-160.

Giussani 2014
Giussani, A., 'Intorno alla "riflessione" del giudicato contro il terzo', *Rivista di diritto processuale*, 2014, p. 1193-1198.

Giussani 2015
Giussani, A., 'Appunti dalla lezione sul giudicato delle Sezioni Unite', *Rivista di diritto processuale*, 2015, p. 1564-1568.

Giussani 2017
Giussani, A., 'Effetti conformativi della sentenza e sospensione del processo', *Rivista di diritto processuale*, 2017, p. 260-267.

Kropholler 1998
Kropholler, J., *Europäisches Zivilprozessrecht, Kommentar zu EuGVÜ und Lugano-Übereinkommen*, Heidelberg: Verlag Recht und Wirtschaft, 1998.

Merlin 2004
Merlin, E., *Il conflitto internazionale di giudicati. Profili sistematici*, Milan: Giuffrè, 2004.

W.H. Rechberger

CROSS-BORDER ENFORCEMENT OF PUBLIC DOCUMENTS AND REGULATION (EU) 2016/1191

1. The European public document[1]

In November 2008 the European Parliament requested the Commission 'to submit to Parliament ... a legislative proposal on establishing the mutual recognition and enforcement of authentic acts.'[2] The draft proposal suggested a new regulation supplementing the already existing regulations on recognition and enforcement of judgments, including public documents such as the Brussels I Regulation No. 44/2001,[3] the Brussels II bis Regulation No. 2003/2201,[4] the European Enforcement Order (EEO) Regulation No. 2004/805[5] and the Maintenance Regulation No. 2009/4.[6] The proceedings for verification of the accuracy of public documents in cross-border cases were abolished. The regulation would apply to all public documents concerning civil and commercial matters, with the exception of those that concern immovable property, which are listed in a public register, or have to be listed, or can be listed therein.[7]

1 Cf. Rechberger 2010, p. 5.

2 European Parliament Resolution of 18 December 2008 with recommendations to the Commission on the European Authentic Act (2008/2124(INI)); cf. Recommendations on the context of the proposal requested P6_TA-PROV(2008)0636.

3 Council Regulation (EC) No. 44/2001 on jurisdiction and the recognition and enforcement of judgments in civil and commercial matters, OJ L 2001/12, 1.

4 Council Regulation (EC) No. 2201/2003 concerning jurisdiction and the recognition and enforcement of judgments in matrimonial matters and the matters of parental responsibility, repealing Regulation (EC) No. 1347/2000, OJ L 2003/338, 1.

5 Regulation (EC) No. 805/2004 of the European Parliament and of the Council of 21 April 2004 creating a European Enforcement Order for uncontested claims, OJ L 2004/143, 15.

6 Council Regulation (EC) No. 4/2009 on jurisdiction, applicable law, recognition and enforcement of decisions and cooperation in matters relating to maintenance obligations, OJ L 2009/7, 1.

7 Cf. Rechberger 2010, p. 5 *et seq.*

As a next step, implementing the Council's Stockholm Programme,[8] the Commission presented a Green Paper[9] in 2010, in which eleven questions were raised concerning national public documents as well as the options to ease the free circulation of such documents. The key points of the proposal concerned the 'free movement of documents by eliminating legalisation formalities between Member States and recognition of the effects of certain civil status records[10]..., so that legal status granted in one Member State can be recognised and have the same legal consequences in another.'

Finally, in April 2013 the Commission presented a proposal for a regulation concerning the abolition of legislation of documents and the necessity to bear an apostille. It further regulated administrative cooperation as well as the introduction of multi-lingual EU standard forms.[11] On 4 February 2014 the European Parliament accepted the proposal upon the first reading, and the final text of the regulation became available on 9 June 2016.[12] The regulation was published in the Official Journal of the European Union on 26 July 2016 and is applicable in general since 16 February 2019 (Article 27(2) Public Documentation Regulation).

According to Article 2(1) of the Public Documents Regulation, the regulation applies to public documents 'which have to be presented to the authorities of another Member State.' Simultaneously, Article 2(4) provides that the regulation *does not apply* to the recognition in a Member State 'of legal effects relating to the content of public documents issued by the authorities of another Member State.'

The Public Documents Regulation comprises those public documents which are issued by EU Member States' authorities and have a probative value - not earlier defined by EU legislation - concerning one of the facts ('establish one or more of the following facts') listed exhaustively in Article 2(1),[13] primarily affecting the legal status of a person. This definition of a public document conversely implies that documents issued by private persons are excluded from the scope of the

8 European Council, *The Stockholm Programme – An open and secure Europe serving and protecting citizens*, OJ C 2010/115, 1. Cf. also Communication from the Commission to the European Parliament, the Council, the European Economic and Social Committee and the Committee of the Regions of 20 April 2010 - Delivering an area of freedom, security and justice for Europe's citizens - Action Plan Implementing the Stockholm Programme, COM (2010) 171 final. Green Paper, Less bureaucracy for citizens: promoting free movement of public documents and recognition of the effects of civil status records, COM (2010) 747 final.

9 Green Paper, COM (2010) 747 final.

10 Examples include administrative documents such as diplomas or patents; notarial acts such as sales deeds for property and marriage contracts; civil status records such as birth, marriage or death certificates; plus judicial documents such as court rulings or documents issued by a court: Green Paper, COM (2010) 747 final, No. 3.

11 Cf. for the competence basis of the Commission Proposal, Woschnak 2015a and *Idem* 2015b, p. 394.

12 European Parliament, Legislative resolution of 4 February 2014 on the proposal for a regulation of the European Parliament and of the Council on promoting the free movement of citizens and businesses by simplifying the acceptance of certain public documents in the European Union and amending Regulation (EU) No. 1024/2012 (COM[2013]0228 – C7-0111/2013 – 2013/0119(COD).

13 Cf. Woschnak 2015a.

regulation; the same is true for public documents issued by the authorities of third countries (explicitly Recital 17 Public Documents Regulation).[14]

'Authority' means, according to Article 3(2) of the Public Documents Regulation, 'a public authority of a Member State, or an entity acting in an official capacity and authorised under national law to issue or receive a public document covered by this regulation or a certified copy thereof.' The originally recommended amendment by rapporteur Rapkay[15] 'including courts or notaries issuing public documents as referred to in point 1 [meaning Article 3(1) of the Proposal], or a Union authority' was seen only as a legal clarification and was not included in the final version.

The definition of a public document (Article 3 together with Article 2 of the Public Documents Regulation) therefore comprises three constitutive elements:

- the issuance of the document by a national authority or an institution competent in public matters (e.g. notaries);
- the probative value of the document, although not defined in greater detail;
- the relation to one of the categories (a)-(m) listed in Article 2(1).

2. About recognition and enforcement of public documents

As is well known, for the term 'public document' within EU law, the judgment of the ECJ C-260/97, *Unibank A/S v. Flemming G. Christensen* is of relevance. In the judgment, the ECJ specified as a criterion for an enforceable document among others:

> Since these documents are enforced under exactly the same conditions as judgments, the authentic nature of such instruments must be established beyond dispute so that the court in the state in which enforcement is sought is in a position to rely on their authenticity. Since instruments drawn up between private parties are not inherently authentic, the involvement of a public authority or any other authority empowered for that purpose by the state of origin is needed in order to endow them with the character of authentic instruments.[16]

What is addressed in this context is the *formal* probative value. Correspondingly, one can find in the literature that public certification has to guarantee the authenticity of the document (guarantee of origin) and its correctness.[17]

By legal definition of a public document in Article 4(3)(a) of the EEO,[18] the case law of the ECJ was codified under secondary law.[19] The definition of Article 4(3)(a)(i) of the EEO clarifies that the authenticity of the document 'relates to the

14 See Austrian Chamber of Notaries 2013, p. 5.
15 Report 'Bernhard Rapkay', Amendment 12, A7-0017/201.
16 ECJ 17.6.1999, C-260/97 Coll 1999, I-3715.
17 Cf. Brenn 2008.
18 Regulation (EC) No. 805/2004 – creating a European Enforcement Order for uncontested claims, OJ L 050, 71.
19 Cf. Rechberger 2008.

signature and the content of the instrument.' In the most recent regulations concerning the law of International Civil Procedure (the Succession Regulation[20] and the Brussels I Recast Regulation, hereafter BIR[21]), the same view of the formal probative value is expressed, when in each of the legal definitions of public documents the following paragraph can be found: 'the authenticity of [the authentic instrument] relates to the signature and the content of the instrument' (Article 3(1)(i) Succession Regulation No. 650/2012, Article 2(c)(i) BIR).

Within the EU acquis, the recognition of public documents was stipulated for the first time in Article 13(3) of the Brussels II Regulation No. 1347/2000[22] (now Article 46 Brussels II bis Regulation). Furthermore, that principle has been standardised in Article 48(1) of the Maintenance Regulation No. 4/2009 and has been included in Article 34 of the Proposal for the Succession Regulation.[23] In the literature the question of 'recognition' of public documents was repeatedly discussed and almost unanimously rejected.[24]

It is specifically unclear *how* the concept of recognition of foreign judgments deriving from a Member State would be applicable. The recognition of foreign judgments would mean that the effect of the decision as an act of public authority (of a court or other state authority) of a Member State will also be extended to the national territory of another Member State. The foreign decision would then develop the same effect nationally as it has in the country of origin.[25] But the same judicial effect as is the case of foreign judgments would simply not exist with public documents, because they do not have any *res judicata* effect nor a declaratory character. However, a 'recognition' of public documents could be interpreted in such a way that the substantive constitutive effect in the country of origin would be nationally extended. Such an extension would also have to be assessed in the same way, as it would be concerning foreign judgments, for example, according to the substantive law determined by the private international law of the state of recognition. The 'recognition' of public documents postulated by the mentioned regulations cannot change anything merely because the recognition should be the same as with judgments and, as already stated, the extension of substantive constitutive effects is simply excluded.[26] Occasionally in the literature the view is expressed that the rules which would be applicable on the form and the effects of

20 Regulation (EU) No. 650/2012 of the European Parliament and of the Council on jurisdiction, applicable law, recognition and enforcement of decisions and acceptance and enforcement of authentic instruments in matters of succession and on the creation of a European Certificate of Succession, OJ L 201/207.

21 Regulation (EU) No. 1215/2012 of the European Parliament and of the Council on jurisdiction and the recognition and enforcement of judgments in civil and commercial matters (recast), OJ L 351/1.

22 Council Regulation (EC) No. 1347/2000 on the jurisdiction, recognition and enforcement of judgments in matrimonial matters and in matters of parental responsibility for joint children. OJ L 160/19.

23 COM (2009) 154 final.

24 Cf. Rechberger 2010, p. 12 *et seq.*

25 Cf. Rechberger 2010, p. 13; Andrae 2010; Geimer 2005.

26 Cf. Rechberger 2010, p. 13.

the legal transaction certificated in the document according to the international private law of the state of recognition were overridden by the 'recognition' of the authentic instrument.[27] As a result, the transaction certificated in the document would be 'immunised' against objections to its legal effectiveness pursuant to the applicable substantive law.[28] Such an understanding of the meaning 'recognition of public documents' led to the result that large parts of international private law were undermined. In all of those areas of law, where the conflicts of law are not harmonised, this would bring with it a severe infringement of the competences of the Member States. This opinion is also expressed by Hess in the 'Heidelberg Report' in which he formulates: 'Therefore, the reference to recognition in Article 46 Regulation 2201/2003 should not be interpreted as an enlarged concept of "recognition" which deviates from the application of the pertinent private international law to authentic instruments.'[29] It is significant that Article 2(2) of the Proposal for the Public Documents Regulation rightly declared the regulation will not apply to the recognition of legal effects relating to the content of public documents issued by the authorities of another Member State (now Article 2(4) of the Regulation).

3. The 'acceptance' of foreign public documents

The purpose of the Public Documents Regulation is to ensure the free circulation of public documents within the Union (Recital 1). This should no longer – as foreseen in the Proposal of the Regulation – be achieved by 'acceptance' but by 'presentation' (Article 2(1) and (2) Public Documents Regulation). Whatever difference might exist between 'presentation' and 'acceptance' of public documents is absolutely unclear and remains so.

The concept of acceptance of public documents was not an original creation of the Proposal, but is contained in the Succession Regulation for the first time. The effect of this acceptance can only be comprehended through the genesis and the legislative application of the concept within the framework of this regulation. The starting point is Article 34 of the 'Proposal for the Succession Regulation'[30] which reads: 'Authentic instruments formally drawn up or registered in a Member State shall be recognised in the other Member States, except where the validity of these instruments is contested in accordance with the procedures provided for in the home Member State and provided that such recognition is not contrary to public policy in the Member State addressed.' Because of this text it was – not unjustly – feared that the Commission might have in mind the *general recognition of legal status*.[31] The consequence of such a shift of the system would be the displacement of the classic conflict of law system, because – as already mentioned above – questions of international private law would be levered out by rules of international

27 Rauscher 2010; Andrae 2010.
28 Rechberger 2010, p. 13.
29 Hess 2008.
30 COM (2009) 154 final.
31 Cf. Geimer 2014.

procedural law. Therefore, the Max Planck Institute[32] suggested deleting Article 34 of the proposal entirely. Finally, it could be agreed during the European legislative procedure[33] that the conflict of law connection mechanism will not be paralysed by the 'recognition' of acts not based on state authority.[34] That was the reason why the legal concept of 'acceptance' was created.[35] The use of this term now presents a targeted and deliberate reduction.[36] Article 59(1) of the Succession Regulation rules: 'An authentic instrument established in a Member State shall have the same evidentiary effects in another Member State as it has in the Member State of origin, or the most comparable effects, provided that this is not manifestly contrary to public policy (*ordre public*) in the Member State concerned.'

The same is true for the 'presentation' of public documents according to the new regulation. It is clear that the intention of the European Regulator is to limit the effects in two ways: public documents cannot develop more rights than in the state of origin, nor can they develop more legal effects than public documents of the accepting state.[37]

4. Conclusion

The definition of 'public document' in Articles 2 and 3 of the Public Documents Regulation contains three constitutive elements: (*i*) issued by a public authority of a Member State, or an entity acting in an official capacity and authorised under national law to issue or receive a public document (i.e. a notary), (*ii*) the probative value of the document, and (*iii*) the connection of the document to one of the thirteen categories listed in Article 2(1)(a)–(m) of the regulation. This is a completely new definition. The central element of this new definition is its *connection to the (formal) probative value of the document*. When looking at the regulation in detail, it turns out that there is no clear separation between a nationally oriented understanding of 'probative value' and an autonomous one created by European law. The 'free circulation' of documents shall be replaced by the mechanism of 'presentation' of documents. But it is absolutely unclear whether that creates an important difference compared to the concept of 'acceptance' of documents which can be found in the European Union Succession Regulation. Adopting this concept would not be a recommended solution, because in the literature many problems, which have been discussed, were caused by the concept of the Succession Regulation. Besides there is no practical experience with the concept of 'acceptance', and as a consequence a final evaluation of the operation of that scheme is not possible.

32 Max Planck Institute 2010.
33 Cf. Lechner 2014.
34 Cf. Simon & Buschbaum 2012; Rauscher 2010.
35 Cf. Janzen 2012.
36 Geimer 2014.
37 *Ibid.*, p. 152.

References

Andrae 2010
Andrae, M., 'Article 48 EG-UntVO', in: Th. Rauscher (ed.), *Europäisches Zivilprozess- und Kollisionsrecht. EuZPR/EuIPR Kommentar,* München: Sellier, 2010, marginal note 6.

Austrian Chamber of Notaries 2013
Austrian Chamber of Notaries, *Stellungnahme zum Vorschlag für eine Verordnung des Europäischen Parlaments und des Rates zur Förderung der Freizügigkeit von Bürgern und Unternehmen durch die Vereinfachung der Annahme bestimmter öffentlicher Urkunden innerhalb der Europäischen Union und zur Änderung der Verordnung (EU) Nr. 1024/2012,* Wien: ÖNK, 2013.

Brenn 2008
Brenn, C., 'Article 57 Brussels I Regulation', in: H.W. Fasching & A. Konecny (eds.), *Kommentar zu den Zivilprozessgesetzen V/1,* Wien: Manz, 2008, marginal note 7.

Geimer 2005
Geimer, R., *Internationales Zivilprozeßrecht,* Köln: Dr. Otto Schmidt, 2005, marginal note 2776.

Geimer 2014
Geimer, R., '*"Annahme" ausländischer öffentlicher Urkunden in Erbsachen gemäß Article 59 EuErbVO*', in: A. Dutta & S. Herrler (eds.), *Die Europäische Erbrechtsverordnung,* München: C.H. Beck, 2014, p. 143-145.

Hess 2008
Hess, B., Pfeiffer, Th. & Schlosser, P. (eds.), *The Brussels I-Regulation (EC) No 44/2001. The Heidelberg Report on the Application of the Regulation Brussels I in 25 Member States,* Munich: C.H. Beck, 2008, marginal note 555.

Janzen 2012
Janzen, U., 'Die EU-Erbrechtsverordnung', *Deutsche Notar-Zeitschrift,* 2012, p. 484-491.

Lechner 2014
Lechner, K., 'Die Entwicklung der Erbrechtsverordnung - Eine Einführung zum Gesetzgebungsverfahren', in: A. Dutta & S. Herrler (eds.), *Die Europäische Erbrechtsverordnung,* München: C.H. Beck, 2014, p. 12 ff.

Max Planck Institute 2010
Max Planck Institute for Comparative and International Private Law, 'Comments on the European Commission's Proposal for a Regulation of the European Parliament and of the Council on jurisdiction, applicable law, recognition and enforcement of decisions and authentic instruments in matters of succession and the creation of a

European Certificate of Succession', *Rabels Zeitschrift für ausländisches und internationales Privatrecht*, 2010, Vol. 74, p. 522 (marginal note 255 *et seq*).

Rauscher 2010
Rauscher, Th., 'Article 46 Brussels IIa-VO', in: Rauscher, Th. (ed.), *Europäisches Zivilprozess- und Kollisionsrecht. EuZPR/EuIPR Kommentar,* München: Sellier, 2010, marginal note 2 (Einf. EG-ErbVO-E marginal note 36 ff.).

Rechberger 2008
Rechberger, W.H., 'Article 4 EEO', in: Fasching, H.W. & Konecny, A. (eds.), *Kommentar zu den Zivilprozessgesetzen V/1,* Wien: Manz, 2008, marginal note 4.

Rechberger 2010
Rechberger, W.H., 'Die Europäische öffentliche Urkunde - ein Eckpfeiler der vorsorgenden Rechtspflege?', in: W.H. Rechberger (ed.), *Brücken im Europäischen Rechtsraum,* Wien: Manz, 2010, p. 5-16.

Simon & Buschbaum 2012
Simon, U. & Buschbaum, M., 'Die neue EU-Erbrechtsverordnung', *Neue Juristische Wochenschrift,* 2012, p. 2393-2398.

Woschnak 2015a
Woschnak, K., *Binnenmarkt und Notariat,* Wien: Manz, 2015.

Woschnak 2015b
Woschnak, K., 'Unionsrechtliche öffentliche Urkunde? - Ein Versuch zum Urkundenrecht der EU', *Österreichische Juristen-Zeitung,* 2015, p. 394 ff.

S. Kraljić

BRUSSELS II BIS AND ABOLITION OF EXEQUATUR: EXPERIENCES AND VISIONS

1. Introduction

We live in an age of nearly unlimited mobility. Migration occurs not only within individual states, but also between states and continents. Mobility has led to a strong international element in family relations. In 2011, out of 122 million marriages in the European Union (EU) approximately 13 per cent had a cross-border dimension.

The rapid development of European private international law and international procedural law in matters of family law has influenced the awareness of key European actors in this field.[1] This jump-started the adoption of regulations representing the fundamental sources of modern European family law at the EU level. The European Court of Human Rights (ECtHR) and the Court of Justice of the European Union (CJEU) have also contributed to the unification of family law in the EU through their decisions.[2]

An important milestone in the field of European procedural family law is Council Regulation (EC) No. 1347/2000 of 29 May 2000 on jurisdiction, the recognition and enforcement of decisions in matrimonial matters and matters of parental responsibility for children of both spouses[3] (hereinafter Brussels II) that entered into force on 1 March 2001. Soon after its enactment, deficiencies in Brussels II regarding the regulation of matters of parental responsibility became apparent. Accordingly, in 2002 the draft of a new regulation was proposed to replace Brussels II, eliminating the deficiencies and providing for equality of all children.[4] Almost immediately then, Brussels II was recast and in 2003 replaced by Council Regulation (EC) No. 2201/2003 of 27 November 2003 concerning jurisdiction and the

1 E.g. the Council of Europe, the Hague Conference on Private International Law and the Council of the European Union.

2 Boele-Woelki 2005, p. 160.

3 OJ L 160/19 of 30 June 2000.

4 Kraljič 2005, p. 92-94.

recognition and enforcement of judgments in matrimonial matters and the matters of parental responsibility[5] (hereinafter Brussels II bis), repealing Regulation (EC) No. 1347/2000. Brussels II bis has been in force since 1 March 2005. The first version of Brussels II dealt only with the parental responsibility of the common children of divorcing parents. This was found to be discriminatory. Therefore, discrimination, which was based on the marital status of the parents, was abolished under the new Brussels II bis, which was given such extended scope that parental responsibility is covered entirely. As a result, Brussels II bis now incorporates the combination of two very important areas of family law: parental responsibility (including the civil aspects of international child abduction) and matrimonial matters.[6]

Since its entry into force, Brussels II bis has represented an important element in the construction of jurisdictional cooperation between the EU Member States. Its contents encompass unified rules on competences for divorce, the ending of cohabitation and the annulment of marriage, as well as on disputes in connection with parental responsibility in cross-border cases. Brussels II bis has also greatly facilitated the free movement of judicial decisions, public documents and agreements in the EU, as it contains provisions on their recognition and execution in the Member States. Namely, it is the first regulation to abolish exequatur (from Latin *exequi* – let it be executed).

With the passage of time, the Commission undertook to assess the operation of Brussels II bis and determine whether there was a need for amendments to rectify any shortcomings. Such need was indeed determined, and a proposal to recast the regulation and address the shortcomings was put forward.[7] With the recast, although the development of the European Area of Freedom, Security and Justice that was established in 1992 by the Treaty on European Union (the Maastricht Treaty) will be followed, and while in that sense the status quo will be maintained, there are positive amendments designed to eliminate deficiencies that had existed.[8] The recast will depart from the concept of mutual trust and strive for the abolition of the remaining obstacles to the free movement of judgments in accordance with the principle of mutual recognition of judicial decisions. The recast will also provide for additional improvement of the protection of the child's best interests by simplification of the procedures and an increase in the effectiveness of the proceedings.[9]

5 OJ L 338, 23 December 2003, p. 0001–0029.

6 Kruger & Samyn 2016, p. 132; Pranevičiene 2014, p. 117; De Boer 2015, p. 11.

7 European Commission, Proposal for a Council Regulation on jurisdiction, the recognition and enforcement of decisions in matrimonial matters and matters of parental responsibility, and on international child abduction (recast), Brussels, 30 June 2016, COM (2016) 411 final, 2016/0190 (CNS), p. 2.

8 OJ C 191, 29 July 1992.

9 European Commission, 'Proposal for a Council Regulation', *supra* n. 7, p. 2.

2. From exequatur to the concept of the free movement of judgments

Before proceeding with the primary subject of this contribution, we shall first distinguish between two frequently confused terms: a mere recognition (exequatur) and enforcement. Recognition refers to the *res judicata* effect of the foreign judgment, which spreads to the country of reception, while enforcement pertains to an act of material execution on assets or committal of persons. Exequatur is the second stage (in the enforcement state), which in sequence follows the first stage (litigation in the state of origin) but precedes the third stage (the enforcement proceedings in the state in which enforcement is sought).[10] Therefore, exequatur may be seen as 'double autonomy'. On the one hand it represents the autonomy of a state, (based on the state's sovereignty), because the enforceability of the judgment must be confirmed by a national court (or other authority) in a special exequatur procedure.[11] In these cases, we can say that the states recognise foreign decisions where it is in their best interests to do so. But a judicial decision may threaten the public policy of the state where the judicial decision is supposed to be recognised.[12] Therefore, it is not surprising that public policy grounds are most frequently invoked as the reason for rejection of the recognition of a foreign decision.[13] At the same time, public policy is a ground for non-recognition where: (*a*) 'a judgment relating to a divorce, legal separation or marriage annulment shall not be recognised, if such recognition is manifestly contrary to the public policy of the Member State in which recognition is sought' (Article 22(a) Brussels II bis); (*b*) 'a judgment relating to parental responsibility shall not be recognised, if such recognition is manifestly contrary to the public policy of the Member State in which recognition is sought, taking into account the best interests of the child' (Article 23(a) Brussels II bis). The second aspect of autonomy arises in the situation where a party does not take steps to enforce the foreign judgment such that the procedure of exequatur is not necessary.[14]

One of the primary objectives behind the abolition of exequatur was to facilitate and enhance the free movement of judgments in the European Justice Area.[15] Specifically, the abolition of exequatur promotes the ideal that the judgments issued in the EU Member State of origin (adjudicatory jurisdiction) will be accepted and enforced in all other EU Member States (jurisdiction to enforce) without additional procedures (intermediary judicial proceedings) for recognition and enforcement of this foreign judgment. The judgment from another EU Member State is now considered to be in the nature of a domestic judgment as opposed to a

10 Sladič 2013, p. 332.

11 Lindfors 2007.

12 Ilešič, Polajnar Pavčnik & Wedam Lukić 1992, p. 132; Schramm 2013/2014, p. 147.

13 Such a provision is also contained within the Slovenian *Zakon o mednarodnem zasebnem pravu in postopku* (Private International Law and Procedure Act (Uradni lis RS, No. 56/99; 45/08) in Article 100 ('A foreign judgment shall not be recognized if the effect of its recognition is contrary to the public policy of the Republic of Slovenia')).

14 García 2010, p. 7.

15 *Ibid.*

foreign judgment which historically had to go through a special, separate procedure to be recognised and enforced in another EU Member State. Therefore, a *titulus executionis* in the EU Member State of origin means that this title shall be enforced in all EU Member States. A foreign *titulus executionis* in one EU Member State is then considered to be a national title by virtue of the principle *nulla executio sine titulo*.[16]

The abolition of the exequatur procedure envisages an immense degree of mutual trust between EU Member States as well as between the courts of EU Member States. In conjunction with the term 'free movement of civil judgments' are also the associate terms 'mutual trust' and 'mutual recognition'. Namely, the mutual recognition of judgments represents one of the key goals of the European Area of Freedom, Security and Justice, which is clearly defined also by the Treaty on the Functioning of the European Union (TFEU).[17] Article 67(4) of TFEU provides that the EU shall facilitate access to justice, in particular through the principle of mutual recognition of judicial and extrajudicial decisions in civil matters.[18] The procedure of exequatur (recognition and enforcement of a judgment in another EU Member State) only served as an obstacle to the free circulation of judgments and resulted in unnecessary costs and delays for the parties.[19]

A crucial question, however, is whether both terms (mutual trust and mutual recognition) are to be used synonymously. According to García, the answer is no, they have to be used separately.[20] García's conclusion is supported by reference to the Hague Programme: Strengthening Freedom, Security and Justice in the European Union (2005/C 53/01)[21] (hereinafter the Hague Programme), adopted in 2004 by the European Council. The Hague Programme, while not referring to the

16 Sladič 2013, p. 332.

17 OJ C 326/47 of 26 October 2012.

18 See also Article 81 TFEU: '1. The Union shall develop judicial cooperation in civil matters having cross-border implications, based on the principle of mutual recognition of judgments and of decisions in extrajudicial cases. Such cooperation may include the adoption of measures for the approximation of the laws and regulations of the Member States. 2. For the purposes of para 1, the European Parliament and the Council, acting in accordance with the ordinary legislative procedure, shall adopt measures, particularly when necessary for the proper functioning of the internal market, aimed at ensuring: (a) the mutual recognition and enforcement between Member States of judgments and of decisions in extrajudicial cases; (b) the cross-border service of judicial and extrajudicial documents; (c) the compatibility of the rules applicable in the Member States concerning conflict of laws and of jurisdiction; (d) cooperation in the taking of evidence; (e) effective access to justice; (f) the elimination of obstacles to the proper functioning of civil proceedings, if necessary by promoting the compatibility of the rules on civil procedure applicable in the Member States; (g) the development of alternative methods of dispute settlement; (h) support for the training of the judiciary and judicial staff.'

19 European Commission, COM (2010) 748 final – Proposal for a Regulation of the European Parliament and of the Council on jurisdiction and the recognition and enforcement of judgments in civil and commercial matters (Recast). SEC (2010) 1547 final – SEC (2010) 1548 final, Explanatory memorandum of 14 December 2010, p. 1, available at: <http://eur-lex.europa.eu/legal-content/EN/TXT/?uri=CELEX%3A52010PC0748>, last accessed 20 June 2019.

20 García 2010, p. 10.

21 OJ C 53/1 of 3 March 2005.

immediate abolition of exequatur, made several references to the topic of mutual recognition, which was already recognised as being fundamental and necessary for the ultimate abolition of exequatur. Departing from the Hague Programme (point 3.4.2), the mutual recognition of decisions represents an effective means of protecting the rights of the citizens and securing the enforcement of such rights across European borders. At the same time, the Hague Programme also warns that minimum standards for aspects of procedural law have to be developed. Directives in the Hague Programme clearly state that in order to ensure the full achievement of the principle of mutual recognition in civil matters (and also in criminal matters) it is also necessary to improve upon the idea of mutual trust. However, these twin objectives may be reached only:

a) by progressive development of a European judicial culture based on the diversity of the legal systems of the Member States;
b) by providing possibilities to all European citizens for access to a judicial system meeting high standards of quality;
c) by the creation of a system that will provide for objective and impartial evaluation of the implementation of EU policies in the field of justice, be fully respectful of the independence of the judiciary and consistent with all the existing European mechanisms (point 3.2 of the Hague Programme).

According to García, mutual trust represents factual and political grounds for the implementation of mutual recognition. However, in the case of the existence of mutual trust, it is important to both improve and build upon the principle of mutual recognition.[22] If we identify mutual recognition as a key goal of the European Area of Freedom, Security and Justice, which also derives from Article 67(4) of TFEU, then mutual trust also might be understood as an obligation of all the authorities of an EU Member State to trust the authorities of another Member State. However, the existence of genuine trust between the authorities of the Member States is not a legal requirement for the effectiveness of the principle of mutual recognition.[23] Following Hazelhorst, mutual recognition can be seen as the practical application of mutual trust - if one EU Member State trusts another, then it should recognise the judicial decisions of the other EU Member State without second-guessing whether they conform to its own national standards. Mutual recognition therefore presupposes and necessarily is premised on mutual trust.[24]

In order to reinforce the principle of mutual trust, common minimum standards have been developed and the EU Member States should respect them so as to ensure the balance of rights of all parties involved in civil proceedings. At the moment, the EU has twenty-eight Member States which have different political, cultural, religious and court systems. Therefore, as already mentioned, the EU Member States should strive to strengthen mutual trust by the progressive

22 García 2010, p. 11.
23 *Ibid.*, p. 24.
24 Hazelhorst 2017, p. 27.

development of a European judicial culture based on the diversity of the legal systems in each of the Member States. Access to the judicial system must be based on high standards of quality (point 3.2 of the Hague Programme). In December 2015 rapporteur Emil Radev, appointed by the European Parliament's Committee on Legal Affairs, presented a 'Working document on establishing common minimum standards for civil procedure in the European Union – the legal basis'. Radev wrote that the 'system of common minimum standards in the form of principles and rules would serve as a basis for convergence of national regulations concerning civil procedure, establishing a balance between the fundamental rights[25] of litigants in the interest of full mutual trust between the judicial systems of the Member States'.[26] Radev stressed that the creation of common minimum standards will be a lengthy procedure and they would have to be formed in two ways. The first method will require the adoption of sector-specific instruments, which will be based on Article 114 of TFEU, and will address civil-procedural aspects of certain types of claims under EU law. The second method will consist in the adoption of horizontal instruments, which will harmonise national civil procedural laws with cross-border implications notwithstanding the subject matter.[27] Two years later, in February 2017, Radev presented a 'Draft Report with recommendations to the Commission on Common Minimum Standards of Civil Procedure in the EU'[28] and emphasised that, 'Common minimum standards should lead to increased confidence in the civil justice systems of all Member States, which, in turn, should lead to more efficient judicial cooperation in a climate of mutual trust. Such common minimum rules should also remove obstacles to the free movement of citizens throughout the territory of the Member States.'[29] The goals framed by Radev in 2015 and 2017 regarding common minimum standards have a key relevance also for the subject-matter of Brussels II bis, especially in cases where children are involved – e. g. in international child abduction cases (e.g. in hearings, the use of the appropriate technology for distance communication).[30] The common minimum standards should be set out in a directive.[31]

Brussels II bis is directly applicable in all EU Member States, except in Denmark (Article 2(3) Brussels II bis), and has priority over national legislation. Brussels II bis contains:

a) rules on jurisdiction indicating the national court that is competent for decisions in matrimonial matters (divorce, legal separation or marriage annulment) and matters of parental responsibility (attribution, exercise,

25 For instance: the right to a fair trial (Article 6 ECHR), the right to respect for private and family life (Article 8 ECHR), the right to marry (Article 12 ECHR), prohibition of discrimination (Article 14 ECHR).

26 Radev 2015, p. 2.

27 *Ibid.*, p. 7.

28 Radev 2017.

29 *Ibid.*, p. 10.

30 *Ibid.*, p. 12 and 18.

31 Kruger & Samyn 2016, p. 161.

delegation, restriction or termination), if there is a dispute with an international element, i.e. if more than one state is involved in the dispute;[32]
b) rules for simplification of recognition and enforcement of judgments, which have been issued in another EU Member State; and
c) a procedure to settle cases in which the child was abducted by a parent from one EU Member State and taken to another EU Member State.

In this contribution, we will tackle point b), as in the past several years, following Regulation (EU) No. 1215/2012 of the European Parliament and of the Council of 12 December 2012 on jurisdiction and the recognition and enforcement of judgments in civil and commercial matters (recast)[33] (hereinafter BIR), there have been efforts aimed at the abolition of exequatur in Brussels II bis, too.

Several years ago the seeds were already planted for the eventual abolition of exequatur. To illustrate this point, as early as 1999[34] the Tampere European Council conceived mutual recognition as a principle of civil justice cooperation, and the EU legislature deemed it a priority to simplify cross-border recognition and enforcement as much as possible and to remove potential obstacles.

Exequatur[35] is a concept specific to private international law. It refers to the decision by a court authorising the enforcement of a judgment, arbitral award, authentic instrument or court settlement entered abroad.[36] Under the exequatur procedure, the judgments from one EU Member State may be given extraterritorial effect in another EU Member State.

Exequatur may also be defined as a protective procedure that restrains the enforcement of foreign judgments under circumstances where such enforcement in the state where enforcement is sought could violate fundamental rights in the country of enforcement. The drawback of the exequatur procedure, however, is that the relevance of a court judgment (which after all is oftentimes difficult, time-

32 Brussels II bis is a procedural instrument and regulates jurisdiction, recognition and enforcement, but does not contain the rules of applicable law on matrimonial matters and parental responsibility. The applicable law in matrimonial matters is covered by Council Regulation (EU) No 1259/2010 of 20 December 2010 implementing enhanced cooperation in the area of the law applicable to divorce and legal separation (hereinafter Rome III) – OJ L 343/10 of 29 December 2012.

33 OJ L 351/1 of 20 December 2012.

34 However, the process of simplifying the recognition and enforcement of foreign judgments may be observed ever since 1968, when the Convention of 27 September 1968 on jurisdiction and the enforcement of judgments in civil and commercial matters (hereinafter the Brussels Convention) was adopted. The Brussels Convention drastically limited the grounds for review of judgments, and in 2001 Brussels I further simplified this procedure. See more on this in Cuniberti & Rueda 2011, p. 288.

35 The term 'exequatur' has to be distinguished from the term 'enforceability'. 'Enforceability' is confined to the state of the court which gave the judgment and 'exequatur' is the procedure which allows the judgment to be enforced abroad. So European Commission, 'European Judicial Network in Civil and Commercial matters Glossary', available at: <http://ec.europa.eu/civiljustice/glossary/glossary_en.htm#Exequatur>, last accessed 9 June 2019.

36 *Ibid.*

consuming and expensive to obtain) is severely diminished if it cannot be enforced in a different EU Member State or may be ultimately enforced but only after further delays and great expense. For these reasons the exequatur procedure rightly was criticised as counterproductive and detrimental to the free movement of court decisions in the EU and its abolition therefore had been put on the EU's agenda since the meeting of the European Council in Tampere in 1999.[37] The abolition of the exequatur procedure between EU Member States for all judgments in civil and commercial matters is the ultimate objective of the 'Draft Programme of measures for implementation of the principle of mutual recognition of decisions in civil and commercial matters' adopted by the Commission and the Council (hereinafter the Draft Programme).[38] Indeed, the Draft Programme proclaimed the principle of mutual recognition as the cornerstone of judicial cooperation.

The process of abolishing all intermediate measures (exequatur) then proceeded during the period covered by the 'Stockholm Programme – An open and secure Europe serving and protecting the citizens' (hereinafter the Stockholm Programme),[39] which also continued to advance the principle of mutual recognition as the cornerstone of judicial recognition.[40] At the same time, the abolition of exequatur should be accompanied by a series of safeguards, namely measures concerning both procedural law as well as conflict-of-law rules. Mutual recognition should, moreover, be extended to fields that are not yet covered but essential to everyday life, e.g. succession and wills, matrimonial property rights and the property consequences of the separation of couples, while taking into consideration EU Member States' legal systems, including public policy,[41] and national traditions in this area. The European Council considers that the process of harmonising conflict-of-law rules at the EU level should continue in areas where it is necessary, such as separation and divorce. It could also include the area of company law, insurance contracts and security interests.[42]

The previously mentioned Draft Programme outlined three stages in the process of abolishing exequatur and since 2000 one gradually moved forward. The first phase ran from 2001 to 2009, during which a series of regulations accepting the principle of abolishment of exequatur was adopted, i.e.:

37 Schramm 2013/2014, p. 144.

38 OJ C 12/1 of 15 January 2001.

39 Council of the European Union, 'Stockholm Programme – An open and secure Europe serving and protecting the citizens', 02.12.2009, available at: <https://ec.europa.eu/anti-trafficking/sites/antitrafficking/files/the_stockholm_programme_an_open_and_secure_europe_en_1.pdf>, last accessed 17 June 2019.

40 Cf. *ibid.*, p. 21.

41 More on public policy, see Requejo Isidro 2014; Kramberger Škerl 2011, p. 133.

42 Council of the European Union, 'Stockholm Programme', *supra* n. 39, p. 25; see also European Commission, 'Communication from the Commission to the European Parliament, the Council, the European Economic and Social Committee and the Committee of the Regions – Delivering an area of freedom, security and justice for Europe's citizens – Action Plan Implementing the Stockholm Programme/COM/2010/0171final/' of 20 April 2010, available at: <http://eur-lex.europa.eu/legal-content/EN/ALL/?uri=CELEX:52010DC0171>, last accessed 21 June 2019.

a) 2003 – Brussels II bis being the first regulation including a provision on abolishment of exequatur (more on this later);
b) 2004 – Regulation (EC) No. 805/2004 of the European Parliament and of the Council of 21 April 2004 creating a European Enforcement Order for uncontested claims[43] (Article 5);[44]
c) 2006 – Regulation (EC) No. 1896/2006 of the European Parliament and of the Council of 12 December 2006 creating a European order for payment procedure[45] (Article 19);[46]
d) 2007 – Regulation (EC) No. 861/2007 of the European Parliament and of the Council of 11 July 2007 establishing a European Small Claims Procedure[47] (Article 20(1));[48]
e) 2009 – Council Regulation (EC) No. 4/2009 of 18 December 2008 on jurisdiction, applicable law, recognition and enforcement of decisions and cooperation in matters relating to maintenance obligations[49] (Article 17(2)).[50]

The five regulations listed above provide that decisions from the EU Member State of origin shall be recognised and enforced in the other EU Member States without the need for a declaration of enforceability and without any possibility of opposing their recognition (that is, without exequatur). A refusal of recognition and enforcement is therefore not possible, because the abolition of exequatur in principle removes any discretion for the national courts, notwithstanding the individual circumstances of a particular case.[51] The first stage of movement away from the principle of exequatur ended in 2009, and at that point the second stage of the implementation of the principle of mutual recognition of judgments and the abolition of exequatur began. The Stockholm Programme embodies the second stage. The Stockholm Programme, as a multi-year programme, stated that the process of abolishing all intermediate measures (exequatur) should be continued and that the abolition of exequatur should be accompanied by a series of safeguards. The Stockholm Programme expanded the idea of abolishing the

43 OJ L 143/15 of 30 April 2004.

44 'A judgment which has been certified as a European Enforcement Order in the Member State of origin shall be recognised and enforced in the other Member States without the need for a declaration of enforceability and without any possibility of opposing its recognition.'

45 OJ L 399/1 of 30 December 2006.

46 'A European order for payment which has become enforceable in the Member State of origin shall be recognised and enforced in the other Member States without the need for a declaration of enforceability and without any possibility of opposing its recognition.'

47 OJ L 199/1 of 31 July 2007.

48 'A judgment given in a Member State in the European Small Claims Procedure shall be recognised and enforced in another Member State without the need for a declaration of enforceability and without any possibility of opposing its recognition.'

49 OJ L 7/1 of 10 January 2009.

50 'A decision given in a Member State bound by the 2007 Hague Protocol which is enforceable in that State shall be enforceable in another Member State without the need for a declaration of enforceability.'

51 Hazelhorst 2014, p. 27.

exequatur principle in the substantive areas of succession and wills, matrimonial property rights as well as with regard to the property consequences of the separation of couples.[52] Then, in 2012 BIR followed and abolished exequatur for judgments handed down in legal proceedings on or after 10 January 2015 (see Chapter III and Article 66 BIR). In 2013, BIR was further bolstered by Regulation (EU) No. 606/2013 of the European Parliament and of the Council of 12 June 2013 on mutual recognition of protection measures in civil matters[53] (Article 4(1))[54] (hereinafter Regulation 606/2013). It has to be stressed, however, that Regulation 606/2013 is inapplicable for measures of protection falling under the umbrella of Brussels II bis (compare Article 2(3) Regulation 606/2013 and Article 21 Brussels II bis).[55]

3. Brussels II bis: experiences and visions

3.1. *Experiences*

In many cases, the abolition of exequatur has been justified mainly because of the added financial burden it imposed along with its time-consuming nature. However, the question arises, whether these savings in expense and time are sufficient reasons to totally abolish exequatur in matrimonial and parental matters.

Namely, Brussels II bis abolished exequatur in two matters relating to parental responsibility, i.e. regarding rights to access (Article 41) and return of the child (Article 42). Contact orders (right to access) are granted in an enforceable judgment given in an EU Member State and shall be recognised and enforceable in another EU Member State without the need for a declaration of enforceability and without any possibility of opposing its recognition if the judgment has been certified in the EU Member State of origin. Even if national law does not provide for enforceability by operation of law of a judgment granting access rights, the court of origin may declare that the judgment shall be enforceable, notwithstanding any appeal (Article 41(1) Brussels II bis). In such a situation, enforceability expands to the full content of the judicial decision.[56] This system is based on the principle of mutual trust between EU Member States given the fact that their respective national legal systems are capable of providing an equivalent and effective protection of fundamental rights,

52 Cuniberti & Rueda 2011, p. 293.

53 OJ L 181/4 of 29 June 2013.

54 'A protection measure ordered in a Member State shall be recognised in the other Member States without any special procedure being required and shall be enforceable without a declaration of enforceability being required.'

55 The difference between protection measures after Brussels II bis and Regulation 606/2013: (*a*) Brussels II bis has not yet abolished exequatur; (*b*) Brussels II bis cross-border enforcement is not restricted to an expiry date of a certificate (see Article 4(4) Regulation (EU) No 606/2013) – so and more, see Dutta 2016, p. 180-181.

56 Rauscher 2015, p. 338.

recognised at the EU level, and precludes any review of the judgment given by the court of the state of origin.[57] In case C-4/14[58] the CJEU held that the

> recovery of a penalty payment, which the court of the EU Member State of origin that gave judgment on the merits with regard to rights of access has imposed in order to ensure the effectiveness of those rights, forms part of the same scheme of enforcement as the judgment concerning the rights of access that the penalty safeguards and the latter must therefore be declared enforceable in accordance with the rules laid down by Brussels II bis.

In the context of Brussels II bis, a foreign judgment which orders a periodic penalty payment is enforceable in the EU Member State in which enforcement is sought only if the amount of the payment has been finally determined by the courts of the EU Member State of origin.[59] The judge of a court of the EU Member State of origin shall issue the certificate[60] in a proposed standard form only if the following minimum requirements are fulfilled:

> a) where the judgment was given in default, the person defaulting was served with the document which instituted the proceedings or with an equivalent document in sufficient time and in such a way as to enable that person to arrange for his or her defense, or, if the person has been served with the document but not in compliance with these conditions, it is nevertheless established that he or she accepted the decision unequivocally; and
>
> b) all parties concerned were given an opportunity to be heard. Exactly who are considered to be 'concerned parties' in this context shall be judged by the national law of the state of origin. As a rule, problems will not arise in cases where the parents are of different sexes, since in all member states such parents have parental responsibility. Problems may arise, however, in cases involving same-sex or unmarried parents, or in cases where a parent was not heard based on national law, while the decision is also related to this parent;[61] and

57 Case C-4/14, *Christophe Bohez v. Ingrid Wiertz* [2015], 9 September 2015 (ECLI:EU:C:2015:563), para 58.

58 In this case, the Belgian court issued a contact order in divorce proceedings, authorizing the father to contact the children who lived with their mother in Finland. The Belgian court also supplemented its judgment with a penalty payment intended to ensure compliance with the rights of access granted to the father. That penalty payment was set at €1,000 per child, which was to be paid to the father for each day of the child's non-appearance. The maximum amount of the penalty payment was set at €25,000. The mother disregarded the contact order, and the father applied for payment of the penalty (C-4/14, para 24).

59 C-4/14, final rules 2-3.

60 The certificate was introduced in order to create safeguards for the protection of the rights of parties in relation to the abolition of exequatur. Before the judge issues a certificate, he/she should ensure that the child, where appropriate, and the parties are given an opportunity to be heard. So Beaumont, Walker & Holliday 2016, p. 232 *et seq.*

61 See more Rauscher 2015, p. 345.

c) the child was given an opportunity to be heard, unless a hearing was considered inappropriate having regard to his or her age or degree of maturity (Article 41(2) Brussels II bis).[62]

Where the rights of access involve a cross-border situation at the time of the delivery of the judgment, the certificate shall be issued *ex officio* when the judgment becomes enforceable, even if only provisionally. If the situation subsequently acquires a cross-border character, the certificate shall be issued at the request of one of the parties (Article 41(3) Brussels II bis).

Return orders included in an enforceable judgment given in a Member State shall be recognised and enforceable in another Member State without the need for a declaration of enforceability and without any possibility of opposing its recognition if the judgment has been certified in the Member State of origin. In the case of a judgment requiring the return of the child mentioned in Article 11(b)(8), even if national law does not provide for enforceability by operation of law, notwithstanding any appeal, the court of origin may nevertheless declare the judgment enforceable (Article 42(1) Brussels II bis). The judge of origin who delivered such judgment shall issue the certificate only if the following minimum requirements are fulfilled:

a) the child was given an opportunity to be heard, unless a hearing was considered inappropriate having regard to his or her age or degree of maturity; and

b) the parties were given an opportunity to be heard; and

c) in issuing its judgment the court has taken into account the reasons for and evidence underlying the order issued pursuant to Article 13 of the 1980 Hague Convention.

In the event that the court or any other authority takes measures to ensure the protection of the child after the child's return to the state of habitual residence, the certificate shall contain details of such measures (Article 42(2) Brussels II bis). As the judgments on the return of the child are immediately enforceable in other EU Member States, there is no possibility of opposing the enforcement in the EU Member State where the enforcement is sought. The court of the EU Member State of origin has the responsibility and is obliged to prove whether the requirements laid down have been achieved.[63] The enforcement procedure is governed by the law of the EU Member State of enforcement. Any judgment delivered by a court of another EU Member State and declared to be enforceable in accordance with Section 2 or certified in accordance with Article 41(1) or Article 42(1) shall be enforced in the EU Member State of enforcement under the same conditions as if it had been delivered in that EU Member State. In particular, a judgment which has been

62 For more on the hearing of the child and a child's right to express his/her opinion, see Kraljić 2016, p. 11-30; Kruger & Samyn 2016, p. 156-158.

63 Hazelhorst 2014, p. 28.

certified according to Article 41(1) or Article 42(1) cannot be enforced if it is irreconcilable with a subsequent enforceable judgment (Article 47 Brussels II bis).

As Brussels II bis impacts family relations between parents and children in fundamental ways, the question that naturally arises is what influence the abolition of exequatur has on human rights. Namely, exequatur, despite its shortcomings previously discussed, may in fact be an effective means of averting violations of human rights, as it prevents the going into effect of a judgment and its eventual (possible) harmful effects outside the state of origin.[64] [65] Exequatur shall provide for the enforcement only of judgments consistent with the principles of the EU and the European human rights system.[66] The importance placed on the value of human rights can be seen also in individual regulations that specifically refer to respect for human rights in their Recitals.[67] Indeed, individual authors have even criticised the abolition of exequatur on the grounds that its elimination may negatively influence the protection of fundamental rights.[68] In *Aguirre Zarraga*,[69] the CJEU denied that the courts of the EU Member State of enforcement have an extraordinary power of review of the judgment issued by the state of origin, even when an infringement of fundamental rights is at stake. The assessment of whether there is such an infringement falls exclusively within the jurisdiction of the courts of the Member State of origin.[70] The possible negative impact that eliminating exequatur could in turn have on actually sanctioning the violation of human rights was expressed especially well in the *Povse* case[71] that was heard by both the ECtHR (*Povse v. Austria*)[72] and the CJEU.[73] It was the first time that the ECtHR and the CJEU had the occasion for a dialogue with regard to the topic of the mutual recognition of judgments.[74] Both proceedings (ECtHR and CJEU) were connected to the abolition

64 Cuniberti & Rueda 2011, p. 293.

65 Public policy was also an important question in a recognition procedure of a foreign court decision (*Sklep II Ips* 462/2009 of 28 January 2010) before a Slovenian court (not under Brussels II bis).

66 Cuniberti 2012, p. 568.

67 E.g. see Recital 29 of Regulation 4/2009: 'In order to guarantee compliance with the requirements of a fair trial ...', and Recital 38 of BIR: 'This Regulation respects fundamental rights and observes the principles recognised in the Charter of Fundamental Rights of the European Union, in particular the right to an effective remedy and to a fair trial guaranteed in Article 47 of the Charter.'

68 So Hazelhorst 2014, p. 27; Cuniberti & Rueda 2011, p. 293-302; Cuniberti 2012; Sladič 2013, p. 336 *et seq.*

69 Case C-491/10, *Joseba Andoni Aguirre Zarraga v. Simone Pelz* [2010], 22 December 2010 (ECLI:EU:C:2010:828), paras. 46 and 70.

70 Case C-491/10, para 72.

71 *Povse* relates to a judgment concerning the custody of a child whose parents had Italian and Austrian nationality. The family resided in Italy. The mother left Italy for Austria despite an Italian judicial decision prohibiting this action. As a result, the father was granted an order for the immediate return of the child. The mother applied for custody at the Austrian court, and the request for enforcement of the return order was also sent to the Austrian court.

72 *Povse v. Austria*, No. 3890/11 of 18 June 2013.

73 Case C-211/10, *Doris Povse v. Mauro Alpago* [2010], 1 July 2010 (ECLI:EU:C:2010:400), para 83.

74 Biagioni 2016, p. 581.

of the exequatur in decisions ordering the child's return based on Brussels II bis. Related to the question of the abolition of exequatur the CJEU decision stated:

> 3. The second subparagraph of Art. 47(2) of Brussels II bis must be interpreted as meaning that a judgment delivered subsequently by a court in the Member State of enforcement which awards provisional rights of custody and is deemed to be enforceable under the law of that State cannot preclude enforcement of a certified judgment delivered previously by the court which has jurisdiction in the Member State of origin and ordering the return of the child. 4. Enforcement of a certified judgment cannot be refused in the Member State of enforcement because, as a result of a subsequent change of circumstances, it might be seriously detrimental to the best interests of the child. Such a change must be pleaded before the court which has jurisdiction in the Member State of origin, which should also hear any application to suspend enforcement of its judgment.

The ECtHR raises the question, however, whether the Austrian courts had to fulfil the obligations flowing from Austria's EU membership by applying the relevant provisions of Brussels II bis as explained by the CJEU.[75] The ECtHR was attempting to arrive at the answer to this question under the so-called 'Bosphorus test',[76] which has three criteria: (*a*) the international organisation (EU in our case) must protect fundamental rights to a degree which is equivalent to the protection given by the European Convention on Human Rights (ECHR) (the so-called presumption of equivalent protection); (*b*) the state had no discretion (if it did, the test is not applicable); (*c*) there are no circumstances which could cause the presumption of equivalent protection to be rebutted. The Bosphorus test could be satisfied, for example, if in a particular case it were proven that the protection of ECHR was manifestly deficient.[77] We could confirm the compliance with points (*a*) and (*c*), but in regard to Article 42 of Brussels II bis Austrian courts had not been exercising any discretion when they ordered the enforcement of return orders. Namely, where the courts of the state of origin of a wrongfully removed child had ordered the child's return and had issued a certificate of enforceability, the courts of the requested state could not review the merits of the return order, or refuse enforcement on the ground that the return would entail a grave risk[78] for the child owing to a change in circumstances since the delivery of the certified judgment. Nevertheless, the ECtHR

75 Hazelhorst 2014, p. 29.

76 The *Bosphorus test* (also *Bosphorus presumption* or *presumption of compliance*) has its origin in *Bosphorus v. Ireland* (No. 45036/98 of 30 June 2005), in which the ECtHR dealt with the question of whether a state may be exempt from responsibility under the ECHR if the state had ceded powers to an international organisation (in the event that the question is related to the relationship between EU law and the ECHR) and fulfilled its obligations under membership in the international organisation, where there was proper provision in that organisation's structure for effective protection of fundamental rights at a level at least 'equivalent' to that of the ECHR (see para 122). The *Bosphorus test* was applied also in cases *Michaud v. France* (No. 12323/11 of 6 March 2013) and *Avotinš v. Latvia* (No. 17502/07 of 23 May 2016). For more about the *Bosphorus test*, see Kuhnert 2006, p. 177-189; Lock 2010; Johansen 2016; Biagioni 2016, p. 584.

77 Hazelhorst 2014, p. 29; Kuhnert 2006, p. 185; Lock 2010; Johansen 2016.

78 For more on grave risk for the child, see Kraljić 2015, p. 59-78.

applied the so-called *Bosphorus presumption* and concluded that the applicant had failed to exhaust all possibilities of review under Brussels II bis. In particular, the ECtHR observed that the applicant had failed to request a review of the return order before the Italian courts and that legal recourse in Italy was in principle available. Further, the ECtHR observed, should any action before the Italian courts fail, the applicants would ultimately be in a position to lodge an application directly with the ECtHR against Italy. The ECtHR could not find any flaws in the procedural protection mechanisms for the observance of the applicants' ECHR rights. The ECtHR stated that simply by fulfilling its obligations as an EU Member State under the Brussels IIa Regulation Austria had complied with the ECHR and the case *Povse v. Austria* was proclaimed as inadmissible (manifestly ill-founded).[79]

3.2. *Visions*

Judicial cooperation in civil law has progressed over the last decade, and the internal market currently functions on the premise of mutual recognition of judgments. The principle of mutual recognition could therefore be identified as a core condition and argument for the abolition of exequatur.[80] The principle of mutual recognition has been gradually bolstered by minimising the barriers that previously existed with respect to the enforcement of foreign judgments throughout the EU Member States. Today, in fact, the significantly improved level of judicial cooperation and trust among the EU Member States has reached a degree of maturity which permits the move towards a simpler, less costly and more automatic system of circulation of judgments, removing the existing formalities among the EU Member States.[81] Notwithstanding this significant progress, the abolition of exequatur must be accompanied by procedural safeguards with the aim of ensuring and protecting core procedural rights (e.g. the right to a fair trial).[82]

In spite of the fact that Brussels II bis made important pioneering steps towards the abolishment of exequatur, as we have seen, the procedure respecting the announcement of executability of a decision filed in another Member State or exequatur, respectively, still represents one of the problematic fields of Brussels II bis that requires further attention. Exequatur, having a double meaning,[83] still imposes undesirable barriers for the free mobility of judicial decisions and causes unnecessary costs (up to €4,000)[84] and delays for parents and their children in cross-

79 *Povse v. Austria,* No. 3890/11 of 18 June 2013; see also Lazić 2015, p. 295-316.

80 García 2010, p. 10.

81 European Commission, 'COM (2010) 748 final – Proposal for a Regulation of the European Parliament and of the Council on jurisdiction and the recognition and enforcement of judgments in civil and commercial matters (Recast). SEC (2010) 1547 final – SEC (2010) 1548 final, Explanatory memorandum' of 14 December 2010, p. 6, available at: <http://eur-lex.europa.eu/legal-content/EN/TXT/?uri=CELEX%3A52010PC0748>, last accessed 20 June 2019.

82 *Ibid.*

83 Ekart & Rijavec 2010, p. 34; Cuniberti & Rueda 2011, p. 303.

84 The costs for obtaining exequatur equally vary throughout the EU. For a straightforward case of exequatur, identifiable costs (which include court and lawyers' fees, costs for service of →

border procedures. The length of time required to obtain exequatur differs among the Member States. Depending on court competences and other complicating factors, securing exequatur may take anywhere from several days to even several months. Additional time burdens include the collection of the documents necessary for the request and the process of translation. Still additional delays occur in cases where a legal remedy is lodged against approval or denial of exequatur. In the individual Member States, procedures of appeal last for up to two years, as the subject-matter of Brussels II bis represents an extraordinarily sensitive field. In everyday life, as well as in law, the time-consuming nature of the procedures may be especially difficult for parents, who quite reasonably expect that decisions regarding their children should take force immediately and without unnecessary delays. Even contradictory situations may arise, such as, for example, where a Member State has to execute rights to contact with a child based on Brussels II bis, and at the same time in the same Member State the decision is appealed against, and perhaps recognition and/or execution of rights to custody over a child given to a parent in the same decision may be refused, in view of the fact that decisions on both rights are regulated by different procedures under Brussels II bis.[85] Further, unnecessary costs, when coupled with the further burdens associated with drawn out procedures, are circumstances that negatively influence the parent-child relationship (especially, e.g., in divorce proceedings) and are counter-productive to the protection of the child's best interests (the principle of the best interests of the child). Therefore, it is not surprising that the possibility of abolishment of exequatur is one of the key questions facing the prospect of whether Brussels II bis should be renewed. Research conducted in 2015 shows that 68 per cent of those questioned believe that all judgments, authentic instruments and agreements concerning parental responsibility should circulate freely among the EU countries without exequatur. Private individuals are the most prominent group that sought to expand the abolition of exequatur (82 per cent), followed by judges and lawyers (71 per cent). Academics were equally divided on the issue.[86]

Those respondents seeking the further expansion of the abolition of exequatur view increased access rights as a positive development. Nevertheless, this view has been criticised to some extent because the system does not always leave sufficient

documents and translations) range from €1,100 (in Bulgaria) to almost €4,000 (in the United Kingdom). On average, €2,200 have to be paid for processing the application. This amount can increase exponentially in a more complex or contested case – so European Commission, 'Commission Staff Working Document Impact Assessment – Accompanying the document Proposal for a Council Regulation on jurisdiction, the recognition and enforcement of decisions in matrimonial matters and the matters of parental responsibility, and on international child abduction (recast)', SWD/2016/0207 final of 30 June 2016, p. 57-58, available at: <http://eur-lex.europa.eu/legal-content/EN/TXT/PDF/?uri=CELEX:-52016SC0207&from=EN>, last accessed 22 June 2019 (hereinafter 'Working Document').

85 *Ibid.*, p. 4.

86 European Commission, 'Study on the assessment of Regulation (EC) No 2201/2003 and the policy options for its amendment – Final report, Analytical annexes', 2015, Brussels, European Union, p. 75 and 152, available at: <http://ec.europa.eu/justice/civil/files/-bxl_iia_final_report_analtical_annexes.pdf>, last accessed 11 February 2019.

leeway to protect the rights of the child which is, after all, the 'object' of the enforcement. If the judgment on access rights is enforceable (albeit only provisionally) and accompanied by the certificate issued by the court of origin (which replaces exequatur by the state where enforcement is sought), it has to be enforced in all other Member States (Article 41 Brussels II bis). According to the case law of the CJEU (*Povse*), even a stay of enforcement proper has to be requested from the court of origin of the judgment, and not in the state where enforcement is sought. However, the defendant parent is not served with the certificate and may learn about its existence only at the moment when enforcement actually starts. As a result, it is de facto impossible for the judgment debtor to challenge the validity or correctness of the certificate in the EU Member State of origin before enforcement takes place, and Brussels II bis as interpreted by the CJEU prohibits any such challenge in the EU Member State where recognition and enforcement are sought.[87] The abolition of exequatur does not mean that the child's right to be heard is abrogated. However, it is more arduous to assert that the child's right to be heard has not been violated because the courts in the EU Member State where enforcement is sought would no longer be able to investigate such claims.[88] A lack of mutual trust within the EU is also recognised as negative in relation to abolishing exequatur proceedings.[89] Namely, mutual trust is an indispensable element necessary for the free movement of judicial decisions in the EU.

Problems also exist in connection with the hearing of the child. In particular, the CJEU in *Aqiurre Zarraga* held that under Brussels II bis a domestic court cannot refuse enforcement of a decision ordering the return of the child, even if a serious violation of a fundamental procedural right has occurred. Article 42(2)(a) is based on the principle that the child has the right to express his/her views,[90] and they must be taken into account as this is appropriate in the light of the child's age and maturity, and if this is in the child's best interest (also Article 41(2)(c)). It must be noted, however, that the national rules and practices on hearing children vary significantly. For example, the age at which a child is considered sufficiently mature to present his/her views ranges from ten to fifteen years. In some EU Member States, judges also hear children who are much younger (e.g. 2 or 3 years old) if they deem this appropriate in specific cases. Also, the term 'hearing' seems to have different meanings in the various legal systems, ranging from 'having been given an opportunity to express him- or herself' (which could take place outside the court) to a formal hearing of the child before a court. Such differences encourage the EU Member States with stricter standards on the hearing of the child than the EU Member State of origin to refuse the recognition and exequatur if the hearing of the child does not meet their own standards. Therefore, this is one of the areas calling

87 European Commission, 'Working Document', *supra* n. 84, p. 57.

88 Scott 2015, p. 31.

89 European Commission, 'Study on the assessment', *supra* n. 86, p. 75.

90 This right can be found also in the Convention on the rights of the child (Article 12) (Uradni list RS-MP, št. 9/92; EU Charter of Fundamental Rights (Article 24(1)) (OJ C 326 of 26 October 2012); European Convention on the Exercise of Children's Rights (Article 3) (Uradni list RS-MP, št. 26/99).

for additional improvements, better solutions and safeguards to protect the child as the most vulnerable party.[91] In a survey conducted in 2015, 78 per cent of respondents think that common minimum standards for the hearing of the child could help in avoiding the refusal of recognition, enforceability and/or enforcement of a judgment from another Member State, whereas just 22 per cent do not do so.[92]

The proposed extension of the abolishment of exequatur, despite its many advantages, should not be at the expense of abandoning traditional safeguards, including those relating to public policy, nor should it involve diluting protection for children (e.g. hearing of the child). The abolition of exequatur should be accompanied by a series of safeguards, especially regarding default judgments, which may be measures in respect of procedural law as well as of conflict-of-law rules (e.g. the right to be heard, the serving of documents, the time required for providing opinions, etc.). The main policy objectives in the area of civil procedural law is that borders between countries in the EU should not constitute an obstacle to the settlement of civil law matters or to initiating court proceedings or to the enforcement of decisions in civil matters. In recent years, major steps have been taken to reach this goal, but additional work is necessary to further build upon gains already established. Some do not believe that the abolition of exequatur could resolve the problems of enforcement of judgments related to parental responsibility.[93] Parental responsibility proceedings should be handled as quickly as possible and the need to apply for a declaration of enforceability is an onerous requirement that causes an additional (time) burden for citizens that simply is not necessary or reasonable. Therefore, the improvements should take into account the possibility of accelerating the proceedings. Problems are also recognised relating to the fact that only some types of decisions are exempted from exequatur proceedings. For example, a decision could contain information relating to different matters in regard to parental responsibility.[94] Accordingly, only part of the decision may be directly enforceable. Thus, a declaration of enforceability is still necessary.

4. Final thoughts

European civil procedural law has faced rapid development over the last decade. In order to achieve the target goal of the free movement of judicial decisions many regulations introduced the abolishment of exequatur. The Commission proposal for Brussels II bis Recast should extend the abolition of exequatur proceedings. On the one hand, such an extension is supported because it would strengthen the efficiency of judicial cooperation between the EU Member States. Yet, abolition of exequatur under Brussels II bis Recast, which regulates the most sensitive family matters (matrimonial and parental matters) must take into account that sufficient procedural guarantees are adopted. But given that the EU Member States are very

91 European Commission, 'Working Document', *supra* n. 84, p. 57-58; see also Scott 2015, p. 31.

92 European Commission, 'Study on the assessment', *supra* n. 86, p. 154.

93 So Scott 2015, p. 34; Kruger & Samyn 2016, p. 160; European Commission, 'Study on the assessment', *supra* n. 86, p. 76.

94 European Commission, 'Study on the assessment', *supra* n. 86, p. 76.

different (legally, politically, religiously, economically), common minimum standards will have immense importance. These standards should, therefore, provide the guarantee of equivalent procedural protection, as well as the protection of fundamental rights, and should build on the further efficiency of judicial cooperation between the EU Member States. Of paramount importance, of course, is the necessity to ensure that the best interests of the children are given the highest priority.

References

Beaumont, Walker & Holliday 2016
Beaumont, P., Walker, L. & Holliday, J., 'Conflicts of EU courts on child abduction: the reality of Article 11(6)(8) Brussels IIa proceedings across the EU', *Journal of Private International Law*, 2016, Vol. 12(2), p. 211-260.

Biagioni 2016
Biagioni, G., '*Avotinš v. Latvia*. The Uneasy Balance Between Mutual Recognition of Judgments and Protection of Fundamental Rights', *European Papers*, 2016, Vol. 1(2), p. 579-596, available at: <http://www.europeanpapers.eu>.

Boele-Woelki 2005
Boele-Woelki, K., 'The Principles of European Family Law: Its Aims and Prospects', *Utrecht Law Review*, 2005, Vol. 1(2), p. 160-168.

Cuniberti 2012
Cuniberti, G., 'Some Remarks on the Efficiency of Exequatur', *University of Luxembourg Law Working Paper* No. 2012-1, 2 February 2012, available at: <https://papers.ssrn.com/sol3/papers.cfm?abstract_id=1998030>.

Cuniberti & Rueda 2011
Cuniberti, G. & Rueda, I., 'Abolition of Exequatur - Addressing the Commission's Concern', *RabelsZ*, 2011, Vol. 75, p. 286-316.

De Boer 2015
De Boer, Th.M., 'What we should not expect from a Recast of the Brussels IIbis Regulation', *NiPR*, 2015, Vol. 33(1), p. 10-19.

Dutta 2016
Dutta, A., 'Cross-border Protection Measures in the European Union', *Journal of Private Int'l Law*, 2016, Vol. 12(1), p. 169-184.

Ekart & Rijavec 2010
Ekart, A. & Rijavec, V., *Čezmejna izvršba v. EU - osrednja tema evropskega civilnega procesnega prava*, Ljubljana: GV Založba, 2010.

García 2010
García, R.A., *Abolition of Exequatur: Problems and Solutions. Mutual Recognition, Mutual Trust and Recognition of Foreign Documents: Too many Words in the Sea*, available at: <https://www.academia.edu/2927201/Abolition_of_Exequatur-_Problems_and_Solutions._Mutual_recognition_mutual_trust_and_recognition_of_foreign_documents_too_many_word_in_the_sea>.

Hazelhorst 2014
Hazelhorst, M., 'The ECtHR's Decision in Povse: Guidance for the Future of the Abolition of Exequatur for Civil Judgments in the European Union. European Court of Human Rights 18 June 2013, Decision on Admissibility, Appl. No. 3890/11 (*Povse v. Austria*)', *Nederlands Internationaal Privaatrecht*, 2014, Vol. 1, p. 27-33.

Hazelhorst 2017
Hazelhorst, M., *Free Movement of Civil Judgments in the European Union and the Right to a Fair Trial*, The Hague: Springer, 2017.

Ilešič, Polaijnar Pavčnik & Wedam Lukič 1992
Ilešič, M., Polaijnar Pavčnik, A. & Wedam Lukič, D., *Mednarodno zasebno pravo – komentar zakona, II. dopolnjena izdaja*, Ljubljana: Časopisni zavod Uradni list Republike Slovenije, 1992.

Johansen 2016
Johansen, S.Ø., *EU law and the ECHR: The Bosphorus Presumption is still Alive and Kicking – The Case of Avotiņš v. Latvia*, 2016, available at: <http://eulawanalysis.blogspot.si/2016/05/eu-law-and-echr-bosphorus-presumption.html>.

Kraljič 2005
Kraljić, S., 'Progresivni razvoj unifikacije procesnega in materialnega prava na področju mednarodnega družinskega prava', in: R. Knez, S. Kraljić & D. Stojanovič ćeds.), *Evropski sodni prostor*, Maribor: Univerza v Mariboru - Pravna fakulteta, 2005, p. 89-96.

Kraljić 2015
Kraljić S., 'Resna nevarnost kot razlog za zavrnitev vrnitve protipravno odpeljanega ali zadržanega otroka', *Pravosodni bilten*, 2015, p. 59-78.

Kraljić 2016
Kraljić, S., '12. člen KOP - pravica otroka do svobodnega izražanja v sodnih in upravnih postopkih', *Pravosodni bilten*, 2016, p. 11-30.

Kramberger Škerl 2011
Kramberger Škerl, J., 'The Abolition of Exequatur in the Proposal for the Review of the Brussels I Regulation', in: V. Rijavec & T. Ivanc (eds.), *Cross-border Civil Proceedings in the EU*, Maribor: Univerza v Mariboru - Pravna fakulteta, 2011, p. 127-151.

Kruger & Samyn 2016
Kruger, T. & Samyn, L., 'Brussels II bis: Success and Suggested Improvements', *Journal of Private International Law*, 2016, Vol. 12(1), p. 132-168.

Kuhnert 2006
Kuhnert, K., 'Bosphorus - Double Standards in European Human Rights Protection?', *Utrecht Law Review*, 2006, Vol. 2(2), p. 177-189.

Lazič 2015
Lazič, V., 'Legal Framework for International Child Abduction in the European Union - the Need for Changes in the Light of Povse v. Austria', in: M. Župan (ed.), *Private International Law and the Jurisprudence of European Courts - Family at Focus*, Osijek: Faculty of Law Osijek, 2015, p. 295-316.

Lindfors 2007
Lindfors, H., 'Cross-border Enforcement in the European Framework', *Scandinavian Studies in Law*, 2007, p. 345-358, available at: <http://www.scandinavianlaw.-se/pdf/51-15.pdf>.

Lock 2010
Lock, T., 'Beyond *Bosphorus*: The European Court of Human Rights Case Law on the Responsibility of Member States of International Organisations under the European Convention on Human Rights?', *Human Rights Law Review*, 2010, Vol. 10, p. 529-545, available at: <https://core.ac.uk/download/pdf/9050852.pdf>.

Pranevičiene 2014
Pranevičiene, K., 'Unification of Judicial Practice Concerning Parental Responsibility in the European Union - Challenges Applying Regulation Brussels II bis', *Baltic Journal of Law & Politics*, 2014, Vol. 7(1), p. 113-127.

Radev 2015
Radev, E., *Working Document on Establishing Common Minimum Standards for Civil Procedure in the European Union - The Legal Basis*, 2015, available at: <http://www.europarl.europa.eu/sides/getDoc.do?pubRef=//EP//NONSGML+COMPARL+PE-572.853+01+DOC+PDF+V0//EN&language=EN>.

Radev 2017
Radev, E., *Draft Report with Recommendations to the Commission on Common Minimum Standards of Civil Procedure in the EU*, 2017, available at: <http://www.europarl.europa.eu/sides/getDoc.do?type=COMPARL&mode=XML&language=EN&reference=PE593.974>.

Rauscher 2015
Rauscher T. (ed.), *Europäisches Zivilprozess- und Kollisionsrecht - Kommentar*, Cologne: Verlag Otto Schmidt, 2015.

Requejo Isidro 2014
Requejo Isidro, M., *Recognition and Enforcement in the New Brussels I Regulation (Regulation 1215/2012, Brussels I Recast): The Abolition of Exequatur*, 2014, available at: <http://www.ejtn.eu/PageFiles/6333/Requejo_Doc.pdf>.

Schramm 2013/2014
Schramm, D., 'Enforcement and the Abolition of Exequatur under the 2012 Brussels I Regulation', *Yearbook of Private International Law*, 2013/2014, Vol. 15, p. 143-174.

Scott 2015
Scott, J.M., 'A Question of Trust? Recognition and Enforcement of Judgments', *NiPR*, 2015, Vol. 1, p. 27-35.

Sladič 2013
Sladič, J., 'The Remedies and Recourses in European Civil Procedure after the Intended Abolition', *Zeitschrift für Europarechtliche Studien*, 2013, Vol. 3, p. 329-358.

II. (Cross-border) Enforcement and the National Legal Context

W. Kennett

LEGAL TRANSPLANTS: JUDICIAL OFFICERS IN POLAND AND THE CZECH REPUBLIC

1. Introduction

1.1. *The contested viability of transplants*

Comparative law literature expresses different views on the feasibility of legal transplants. Alan Watson, whose book *Legal Transplants: An Approach to Comparative Law* generated this controversy, suggested that 'the transplanting of individual rules or of a large part of a legal system is extremely common. ... Most changes in most systems are the result of borrowing.'[1] At the opposite extreme, Pierre Legrand has concluded that legal transplants are impossible since

> a rule receives its meaning from without and if one accepts that such investment of meaning by an interpretive community effectively partakes in the ruleness of the rule ... it must follow that there could only occur a meaningful 'legal transplant' when both the statement as such and its invested meaning – which jointly constitute the rule – are transported from one culture to another.[2]

It is nevertheless clear that law reform projects sometimes import legal institutions, or principles, or pieces of legislation in their entirety, from a foreign legal system. The issue in such cases is not whether an attempt has been made to transplant legal rules, but rather what the consequences of the transplant have been. Jaakko Husa notes:

> It would be essential to observe the societal context of law, or the result could be transplant rejection in the new system. In the case of a legal loan it is influence that takes place in a *mutated form*. Here is the thing: a mutated loan is still a loan although in

1 Watson 1974, p. 95. The book did not attract much attention when first written. Watson described it as having fallen 'stillborn from the press': Watson 2007, p. 9. See also Cairns 2012/2013. Legal transplants have since become a central topic of comparative law, and Watson's text the starting point for debate.

2 Legrand 1997, p. 111, 116-117.

> some respect it is a loan gone wrong. The success of a loan is not the same thing as making a loan as such because one can certainly copy a rule or an institution from another country, but whether it really works in the receiving system is quite another question.[3]

A transplant may have an effect entirely different from that anticipated, because of the surrounding political, legal and social culture. For that reason, Teubner's description of transplants as 'legal irritants' is helpful.[4] A transplant will create disturbances in the legal culture, and adjustments to existing rules and institutions – but is most unlikely to perform precisely the same role in the importing jurisdiction as it does in the exporting one. The present contribution is the fruit of an ongoing research project, looking at the 'transplantation' of enforcement institutions and the success of the resulting 'mutated loans'.

1.2. *The tasks of enforcement law*

There are three basic models of enforcement law – enforcement by a court, by an independent enforcement professional (Judicial Officer), or by an administrative body – but given the various hybrid variants of these models that can be found, it may be preferable to see enforcement as made up of a number of distinct tasks, which may be allocated to a judicial or a non-judicial authority. The choices made as to the allocation of these tasks differ from one jurisdiction to another: in some jurisdictions, most tasks are performed by a court (e.g. Austria), in others by a non-judicial authority (e.g. Sweden, France), with a range of other options in between. In this section, Austria and France will be used to illustrate the two 'poles', with illustrations from other jurisdictions where relevant.

The tasks central to civil enforcement are outlined below.

1.2.1. The issue of an enforcement title (*titre exécutoire*)

This is the starting point for enforcement. An enforcement title may be the judgment of a court, but a variety of other titles exist. In the present context, it should be noted that Judicial Officers may be competent to issue an enforcement title in some circumstances. Thus, for example, a French *huissier de justice* can issue an enforcement title in proceedings relating to a dishonoured cheque.[5] An enforcement authority, whether court, Judicial Officer or other authority – may thus perform a dual role in the issuance and enforcement of titles. It is important to distinguish between these two procedures.

3 Husa 2015.

4 Teubner 1998, p. 11-32.

5 See Article L. 131-73 Code monétaire et financier.

1.2.2. Authorisation for enforcement

Before an enforcement title can be enforced it must bear some sign that it is indeed enforceable. Authorisation may be given by the competent authority that issued the enforcement title. For example, in France the Registry at the first instance court that hands down a judgment affixes the *formule exécutoire* to its judgment to signify that it may proceed to enforcement, while a notary affixes this certification to the authentic instrument it has drawn up. Clothed with a *formule exécutoire*, the judgment can then be taken to the non-judicial authority (*huissier de justice/gerechtsdeurwaarder*) who will undertake enforcement action. In many jurisdictions, however, rather than being a 'final' act by the initial decision-maker, authorisation for enforcement is instead the first (or one of the first) stages in the enforcement process. In Austria, the enforcement court (the *Bezirksgericht*: potentially a different section of the court that originally handed down the enforcement title) will check whether the criteria for enforceability are met, and issue a declaration or certificate to that effect.

In some circumstances, protective measures may be taken where there is no judgment or authentic instrument to enforce. For example, Article L511-2 of the French *Code des procédures civiles d'exécution* permits protective measures to be taken without prior judicial authorisation if the creditor is in possession of an enforcement title without the *formule exécutoire*, but goes even further than this and allows such measures to be taken where there is non-payment of an accepted bill of exchange, promissory note, a dishonoured cheque or rent remaining unpaid under a written tenancy of immovable property. The Judicial Officer who implements such protective measures is trusted to act independently without specific judicial authorisation.[6]

1.2.3. Service of documents relating to enforcement

Service on the debtor of documents relating to the various steps in the proceedings is an essential part of enforcement action. In the French system, a distinction is made between *signification* and *notification*. Documents requiring *signification* are formally served by a Judicial Officer, whereas *notification* may be by less formal methods such as the post. *Signification* is required for many procedural acts, including, notably, the document instituting the proceedings, the judgment and any enforcement measures. By contrast, in Austria service of documents relating to enforcement is regularly undertaken via postal channels.

1.2.4. Creditor application for enforcement

Enforcement is not automatic. It is subject to the principle of party initiative. There must therefore be an initial application for enforcement by the creditor. The extent

6 Proceedings must be introduced by the creditor within a short timeframe after the protective seizure.

to which the enforcement proceedings must be driven forward by the creditor, and the scope for the creditor to choose a specific method of enforcement, nevertheless vary among the systems.

1.2.5. Obtaining information about a debtor's assets

In the era of electronic access to information, many jurisdictions have created systems allowing extensive access to debtor information. This may include information from tax authorities, social insurance organisations, banks, vehicle licencing bodies and local councils, as well as easy access to registers of securities and immovable property. Access is available to the competent authority - whether it is a court or a non-judicial authority. Twenty years ago, in the early stages of digitalisation, information access for the enforcement of civil enforcement titles was more limited, but under development. In the 1990s Judicial Officers in Belgium and the Netherlands had established both direct and indirect access to databases,[7] whereas French Judicial Officers faced a more complex, slow and unreliable procedure for obtaining information via the *procureur de la République*.[8] Now, most European jurisdictions have either direct online access to databases of relevant information or a right to information from, for example, banking authorities or social insurance organisations - a right which can be exercised via electronic communication with the information holder. Nevertheless, some legal systems continue to allow rather limited access to information. Enforcement agents may be dependent on the knowledge of creditors, or even private investigators. Access to information is usually granted once an enforcement title has been obtained, but information may sometimes be available at an earlier stage in proceedings.[9]

1.2.6. Choice of enforcement method

A choice must be made from the various enforcement methods available, based on available information. Many jurisdictions confer this choice on the creditor as a matter of principle - sometimes specifically subject to the principle of

[7] For example, Dutch Judicial Officers had access to local authority civil status and residence information in the late 1990s and were seeking access to social insurance records. In Belgium, Judicial Officers had access to the register of civil status and could obtain social insurance information indirectly through an application to *Banque-carrefour*, the institution controlling data access. In each case, the information was only available for enforcement purposes rather than in pursuit of the Judicial Officer's other business activities.

[8] Established by Articles 39 and 40 of L. 91-650.

[9] Some legal systems are very open and allow broad access to personal information. This is routinely true in Sweden, where e.g. personal tax records are public. Another example is Portugal, where information gained about a debtor in earlier enforcement proceedings is made publicly accessible via PEPEX: see IMF Working Paper WP/15/279 'Reforming the Legal and Institutional Framework for the Enforcement of Civil and Commercial Claims in Portugal', available at: <https://www.imf.org/external/pubs/ft/wp/2015/wp15279.pdf>, last accessed 25 June 2019.

proportionality.[10] And creditors may certainly be aware of assets of the debtor that could be seized, either because of their general business dealings, or perhaps because the asset in question originated with the creditor. In some jurisdictions, however, there is a hierarchy of enforcement methods and the order in which they are attempted is prescribed by law.[11] Alternatively, the creditor may leave it to the competent enforcement authority - with their privileged access to information - to make the choice.

1.2.7. Planning of the enforcement method

This step is included in the list of enforcement tasks because there may be several different types of personnel within the competent authority, with different responsibilities. One may determine or manage the method of enforcement, and another execute that method. For example, a Judicial Officer may decide to send an enforcement agent to seize movable property, and the enforcement agent may be responsible for the seizure itself. Similarly, where enforcement is undertaken by a court, one type of court official may delegate enforcement tasks to another.[12] Alternatively, a creditor's choice of enforcement method may determine the individual enforcement agent responsible for that method of enforcement, who will undertake all aspects of planning and execution. An analysis of enforcement must take this division of responsibilities into account.

1.2.8. Removal and sale of assets

Once assets have been seized, a procedure may be initiated for realisation of the value of the asset. This may be the task of a Judicial Officer or an external agency, depending on the type of goods, the degree of specialisation relevant and the particular range of functions performed by the Judicial Officer in question. E-auctions are increasingly used. These may be organised via a specific digital platform created for enforcement purposes, but in some jurisdictions eBay or other commercial sites are also an option.

1.2.9. Division of assets or the realised value of assets

Sometimes several creditors may have claims to be satisfied out of the same asset. In such cases there will be a procedure for the division of the money realised. Where a court is responsible for enforcement, this will be a judicial task. In jurisdictions where enforcement is done by a Judicial Officer, the officer will often deal with the

10 The approach also advocated in the CEPEJ Guidelines.

11 This is true of the Czech Republic: see further *infra* at text accompanying n. **Fout! Bladwijzer niet gedefinieerd.**.

12 As may be the case with the relationship between *Rechtspfleger* and *Gerichtsvollzieher* in Austria.

division of the proceeds from the sale of an asset, but court involvement may also be necessary, e.g. in the case of immovable property.[13]

1.2.10. Dealing with challenges to enforcement

Finally, enforcement will often occur in a highly charged atmosphere, and those responsible for enforcement are liable to be the subject of complaints. Responsibility for dealing with such complaints may be allocated to several different authorities, whether in tiered or parallel procedures. For example, there will probably be an initial complaints procedure directed to the enforcement authority that undertook the action against which the complaint is made. There may be an ombudsman who can review cases, or a complaint may be made to a professional organisation, which can undertake disciplinary action if required. The challenge to enforcement may also take the form of court action if there is a question of ownership of the asset seized, if it is alleged that the enforcement agent has acted unlawfully, or if there is some other reason to object to enforcement.

2. The Judicial Officer model

Historically, transplants of enforcement systems have not been unusual. The French Judicial Officer (*huissier de justice*) model of enforcement professional has been widely adopted around the world, both as a result of colonisation and as a result of a positive choice to adopt that model.[14]

The Judicial Officer is one of several French professions to have obtained its original strength and security from the sale of offices by the French state under the *ancien régime*, which rendered these offices valuable and heritable. *Huissiers* were originally ushers and messengers for medieval councils – which had legislative, judicial and executive functions – and so had responsibility for the service of documents and the exercise of state force from the medieval period.[15] Following the French Revolution, their economic fortunes waned for a long period during the nineteenth century, but the Napoleonic legislation also favoured them by unifying their role and providing a national structure and the foundations on which a single profession could grow. Their function was put on a statutory footing by a decree of 14 June 1813, and a professional association was formed in 1842.

Sensing that they attracted less respect than members of the other legal professions, Judicial Officers set about improving their level of qualifications and

13 For France, see Articles R251-1 *et seq.* and R-331-1 *et seq.* of the Code des procedures civiles d'exécution.

14 France is the country of origin of this model and so is used by way of example here, but the profession also has strong forms in Belgium and in the Netherlands. Regulation in Belgium has remained somewhat conservative to date, and the profession thus retains more of its traditional features, whereas in the Netherlands there has been greater deregulation and diversification. On the Netherlands, see Van Rhee 2010 and Jongbloed 2010.

15 For further historical background, see Raynouard 2016, p. 15-25; Chambre Nationale des Huissiers de Justice, 1995; further Mathieu-Fritz 2005.

training beginning in the late nineteenth century and this bore fruit throughout the twentieth century. The National Chamber of Judicial Officers was established by a law of 20 May 1942, and the status and functions of the professional organisation were further specified in an Ordonnance of 20 December 1945. Professional chambers at departmental, regional and national levels have training, supervisory and disciplinary functions, while the National Chamber became a single voice to represent the profession to the state. A training institution was established in 1960 (École Nationale de Procédure, ENP), and a decree of 1975[16] introduced the requirement that a candidate to the profession should have a *maitrîse* in law or an equivalent qualification. In terms of securing greater security for the profession, social insurance and pension funds were put in place by the end of the 1960s. Meanwhile, the status and functions of Judicial Officers were put on a statutory footing by Décret No. 56-222 of 29 February 1956, since variously amended, which established their exclusive and non-exclusive functions, permitted forms of organisation, and professional obligations and liability. Between the 1940s and 1970s, therefore, the profession took the basic shape that has become the model for transplantation – as explained further in the next section.

The 1950s also saw the establishment of the International Union of Judicial Officers (UIHJ), which held its first international congress in 1952 with seven members, and which has grown to a membership of the representatives of eighty-six states.[17] The International Union has campaigned vigorously for the wider adoption, or transplantation, of the Judicial Officer model and is well respected – particularly within the European Union and the Council of Europe, and in West Africa.

3. Transplanting the model

3.1. An identifiable structure

Pressure to improve judicial efficiency and contract enforcement has been a key motivation for the transplantation of institutions and rules relating to enforcement. The ability to enforce contracts is regarded as an important factor encouraging investment, and this has spurred legal change in Eastern Europe, where enforcement was a court process – and one that proceeded with glacial slowness and with few incentives for efficiency.

In work subsequent to *Legal Transplants*, Watson has suggested that successful transplantation did not depend on the detail of the rules and their suitability to the social, political, geographic or other features of the importing state, but rather on factors that made the rule or institution easy to identify, isolate and import. Thus, he notes the impact of Gaius' *Institutes* and, following the same structure, Justinian's

16 Décret 75-770 of 14 August 1975.

17 See further the website of the UIHJ at: <http://www.uihj.com/en/-background_1019810.html>, last accessed 25 June 2019.

Institutes – the 'nutshells' of Roman law – on later generations and on the reception of Roman law in Western Europe.

At the very least, without these treatises the reception would have been incomparably more difficult, hence much slower, and it would have occurred in a very different way. But in fact, Justinian's *Institutes* existed and were the basic text for beginning law students throughout Europe for hundreds of years, and gave them their concepts and structures.[18]

Similarly, Blackstone's *Commentaries on the Laws of England* are hailed by Watson as crucial to the successful transplantation of the English common law throughout the United States. They represented a statement of the law that was systematic, relatively simple and of portable size.[19]

It is interesting to look at the Judicial Officer enforcement model in the light of these considerations. It can be seen as offering a 'bolt on' module to the court system – not requiring integration within that system. The framework for creating the profession is also easily identifiable: a set of regulations on competences, qualifications, training, supervision, discipline, remuneration and other features of the profession are available for adoption. Thus, the concentrated, professional model has proved relatively easy to package and market.

But other important factors have also favoured transplantation. It has been observed that, '[I]n certain, highly technical, sectors, the presence of a single proponent can promote uniformity. The fact that the proponent also grants credits and other economic aids may guarantee the adoption of the proposed model.'[20] Contract enforcement in general features significantly in the World Bank's *Doing Business* reports, and so there are certainly incentives to find ways of improving the efficiency of enforcement. There are, however, no particular recommendations for the way that judgments should be executed in the *Doing Business* reports. Rather, the reports frame contract enforcement from the start of proceedings to enforcement as a question of the efficiency of court procedures, with very little specific focus on the stage of execution of judgments, and no advocacy for a Judicial Officer model.[21]

But there have been other proponents of the model. In introducing its International Congress in 2015, the then President of the UIHJ Leo Netten stated:

> The UIHJ is in contact with the major international organisations and legal institutions. For several years, the UIHJ has developed special relationships with influential organisations in the economic field. This strategy has helped position the profession of judicial officer both as a key player in the economic development and as a guarantor of legal security worldwide. …

18 Watson 1994, p. 1-23, 10.

19 *Ibid.*, p. 12 *et seq.*

20 Ajani 1995, p. 93-117, 112.

21 In various reports where improvements in contract enforcement are highlighted, however, reference is made to the introduction of a Judicial Officer (or private bailiff) model. See, for example, World Bank 2013, p. 92 and World Bank 2014, p. 40.

> The agencies specialised in economic development have realised that a country can[not][22] take root if it cannot guarantee a definite level of legal certainty for economic operators, enterprises and citizens. Financial aid is subject to the implementation of structural legal reforms to meet their specific requirements developed from models, and model laws. The main organisations and institutions have also understood that to be effective, these models and model laws shall be designed in collaboration with professional organisations such as the UIHJ. …
>
> [F]or fifteen years, the UIHJ took part in more than one hundred European and international projects in this area, alongside these large organisations and institutions. The UIHJ was particularly active in the development of the CEPEJ Guidelines on enforcement.[23]

Given that the UIHJ has had significant input into the European Commission for the Efficiency of Justice (CEPEJ) work on enforcement of judgments, and has put its expertise at the disposition of the justice ministries of transition economies, it is no surprise that many East European jurisdictions have adopted a Judicial Officer model in the reform of their enforcement law. There are distinct differences between the various systems, some of which will be explored below, but a Judicial Officer model is now in place in most East European states: including Poland, the Czech Republic, Slovakia, Hungary, Romania, Estonia, Lithuania, Latvia and Bulgaria. A Judicial Officer model was also given serious consideration in Slovenia, but ultimately a court-based model has been retained, with reforms that have led to major improvements in efficiency.[24]

It is not only Eastern Europe where these reform pressures have been felt. Portugal has also introduced a new system, which is clearly identified as having been 'imposed' by the Troika in order to improve the efficiency of enforcement.[25]

3.2. *Transplanting the model: the view from the UIHJ and CEPEJ*

It was suggested above that the ease of packaging and marketing the Judicial Officer model has been influential in its adoption in much of Eastern Europe. Although it is somewhat anachronistic to refer to the CEPEJ Guidelines for a better implementation of Recommendation Rec (2003) 17 of the Committee of Ministers to Member States on enforcement,[26] since they were adopted in 2010 after the main wave of creation of Judicial Officers in Eastern Europe, they demonstrate the way in which the principal features of the model can be stated without difficulty.

22 The English version of this text says 'can', but this is a mistranslation of the French original.

23 'The Judicial Officer, Link between Law and Economy – A New approach to Enforcement': available at: <http://www.uihj.com/en/introduction_2163584.html>, last accessed 18 June 2019.

24 Although the law on civil enforcement in Slovenia is outside the scope of this contribution, I am grateful to Professor Vesna Rijavec and Dr Andrej Ekart for their generosity with their time and willingness to discuss the subject with me in April 2017.

25 Correia & Videira 2015, p. 37-49.

26 Guidelines for a Better Implementation of the Existing Council of Europe's Recommendation on Enforcement, 17 December 2009 CEPEJ (2009) 11REV2.

The Guidelines are intended to apply to both state employees and independent professionals, and have some specific provisions for each. Among those that are of particular relevance for Judicial Officers there is the suggestion that, where enforcement agents carry on their profession as a private practice, Member States should ensure that there is sufficient competition and clearly defined geographical competence.[27] Rules on territorial competence and promoting adequate competition are therefore indicated. The Guidelines go on to suggest that enforcement agents should have sole competence for the enforcement of judicial decisions and other enforceable titles or documents, and for implementation of all the necessary enforcement procedures.[28] At Guideline 34 they provide a list of secondary activities which may be considered compatible with the status of Judicial Officer 'tending to safeguard and secure recognition of parties' rights and aimed at expediting the judicial process or reducing the workload of the courts.' The secondary activities highlighted as compatible include: debt recovery, working as an auctioneer, seizure of goods, the recording and reporting of evidence (*constat d'huissier*), serving as court ushers, the provision of legal advice, the conduct of bankruptcy procedures, representing parties in the courts, drawing up private deeds and documents, and teaching. Additionally, Guideline 20 specifically indicates that it should be possible to entrust enforcement agents with the service of notices - traditionally an exclusive competence of Judicial Officers in France, Belgium and/or the Netherlands (the Donor States), but now one subject to erosion. The secondary activities listed in Guideline 34 are - to a greater or lesser extent - activities undertaken by Judicial Officers in the Donor States, and they constitute important areas in which Judicial Officers can compete with other professions. As will be seen below, this is an area in which the transplantation of the model is particularly difficult - and yet in the Donor States this mix of competences has been important as a way of offsetting the lower income that comes from the obligatory exercise of exclusive competences.

The Guidelines suggest that 'enforcement agents should be organised in a professional body representing all members of the profession, thereby facilitating their collective representation and the gathering of information'[29] and that membership of such a professional body should be compulsory in states which have established a Judicial Officer profession.[30] Clear regulation of the status and degree of autonomy of enforcement agents is recommended.[31] As to training, candidates for the position of enforcement agent should be of a standard and training commensurate with the complexity of their tasks, to increase the trust of users in the justice system, and should undergo compulsory continuous training.[32]

27 Guideline 14.
28 Guideline 33.
29 Guideline 29.
30 Guideline 30.
31 For example, should an enforcement agent be free to choose the method of enforcement to be adopted (on the basis of his experience and privileged access to information)?
32 Guidelines 25 and 26.

Professional codes of conduct are advocated in Guideline 38, which also highlights desirable professional standards such as ethical rules,[33] the information to be given to parties by enforcement agents concerning the enforcement procedures and the factors important to smooth enforcement.[34] Elsewhere the Guidelines deal with issues relating to the obligation to provide a universal enforcement service, subject to situations where there is a conflict of interest.[35]

The Guidelines also address some issues of financial regulation, such as the need for a separate client account, and for professional and liability insurance, as well as for financial inspection.[36] They then devote attention to the regulation of fees and the need for clear and transparent fee scales and charges.[37] Data protection issues are also addressed. One might expect much of the relevant regulation in this respect to be provided by general data protection legislation, but the Guidelines specifically draw attention to the need to regulate the reuse of information concerning debtors. Thus, there is a need to establish what debtor information, if any, may be retained and used if several creditors are pursuing claims against the same debtor – or one creditor has several claims against the same debtor. A clear legal framework needs to be established for such reuse of information, including time limits for the retention of information.[38]

Since completing the work on the CEPEJ Recommendation and Guidelines, the UIHJ has been active in developing a Global Code of Enforcement, a draft of which it presented at the World Bank 'Law, Justice and Development' Week in April 2014,[39] and which promotes similar principles.

3.3. *Transplanting the model: a view from the Recipient States*

3.3.1. Introduction

The following observations on the process of the transplantation of the model are drawn from recent visits to Poland and the Czech Republic (the Recipient States). They represent initial findings and lines of further enquiry.

A first observation is that, while reforms to enforcement have undoubtedly introduced a Judicial Officer model, that model has a domestic character. It is the Judicial Officer *concept* that has been transplanted, into new soil – rather than the

33 On behaviour, professional secrecy and the criteria governing the choice of enforcement action, etc.

34 E.g. predictability and proportionality of costs and lead-times and cooperation between enforcement agents.

35 Guideline 35.

36 Guideline 36.

37 Guideline 47 *et seq.*

38 Guideline 46.

39 'The UIHJ and the Draft Global Code of Enforcement at the "Law, Justice and Development" Week of the World Bank', *LJD* (*Law, Justice and Development*), 1 November 2014; available at: <http://www.globalforumljd.org/press/2014/uihj-and-draft-global-code-enforcement-law-justice-and-development-week-world-bank>, last accessed 25 June 2019.

specific details of legislation. The concept requires the introduction of certain types of regulatory legislation (on qualifications, training, professional organisation, exclusive and non-exclusive competences, supervision, disciplinary matters, remuneration, etc.), but in each jurisdiction that legislation has also been shaped by domestic considerations. The pre-existing legal culture has had a significant impact on the transplant.

Features of the pre-existing legal culture that have had a particularly noteworthy effect on the creation of the institution of Judicial Officer are the conceptions of the role of the courts in the enforcement process and the conception of enforcement agents as public servants – with a consequential impact on questions of competition and on the range of competences that are appropriate to Judicial Officers, and the weakness of the professional body in negotiations with the government.

3.3.2. Poland[40]

3.3.2.1. Introduction

The initial legislation creating a Judicial Officer in Poland, and reforming the law on civil enforcement, was adopted in 1997. Prior to the adoption of the new law, enforcement was a court-based process, and enforcement agents were low ranking court officers. They did not need any education beyond the high school level. The new legislation introduced a system that was influenced by the French model, but did not initially create Judicial Officers as independent professionals. Instead they became functionaries somewhat similar to the German *Gerichtsvollzieher* – they were employed by the court but had their own offices and their own staff. This interim situation lasted until a review was conducted in 2002. Thereafter Judicial Officers became independent professionals, relying on the fees recovered for their services. The legislation regulating the profession has been the subject of numerous amendments,[41] adjusting the rules to deal with problems that arise and with a view to ensuring that the initial transplant is better adapted to its new legal and political environment.[42]

Under the 1997 reforms, a law degree is necessary for access to the profession,[43] plus an additional two-year training programme. The training

[40] The description of the general lines of the Polish legislation that is presented in this section is largely derived from an interview with Rafał Fronczek, the President of the Polish National Chamber, in January 2017.

[41] There have been about 40 amendments since 1997 and a major revision of the legislation is currently before the Sejm.

[42] The appropriate future direction of enforcement regulation is nevertheless fiercely contested between the government and the profession as discussed further in the paragraphs that follow in the text.

[43] This involves a five-year programme of study. For the first 10 years after the reform, a degree in administration was also accepted as a route into the profession, but this option was removed in 2007.

programme is provided by the professional body, with the support and assistance of the office employing the trainee. Training is completed by a final exam, and successful trainees thereafter become a Judicial Officer Candidate. Two further years of supervised practice are required in order to become a Judicial Officer, but a Judicial Officer Candidate may alternatively continue to work as an employee of a Judicial Officer. Appointments to an office, within the area of a specific district court, are made by the Minister of Justice.

Polish Judicial Officers are authorised to issue an enforcement title in one particular situation - which does not owe anything to the Donor States. Under Article 761(1) of the Code of Civil Procedure an enforcement authority, including a Judicial Officer, may order participants to proceedings to provide explanations in order to obtain information that may be necessary to conduct execution proceedings, and under Article 762(1) the enforcement authority may, at the creditor's request or *ex officio*, fine a person[44] who refuses without just cause to provide the explanation or information required, or who deliberately provides a false explanation or information. A debtor is also required to notify the enforcement authority of a change of residence for any period lasting more than one month once execution has commenced,[45] and failure to do so attracts the same fine. Resistance to enforcement also attracts a fine under Article 764.

Judicial Officers are highly regulated. They are subject to administrative supervision and inspection by the president of the district court for the location where they have their office and by the Minister of Justice. Their actions are also subject to judicial scrutiny. They are regulated by their professional body.

3.3.2.2. *The role of courts in the enforcement process*

In the Donor States (as noted above in Section 1.2.2), certification of the enforceability of a judgment is provided by the court that decided the case, which appends the *formule exécutoire* to the judgment.[46] A Judicial Officer is authorised to enforce a title so certified, and thus will proceed with the various enforcement tasks within his/her competences without the need for any further court intervention. The onus will typically be on the judgment debtor, or a third party, to oppose enforcement if there is a reason to do so, although the Judicial Officer may in some situations need to seek the assistance of the court.

In Poland, under the current legislation, a similar situation prevails in principle. The *formule exécutoire* (typically translated as 'writ of execution') in relation to a judgment is also usually issued by the court of first instance where the case has been pending.[47] According to Article 781 of the Code of Civil Procedure (CCP), applications for a writ of execution 'shall be adjudicated by the court immediately, in no case later than within three days from the day on which they are

44 Up to 2,000 Polish zlotys.

45 Article 761(3).

46 In the case of notarised instruments, it is the notary who appends the *formule exécutoire*.

47 Or the court of second instance if the case is still pending there. There are various further exceptions in the procedural code: see Article 781 *et seq*. CCP.

filed.' This provision is, however, notoriously honoured in the breach, and it may take several months for a writ of execution to be issued.

Where proceedings are brought to challenge enforcement, they will also progress at a stately pace.[48] Court proceedings in relation to enforcement are common in practice, many of them being concerned with immovable property.[49]

3.3.2.3. *Conception of Judicial Officers as public authorities*

In the Donor States, Judicial Officers are viewed as holding a neutral position between the creditor and the debtor. They are representatives of the state, but are nevertheless independent liberal professionals. This is particularly evident from the fact that, to a greater or lesser extent, they can exercise a variety of non-exclusive competences – the 'secondary activities' of the CEPEJ Guidelines. Their offices have a financial value, and so an entrant to the profession has to raise the capital to invest in purchasing the business. In recent years deregulatory pressures have been strong: there has been greater commercialisation, digitalisation, rationalisation and the adoption of corporate forms. New entrants to the profession now often buy a share in a legal person, rather than become the sole owner of a business.[50]

In Poland, however, the idea of Judicial Officers as independent professionals is controversial, in spite of the origins of the transplant, the professional organisation and rules introduced, and the fact that Judicial Officers are paid by fee income, not salary. Rather, there are frequent assertions that Judicial Officers are public authorities. This has manifested itself in several ways. First, there is an unwillingness to extend the range of activities that may be pursued by Judicial Officers: they are limited to their exclusive enforcement activities (with very limited additional competences discussed below, in Section 3.3.2.4). Broader competition is not permitted since it is not considered to be in keeping with their public authority status.

A second area in which the question of whether Judicial Officers are public authorities or business entities has arisen is in relation to the obligation to charge VAT. It was established by the European Court of Justice in 1987 in Case 235/85, *Commission of the European Communities v. Kingdom of the Netherlands*,[51] that Judicial Officers and notaries in the Netherlands carried out their economic activity 'independently' for the purposes of the relevant VAT Directive. It was vigorously

48 Although it is only an isolated example, I visited an enforcement court in January 2017 at which evidence was being heard in interpleader proceedings. Four witnesses were called. Two attended. The case was adjourned to hear the other two, with the next hearing scheduled for June. It was plausible that the judge might call for further evidence. Argument in the case would then be scheduled for a later date.

49 For example, the judge hearing the enforcement case mentioned in *supra* n. **Fout! Bladwijzer niet gedefinieerd.** had a caseload of c. 500 cases, of which ca. 10 per cent were enforcement-related (about half being related to immovable property, and the other half being complaints against Judicial Officers).

50 Raynouard 2016, p. 35 *et seq.*

51 ECLI:EU:C:1987:161. See also in relation to Slovak Judicial Officers, Case C-456/07, *Karol Mihal v. daňový úrad Košice V*, ECLI:EU:C:2008:293.

argued by Polish Judicial Officers and the Ministry of Justice that the position was different under Polish law, and conflicting court decisions on this point emerged[52] – but the Supreme Administrative Court issued a Resolution on 6 March 2017[53] to the effect that a Judicial Officer works 'in the form of an independent economic activity, performed within the framework of a liberal profession' and so is liable to VAT.

3.3.2.4. *Entrepreneurship and competition*

Judicial Officers in the Donor States engage in varying levels of competition. The potential for competition can arise in two ways: first there is the question of the number of Judicial Officers competing within a given area of territorial competence, and, second, Judicial Officers may compete with one another and with other service providers in relation to their secondary activities.

Traditionally there was limited competition within the areas of territorial competence. Only a small number of Judicial Officers would be appointed to one territorial unit. In the last twenty years, however, that has changed. In 2001, Judicial Officers in the Netherlands became eligible to exercise their competence in enforcement activities throughout the whole national territory.[54] Judicial Officers in France have an expanded area of territorial competence as from 1 January 2017 under the Loi Macron.[55] They have national competence in relation to the *constat d'huissier*, small claims actions and public auctions, and an enlarged area of competence for service and enforcement activities, extending to the territorial jurisdiction of their local court of appeal.[56] At the same time, in each of these jurisdictions, the offices of Judicial Officers who are successful in a competitive environment have been able to expand to meet the demand for their services, and this has been facilitated by the introduction of corporate forms of ownership of the business.[57]

The picture is rather different in Poland: the traditional framework of limited competition within an area of territorial competence has been retained. In fact, the

52 In favour of imposing VAT: the Regional Administrative Court in its judgments in Gdansk on 25 May 2016, Ref. I SA / Gd 330/16; Kielce on 30 June 2016, Ref. I SA / Ke 295/16; Opole on 2 August 2016, Ref. I SA / Op 243/16; Gorzow UK on 11 August 2016, Ref. I SA / Go 175/16; Wroclaw on 25 August 2016, Ref. I SA / Wr 281/16; Krakow on 7 October 2016, Ref. I SA / Kr 825/16. Against imposing VAT: the Regional Administrative Court in its judgments in Poznan on 14 June 2016, Ref. I SA / Po 309/16; Rzeszów on 30 June 2016, Ref. I SA / Rm 373/16; Lodz on 6 July 2016, Ref. I SA / LD 338/16, I SA / LD 342/16, I SA / LD 349/16, I SA / LD 353/16, I SA / LD 354/16, I SA / LD 355/16, and SA / LD 362/16, I SA / LD 363/16, I SA / LD 364/16 and I SA / LD 367/16 and of 27 July 2016, Ref. I SA / LD 501/16; Bydgoszcz on 9 August 2016, Ref. I SA / Bd 330/16.

53 Resolution I FPS 8/16 of the Supreme Administrative Court: available at: <http://orzeczenia.nsa.gov.pl/doc/470EBE2BCC>, last accessed 25 June 2019.

54 Article 3, Wet van 26 januari 2001 tot vaststelling van de Gerechtsdeurwaarderswet.

55 Loi Macron: Loi n° 2015-990 du 6 août 2015 pour la croissance, l'activité et l'égalité des chances économiques.

56 Article 54 Loi Macron, modifying Ord. no. 45-2592 of 2 November 1945, Article 3(1).

57 For France, see Raynouard 2016, p. 35 *et seq*.

appropriate regulation of territorial competence has been the subject of debate and experimentation, and the current approach is the culmination of a series of amendments to the legislation. The starting point, in 1997, was that the territorial competence of the Judicial Officers was restricted to the circuit of the local appellate court. In 2002, the law was amended. Before Judicial Officers could work outside the area of competence of their local district court, they had to meet set targets as to the level of backlog in their caseload. A further restriction was introduced in 2004. In cases involving enforcement against immovable property, a creditor could not choose a Judicial Officer outside the district in which the immovable property was situated.

Following this series of restrictions, legislation in 2007 moved in the opposite direction. The restriction of Judicial Officers to the circuit of an appellate court was removed. National competition became possible – provided that the Judicial Officer concerned met the targets necessary to permit him to work outside the territorial jurisdiction of his district court: his backlog of cases should not be more than a certain proportion of his entire caseload. In 2015, a more restrictive approach began to return. A Judicial Officer had to meet further efficiency requirements before accepting cases outside the jurisdiction of the district court, and furthermore, he could not accept more than 10,000 cases outside that jurisdiction. Finally, the legislative wheel turned full circle. Legislation in 2017 has caused the situation to revert to that prevailing in 1997 – Judicial Officers are restricted to working within the territorial jurisdiction of their local appellate court.

The changes reflect the difficulty of moving from a non-competitive to a competitive approach to the provision of enforcement services, and of finding the right level of competition and the right incentives. But they also reflect ambivalence about the desirability of competition, and Polish disillusionment with the country's transition to capitalism. The re-imposition of restrictions on territorial competence results from concerns about whether competition is operating in a way that produces optimum results, fears that excessive competition may drive some Judicial Officers out of work[58] and doubts on the part of the Ministry of Justice as to whether Judicial Officers with a large caseload could properly monitor their caseload, and so discharge their responsibilities as state authorities.

In fact, it became apparent that the regulations on backlog indicators were providing perverse incentives. The thinking behind the introduction of this restriction on competition was that a Judicial Officer with a significant backlog was inefficient and should not therefore be competing for more work outside of his local district. In fact, however, a Judicial Officer with a growing backlog of cases had an incentive to take on more new cases,[59] so that the backlog remained a small proportion of his overall caseload – a proportion below the threshold that would enable him to continue to compete nationally.

58 In 2015, 10 per cent of offices were responsible for 65 per cent of enforcement work, and 20 per cent of offices were responsible for 80 per cent of enforcement work, and yet it was not the most efficient offices that were attracting more business.

59 In addition, Judicial Officers are not allowed to advertise their business. The factors which drew additional business to poorly performing Judicial Officers are not evident.

As to competition in the area of secondary activities, the Ministry of Justice is opposed to Judicial Officers extending their range of functions. The professional association has been arguing for several years that Judicial Officers should be allowed to offer amicable debt recovery services – an idea which has the support of the Ministry of Development and CEPEJ – but this argument has not been accepted so far. In fact, this is not such an unusual situation: according to a large survey conducted by the UIHJ, about 50 per cent of countries operating a Judicial Officer system of enforcement adopt the same approach.[60] There is a concern that debtors will be confused about the role the Judicial Officer is acting in: debt recovery agent for the creditor, or manifestation of the state. Nevertheless, in some jurisdictions this forms an important feature of the work of Judicial Officers, and may be linked to a right to represent creditors in small claims cases.

There are, however, two specific 'secondary' activities for which Polish Judicial Officers are given competence. The first of these is the service of documents. CEPEJ Guideline 17 states that:

> Notices to parties concerning the enforcement of judicial decisions or enforceable titles or notarised or other documents are an essential aspect of the law of enforcement. Due notification of parties is a necessary element of a fair trial, in the sense of Article 6.1 of the European Convention on Human Rights.

The Guidelines go on to add, '[I]t should be possible to entrust enforcement agents with the service of notices.' In the Donor States, service has traditionally been a central part of the role of the Judicial Officer, and the exclusive right to serve key documents in civil proceedings is the foundation on which their role was built.[61] In Poland, however, in common with other jurisdictions with court-based enforcement systems, postal methods of service are the norm, and the rules governing postal delivery are adapted to ensure that procedural guarantees of due service are observed.

Polish Judicial Officers have been given the right to serve documents, but it is not an exclusive right in relation to all documents.[62] This competence is therefore of limited value: the legal culture into which it has been transplanted is not receptive. There are limited incentives to replace the cheap availability of postal service with the more expensive option offered by Judicial Officers.[63] The argument that service via a Judicial Officer is more secure than postal service and should be employed, at the very least, for the initiation of a claim, is being advanced by the profession, but so far without any support from the state.

The other secondary activity recognised in Polish law is the opportunity for Judicial Officers to provide 'preconstituted proof' via a written report (cf. *constat*

60 This includes the Donor States. In fact, for some Judicial Officers, the amicable recovery of debts represents their main activity.

61 A foundation now subject to serious challenge in the digital age.

62 Hence its designation here as a 'secondary' activity.

63 Service via a Judicial Officer is about 10 times the cost of postal service, but at c. €10 it is extremely cheap in comparison with *signification* in the exporting jurisdictions (referred to in Section 1.2.3).

d'huissier). Again, however, this is a service which is foreign to Polish legal culture and so remains greatly underutilised - although not entirely a dead letter. Competence was conferred on Judicial Officers through brief reference in the 1997 legislation establishing the profession, but was not further implemented by means of regulations, and was not specifically introduced into the Code of Civil Procedure. The lack of linkage between the regulations establishing the competences of Judicial Officers and the procedural code renders the *constat* obscure as a method of proof. Nevertheless, evidence provided by means of a public instrument is regulated in the Civil Code,[64] and the *constat* is a form of public instrument - so the connection has been made in some cases and accepted by the courts.

3.3.2.5. *Regulation of fees*

Appropriate incentives are key to the good functioning of a system of enforcement - although they are extremely difficult to maintain. Incentives can come from a variety of sources, but fees are, of course, the most obvious and significant. In introducing a fee system for the Polish Judicial Officer profession, the French approach to tariffs was rejected as being overcomplicated. A home-grown system was devised, under which the starting point for calculating fees is average income (which is officially published each year).

By far the most important element in the fee system (in relation to pecuniary claims) is the proportional fee - an amount determined by reference to the sum recovered in the enforcement proceedings. The fee is a percentage of the amount recovered - but within limits imposed by average income. The fees recoverable also vary based on the method of enforcement. For example, where enforcement involves the seizure of goods or immovable property, the proportional fee is 15 per cent of the amount recovered, with a minimum of 10 per cent of average income, and a maximum of thirty times average income. In the case of the seizure of a bank account, or an attachment of earnings, the proportional fee is 8 per cent of the amount recovered, with a minimum of 5 per cent of average income and a maximum of ten times average income.

This recognition of the role of average income is an indication of the attention paid by the Polish legislator to social factors. Concerns about the cost of enforcement have led to a further innovation which is problematic from the perspective of Judicial Officers. Two ideals clash in the regulation of enforcement fees. On the one hand, it is reasonable to take the view that neither creditors nor debtors should be unreasonably burdened with enforcement costs, and so the fees charged should not be disproportionate to the level of service that is necessary, and actually provided, in their individual case. On the other hand, Judicial Officers are frequently employed in enforcement cases which ultimately prove unsuccessful because of the debtor's lack of assets. Since they have a legal obligation to render their services whenever requested to do so, in the absence of fee income which can compensate for this they will remain unremunerated in cases of unsuccessful

[64] Articles 565-569.

enforcement - which is ultimately unsustainable. It is therefore also reasonable to take the view that the fee income for Judicial Officers should not be dependent on the level of service provided in an individual case, but should be spread in an equitable way across debtors and also, where the debtor cannot pay, creditors who have the benefit of a well-functioning enforcement service.

A threat to this distribution of fee income across the full range of cases is posed by legislation introduced in 2010 that gives enforcement courts the power to lower the fees charged by the Judicial Officer in any given case by up to 10 per cent, on the request of the debtor.[65] The justification for lowering fees may be the fact that enforcement was straightforward in that case - for example, the Judicial Officer was able to attach a bank account - and so did not have to expend a degree of effort that justifies the fee charged. This focus on the individual case does not take account of the situations in which Judicial Officers are legally obliged to undertake work which remains unremunerated - or which is not remunerated at a level commensurate with the effort involved.

From the perspective of the observer of a mutated transplant, it is clear that although the *concept* of an independent professional Judicial Officer, paid from enforcement fees, has been transplanted, the realisation of that concept in the context of fee regulation has been domesticated. The potential for fee reductions also illustrates ambivalence on the part of the Ministry of Justice about its support for an enforcement agent who is a member of a liberal profession.

3.3.2.6. Relationship with the government

Several of the issues discussed above have indicated that Judicial Officers are in a weak position vis-à-vis the Polish government. This is not surprising. The profession is a new one, and is small in size.[66] In trying to achieve recognition of its work and build a viable professional profile, it faces opposition from powerful creditors - such as banks - who want to resist the imposition of fees on creditors, and a government and society which has a more natural sympathy for debtors and distrust of functionaries.

The profession is also regulated by the district courts in addition to self-regulation. Distrust of the professions and the promotion of competition have led to greater use of external regulators in many jurisdictions, but here the choice of district courts as supervisors is an indicator of the view of Judicial Officers as public functionaries.

Taking a step back from Poland, it is certainly a matter open to debate as to the 'appropriate' level of competition among Judicial Officers, and between Judicial Officers and other providers of 'secondary activities'. A certain level of competition is desirable, in order to promote efficiency, but deregulation - unless it is combined with stringent disciplinary and other measures to ensure proper respect for the

65 Information supplied by Rafał Fronczek.
66 There are approximately 585 Judicial Officers; see Schadl 2015, p. 97-124, 111.

rights of debtors - can lead to cut-throat competition and a reduced level of service in rural areas, or where assets are difficult to access.

In the Donor States, Judicial Officers have enjoyed a moderate or high level of esteem in their dealings with their respective Ministries of Justice. In particular, the corporatist nature of the French state has led to a close relationship between the Ministry of Justice and the legal professions, which has helped to dilute if not to prevent reforms.[67] Consumer lobbying has also been channelled in a way that has reduced its impact. By contrast, in the former Eastern Bloc countries, Judicial Officers do not have the same support from the Ministries of Justice. They are seen by society not as an essential part of the system of justice, or as a vital element in a capitalist society in which the security of property rights is fundamental, but rather as someone who attacks the debtor. Debtors typically attract the compassion of society, and sympathy for the fact that they are combatting state authorities. The rights of the creditor are less appreciated. The legislature can be complicit in this, preferring to blame Judicial Officers for the defects in legislation, and thus deflect the blame.[68] A recent example of this in Poland can be seen in a change in the law designed to give greater benefits to families with children. The new benefits were specifically stated to be exempt from enforcement action. But the legislation did not provide any way of enabling Judicial Officers to identify these benefits. If the money was paid into a bank account, there was nothing to alert a Judicial Officer as to its source. The professional association highlighted this as a problem at an early stage in the legislative process, but the Ministry of Justice left it as a matter to be resolved by the Judicial Officers. The association intervened before the Prime Minister and the President, and eventually the President drew up a law requiring banks to open a new account - exempt from seizure - into which the benefit should be paid.

The current government (Law and Justice Party) has presented a law reform project to the Polish Parliament (the Sejm) which would significantly amend the 1997 Act, imposing greater responsibilities on Judicial Officers, and increasing control over them while at the same time reducing their remuneration.[69] Public sympathy for debtors weakens the position of Judicial Officers in their negotiations with the government, although organised consumer protection associations are few in number and rather small.

67 Of course, this relationship has been closer during some administrations than others. See further Mathieu-Fritz 2005, p. 192 *et seq*. The profession in France is currently adjusting to significant deregulation: see Raynouard 2016. Digitalisation is also challenging the traditional role of Judicial Officers in serving documents.

68 The Polish government and legislature are, of course, not alone in this. The English law on enforcement has suffered from legislative inaction for decades, despite a number of reviews of this area of law. Public authorities are very willing to allow enforcement agents to take the blame for harsh enforcement action, in which they are complicit.

69 The Bill was submitted to the Sejm on 24 May 2017, and at the time of this writing had been referred to the Justice and Human Rights standing committee.

3.3.3. The Czech Republic[70]

3.3.3.1. Introduction

The enforcement legislation in the Czech Republic is based on the legislation introduced in Slovakia in 1996 importing a Judicial Officer model of enforcement. It was recognised that enforcement in the Czech Republic was very inefficient,[71] and so a law which seemed to be working effectively was used to guide reforms. The Czech legislation, Act no. 120/2001 Coll. (hereinafter the Code of Execution), is nevertheless different from that in Slovakia. It is less comprehensive, and instead requires cross-referencing to the Code of Civil Procedure. The CCP dates from 1963, and it assumes that enforcement will be carried out by a court. The new law on enforcement therefore combines elements of a Judicial Officer model with elements of a court-based model. In fact, the two systems of enforcement run in parallel, since the government did not want to abolish the existing court-based system, but creditors do not use the court-based system for methods of execution for which a Judicial Officer can be employed. Appointments to the profession are made by the Ministry of Justice and there are currently just under 160 Judicial Officers.

A Master's degree in law is required for access to the profession, followed by three years of supervised practice and a professional examination. As in Poland, in view of the small number of offices available, many of those who pass the exam (described as Candidates) will remain employees of existing Judicial Officers. Although some offices are very small, the largest one has about 200 employees, including Executors (who undertake the necessary visits to debtors' premises) and a range of administrators. Enforcement procedures are substantially digitalised, so that much of the work can be done by administrators and the role of the Judicial Officer is strategic and managerial.

The professional organisation – the National Chamber – has its seat in Prague. It is competent to issue regulations governing the profession to supplement the primary legislation and has adopted rules on, for example, professional ethics, competition between Judicial Officers, the education of trainees and complaints against Judicial Officers. Supervision of the profession is undertaken by four different bodies. Complaints are handled by the National Chamber, the Ministry of Justice, the president of the enforcement court for the domicile of the debtor concerned and the president of the district court for the office of the Judicial Officer concerned. Inspections are also conducted by all of these except the aforementioned enforcement court – which only deals with individual cases. Where disciplinary proceedings are required, the National Chamber has a disciplinary board that deals

70 Much of the information that follows in the text is based on interviews conducted in March 2017. I am grateful to Antonín Toman and Jan Krejsta for their willingness to give me their time and patiently answer my questions, and also to Me Mathieu Chardon, Dr Juraj Podkonický and Petr Ustohal for helping me to arrange these interviews.

71 No reliable statistics exist, but it is believed that only ca. 3 per cent of debts were collected.

with candidates and trainees, while Judicial Officers must come before a disciplinary board attached to the Supreme Administrative Court.[72]

The procedure for enforcement begins with an application to a Judicial Officer. The Judicial Officer has fifteen days in which to check whether it is formally correct and must then seek authorisation from the court before proceeding to enforcement. This processing is free to the creditor and is done electronically, and so is a cost borne by the Judicial Officer.[73] The court has fifteen days in which to dismiss the application if it considers that there is a defect in it. Otherwise, it will authorise enforcement.

Once enforcement has been authorised, the Judicial Officer can start identifying assets and seize the debtor's property. On average, this can take about two months. There is good access to information about the debtor's assets, from sources such as banks and social insurance organisations, but again the cost of this is borne by the Judicial Officer and the information providers.[74] It is only once the assets have been seized that the Judicial Officer will issue an execution order to be served on the debtor.[75] A separate execution order must be issued for each method of enforcement, but the Judicial Officer can issue as many orders as are needed. On service of the execution order, the debtor is given a final opportunity to pay before forced execution. If payment is made at this stage, the fee for enforcement – a 15 per cent proportional fee on the amount recovered[76] – is halved.[77]

Where it is necessary to proceed to forced execution, the order in which assets are realised is prescribed by law:

a. debtor's bank account;
b. account of debtor's spouse;[78]
c. attachment of earnings or other third-party debts;
d. suspension of driving licence;[79]
e. movables and immovable property not used as a residence; seizure of an enterprise;
f. immovable property used as a residence.

72 This board has six members: two judges (from the Supreme Court and the Supreme Administrative Court), two Judicial Officers, one representative from another legal profession, and one ombudsman.

73 See below for a discussion of the remuneration of Judicial Officers in the Czech Republic. The fees recovered from the debtor are expected to cover this expense – but in many cases no fees are recovered.

74 In the case of information providers, there is no mechanism for them to be paid out of any money recovered from the debtor.

75 However, the Code of Civil Procedure requires that the debtor has already been served with the judgment being enforced.

76 Subject to a prescribed minimum amount, and a reduction in the proportional fee for larger debts

77 The expenses claimable remain the same however.

78 The rules on this, introduced into the Civil Code in 2014, are complex.

79 Only used in relation to the enforcement of a maintenance claim relating to a minor.

If enforcement is challenged, the courts may become involved and give directions as to the way in which it should proceed. This regulation was introduced because of concerns that Judicial Officers might be using methods of enforcement that were disproportionate in the circumstances, such as a seizure of immovable property - with consequent eviction of the debtor - for a relatively small debt.[80]

3.3.3.2. *The role of the courts in the enforcement process*

As noted above, the possibility of applying to the courts for the various enforcement methods available remains part of the Czech legal system, but is not generally used.[81] Given that the 1963 Code of Civil Procedure assumes that enforcement will be court-based, the legal relationship between the courts and Judicial Officers is an awkward one: some of the provisions of the CCP are not well adapted to the introduction of the institution of Judicial Officer, and the law is complicated to understand even for the courts and lawyers. From the 'transplant' perspective, it is surprising that, after receiving an enforcement application from a creditor,[82] a Judicial Officer has to obtain authorisation from the court before taking any steps to enforce the *titre exécutoire*. The lack of independence of the Judicial Officer, as well as the delay in enforcement proceedings caused by this additional procedural step, are forms of 'mutation' of the transplanted institution.

3.3.3.3. *Entrepreneurship and competition*

The two areas in which competition was discussed above were territorial competition, and competition in respect of secondary activities. In relation to territorial competition, the 2001 legislation gave Judicial Officers - who must be natural persons[83] - competence to act throughout the whole of the Czech Republic.[84] This has proved to be problematic as far as Judicial Officers are concerned, with arguments that it has led to an undesirable level of competition. This concern is expressed in many jurisdictions in relation to the competence of Judicial Officers, and the trend is towards greater competition. In such circumstances, it is not surprising that the Czech government has not been receptive to suggestions that the territorial competence of Judicial Officers should be restricted - although, as noted above, such restriction has occurred in Poland. Nevertheless, appropriate regulation of fees is important to create the right incentives and avoid bad practices. Czech Judicial Officers are expected to do a significant amount of preparatory work even in cases where there may prove to be no assets to attach. Although in principle they

80 This was dismissed as an urban myth by my information sources.

81 The locally competent enforcement court is the court in whose district the debtor has his place of residence.

82 Which must be accompanied by an enforcement title, already bearing a certificate of enforceability provided by the body that issued it: Article 41 Code of Execution.

83 Article 1(1) Code of Execution.

84 If any disputes arise relating to the enforcement action, the competent court is the court for the permanent residence of the debtor (Article 45(2) Code of Execution).

are permitted to ask creditors for a payment to cover such initial work,[85] in practice the level of competition is such that no up-front payment is requested.

Czech Judicial Officers are also restricted in the range of secondary activities they can perform. In principle, Judicial Officers are not authorised to conduct any activity other than enforcement,[86] but a few other activities are specifically permitted. As in the case of Polish Judicial Officers, Czech Judicial Officers are permitted to draw up a *constat technique* and they are permitted to serve documents, but in practice these competences are not very significant. For the service of documents, every public authority and every legal person has to have a data box,[87] which must then be used for service. If a debtor or creditor does not have a data box, postal service is used, and is regulated in such a way as to provide the necessary guarantees of due service.

Until 2013 Judicial Officers had an additional potentially lucrative competence in that they could draw up authorised instruments. Czech notaries were, however, able to argue successfully that they should be the entities with sole competence to issue such instruments, and so the law has been changed to give effect to this. However, a new competence has recently been granted to Judicial Officers in the field of insolvency. Insolvency administration is a specialised profession under Czech law, and Judicial Officers are not permitted to undertake this work. As of 1 July 2017, however, they have been authorised to assist debtors to draw up an insolvency petition if they have been certified by the Ministry of Justice as competent to do so.[88]

3.3.3.4. *Regulation of fees*

Fees are regulated in Articles 90 *et seq.* of the Code of Execution and Regulation 330/2001. Article 90 of the Code of Execution sets out the principle of remuneration and recovery of expenses and permits the Judicial Officer to contract with a creditor for additional remuneration. The regulation specifies the applicable tariffs and provides for the recovery of expenses. The main element of remuneration for a Judicial Officer is a proportional fee, based on the sum of money recovered.[89] The fee is subject to a minimum amount of 2,000 CZK and is set at 15 per cent of the amount recovered up to 3 million CZK, after which it is reduced in stages.[90] No additional remuneration is recoverable for the recovery of amounts over 250 million CZK. In relation to expenses, the starting point is a lump sum payment, currently

85 Article 90 Code of Execution.

86 Article 3 Code of Execution, with exceptions for scientific, publishing, pedagogical, interpreting, expert and artistic activities and work within state consultative and other bodies.

87 A natural person can have one if they want to.

88 The rationale for this is apparently an attempt to prevent abuse by some insolvency administrators who encourage debtors to petition for insolvency when it is not appropriate for them to do so.

89 Provision is, of course, also made for other forms of enforcement, such as evictions and the recovery of goods.

90 Article 6 Regulation 330/2001.

set at 3,500 CZK. Amounts greater than this can be claimed if they are supported by evidence.[91]

As noted above, the emphasis on a proportional fee means that there is a problem with 'free riders'. Enforcement action can be started without any cost to the creditor. Judicial Officers occupy a weak bargaining position in comparison with banks and public authorities and so are unable to argue effectively for upfront payments – whether as a matter of regulatory obligation or individual contract. In addition, the minimum amount that can be claimed has recently been reduced. As a result, a number of Judicial Officers have left the profession and it has proved difficult to replace them. It is hard to say whether this is problematic or not. Large creditors prefer to deal with a small number of Judicial Officers with national territorial competence, but Judicial Officers also need to be in a sufficiently strong position to treat debtors fairly and not simply act as an agent of the creditor.

A further problem for Judicial Officers is that it is fairly easy to live in the 'grey' economy – avoiding the need to have property, a bank account or any declared employment. There is a formal register of domicile, but often it does not reflect actual residence. In these circumstances a growing number of debtors are skilled at avoiding enforcement. The number of enforcement proceedings open against such professional debtors is increasing,[92] with Judicial Officers having little hope of recouping any expenditure involved in initiating such proceedings.

3.3.3.5. *Relationship with the government*

As in Poland, the relationship between Judicial Officers and the government has proved to be a difficult one. Parties on the left wing have typically favoured debtors over creditors and Judicial Officers, but this tendency has become more widespread within politics. Initially, when the legislation establishing the institution of Judicial Officer was introduced in 2001 there was great enthusiasm for the new law, and a high rate of debt recovery was claimed.[93] But by about 2008 politicians had become more alert to debtor concerns[94] and began to introduce further debtor protections.

The view of the National Chamber of Judicial Officers is that the politicians have overreacted to debtor lobbying and risk deterring creditors from investment in the Czech Republic. There is agreement that some aspects of the enforcement legislation are unsatisfactory – and notably the unsuitability of some of the

91 *Ibid.*, Article 13.

92 For example, there may be 20-30 procedures against one debtor. A register of enforcement proceedings – established under Article 125 of the Code of Execution and Act no. 329/2008 Coll. – is maintained by the National Chamber of Judicial Officers, and it can be consulted by the public for a small fee (50-60 CZK). This contains information about the commencement and termination of enforcement proceedings (once the 30-day period for voluntary compliance has ended) and also about any auctions conducted.

93 A success rate of 60 to 70 per cent has been suggested, but this raw information is not meaningful without further specificity.

94 There are some very active debtor NGOs, of which the most prominent is *Clovek v. Tísni* ('People in Need', available at: https://www.clovekvtisni.cz/en/social-work, last accessed 25 June 2019).

provisions in the CCP, and the mismatch between that legislation and the Code of Execution – and that the level of competition has contributed to improper practices on the part of some Judicial Officers, but it is thought that part of the problem lies in the great difference between the very inefficient enforcement practices of the courts, and the contrasting efficiency of Judicial Officers, which has led to an unjustified level of outrage that has unsettled politicians. In such circumstances, Judicial Officers are an easy target, whereas the proper balancing of the economy requires a wider range of adjustments. For example, although it is easy to get into debt, and loans are widely advertised, creditors have not been required to take responsibility for their lending, which has put all the pressure on Judicial Officers when creditors have tried to recover the sums lent. Recently, there has been better recognition of the importance of creditor responsibility and the introduction of some consumer credit regulation, but creditors can still start enforcement proceedings without having to pay any deposit or fee and so have no incentive to improve their debt collection practice.

4. Conclusions

4.1. *Reviewing the enforcement tasks*

In respect of the enforcement tasks outlined in Section 1.2 above, Judicial Officers in Poland and the Czech Republic have limited competence to issue *titres exécutoires* – somewhat less than their counterparts in Western Europe (Section 1.2.1). They also have more limited competence in relation to protective seizure of assets. Thus, for example, a French *huissier de justice* is permitted to seize assets as a protective measure on the strength of certain types of title – including a foreign judgment – whereas proceedings for protective measures are required in Poland and the Czech Republic, and may progress slowly. Polish Judicial Officers have exclusive competence for the enforcement of (civil law) titles to which a certificate of enforceability has been appended (Section 1.2.2), while those in the Czech Republic share that competence with the courts in principle, but have near exclusive competence in practice.[95] In this respect their role is similar to that of Judicial Officers in the Donor States. An important difference arises with regard to the service of documents (Section 1.2.3), which has until now been a major bulwark of the profession in the Donor States, but which is usually carried out by post in Poland and the Czech Republic. In both Donor and Recipient States, however, enforcement is undertaken on the initiative of the creditor (Section 1.2.4) – although the requirement for court authorisation is an unusual and unexpected step in the Czech Republic, illustrating the subordinate role of Judicial Officers and the complexity of coordinating the CCP and the Code of Execution.

In both Donor and Recipient States the Judicial Officer has privileged access to information about the debtor's assets, and in this context it seems that Judicial

95 In both cases this is subject to a role for the courts in relation to immovable property, where there are interests at stake that require judicial intervention.

Officers in the Recipient States have the advantage of particularly good access to information. Two reasons may be suggested for this. First is the fact that there has been huge investment in digitalisation of administrative and judicial systems and procedures, with the support of the EU, which has facilitated online data access. Second, the Recipient States do not have the same traditions of privacy of private individuals as the Donor States and have not faced the same resistance to granting data access.

The choice of the method of enforcement (Section 1.2.6) is largely a matter between creditor and Judicial Officer in Poland under the current law - as in the Donor States - but is strictly regulated in the Czech Republic, while the remaining enforcement tasks (Sections 1.2.7-1.2.9) are largely allocated to Judicial Officers, or delegated by them to employees - although there may also be the involvement of external agents (such as auctioneers) or the courts. Challenges to enforcement (Section 1.2.10) may be dealt with via an internal complaints procedure, as well as via complaints to the National Chamber, or court action. In both Poland and the Czech Republic, however, additional administrative supervision by the district courts emphasises the way in which the view of Judicial Officers as part of the public, judicial system continues to influence regulation.

In respect of the enforcement tasks, therefore, there are differences, but not dramatic ones, between Donor and Recipient States (particularly given that the Donor States differ amongst themselves as to the precise organisation of these tasks). Furthermore, the Recipient States have followed the Donor States in relation to a professional structure under a National Chamber with training, supervisory and disciplinary functions, and in relation to high entry qualifications to the profession.

4.2. *Reviewing the surrounding legal culture*

> A transplant is more likely to be successful if two legal systems are based on a similar conceptual understanding of the law, say, because they belong to the same legal family. Reference may also be made to research in political science on the key conditions for the transferability of policies, for example, that countries need to be ideologically and psychologically compatible.[96]

Looking beyond the enforcement tasks to the place of Judicial Officers in the Recipient States, it is apparent that the role of a Judicial Officer as both enforcement agent and business person - which is central to the conception of Judicial Officers in the Donor States - is not replicated in Poland and the Czech Republic. Nor do they seem, on initial investigation, to have the same status vis-à-vis the government, or the same freedom of action. In both states, Judicial Officers have very limited competences beyond the enforcement of *titres exécutoires*, and in Poland in particular there is a strong emphasis on their role as public servants and a corresponding desire to exercise close supervision of their activities. In some respects, Judicial Officers in Poland and the Czech Republic have advantages - such

96 Siems 2014, p. 133-134, 138.

as good access to information – but the fledgling profession is finding it difficult to flourish.

The conclusion to this contribution is not the place to start a detailed discussion of the legal and political cultures that may have influenced and continue to influence the success of a transplant. But it is evident that these cultures are bringing about a mutation of the transplanted institution. The neoliberal agenda has contributed in various ways to the process of propagation of the Judicial Officer model, not least in contributing to expanding consumer credit and the contracting out of public debt collection – which increased the workload, wealth and prominence of Judicial Officers in the Donor States – as well as more generally in its emphasis on globalisation and the creation of legal institutions favourable to the market. Poland was the poster child for successful transition to a capitalist economy. But harsh austerity policies, in the interest of economic reform and attracting international investment, have quickly led to a turn to nationalism and populism. The current Law and Justice Party is socially conservative, but economically left of centre with welfarist, community-centred policies. At the same time, Polish legal culture is 'hyperpositivist'[97] and bureaucratic – emphasising certainty and the strict application of rules.[98] Meanwhile, the Czech Republic, which is proving to be a more enduring economic success story,[99] displays a more moderate form of nationalism. It too, however, is politically detached from Western Europe and is currently torn between pro-Russian and pro-European influences. And it too has a positivistic legal culture.[100]

The interplay of these various factors remains to be explored – but it is necessary to do this also in the context of 'mutations' of the Judicial Officer model in the Donor States. Neoliberalism, although an increasingly contested ideology, continues to be a dominant force in these countries. There is continuing momentum towards deregulation and increased competition – most recently manifested in the changes to French enforcement law in the wake of the Loi Macron.[101] Judicial Officers are 'une profession en mouvement'[102] – but whether they are all moving in the same direction is another question.

97 Manko 2013; Bobek 2015.

98 Muszyńska, Nováková & Van Rossum 2012.

99 Though heavily dependent on manufacturing exports.

100 Illustrated notably by the refusal of the Czech Supreme Court to follow rulings of the Constitutional Court unless they are firmly based on legislative texts: see, e.g., Kühn 2011, Ch. 5.

101 See Resolution I FPS 8/16, *supra* n. 53.

102 See Raynouard 2016.

References

Ajani 1995
Ajani, G., 'By Chance and Prestige: Legal Transplants in Russia and Eastern Europe', *American Journal of Comparative Law*, 1995, Vol. 43(1), p. 93-117.

Bobek 2015
Bobek, M. (ed.), *Central European Judges Under the European Influence: The Transformative Power of the EU Revisited*, Oxford: Hart Publishing, 2015.

Cairns 2012/2013
Cairns, J.W., 'Watson, Walton, and the History of Legal Transplants', *Georgia Journal of International and Comparative Law*, 2012/2013, Vol. 41(3), p. 637-696.

Chambre Nationale des Huissiers de Justice 1995
Chambre Nationale des Huissiers de Justice, *Hostarii*, Paris: Editions Juridiques et Techniques, 1995.

Correia & Videira 2015
Correia, P. & Videira, S., 'Troika's Portuguese Ministry of Justice Experiment: An Empirical Study on the Success Story of the Civil Enforcement Actions', *International Journal for Court Administration*, 2015, Vol. 7(1), p. 37-49.

Husa 2015
Husa, L., *A New Introduction to Comparative Law*, Oxford: Hart Publishing, 2015.

Jongbloed 2010
Jongbloed, A.W., 'The Dutch Court Bailiffs Act Eight Years After its Introduction', in: C.H. van Rhee & A. Uzelac (eds.), *Enforcement and Enforceability: Tradition and Reform*, Antwerp: Intersentia, 2010, p. 179-206.

Kühn 2011
Kühn, Z., *The Judiciary in Central and Eastern Europe (Law in Eastern Europe)*, The Hague: Martinus Nijhoff, 2011.

Legrand 1997
Legrand, P., 'The Impossibility of "Legal Transplants"', *Maastricht Journal of European and Comparative Law*, 1997, Vol. 4(2), p. 111-124.

Manko 2013
Manko, R., 'Survival of the Socialist Legal Tradition? A Polish Perspective', *Comparative Law Review*, 2013, Vol. 4(2), p. 1-28.

Mathieu-Fritz 2005
Mathieu-Fritz, A., *Les huissiers de justice*, Paris: Presses Universitaires de France, 2005.

Muszyńska, Nováková & Van Rossum 2012
Muszyńska, B., Nováková, P. & Van Rossum, W., 'Fighting Corruption in Polish and Czech Legal Cultures', *Comparative Law Review*, 2012, Vol. 3(1), p. 1-34.

Raynouard 2016
Raynouard, A., *Huissiers de Justice: Monographie d'une Profession en Mouvement*, Paris: Editions Juridiques et Techniques, 2016.

Schadl 2015
Schadl, G., 'The Organization System and Rules of Judicial Execution in Europe', *Acta Univ. Sapientiae, Legal Studies*, 2015, p. 97-124.

Siems 2014
Siems, M., 'The Curious Case of Overfitting Legal Transplants', in: M. Adams & D. Heirbaut (eds.), *The Method and Culture of Comparative Law: Essays in Honour of Mark Van Hoecke*, Oxford: Hart Publishing, 2014, p. 133-146.

Teubner 1998
Teubner, G., 'Legal Irritants: Good Faith in British Law or How Unifying Law Ends up in New Divergences', *Modern Law Review*, 1998, p. 11-32.

Van Rhee 2010
Van Rhee, C.H., 'The History of the "Huissier de Justice" in the Low Countries', in: C.H. van Rhee & A. Uzelac (eds.), *Enforcement and Enforceability: Tradition and Reform*, Antwerp: Intersentia, 2010, p. 161-177.

Watson 1974
Watson, A., *Legal Transplants: An Approach to Comparative* Law, Edinburgh: Scottish Academic Press, 1974.

Watson 1994
Watson, A., 'The Importance of Nutshells,' *American Journal of Comparative Law*, 1994, p. 1-23.

Watson 2007
Watson, A., 'Law and Society', in: J.W. Cairns & P.J. Du Plessis (eds.), *Beyond Dogmatics: Law and Society in the Roman World*, Edinburgh: Edinburgh University Press, 2007, p. 9-36.

World Bank 2013
World Bank, *Doing Business 2013: Smarter Regulations for Small and Medium-Size Enterprises*, Washington DC: International Bank for Reconstruction and Development/The World Bank, 2013.

World Bank 2014
World Bank, *Doing Business 2015: Going Beyond Efficiency*, International Bank for Reconstruction and Development/The World Bank, 2014.

J. Valdhans
T. Kyselovská

RECOGNITION AND ENFORCEMENT OF FOREIGN JUDGMENTS ACCORDING TO CZECH LAW

1. Introduction

In this contribution we will address the basic underlying principles of recognition and enforcement of foreign judgments in the Czech Republic. The area of recognition and enforcement is part of private international law. This premise alone sometimes presents challenges for competent national authorities who are in charge of dealing with foreign judgments in their territory. Nevertheless, the processes correspond to each other. It is important to distinguish the differences between them and to apply them in the relevant order using the relevant instruments.

Our focus in this contribution will be, in particular, the recognition and enforcement of judgments coming to the Czech Republic from third, non-Member States of the European Union (EU). We will analyse the relevant Czech private international law rules and procedural rules on enforcement in the Czech procedural codes. Furthermore, the necessary information concerning EU legal regulations will be included. Particular Czech legal instruments will also be compared with their EU legal counterparts.

2. Recognition and enforcement of foreign judgments

To understand the recognition and enforcement of foreign judgments, it is necessary to define the most important terminology, i.e. the principle of territoriality, recognition and enforcement.[1]

The decision of a court represents an act of official authority bestowed by a state power and provides protection to the rights and duties of the subjects of the law. It demonstrates the sovereignty of the issuing state and represents a

1 For more in-depth theoretical and doctrinal analysis of private international rules for the recognition and enforcement of foreign judgments, see Valdhans & Kyselovská 2016, p. 157-172.

combination[2] of substantive and procedural rules.[3] As such, it has legal effects only in the territory of the issuing state,[4] which means that its effects are *territorially* limited. The decision of a court of one state cannot be used as a relevant legal title in another state unless certain steps are realised. Two legal processes with different effects – recognition and enforcement – represent these steps.

First, the foreign court decision has to be recognised in the state of further enforcement. The term *recognition* can be understood in two ways. It can represent the process of recognition, i.e. the legal procedure where the court usually examines the conditions established by the *lex fori* which are necessary to grant a foreign judgment legal effect in the state of recognition. The second meaning represents the result of the whole process, i.e. the situation where a foreign judgment is granted legal effect in the state of recognition and can be subject to enforcement.[5]

The method by which each state handles the recognition process differs. In general, it is possible to distinguish three methods of recognition:[6]

- Exequatur (the state agrees to the enforceability of a foreign judgment in its territory under certain conditions);
- Registration (the execution of a foreign judgment is correlative to registration, again under certain conditions – this method is similar to exequatur);
- Transformation (a foreign judgment has to be transformed – incorporated – into a new domestic judgment. It is not the foreign judgment that is executed, but the domestic judgment. This method is hostile towards foreign judgments).

If a state is more intent on cooperation with other states, the more favourable method of recognition is used. Therefore, the most favourable mechanism may be expected among the EU Member States. Although Member States cooperate very closely in judicial issues, the principle of sovereignty is still very important, indicating that a judicial decision is a manifestation of the said principle of one state and does not automatically have any legal effects in the territory of another Member State. Therefore, it is still necessary to recognise this decision in order for the judgment to be enforceable in the territory of another state. The advantage of close cooperation between Member States is that recognition does not require separate proceedings and is realised automatically. Therefore, from a practical point of view, one who is not familiar with private international law theory may conclude that the process of recognition is not a necessary part of the whole process of both the recognition and the enforcement of a foreign judgment. Actually, the opposite is

2 For the decision to be issued many conditions have to be fulfilled, which may differ in many ways from state to state.

3 Steiner 1970, p. 244.

4 Basedow *et al.* 2012, p. 244; Cheshire, North & Fawcett 2008, p. 611; Steiner 1970, p. 241; Heyer 1963, p. 112.

5 Pauknerová *et al.* 2013, p. 104-105.

6 Heyer 1963, p. 112.

true: the process of recognition, with its impact of granting or extending (depending on the concept) legal effects in the state of enforcement, still remains the essential mechanism of private international law.

Enforcement refers to the mechanism of execution in the state of recognition. By the mechanism of execution we mean the authorities providing execution, and the means of execution or objections against execution. It is necessary to bear in mind that recognition is *sine qua non* for enforcement. Put in different words – one cannot enforce something that does not exist in the sense of not having legal effects.

The instruments of recognition and enforcement are often mixed together; when the desired result of the whole process of dealing with the foreign judgment is taken into account, this simplification can be understood. Nevertheless, merging these two legal instruments, or the legal procedures behind them, represents an error and a misunderstanding.

3. Legal sources for recognition and enforcement in the Czech Republic

Every state has its own rules for the recognition and enforcement of foreign judgments. This stems from the principles of territoriality and sovereignty. Since the area of recognition and enforcement of foreign judgments is also regulated by international conventions (bilateral or multilateral) and EU regulations, the national rules have to yield wherever international conventions or EU regulations claim precedence.

National laws usually contain the strictest (restrictive) legal regulation of recognition and enforcement, based on territorial and doctrinal concepts. International treaties typically represent cooperation between Member States and are used to establish a better regime of dealing with judgments issued by a court from another Member State. Finally, the European Union represents a closely co-operating entity with coercive powers vis-à-vis the Member States and has the possibility to adopt its own legal regulations.

The recognition of foreign judgments in the Czech Republic is regulated at the national, international and EU level. The national level is represented by Act No. 91/12 Coll. on private international law (PILA). As mentioned above, the application of PILA is limited because of the EU legislation and international conventions; it applies only if EU regulations or international conventions are not directly applicable (§ 2 PILA). PILA is applicable for the recognition of judgments from non-EU Member States with which the Czech Republic has no legal cooperation established by international convention. The Czech Republic is a contracting state to many bilateral conventions on cooperation and mutual judicial assistance, mainly with the states that belonged to the former socialist bloc.[7]

7 A complete list of the bilateral and multilateral international conventions on judicial assistance and mutual cooperation binding for the Czech Republic, is available at: <http://www.mzv.cz/public/fc/a3/3a/2519811_1769487_seznam_vyhlasenych_mezinarodnich_smluv.pdf>, last accessed 20 December 2019.

Enforcement, on the other hand, is regulated at the national level only. None of the uniform legal regulations (international conventions, EU regulations) address enforcement itself. In the Czech Republic, enforcement is regulated by Act No. 99/1963 Coll. of the Civil Procedural Code (*Občanský soudní řád*) and by Act No. 120/2001 Coll., on Judicial Executors and Enforcements, of the Enforcement Code (*Exekuční řád*). The difference between the two will be discussed below.

The remarkable combination of uniform rules and national rules creates a complex relationship between the processes of recognition and enforcement. From our point of view, it is the interconnection between the legal regulation of recognition and the legal regulation of enforcement which constitutes the biggest problem for legal practice. We can mention, for example, a combination of reasons why recognition can be refused and reasons why enforcement can be stopped or postponed. Each of them are set down in different legal provisions.

What are the conceivable combinations, not only in the Czech Republic, but also in other EU Member States?

a) A judgment from a *third state* with which *no international convention* has been concluded. In this case, the national rules of the state where the enforcement is sought are used; no uniform rules are taken into account. Both recognition and enforcement are covered by the national rules. This does not mean that these rules are gathered together in one regulation. In the Czech Republic, in this case the recognition (the whole process including the reasons for refusal of recognition) is regulated by the rules in PILA and the enforcement by the rules in the Civil Procedural Code.
b) A judgment from a *third state* with which an *international convention* (bilateral or multilateral) has been concluded. The process of recognition is regulated by the international convention and the national rules together. The national rules cover the procedural part (which court, the type of procedure, the type of decision, i.e. the process itself) and the convention usually covers only the reasons for refusal of the foreign judgment, which are either limited or absent. The enforcement is governed by the national rules only.
c) A judgment from an *EU Member State* regarding '*general*' issues. The recognition and, if applicable, the declaration of enforceability are regulated by EU legal rules (e.g. the Brussels I Recast Regulation, hereafter BIR), the enforcement (including the reasons against enforcement) is regulated at the national level.
d) A judgment from an *EU Member State* regarding '*special*' issues (e.g. issues governed by international transport conventions such as CMR, COTIF, etc.). The recognition is covered by the EU regulation (the type of procedure, the process itself), and the grounds for refusal of recognition are governed by international convention (limited or absent). Finally, the enforcement itself is regulated at the national level.

4. Recognition and enforcement of foreign judgments in the Czech Republic – theoretical remarks

Regulation of the recognition and enforcement of foreign judgments in PILA is complex; all aspects of recognition and enforcement are dealt with, as well as all types of decisions (judgments, arbitral awards, notarial deeds and public deeds).[8] The rules for the recognition and enforcement of foreign judgments are in accordance with international and European standards.

PILA contains both a general rule and special provisions for the recognition and enforcement of foreign judgments. The general rule for recognition and enforcement is provided for in §§ 14-19 PILA. Rules in §§ 14-16 are applicable for the recognition and enforcement of judgments if any EU regulation or international convention is applicable. Provisions in §§ 17-19 are applicable in proceedings on the recognition and enforcement of foreign judgments which are governed by directly applicable provisions of EU law or international conventions that require a declaration of enforceability[9] and link EU law and international conventions to national judicial procedures.

Czech private international law is based on limited control of foreign judgments. Current legal regulation in PILA represents a mechanism only slightly amended in comparison to the previous Act.

4.1. *Recognition*

We would like to stress that in this contribution we focus on Czech rules on the recognition of foreign judgments from third, non-Member States of the EU (the recognition and enforcement of judgments from EU Member States is dealt with in many articles and books).

Foreign judgments are recognised automatically without any special procedure being required. However, this does not mean that foreign judgments are (without recognition) treated the same as domestic ones.

Recognition under PILA gives foreign judgments the same legal effect as Czech judgments in the Czech Republic. It is not, as in the case of the recognition of a decision from a Member State according to unified EU standards, the extension of effects from the country of origin to the territory of the Czech Republic, but the recognition of effects as if it were a Czech decision (the foreign judgment is equated to a Czech decision and is adapted to Czech procedural conditions).[10]

The effect of the recognition is the same as the situation that would have arisen if the subject matter had been decided by a Czech authority.[11] The legal effects are *ex tunc*.[12] A recognised decision constitutes *res judicata*. The decision on recognition is a

8 Rozehnalová *et al.* 2015, p. 68.
9 Pauknerová *et al.* 2013, p. 104.
10 Vaške 2007, p. 428. Decision by the Supreme Court of the Czech Republic, 27 August 1987, Cpjf 27/86.
11 Kučera *et al.* 2015, p. 338.
12 Vaške 2007, p. 428.

declaratory decision. There is no new legal right granted by the recognition of the foreign judgment, consequently it cannot have constitutive effects. If we compare the Czech approach to EU law, the same situation exists under the Brussels I Regulation (44/2001) – the exequatur meant nothing more than that the foreign decision was enforceable 'also' in the territory of the state of enforcement – there are no additional legal rights created as a result of it. Exequatur is a procedural decision only and therefore has no constitutive effects in the state of enforcement. The new BIR (1215/2012) expresses a change in procedural steps in dealing with foreign judgments in comparison with the former Brussels I Regulation (44/2001). This is seen in how the abolishment of exequatur is expressed. It shows that no process of granting enforceability to the foreign judgment is needed and that this procedural step is realised against the background of the next step, which is the enforcement itself. The meaning is not to express that recognition is not needed (that the enforcement may proceed without any further step), but to express that the procedural step of granting enforceability is not needed any more.

A positive condition for the recognition of foreign judgments under PILA is their 'legal force' *(právní moc)*. According to the general rule in § 14 of PILA, foreign judgments and rulings from foreign authorities concerning any rights and obligations, whose private law character would mean that they would be subject to the jurisdiction of Czech courts, as well as foreign judicial settlements and foreign notarial or other legal instruments, will be effective in the Czech Republic if they have come into legal force according to the confirmation of the appropriate foreign authority and if they have been recognised by the Czech public authorities.

Therefore, it is not possible to recognise provisional decisions. The concept of 'legal force' must be interpreted according to Czech law: legal force is related to the irreversibility of the decision (it is impossible to challenge such a decision by an ordinary legal remedy), and, therefore the decision is legally binding for the parties. Legal force must be proven by a certificate issued by the relevant foreign authority (other means are not allowed). This can be either in the form of an individual document or in the form of a special clause written on the foreign decision. However, the certificate of enforceability itself does not confirm the legal force of a decision.

In addition, it is clear (although not expressly stated in PILA) that the decision must be enforceable in the state of origin. The fulfilment of this condition is controlled according to the law of the country of origin. Negative conditions are expressed in the form of grounds for refusal of recognition.

Grounds for refusal of recognition are governed by § 15 of PILA:

a) The matter falls under the exclusive jurisdiction of the Czech courts, or the proceedings could not have been undertaken by an authority in a foreign state if the provisions pertaining to the jurisdiction of the Czech courts had been applied when assessing the jurisdiction of the foreign authority, unless the participant in the proceedings, against whom the judgment is given, has voluntarily submitted to the jurisdiction of the foreign authority;

b) If proceedings are underway before a Czech court with regard to the same legal relations and if said proceedings commenced prior to the proceedings abroad, in which the judgment whose recognition is sought was issued;
c) If a Czech court has already issued a valid judgment about the same legal relation or if the valid judgment of a court of a third state has already been recognised in the Czech Republic;
d) If a participant in the proceedings, with regard to whom the judgment is to be recognised, has been deprived of the ability to duly participate in proceedings before a foreign authority, especially if said participant has not received a summons or a motion to commence the proceedings;
e) Any such recognition would clearly contravene public order; or
f) Reciprocity has not been guaranteed; reciprocity is not required if the foreign judgment is not aimed at a citizen of the Czech Republic or a Czech legal entity.

The above-mentioned grounds are applicable to all types of foreign judgments in civil matters. These grounds have to be examined *ex officio*. The only exception to this rule is letter d) above, which is only taken into account if the participant in the proceedings against whom the foreign judgment should be recognised so requests. Letters b) and c) must be pleaded in court proceedings by the interested party only if the court is not familiar with the necessary facts (§ 15 para 2 PILA).[13]

Even though we focus on the recognition of judgments from non-Member States of the EU, it is interesting to compare the Czech regulation with provisions in BIR. The main difference between PILA and BIR is in regard to reciprocity: the principle of reciprocity is not expressly stated in BIR. Nevertheless, cooperation in judicial matters among the Member States of the EU is based on the principle of mutual trust. It is safe to say that the regulation in PILA is stricter, because it is based, *inter alia*, on the principle of (material) reciprocity.[14] However, reciprocity represents the only main difference among the grounds for refusal of recognition between the national rules and EU rules. In this sense the Czech legal regulation is, and even in the past was, very progressive.

Recognition of monetary claims is not initiated by a separate request. Rather, it is carried out by the competent court hearing the case for which recognition is relevant. No specific rules of jurisdiction are prescribed. If the purpose is the enforcement of the decision, the district court in the place of the domicile of the defendant has jurisdiction. Since in these cases recognition is not the subject of a separate decision, nor is the declaration of enforceability, it is not possible to file the application for recognition through an executor.[15]

Recognition of non-monetary claims is initiated by a separate claim, and it is riled on by a special decision, unless the law prescribes that the foreign decision is

13 Pauknerová *et al.* 2013, p. 109-112.
14 *Ibid.*, p. 113. For more information on recognition and enforcement of judgments in the Czech Republic, see Rozehnalová *et al.* 2015, p. 59 *et seq.*
15 Judgment of the Supreme Court NS 30 Cdo 1349/2016.

recognised without a special decision, in which case the process would be the same as in a) (*supra*). The declaration of any such recognition pertains to the locally appropriate court, i.e. the general court of the party requesting the recognition, or otherwise to the district court, in whose district any fact which is significant for the act of recognition has occurred or could occur, unless PILA states otherwise. The Act states otherwise in matters of the dissolution of a marriage, legal separation, the declaration of a marriage as invalid and the designation of whether or not a marriage exists where at least one of the participants in the proceedings is a citizen of the Czech Republic and under the jurisdiction of the Supreme Court.

4.2. *Enforcement*

In Czech procedural law, there are two means for the enforcement of judgments in civil and commercial matters: (1) judicial enforcement by courts (*vykonávací řízení soudní*); (2) (non-judicial) enforcement (*exekuční řízení*) by executors (*exekutoři*).

Judicial enforcement is regulated by Act No. 99/1963 Coll. of the Civil Procedural Code (*Občanský soudní řád*). (Non-judicial) enforcement is regulated by Act No. 120/2001 Coll., on Judicial Executors and Enforcements, of the Enforcement Code (*Exekuční řád*).[16]

The rules for territorial jurisdiction of the courts in judicial enforcement proceedings can be found in § 252 of the Civil Procedural Code. Unless otherwise stipulated, the court of the debtor is competent to enforce the decision. There are several exceptions to this rule in § 252, para 2 of the Civil Procedural Code. The rules for territorial jurisdiction in (non-judicial) enforcement proceedings can be found in § 45, para 2 of the Enforcement Code.

The Czech enforcement law is characterised by the principle of the free disposition of the parties.[17] Any enforcement procedure is started by the claimant. The claimant whose claim is not satisfied can choose between judicial enforcement under the Civil Procedural Code and (non-judicial) enforcement under the Enforcement Code. Both codes have their advantages and disadvantages[18] and it is up to the claimant to choose the best option.[19] [20] In practice, enforcement under the Enforcement Code is used more often because enforcement under the Civil Procedural Code is rigid. The legal regulation of enforcement under the

16 The executor, according to this code, carries out the enforcement activities independently. Enforcement is performed by the executor nominated by the entitled party in the action for execution and authorised to perform execution in the court decision. Acts by the executor are considered to be acts of the court.

17 Winterová & Macková 2015, p. 25.

18 The intention was to move most of enforcement to the Enforcement Code – see Zahradníková *et al.* 2015, p. 353.

19 Winterová & Macková 2015, p. 21.

20 The general provisions in the Civil Procedural Code do not apply to decisions on the upbringing of minors, given the different (non-property) nature of the obligation enforced; some relevant provisions can be found in other legal acts, such as Act No. 292/2013 Coll., Special Judicial Proceedings.

Enforcement Code was introduced to overcome the shortcomings of the Civil Procedural Code.

As to enforcement in civil and commercial matters, the Civil Procedural Code is *lex generalis,* and the Enforcement Code *lex specialis.*[21] Unless otherwise provided by the Enforcement Code, the provisions of the Civil Procedural Code apply *mutatis mutandis* in enforcement proceedings (§ 52 para 1 Enforcement Code).

The two codes differentiate between various types of enforcement procedures, depending on the character of the claim: monetary claims on the one hand and non-monetary claims on the other. The list of enforcement instruments is exhaustive; a decision may only be enforced in the manner provided by the Civil Procedural Code (§ 257 Civil Procedural Code and § 59 Enforcement Code). The legislator has tried to find a balance between the right of recovery of the creditors and the right of the debtor to a dignified existence. Some assets are protected from enforcement.

An enforcement may be ordered only to the extent and amount that is stated in the claim that is to be enforced. Judicial and (non-judicial) enforcement must be in accordance with the principle of proportionality (§§ 263 and 264 Civil Procedural Code, § 58 Enforcement Code).

The main purpose of the proceedings is to enforce an obligation imposed by a court decision that has legal effect, against a debtor who refuses to fulfil this obligation voluntarily. The law has to protect the rights and rightful interests of both parties: the debtor and the creditor. The legislator has to seek a balanced approach. It is necessary to provide for effective and fast enforcement. After all, there is a judgment by the court on the merits of the relevant case. Nevertheless, the rights of the debtor, i.e. the person who refuses to fulfil his/her obligation, have to be protected. The law must protect the right to a dignified life after enforcement. The debtor has several legal remedies at his disposal:

- Right to appeal (§ 254 Civil Procedural Code). The right to appeal is limited and the appellate process is different from the initial proceedings (§ 254 paras 4-8 Civil Procedural Code);
- Right to request postponement of the enforcement of a judgment (§ 266 Civil Procedural Code); upon petition, the court is authorised to defer implementing the decision if the obliged party, not at fault, has momentarily found himself/herself in such a position that the immediate enforcement of the decision could bring very adverse effects for the obliged party or members of his family, and the entitled party (creditor) would not experience any serious harm by the suspension of the enforcement of the decision;
- Right to stop the enforcement for reasons prescribed by law (§ 268 Civil Procedural Code);
- Right to actions under § 267a Civil Procedural Code (*odporová žaloba*).

21 Winterová & Macková 2015, p. 22.

All of these actions are at the disposition of the debtor, and it is up to him/her whether or not to use them.[22]

However, in the enforcement procedure it is not possible to suspend the proceedings and to waive missing a deadline (§ 254 para 2 Civil Procedural Code). Also, it is not possible to file an action for retrial. An action for nullity can only be brought exceptionally (§ 254 para 2 and § 229 para 4 CCP), and the same is true for an extraordinary remedy (§ 237 CCP).

5. The practical side of recognition and enforcement procedures in the Czech Republic

In this contribution, we originally discussed Czech law in general terms before shifting to a more concrete analysis regarding the mechanisms of recognition and enforcement. Now we will discuss this matter from a practical point of view. While before we focused primarily at the national level of legal regulation, now we also include elements of EU law.

The goal of each creditor who holds a judgment that is not complied with on a voluntary basis is forced execution. A prerequisite for the enforcement of a foreign judgment is its recognition. As we have described above, recognition represents the mechanism through which the foreign decision is controlled by the state of recognition. The intensity of the control and protection varies depending on whether the decision is from a state with which an international agreement has been concluded or a different form of cooperation has been established. It is evident that the control is more liberal where it concerns states with which some form of cooperation has been established.

The control includes the elements mentioned above, e.g. public order, procedural discrepancies and *res judicata*. It is not possible to take into consideration other grounds, e.g. fulfilment of the obligation in dispute and set-off. These are grounds against enforcement - therefore it is possible to invoke these grounds after the decision is recognised and declared enforceable. We acknowledge the difficulty in distinguishing these steps in practice because of the technical interconnection between them. Still, the classification and structuring of these steps is of fundamental importance.

We would like to return to the above-mentioned differentiation with regard to the processes of recognition and enforcement depending on the country of origin of the foreign decision and complement it from the perspective of the Czech Republic:

a) Judgment from a *third state* with which *no international convention* has been concluded. Recognition is completely regulated by PILA (the process and the grounds for refusal which are taken into account *ex officio*). Enforcement is regulated by the Civil Procedural Code, including the grounds for terminating or postponing enforcement. National legal grounds are used, which means that different grounds can be invoked in different states. This

22 Winterová & Macková 2015, p. 26.

statement also applies to the cases under points b) to d) below. However, it is not possible to realise enforcement under the Enforcement Code, because according to § 37(2)(b) of the Enforcement Code this method of enforcement can be executed only when recognition is part of a separate decision, or a declaration of enforceability has been granted.

b) Judgment from a *third state* with which an *international convention* (either bilateral or multilateral) has been concluded. The process of recognition is regulated by the international convention (the grounds for refusal) and PILA (process) together. Enforcement is governed by the Civil Procedural Code, unless the international convention requires a declaration of enforceability. In the latter case, enforcement under the Enforcement Code is also possible.
c) Judgment from an *EU Member State* regarding *general* issues. Recognition and, if applicable, a declaration of enforceability are regulated by EU rules (e.g. BIR), enforcement (including the grounds against enforcement) is regulated at the national level by the Civil Procedural Code and/or the Enforcement Code. The Enforcement Code can be used even if a declaration of enforceability is no longer required by BIR. An extensive interpretation of § 37(2)(b) of the Enforcement Code is used. According to this provision, the creditor may apply for the enforcement of a foreign judgment via an executor if the judgment is declared enforceable according to EU provisions. According to BIR, however, no declaration of enforceability is needed. Nevertheless, if it is possible to use executors in cases of a foreign judgment accompanied by a declaration of enforceability, then executors can be used *a fortiori* in cases of foreign judgments where the declaration of enforceability has been revoked.[23] The unified process of recognition under the EU rules is complemented by national elements in the process of enforcement. Therefore, the whole process of 'handling' the foreign court decision is not entirely homogenous and unified among the EU Member States.
d) Judgment from an *EU Member State* regarding *special* issues (e.g. issues governed by international transport conventions such as CMR, COTIF, etc.). Recognition is covered both by the EU regulation (process) and by the international convention (grounds for refusal). Finally, the enforcement itself is regulated by the Civil Procedural Code and/or the Enforcement Code.

6. Conclusion and critical remarks regarding the current legal framework in the Czech Republic

Czech national regulation of recognition is not to be criticised. In comparison with EU regulation in the Brussels Convention/Brussels I Regulation, Czech regulation in PILA has been significantly more modern since the 1960s than EU regulation. The

23 The same conclusion also in Bříza & Břicháček 2014, p. 768, 119.

automatic recognition of monetary claims, without the necessity of separate proceedings, was well known in Czech law much earlier than before the Brussels Convention.

What *can* be criticised is the inadequate link between the legal regulation of recognition and enforcement of foreign judgments concerning monetary claims from third countries. As mentioned above, two types of enforcement exist in the Czech Republic - judicial enforcement and executors. Judicial enforcement is hardly ever used due to its rigidity. According to the wording of the Enforcement Code and follow-up case law, creditors are not able to use the services of the executors in cases of monetary foreign judgments, which represent undoubtedly the largest number of foreign judgments from third countries. This deficiency spoils the simplicity and modernity of the PILA regulation of recognition, resulting in the application of the rigid and out of date regulation of enforcement in the Civil Procedural Code.

References

Basedow *et al.* 2012
Basedow, J. *et al.*, *Max Planck Encyclopedia of European Private Law*, Oxford: Oxford University Press, 2012.

Bříza & Břicháček 2014
Bříza, P. & Břicháček, T., *Zákon o mezinárodním právu soukromém. Komentář*, Prague: C.H. Beck, 2014.

Cheshire, North & Fawcett 2008
Cheshire, G., North, P. & Fawcett, J., *Private International Law*, Oxford: Oxford University Press, 2008.

Heyer 1963
Heyer, J., *Výkon cizozemských rozsudků*, Zprávy advokacie, 1963.

Kučera *et al.* 2015
Kučera, Z. *et al.*, *Mezinárodní právo soukromé*, Pilsen: Aleš Čeněk, 2015.

Pauknerová *et al.* 2013
Pauknerová, M. *et al.*, *Zákon o mezinárodním právu soukromém. Komentář*, Prague: Wolters Kluwer, 2013.

Rozehnalová *et al.* 2015
Rozehnalová, N. *et al.*, *Czech Private Int'l Law*, Brno: Masaryk University, 2015.

Steiner 1970
Steiner, V., *Některé teoretické koncepce řešení otázky uznání a výkonu cizího rozhodnutí*, Časopis pro mezinárodní právo, 1970, p. 244.

Valdhans & Kyselovská 2016
Valdhans, J. & Kyselovská, T., 'Selected Issues of Recognition and Enforcement of Foreign Judgments from the Perspective of EU Members',in: V. Rijavec (ed.), 24th *Conference Corporate Entities at the Market and European Dimensions (May 19th-21st 2016, Portorož, Slovenia, Conference Proceedings)*, Maribor: University of Maribor Press, 2016, p. 157-172.

Vaške 2007
Vaške, V., *Uznání a výkon cizích rozhodnutí v České republice*, Prague: C.H. Beck, 2007.

Winterová & Macková 2015
Winterová, A. & Macková, A., *Civilní právo procesní. Část druhá, Řízení vykonávací, řízení insolvenční: vykonávací řízení obecně, soudní výkon rozhodnutí, exekuční řízení, způsoby výkonu, způsoby řízení úpadku, mezinárodní a evropské insolvenční právo*, Prague: Leges, 2015.

Zahradníková *et al.* 2015
Zahradníková, R. *et al.*, *Civilní právo procesní*, Pilsen: Aleš Čeněk, 2015.

F. Fernhout

ENFORCING FOREIGN TITLES REGARDING MONETARY CLAIMS IN THE NETHERLANDS

Even after the adoption of the Brussels I Recast Regulation (hereafter BIR),[1] enforcing foreign titles in the Netherlands can be quite adventurous. There are three reasons for this. Obviously, the regime instituted by the regulation does not cover all titles, since arbitral awards and titles from outside the European Union are not included. Moreover, the Dutch system of enforcement may be a bit surprising in its efficiency and straightforwardness. Additionally, this efficiency has its counterpart in an intricate maze of procedures to protect the interests of the debtor, other creditors and third parties. This contribution will give a summary of what can be expected when an attempt is made to enforce a foreign title regarding a monetary claim in the Netherlands.

1. General overview of enforcement of titles in the Netherlands

1.1. *Outline of the Dutch system*

Dutch rules regarding the enforcement of titles can be found in the Code of Civil Procedure (CCP),[2] starting with Article 430 and ending with Article 584r.[3] Many

1 Regulation (EU) No. 1215/2012 of the European Parliament and of the Council of 12 December 2012 on jurisdiction and the recognition and enforcement of judgments in civil and commercial matters (recast).

2 Currently, civil procedure in the Netherlands is in the middle of a reform process due to the introduction of digital litigation. The project known as KEI (*Kwaliteit en Innovatie* (Quality and Innovation)) has been enacted (Dutch Bulletin of Acts, Orders and Decrees (*Staatsblad*) (hereinafter DBAOD) 2016), 288-294, and Government Gazette (*Staatscourant*) 2016, 39486), but had to be repealed in the course of 2019 (Parliamentary Proceedings (*Kamerstukken*) II 2018/19, 35175, 2). A new approach is on its way that will be based on voluntary digital communication without changing internal procedures (Parliamentary Proceedings II 2019/2020, 29279, 562). Although it is unclear in which way digital litigation is going to be implemented, it is highly unlikely that these changes will affect the substance of procedures regarding enforcement. Another Act that has not yet entered into force (Act on the Simplification of Exempted Income, DBAOD 2017, 110) will simplify the rules regarding →

other regulations, for instance those regarding tax law and administrative law, refer to these provisions in the CCP for enforcement.

These enforcement regulations all start from the principle that no court interference is needed to enforce a title that has been issued by the designated authorities. The creditor[4] is given the power to take all steps necessary to recover the debt from the debtor without the need to apply for any kind of permission. All measures can be taken at once (Article 435(1) CCP), making it possible to, for instance, attach wages, bank accounts, movables and immovables at the same time.[5] However, all those steps can only be taken by a public civil servant, the judicial officer (*gerechtsdeurwaarder* (bailiff)), in his capacity as an enforcement officer. The judicial officer has an obligation to provide the services requested by the creditor, unless these would be unlawful. Handing over the enforceable title to the judicial officer empowers him to take any steps necessary for the enforcement (Article 434 CCP).

Once the creditor (which could also be the state or any administrative organ) obtains an enforceable title, he is entitled to give the judicial officer appropriate instructions, depending on the assets of the debtor that are deemed to be most suitable for the recovery of the money owed. The CCP describes in detail which steps have to be taken by the judicial officer to recover the claim in the title.[6] These steps depend largely on the type of asset of the debtor that has been chosen by the creditor to sell off. There are for instance separate rules for the enforcement of titles

garnishment of periodic payments. The exemption for low incomes will be increased from 90 per cent to 95 per cent of the social security minimum, while at the same time 5 per cent of the incomes below the social security minimum may always be attached. The implementation of this act is delayed and is not to be expected before 2021 (Parliamentary Proceedings II 2018/19, 26448, 622 (annex *SUWI Jaarverslag 2018*)). A third Act that will modernise attachment in general (Attachment and Enforcement Modernisation Act, Parliamentary Proceedings 2018/19, 35225, 2), has still be approved by Parliament but will certainly enter into force in the beginning of 2021. The changes will be discussed where necessary.

3 In what follows in the text, the focus will be on the enforcement of titles regarding monetary claims. Other claims (such as a claim regarding the delivery of a certain object) will not be discussed systematically.

4 In Dutch law there is a sharp distinction between the creditor as such (*crediteur, schuldeiser*) and the creditor who started enforcement (*executant*). In this contribution, the term 'creditor' usually has the latter meaning. It will be clear from the context when the more general meaning is intended.

5 The Attachment and Enforcement Modernisation Act will remove the words "at once", but only to express that attachment may not be used for other purposes than debt recovery (Parliamentary Proceedings 2018/19, 35225, 3, p. 35-36).

6 Most steps are the exclusive domain of the process server. However, the detailed procedures that have to be followed sometimes designate other authorities with specific tasks. For instance, in the case of attachment of shares, the first instance court will have to decide on the way the public sale will take place (Article 474g CCP). The public sale of attached immovables, ships and airplanes is held by a notary, the first instance court and a judge of instruction, respectively (Article 514 and following CCP). In the case of garnishment of claims of the debtor on third parties, the creditor will have to file an application asking the first instance court to determine the amount garnished when he chooses to dispute the declaration of the third party.

against real property, movable property, ships, airplanes, shares, insurance rights and claims on third parties. Any property rights not explicitly mentioned in the CCP (such as air miles and stock market options) are covered by Article 474bb CCP (the catch-all clause).

Enforceable titles are specified in the law. There are some general provisions (such as Article 430 CCP, designating judgments and notarial deeds as enforceable titles, provided that they have been issued as such, bearing the heading 'In the name of the King')[7] and many specific provisions. No extra recognition or decision by the court is required, unless the title is not Dutch and does not fall within the scope of EU regulations or other instruments that provide for this recognition and enforceability.

This results in a system that can only be qualified as fully private. All steps taken by the judicial officer and consequently all steps taken by other authorities in enforcing the title primarily depend on decisions of the creditor. In the same way, in performing their supervisory tasks the courts depend exclusively on the initiative of the debtor, the judicial officer or (sometimes) third parties. The courts do not have any *ex officio* authority and are not allowed to issue any decisions on their own motion.

The system is also private in the sense that no public money is involved. The judicial officer and anything he does has to be paid upfront by the creditor.[8] Judicial officers do not receive additional payments from any administrative body. The tariffs the judicial officer may charge are fixed in a decree (Article 434a CCP).[9] The costs incurred by the creditor can be fully recovered from the proceeds of the enforcement (Article 474 CCP for non-registered movables, Article 524 for immovables). Only when the judicial officer or the notary embezzles the money recovered in the process of enforcement is the state jointly liable (Article 480 CCP for the judicial officer, Article 551(4) CCP for the notary).

1.2. *Methods of enforcement*

Seen from a more general point of view, there are three methods of enforcement of titles regarding monetary claims.

The first method is the attachment of any asset of the debtor, followed by a public sale. The creditor recovers his costs and his claim from the proceeds of the public sale. There are intricate and quite complicated rules for the procedures to be followed depending on the nature of the attached property right, of which a more detailed account will be given in Section 4 below.

7 In Dutch, 'In naam van de Koning'. Older enforceable titles will bear the title 'In naam der Koningin' (In the name of the Queen), which obviously depends on the monarch on the throne. See *infra* n. 21.

8 Legal aid cases are excepted. When the creditor is entitled to legal aid, all of the process server's costs are covered by the legal aid system (Article 40 *Wet op de rechtsbijstand* (Act on Legal Aid)).

9 *Besluit tarieven ambtshandelingen gerechtsdeurwaarders* (Decree on bailiff fees for official acts) of 4 July 2001 (DBAOD 2001, 325, as subsequently changed).

The second method of enforcement is attachment of ready money. The judicial officer who attaches ready money has an obligation to open a special bank account and deposit the money into this account (Article 445 CCP). The creditor and debtor are jointly entitled to the balance of the account until the money has been divided.[10] The bank becomes the sequestrator. The judicial officer decides what has to be paid, when and to whom, and is empowered to make these payments (Article 861 CCP).

The third method of enforcement is garnishment of claims of the debtor on a third party (the garnishee). The garnishee is asked by the judicial officer to fill out a declaration of what he still owes to the debtor (Article 476a CCP). What is mentioned in the declaration of the garnishee (usually money, but it could be goods) should be paid or handed over to the judicial officer (Article 477(1) CCP).[11] The judicial officer is entitled to pay money recovered in this way directly to the creditor. When the creditor disputes the amount declared by the garnishee or when the garnishee refuses to submit a declaration, a special procedure of the creditor against the garnishee is provided (Article 477a(1) and (2) CCP). If necessary, the garnishee is ordered to pay the correct amount (or to deliver the goods), thus giving the creditor a title that can be enforced directly against the garnishee.

There are two indirect means of enforcement, *astreinte* (Article 611a-611i CCP) and civil imprisonment (Article 585-600). These indirect means of enforcement do not apply to monetary claims with the exception of enforceable titles ordering the payment of maintenance based on Book 1 of the Civil Code (Article 585 sub b CCP). In the case of non-compliance with such an order, civil imprisonment may be requested and, if granted, enforced.[12]

1.3. Underlying principles

The following principles can be distinguished as underlying all regulations regarding the enforcement of enforceable titles.

All enforcement measures can only be taken by Dutch judicial officers and all decisions are taken by Dutch courts. Attachment and enforcement are exclusively governed by Dutch law. Attachment and garnishment thus have to follow the Dutch rules, all with the exceptions following from international law with direct effect.[13] In short, the principle of territoriality applies.

10 As can be understood from *Hoge Raad* (Supreme Court), 12 January 2011, ECLI:NL:HR:2001:AA9441, *NJ* 2001, 371, which judgment concerned an account especially opened by a notary on behalf of his clients, in which case Article 25 of the Notary Act applies. This rule was confirmed in HR 23 June 2017, ECLI:NL:HR:2017:1139 for all accounts held by notaries, lawyers (solicitors), accountants and judicial officers on behalf of their clients. Since the creditor and debtor are jointly entitled, the statute of limitations does not apply to any claims regarding this joint entitlement.

11 For special cases there are special rules. A life insurance policy for instance will be converted first to a surrender value (Article 479m CCP).

12 Civil imprisonment for a monetary claim regarding maintenance will not be discussed in this contribution. Only a few cases have been reported over the years.

13 Article 13a General Provisions Act (*Wet Algemene Bepalingen*).

As a consequence, the objects (in a general sense) on which enforcement is sought have to be located in the Netherlands. In the case of the attachment of a claim (garnishment), it is difficult to determine what the location of the claim is. Several possibilities occur that may entail extraterritorial consequences. In this respect, the *Lindeteves* judgment of the Dutch Supreme Court still gives the two applicable rules.[14] In the first place, according to this judgment the garnishee has to be domiciled or seated in the Netherlands as defined by Articles 1:10-1:14 of the Civil Code. This implies that the place where the claim has to be paid is not decisive for its location. In the second place, if the claim has to be paid in another country, Dutch enforcement has to be recognised in the other country. This recognition should ensure that the garnishee cannot be forced to pay twice.

The next principle to be identified is the principle of efficiency. In the process of enforcement, no court interference is foreseen unless one of the persons concerned (including the judicial officer) submits an application. A point of departure is that all decisions are made by the creditor alone or – on his behalf – by the judicial officer. For the implementation of these decisions, the creditor has to make use of the services of a judicial officer. The judicial officer is bound to provide these services, unless this would amount to unlawful acts. In other words, the legislator is of the opinion that debtors have to pay their debts and that the law should give the creditor efficient means to effectuate involuntary collection of his claims. The law should be such that no debtor should have the feeling of being beyond the reach of his creditors.[15]

The last principle is the protection of the debtor and third parties against unwarranted enforcement. In the first place, their interests are guaranteed by the step-by-step procedure that the judicial officer has to follow in the event of enforcement. These steps aim, for instance, to ensure that the debtor is fully aware of the measures being taken and has all the opportunities to comply voluntarily. Therefore, any enforcement should start with serving by writ the title on the debtor (Article 430(3) CCP) and a summons by writ to pay within a period of at least two days (Article 439(1) CCP). All steps following have to be served on the debtor by the judicial officer (e.g. the attachment itself and the day of the public sale).[16] Moreover, the debtor has full access to the first instance court in summary or ordinary proceedings to dispute the enforcement (Article 438 CCP) (Section 4 below), apart from many specific actions that are available. To ensure that the debtor will always be able to provide for his own costs of living, several goods are exempted from attachment (Articles 447-448 CCP) and periodical payments are exempted up to 90 per cent of the applicable social security allowance (Article 475d CCP).[17] When third

14 HR 26 November 1954, *NJ* 1955, 698 (*Lindeteves/Meilink*).

15 Parliamentary Proceedings (*Kamerstukken*) II 2016/17, 34628, 3, p. 12.

16 After enactment of the Attachment and Enforcement Modernisation Act, this also applies to the website where the internet auction will be held.

17 The Act on the Simplification of Exempted Income (*supra* n. 2 above) will increase this to 95 per cent, while at the same time 5 per cent of the incomes below the social security minimum may always be attached.

parties are involved, they have to be notified as well (as is foreseen in many provisions).

1.4. *Writs and the object of enforcement*

As already mentioned, the debtor and possibly also others, for instance the garnishee, have to be notified of every step taken during the enforcement of a title. Notification has to be done by writ, served by a judicial officer. For attachment itself, a writ is always needed as well.

When a notification has to be served by writ the general rules for writs apply, which can be found in Articles 45-66 of the CCP. As regards the contents of the writ, the parties should be specified, and the writ should specify what it is about. Particular attention is paid to the way the writ is served. This has to be specified in detail (including date and place) in order to make it possible to verify whether the writ was served according to the applicable rules. The most secure way of serving is to the addressee in person, but this is not always possible. In those cases, the writ may be handed over to a co-occupant or member of the family or it may be left in an envelope with specific directions on the outside. Separate provisions are given for the service on different types of legal persons, heirs, legal or moral persons without permanent or temporary residence in the Netherlands, members of the Royal Family and spouses in the case of divorce procedures. The judicial officer is not allowed to serve a writ on Sundays, recognized holidays, after 8 p.m. and before 7 a.m. Article 65 of the CCP states that non-compliance with these rules entails nullity when this is specified in the applicable provision, but Article 66 of the CCP limits this to cases in which the addressee has been unreasonably prejudiced by the failure to comply with the rules for serving writs.

Due to the step-by-step procedure to be followed, there are at least sixty different writs. Some of these writs hardly ever occur, because they are associated with a very specific stage of a very specific form of attachment. However, some writs are important enough to be mentioned explicitly in this general overview. The first two are the writs with which every attachment commences, which have already been mentioned above. The third is the writ with which the attachment itself is effectuated. The rules for these writs depend on the object that is being attached. Sometimes a writ alone is enough to create the attachment (for instance in the case of registrable property),[18] in other cases the judicial officer has to see and designate the attached property or has to be on board (in the case of ships). For garnishment, the writ has to be served on the garnishee, but the judicial officer does not have to verify whether the attached claim or goods actually exist. The fourth writ to be mentioned here is the writ with which the debtor is notified of the attachment (Article 443 CCP). The notification should also be served on third parties if they are involved (the garnishee and the sequestrator).

[18] After enactment of the Attachment and Enforcement Modernisation Act, this will also apply to attachment of registered vehicles (Article 442 CCP (new)).

There are some special rules for the contents of the writs with which the attachment is effectuated and with which the debtor and others are notified of the attachment. Non-compliance sometimes entails nullity. Examples can be found in Articles 439 (chosen domicile at the judicial officer's office), 440 (contents of the writ with which attachment is effectuated) and 475 of the CCP (contents of the writ with which garnishment is effectuated). These nullities are absolute. Failure to comply with the rules will make the judicial officer liable to the creditor.

The object of the enforcement is fully determined by the title itself,[19] and the judicial officer will refuse to enforce any obligations not clearly mentioned in the title. Conditional obligations mentioned in the title can be enforced once the condition has been fulfilled. If there is any proof of this in the form of documents, these documents should best be served on the debtor together with the title itself although no obligation in this respect exists. When the enforcement of a conditional obligation is disputed by the debtor in court, stating that the conditions have not been fulfilled, the burden of proof is with the creditor.[20]

Enforceable titles follow the creditor after transfer of the claim (Article 6:142 Civil Code). The same title can be used without any modification – thus still mentioning the original creditor – but the transfer of the claim has to be served on the debtor by writ (Article 431a CCP). The title can also be used against the successors of the debtor, since the creditor is allowed to recover his claim from the estate of the deceased (Article 4:184(1) Civil Code).

1.5. *Enforceable titles*

The Code of Civil Procedure distinguishes three categories of enforceable Dutch titles: court judgments, authentic instruments and other titles designated by law as enforceable.

Court judgments are enforceable when they carry in a heading at the top of the judgment the words 'In the name of the King' (*In naam van de Koning*).[21] These words are added by the court clerk, and if needed, the creditor is provided with several copies bearing the same heading (Article 231 CCP). No distinction is made between the judgments of civil, administrative or criminal courts, nor between the type of judgments. The enforceable version (*grosse*) of the judgments is only issued to the creditor (which, incidentally, could be either party). No costs are charged for the issuing of these copies of the judgment.

Authentic instruments are instruments in the required form made by a civil servant or someone else with the power to do so according to an obligation

19 However, there are some exceptions for Dutch titles. In the case of a costs order in a judgment, the creditor is also allowed to recover specific costs made after the judgment (for instance costs incurred by informing the other party by letter of its obligation to pay), even though these costs are not mentioned in the title (HR 19 March 2010, ECLI:NL:HR:2010:BL1116, *NJ* 2011, 237).

20 HR 12 July 2013, ECLI:NL:HR:2013:BZ3640, *NJ* 2013, 435, Section 3.9 sub b.

21 Article 1 of the Act of 22 June 1891, DBAOD 1891, 125, provides that the word 'King' is changed to 'Queen' whenever a Queen is the head of state.

provided by law to report in that way about their observations or actions (Article 156(2) CCP). Notarial deeds are authentic instruments, but also writs issued by a judicial officer, acts of the registrar of the Registry of Births, Deaths and Marriages, and court minutes drawn up by judge and court clerk. These titles become enforceable when they carry the words 'In the name of the King'. A special provision allowing the author of the instrument to add these words is needed. For notaries, this provision can be found in Article 50 of the Notary Act.

The other enforceable titles come in a wide variety. They do not always carry the words 'In the name of the King'. In the context of debt recovery, the most important of these is in the first place the settlement reached in court, written down in the court minutes and signed by the parties. These minutes are then issued in an enforceable form (Article 89(1) CCP), which means that the words 'In the name of the King' are added at the top) and consequently can be directly enforced. In this category also fall Dutch arbitral awards for which the summary proceedings judge has issued a permission of enforcement (exequatur, Article 1062 CCP), and eventually all foreign titles that are or have been recognised (to be discussed in Section 2 below).

1.6. *Protective measures*

In general, any type of enforcement may be preceded by protective measures aimed at freezing the assets of the debtor before an enforceable title has been obtained. Attachment as a protective measure follows the rules of attachment in the event of enforcement. For that reason, attachment is divided into a protective stage and an enforcement stage. In the protective stage, the assets of the debtor are frozen to secure the rights of the creditor. Once these rights have been established in the form of an enforceable title, the attachment enters the second phase and recovery of the claim will be realised by the judicial officer, provided that the assets are sufficient.

Since in the case of a protective measure the rights of the creditor have not been established yet, preliminary permission of the court is required.[22] The application for this permission has to be submitted in the form of a petition to the summary proceedings judge of the first instance court of the debtor[23] or the place where the goods to be attached actually are located (Article 700(1) CCP). Legal representation by counsel is mandatory. The decision is given *ex parte*, although the court has the power to order a hearing (a power that is seldom used). The courts have issued a set of recommendations (the *Beslagsyllabus* (Attachment Outline)) that are followed by all courts when deciding on these petitions.

The petition should specify and summarily give evidence of the claim of the creditor and describe the goods to be attached. For some types of attachment, the creditor has to state and summarily show that the debtor is likely to make the goods

22 The exception created for titles falling within the scope of BIR will be discussed in Section 3.4 below.

23 Throughout this contribution, 'the court of the debtor' is used as shorthand for 'the court within the district of which the debtor has his residence or where the debtor, in the case of a legal person, has its seat, all as meant in Articles 1:10-1:14 of the Dutch Civil Code.'

to be attached disappear and thus to frustrate attempts to collect the debt.[24] Usually the permission is issued on the petition itself, specifying the amount for which the attachment is allowed and the period within which proceedings have to be started to obtain an enforceable title.[25] This period is mostly set by the summary proceedings judge at fourteen days for proceedings in the Netherlands and thirty days for proceedings abroad, to count from the moment of attachment. When this period is not respected, the attachment expires. Once the enforceable title has been obtained, enforcement may continue without the necessity of attaching the goods again (Article 704 CCP).

Since the permission for protective measures is granted *ex parte*, it is relatively easy to obtain it.[26] Moreover, since the issuing of the permission is done on the petition itself, the procedure is swift. In most courts there are judges available to grant these permissions instantly (in some courts even seven days a week, twenty-four hours a day). Such arrangements may be needed when, for instance, a ship to be attached is on the point of leaving the harbour. The debtor can always commence summary proceedings to have the attachment lifted or get an injunction against the creditor (Article 705 CCP).

1.7. *Competent courts*

Court intervention with regard to enforcement has been assigned to the civil courts. A brief explanation as to how the jurisdiction of these courts is organised is presented below.

The Netherlands has a three-tiered court system. Almost all cases start at the court of first instance (*Rechtbank* (District Court)) located in eleven separate districts. At the second tier, the appellate courts (*Gerechtshof* or in short *Hof*) are distributed over four regions. The procedure in appeal amounts to a full reconsideration of the first instance decisions, including examination of the facts if necessary. At the apex of the pyramid sits the Supreme Court (*Hoge Raad*), which is a cassation court. Leave to appeal or to commence cassation proceedings against final judgments is not required.

Within the first instance courts several sections have to be distinguished. Summary proceedings are always assigned to the summary proceedings judge (*voorzieningenrechter*, hereinafter also SPJ). The procedure before the SPJ is mostly informal, quick and not too expensive. When no summary proceedings are foreseen, the case is dealt with by the cantonal judge (*kantonrechter*) or the non-cantonal judge (single judge) or non-cantonal chamber (three judges). The cantonal judge has

24 This is not a requirement for the protective attachment of claims (Article 719 CCP) and ships (Article 728 CCP).

25 Specific proceedings are not prescribed. Any procedure that will lead to an enforceable title will do. Thus a counterclaim in current litigation, a claim of a victim within a criminal procedure and also litigation in other countries have been accepted.

26 After enactment of the Attachment and Enforcement Modernisation Act, the court will also have to ascertain whether the expected proceeds of the execution will most likely be lower than the costs of enforcement.

exclusive jurisdiction for claims up to €25,000 and for all monetary claims regarding specific agreements, such as labour contracts and leases (Article 93 CCP). Legal representation before the cantonal judge is not mandatory.

For enforcement procedures, in almost all cases the first instance court has jurisdiction.[27] To dispute enforcement, the debtor and third parties have the choice between summary proceedings before the summary proceedings judge and ordinary proceedings (Article 438 CCP). Apart from this, the legislator seems to make a distinction between weighty decisions (over which the court itself has jurisdiction, such as the permission to enforce a foreign judgment, Article 985 CCP) and decisions that are needed to ensure a fast but fair enforcement. In the latter case, the summary proceedings judge has been assigned to decide on the actions concerned.[28]

Territorial jurisdiction is always assigned to the court in the territory of which the enforcement is taking place or will take place. When such a court cannot be determined, the normal rules should be followed. In the case of a procedure starting with a writ of summons (*dagvaarding*), the application should be addressed to the court of the defendant (Article 99 CCP, with some alternative possibilities). In the case of a procedure starting with a petition, the application should be submitted to the court of the claimant (Article 262 CCP, with some alternative possibilities). The choice between the two procedures is determined by the applicable provisions regarding the remedy sought (as is stated in Articles 78 and 261 CCP).

Judgments regarding monetary claims are subject to appeal to the appellate court, unless the amount on which the judge had to decide was in total[29] not more than €1,750 (Article 332(1) and (2) CCP).[30] As mentioned, appeal in the Netherlands amounts to a full review,[31] possibly including a new examination of the facts. First instance judgments that cannot be appealed and judgments in appeal are open to the procedure of cassation at the Supreme Court (*Hoge Raad*). The review in cassation is on the law only, not on the facts. In the case of an application for cassation against a first instance judgment the cassation grounds are limited.[32] Against default judgments the remedy of opposition is available, which is brought before the court that issued the judgment.[33] Opposition against judgments in

27 An exception can, for instance, be found in Article 1076(6) CCP, according to which an application for permission to enforce certain foreign arbitral awards has to be submitted to the appellate court acting as court of first instance.

28 A quick count yields 40 such provisions. Many of these will be specified in the footnotes to Section 4 below.

29 A peculiar rule adds that to calculate the total, eventual counterclaims have to be included (Article 332(3) CCP).

30 Claims based on family law (maintenance) follow the rules of petition cases. In those cases, appeal is not limited to a certain amount (Article 358 CCP). In the case of a decision by default regarding maintenance, opposition is not possible, only appeal.

31 The rule *Quantum appellatum, tantum devolutum* applies.

32 Article 80(1) Act on the Judiciary. In HR 16 March 2007, ECLI:NL:HR:2007:AZ1490, *NJ* 2007, 637, violation of Article 6 ECHR was added as an extra-legal cassation ground.

33 Article 147 CCP for first instance judgments and Article 353 CCP for judgments on appeal, confirmed by HR 4 October 2013, ECLI:NL:HR:2013:CA3741, *NJ* 2014, 142.

cassation is, apart from some rare exceptions, not possible (Article 425 CCP). All remedies have to be introduced by a writ of summons, not by a petition.[34] These remedies are all ordinary remedies as defined by EU law.[35]

Apart from these ordinary remedies, the extraordinary remedies are repeal, third party opposition and cassation in the interest of the law. Extraordinary remedies are only available after the expiration of all delays for ordinary remedies. The difference between ordinary and extraordinary remedies lies also in the suspending effect of the ordinary remedies. As long as an ordinary remedy is pending, the judgment is not enforceable.[36] However, in practice this hardly plays any role when we focus on final judgments. Courts have the power to declare their judgments immediately enforceable, and this is the rule, not the exception. On the other hand, the debtor always has the possibility to submit an application to lift this immediate enforceability at various stages of the procedure. This means that it will have to be decided on a case by case basis whether or not a title that is still under review is enforceable. When it comes to interlocutory judgments, generally no declaration of immediate enforceability is given. Filing a remedy thus suspends the decision.

The remedies of appeal and review in cassation are available against both interlocutory judgments and final judgments. For remedies against interlocutory judgments, in most cases leave to appeal or to commence cassation is needed (Articles 337(2) and 401a(2) CCP). The application for this leave has to be submitted to the court that will give or gave the judgment against which the remedy will be directed.[37] For many interlocutory judgments and other decisions, a special provision excludes the possibility of appeal, review in cassation or both. These exclusions have to be set aside when the court followed the wrong procedure or the right to a fair trial has been violated.[38] Court acts of a mere administrative nature are not subject to remedies.[39]

1.8. Time limits in the CCP

Time limits in the Dutch Code of Civil Procedure are usually expressed in days, weeks and months. Days and weeks correspond to a number of one and seven days, respectively. Months are a bit more complicated (see following paragraph). In general, a deadline ending on a Saturday, Sunday or recognised holiday will be

34 It has to be noted that as of 1 March 2017 the new KEI procedure entered into force for (amongst others) monetary claims in cassation. The procedure has to be introduced via a digital form, after which a notification sheet will be produced by the digital system provided by the Supreme Court. This notification sheet has to be served on the other party. Otherwise, the cassation procedure did not change.

35 ECJ 22 November 1977, ECLI:NL:XX:1977:AC6101.

36 Article 145 CCP for opposition; Article 350 CCP for appeal; Article 404 CCP for an application for cassation.

37 Asking for leave after the judgment is based on HR 23 January 2004, ECLI:NL:HR:2004:AL7051, *NJ* 2005, 510.

38 HR 1 April 2011, ECLI:NL:HR:2011:BP2312, *NJ* 2011, 220.

39 HR 6 October 2017, ECLI:NL:HR:2017:2568.

extended to the first day that is not a Saturday, Sunday or recognised holiday.[40] A time limit of three days or more has to be extended in such a way that at least two working days fall within it.[41]

The time limit within which proceedings for a remedy against a decision may be initiated usually starts on the day after the pronouncement of the decision.[42] If the time limit is expressed in months, the last day of the time limit will be the corresponding day in the relevant subsequent month. If such a day does not exist, it will be the last day of the month.[43] Thus, a time limit of three months for an appeal against a judgment pronounced on 30 November will expire on 28 February in a ordinary year and on 29 February in a leap year.

2. Enforceability of foreign titles

This section will distinguish foreign titles into several categories with regard to their recognition, enforceability and the conditions that have to be met to enter the stage of actual enforcement. This will be preceded by a short explanation of the relationship between recognition and enforceability under Dutch procedural law. Foreign titles falling within the scope of BIR will be discussed in Section 3 below.

2.1. *Recognition and enforceability*

The recognition of the contents of a foreign decision as such can be foreseen in international instruments that are binding for the Netherlands or in a rule of Dutch law. The conditions will not be the same in every case and will have to be tested by the court in the event that an application for enforcement has been submitted. In other procedures, the question of whether a foreign decision has to be recognised could arise as well, for instance in cases related to family law. Dutch doctrine does not object to recognition on a case-by-case basis. There is no general theory related to the recognition of foreign judgments. This is understandable from the fact that Article 431 of the CCP draws a sharp line excluding all foreign judgments from enforcement when this has not been foreseen in a rule of national or international law. From this it is understood that foreign judgments, including judgments with constitutive effects, do not bind the parties under Dutch law. In the past, some exceptions were accepted in matters of family law, and these have been codified now in Book 10 of the Civil Code (which entered into force in 2012).

If the recognition of the title is foreseen in national or international law, an application for permission of enforcement may be submitted, unless a specific rule states otherwise. The court will not pronounce the recognition of the title explicitly,

40 Article 1(1) Statute Containing General Provisions Regarding Time Limits (*Algemene termijnenwet*).

41 *Idem*, Article 2.

42 This is correct for all non-default judgments and for the parties who have appeared in a procedure that was started by a petition. Other cases are more complicated (Articles 139 and 358(2) CCP).

43 HR 1 September 2017, ECLI:NL:HR:2017:2225.

but will examine this question from the perspective of whether or not the title is enforceable. The application for enforcement is denied when the title is not recognisable under Dutch law. The court does not have the power to retry the case (for instance Article 985(1), second sentence, CCP) and thus has to accept the correctness of the foreign decision. This interdiction of *révision au fond* is stated in the Code of Civil Procedure and thus applies even when the international instrument recognising the judgment does not provide for it.[44] Explicit decisions about recognition can only be obtained when starting a special writ of summons procedure, which hardly ever happens.[45]

2.2. *Foreign judgments in general*

Unless a national or international rule that provides for the recognition and possible enforcement of certain foreign judgments stipulates otherwise, these foreign judgments cannot be invoked in a Dutch context (Article 431(1) CCP) and thus cannot be enforced. This general rule includes the judgments of international courts. To recover the claim, the same lawsuit should be initiated again before Dutch courts (Article 431(2) CCP).[46] However, the Supreme Court case law has mitigated this rule, since it could mean that the same work has to be done all over again. Consequently, a Dutch court is allowed to follow the foreign decision without an examination of the merits of the case when (*i*) the jurisdiction of the foreign court is acceptable according to international standards;[47] (*ii*) the proceedings have been fair; (*iii*) the decision is not contrary to Dutch public policy; (*iv*) there is no conflict with a decision of a Dutch court relating to the same subject matter and (*v*) the foreign title is still intact.[48] In this way (labelled as 'a masked exequatur procedure') a review as to the substance of the case can be avoided.

2.3. *Foreign judgments under an instrument other than BIR*

When the recognition of a judgment of a court of another state is foreseen in a national or international rule, the procedure of Article 985 of the CCP has to be

44 Parliamentary Proceedings II 1963/64, 7179, 6, p. 2.

45 However, in the case of foreign arbitral awards recognition and enforceability are both explicitly pronounced and an application can be limited to recognition only (Article 1075(1) CCP).

46 In the case of judgments covered by BIR, this approach is not necessary and even forbidden, also in cases in which it is cheaper to start the same procedure again instead of applying for recognition and enforcement (European Court of Justice (ECJ) 30 November 1976, 42/76, *NJ* 1977, 484).

47 This was, for instance, not the case in *Rechtbank* (First Instance Court, hereinafter Rb) Arnhem 31 October 2012, ECLI:NL:RBARN:2012:BY4312, where the Chinese court based its jurisdiction on the place where the contract had been concluded.

48 HR 26 September 2014, ECLI:NL:HR:2014:2828, *NJ* 2015, 478. This decision is a refinement of the rules already set out in HR 14 November 1924, *NJ* 1925, p. 91.

followed in cases that are not covered by a rule that says otherwise.[49] The procedure amounts to obtaining permission for enforcement. The following will give more details about this procedure. In some cases a special procedure is foreseen, governed by a separate act.[50]

The application under the general rule of Article 985 of the CCP should have the form of a petition. A petition is a document with which an originally non-contentious procedure is started. In these procedures, the court is more active than in procedures commenced by writ of summons. The first instance court has subject-matter jurisdiction. Representation by counsel is mandatory for both parties (Article 986(1) CCP). Since no special rules have been enacted, the general rules regarding territorial jurisdiction apply. This means that the application has to be submitted to the court of the applicant (Article 262 CCP) or to the court in The Hague for applicants without domicile or seat in the Netherlands (Article 269 CCP).

The petition should be accompanied by a certified copy of the judgment, and documents from which it may be determined that the judgment is enforceable under the law of the country in which the judgment has been given (Article 986(2) CCP). Proof should be provided that the title is enforceable in the country of origin. Certified translations may be requested by the court (Article 986(3) CCP). The other parties should be convoked by the applicant by writ in order to be heard (Article 986(3) CCP).

For applications emanating from the EEX Convention (Brussels Convention [1968] on Jurisdiction and the Enforcement of Judgments in Civil and Commercial Matters), the 1988 Lugano Convention and the 2007 Lugano Convention, the same rules apply when it comes to the documents in which permission has to be asked and to jurisdiction.[51] Since these procedures hardly ever occur, further details, including the remedies, will not be discussed.

Defences can only be based on the instrument or rule in which recognition of the title is foreseen. A *révision au fond* is never allowed (Article 985 CCP), but obviously the court will have to verify whether the requirements for enforceability have been met. The decision is issued as soon as possible. It is given in the form that

49 This procedure does not apply to the judgments of international bodies, unless a separate rule provides for that (as in Article 5a of the Act of 16 July 1869, as changed by DBAOD 1964, 381, regarding the decisions of the Central Commission for the Navigation of the Rhine).

50 These acts are: (1) Implementation Act of 24 December 1958, DBAOD 1958, 677, implementing the Convention of 1 March 1954 on civil procedure; (2) Implementation Act of 4 May 1972, DBAOD 1972, 240, implementing the EEX Convention (still relevant for judgments from the territories mentioned in Recital 9 of Regulation (EU) No. 1215/2012 (hereinafter BIR)); (3) Implementation Act of 26 March 1992, DBAOD 1992, 141, implementing the 1988 Lugano Convention, declaring applicable the rules of Articles 2-10 of the Implementation Act of 4 May 1972, mentioned earlier; (4) Implementation Act of 2 July 2003, DBAOD 2003, 290, as changed by DBAOD 2014, 40 and 540, implementing the 2007 Lugano Convention.

51 This is covered by the Acts mentioned in the foregoing footnote.

is in conformity with the procedure that has to be followed. In these procedures (starting with a petition) the court gives a decision, not a judgment.[52]

Opposition to the decision based on the procedure of Article 985 of the CCP is not possible. The losing party may file an appeal with the appellate court within a month after the day of pronouncement of the decision (Article 989(2) CCP). The decision of the appellate court may be challenged in cassation within a month after pronouncement (Article 989(3) CCP).

2.4. *Arbitral awards*

For a foreign arbitral award for which recognition has been foreseen in an international instrument, an application in the form of a petition has to be submitted directly to the appellate court (Articles 1075 and 1076 CCP). Apart from that, the same procedure is followed as discussed above for foreign titles not covered by BIR.

Recognition and enforcement are also allowed in cases in which this has not been foreseen in an international instrument. No proof of enforceability of the award in the country of origin has to be submitted (Article 1076(6) CCP). The court will have to deny the petition (*a*) in the event of the absence of a valid arbitral clause; (*b*) if the arbitration court was not composed according to the applicable rules; (*c*) if the arbitration court took decisions outside the scope of the arbitration clause; (*d*) if remedies are still open or pending; and (*e*) if the arbitral award has been quashed in the country of origin (Article 1076(1)(A) CCP). The public policy ground applies as well (Article 1076(1)(B)). Each ground knows some extra conditions (Article 1076(2)-(5)).

In both cases, the only remedy is appeal in cassation, which has to be submitted within three months after the pronouncement of the decision (Articles 1075(2) and 1076(6) CCP).

3. Recognition and enforceability of titles falling under BIR

BIR has been implemented in the Netherlands by amending the Implementation Act for Brussels I,[53] giving it the new title Implementation Act EU-Execution Regulation and Lugano Convention (hereinafter IAB IA). Since EU regulations have direct binding force in the Netherlands (Articles 93 and 94 Dutch Constitution)[54] only those parts of BIR had to be implemented which are in need of specific national rules. This implementation and current practice will be discussed in this section in relation to the enforcement of foreign titles.

52 Decisions have to be distinguished from judgments, with which a procedure starting with a writ of summons is decided.

53 The amendments can be found in DBAOD 2014, 40 and 540. A future amendment (DBAOD 2016, 290) is part of the KEI project, but will probably be repealed (*supra* n. 2).

54 This is slightly controversial, since some scholars base the direct binding force of EU law on the *Van Gend & Loos* judgment of the European Court of Justice (ECJ 5 February 1963, ECLI:EU:C:1963:1).

3.1. *Automatic recognition*

The most important innovation of BIR is the automatic recognition of foreign judgments that are enforceable in the state of origin. Thus enforceability no longer depends on a national court judgment granting permission to enforce the title (Article 41 BIR). Under this new rule, the creditor has direct access to the Dutch judicial officer. Only the original judgment and the certificate discussed below are needed (and in the case of a title ordering protective measures ordered *ex parte* – titles falling outside the scope of this contribution – proof of service of the judgment) (Article 9 IAB IA).

3.2. *Certificate of Enforceability*

Article 53 BIR requires a certificate of enforceability, which should be obtained from the court of origin. The certificate has to be issued using a form that is attached to the regulation. This implies that foreign certificates will be easy to interpret and recognise.

Article 43 of BIR provides for an obligatory service of the certificate prior to the first enforcement measure. The Dutch judicial officer will have to ensure that this requirement has been met. If service took place in another country, it is up to the creditor to supply proof of this. This proof has to be submitted to the Dutch judicial officer charged with the enforcement. The organisation of Dutch judicial officers (*Koninklijke Beroepsorganisatie van Gerechtsdeurwaarders* (Royal Dutch Organisation of Bailiffs)) commented on this and did not see any difficulties. In the event of questions regarding prior service, it is simply a matter of gathering information.[55]

When the certificate is outdated because of later developments, which could for instance happen when the judgment has been quashed on appeal, it is up to the debtor to use the available remedies against enforcement. These remedies will be addressed in Section 4 below.

3.3. *Protective measures*

The problems that arise from Article 43 of BIR (obligatory notification of the debtor before any measure of enforcement can be taken with the possibility that the debtor will make enforcement fruitless) are solved in two ways.

Firstly, Article 40 empowers the creditor to take protective measures after obtaining an enforceable judgment. This means that the creditor with a judgment falling within the scope of this article will have the possibility to seek any protective measures that Dutch law provides without any discretionary powers for the summary proceedings judge of Article 700 of the CCP. The judgment and the

55 Advice of the Royal Dutch Organisation of Bailiffs of 28 February 2013, p. 3.

certificate will be sufficient and no permission has to be sought, as can be concluded from the fact that the direct effect of this provision overrules Dutch law.[56]

Secondly, in principle enforcement is only possible after a period of at least two days during which the debtor has the possibility to comply voluntarily (Article 439(2) CCP). Article 9 of IAB IA changes this to one month after service of the certificate for debtors domiciled or seated in the Netherlands and to two months for other debtors. However, both articles give the creditor the possibility to instruct the judicial officer to apply for the shortening of this period, which may even be done orally. Possible problems arising from the notification of the debtor can thus be prevented and solved. However, it has to be noted that the shortening of these periods is not possible in the case of certain categories of debtors, such as consumers and employees (Article 9(4) IAB IA).

4. Remedies regarding and during enforcement

The debtor, third parties and other creditors have the right to object to the way the title is enforced and to the enforcement as such. The numerous possibilities to influence the means of enforcement will be briefly described below. Subsequent sections will deal with objections to the enforcement itself.

4.1. *Influence of the debtor, third parties and other creditors on enforcement*

As seen in Section 1 above, enforcement in the Netherlands varies to an enormous extent, since the steps to be taken depend on the assets subject to enforcement. Various actions are made available to the persons involved in the process of enforcement. These actions often constitute separate proceedings, since enforcement in the Netherlands is a process, not a procedure. This means that the general rules for remedies as described above apply, unless otherwise provided.[57]

The possibilities awarded to the debtor, third parties and other creditors come in a wide variety. They can be grouped as follows:[58]

1. protection of third parties against enforcement on assets or the use of assets in regard to which the third party claims or has exclusive rights;[59]

56 This must be the basis of the remark in the Dutch Parliamentary Proceedings that Article 40 does not need to be implemented (Parliamentary Proceedings II 2012/13, 33676, 3, p. 16 (table)). The same interpretation has been defended by the Royal Dutch Organisation of Bailiffs in its advice to the government (Advice of 28 February 2013, p. 15).

57 As being too detailed, no specifications of these exceptions will be given.

58 The sections that are not relevant to the enforcement of monetary claims will not be included (Articles 491-500 CCP: enforcement of an order to hand over a movable object; Articles 555-558: enforcement of an eviction order; Article 582 CCP: enforcement of an order to hand over a ship; Article 584r CCP: enforcement of an order to hand over an aircraft).

59 *Group I.* Article 435(3) CCP: notification of opposition to the process server; when submitted in time, enforcement will be stayed until a court decision has been obtained. Article 444b(2) CCP: when the movables to be attached are located in a closed place belonging to the third party (e.g. goods in a closed locker), the third party can apply to the process server for →

2. protection of garnishees;[60]
3. protection of other creditors with equal or better rights;[61]

security to cover possible damage. Article 456 CCP: in a procedure starting with a writ of summons, the third party can try to prevent the public sale of his non-registered movables. Article 474bb(4) CCP: the third party and the debtor may apply (by writ of summons) for an order to stop enforcement if the public sale of non-claimable rights will cause an unreasonable prejudice. Article 474g(2) CCP: opposition by petition against the sale of shares in public and private limited companies by a third party. Article 479p(1) CCP: application by writ of summons by the beneficiary or debtor to get an injunction against the creditor who wants to convert a life insurance policy to its surrender value.

60 *Group II.* Article 477a(2) CCP: application for security by the garnishee against the creditor who submitted an application against the garnishee because his declaration was supposedly inadequate (to be submitted as a motion before defences on the merits). Article 477b(3): convocation by writ of the debtor by the garnishee in a procedure about obligations of the garnishee to the debtor in a lawsuit between the creditor and the garnishee.

61 *Group III.* Article 458 CCP: the later creditor who does not have to respect a right that has to be respected by the first creditor may take over enforcement by announcing this to the first creditor, the debtor and possible third parties. Article 459 CCP: when the first creditor refrains from pursuing a public sale, the later creditor may take over enforcement by announcing this to the first creditor and the debtor. Article 459(3) CCP: when multiple creditors want to take over enforcement by public sale, each of them may submit a petition to the SPJ to change the hierarchy of enforcement between the creditors. Article 461a CCP: the pledgee may take over enforcement on an asset that has been given in pawn (*pignus*) by announcing this to the creditor. Article 461b CCP: a creditor may submit a petition to the SPJ asking for a final date for the public sale to be respected by the pledgee who took over enforcement. Article 461c CCP: the pledgee who wants the pawn to be included in the public sale of immovable property will have to announce this by writ to the creditor. Article 478(4) CCP: application (by motion) of a creditor for leave to intervene in a procedure about the obligations of the garnishee to the debtor in the event that there are multiple creditors. Article 509(1) CCP: in the case of attachment of an immovable that has been mortgaged, the mortgagee may take over enforcement by public sale by announcing this by writ to the creditor. Article 513(2) CCP: in the case of attachment of an immovable by multiple creditors, any creditor may submit a petition to the SPJ to obtain the right to pursue enforcement instead of the first creditor (only to be granted in cases of conspiracy or negligence). Article 518(1) CCP: application by petition to the SPJ of the notary or any party regarding a conflict about the conditions, date, time or place of public sale of an attached immovable. Article 527 CCP: in the event that the buyer of an immovable does not pay, each interested party may ask the creditor to sell the immovable again at the expense of the buyer (no form prescribed). Article 539 CCP: in the case the public sale of an immovable has been suspended by opposition, each interested party (by writ) and the notary (no form prescribed) may apply to the SPJ to get the stay of execution lifted. Article 545(1) CCP: in the event that a mortgagee took over enforcement but does not proceed, any creditor or mortgagee may ask the SPJ by petition to fix a term for sale. Article 548(1) CCP: each interested party may submit a petition to order a private sale instead of a public sale of a mortgaged immovable. Article 569(2) CCP: in the case of a lack of due dispatch when enforcing a title on a ship, each creditor may submit a petition to the SPJ to get permission to take over enforcement. Article 584j(2) CCP: after publication of the list of rights and claims in the case of the public sale of an aircraft, each interested person may submit objections against this list (no form prescribed; in absence of an agreement, the parties will be referred to the court). Article 584l(1) CCP: in the case of the sale of an aircraft, a third party with a claim higher in the list may take over enforcement by announcing this to the creditor by registered letter. Article 584q(1) CCP: in the event that →

4. protection of other creditors with regard to the proceeds of enforcement;[62]
5. protection of the debtor with regard to the conditions of public sale;[63]
6. protection of the debtor with regard to other ways of realising the value of an asset.[64]

A short description is given in the footnotes of the actions falling within each group. The details of the relevant regulations have been left out. In general, for all court procedures mentioned, legal representation by counsel is mandatory, unless the application may be filed with the cantonal judge.[65] The suspensive force of any action is normally otherwise absent and should be applied for. In all cases, once enforcement has started, the court where enforcement takes place or will take place is the competent court for all applications (Article 438a(1) CCP). If such a court is absent, for petitions the court of the applicant (Article 262 CCP) and for writs of summons the court of the defendant (Article 99 CCP) is the competent court. In cases commenced by petition, all convocations are sent out by the court clerk (Article 271 CCP), unless otherwise indicated in the law. In cases commenced by writ of summons, the convocation is part of the writ itself.

the public sale of an aircraft violated one of the provisions of Article 584a-584r CCP, anyone prejudiced may apply for nullification of the sale and property transfer by writ of summons.

62 *Group IV.* Article 484(1) CCP (movables), Article 552(1) CCP (immovables): in the event that the creditors do not agree on the way the proceeds of the sale have to be divided, each of them may submit a petition to the SPJ asking for the appointment of a judge of instruction. Article 484(1) CCP: opposition of a creditor against the distribution list regarding the proceeds of enforcement determined by the judge of instruction (no form prescribed; when no settlement is reached, the parties are referred to the court).

63 *Group V.* Article 462 CCP: the debtor may apply for an earlier date of the public sale by submitting a petition to the SPJ. Article 463: the debtor may apply for substituting the public sale of bearer shares to a public sale at the stock exchange by submitting a petition to the SPJ. Article 463a CCP: the debtor may apply for a change of terms, date, time or place of the public sale by submitting a petition to the SPJ. Article 465 CCP: the debtor may apply for the shortening of the period between the announcement of the public sale by bill-posting and the public sale itself to less than four days by submitting a petition to the SPJ. Article 474bb(4) CCP: see the first group. Article 475e CCP: in the case of garnishment of periodical payments, the debtor domiciled outside the Netherlands may submit a petition to the cantonal judge asking for the determination of the exempted amount to cover his own costs of living. Article 475f CCP: same as Article 475e CCP in the case of periodic payments for which no exempted amount is mentioned in the law. Article 476(2) CCP: notification of the debtor to the garnishee that opposition has been made to garnishment of periodical payments in order to obtain suspending effect. Article 518(1) CCP: see group III. The Attachment and Enforcement Modernisation Act will extend these remedies to sale by means of an internet auction.

64 *Group VI.* Article 479n(2) CCP: notification of the debtor to the creditor that he wants to raise a loan on the life insurance policy attached in order to pay the creditor who wants to convert the policy to the surrender value (to be done by registered letter). Article 479p(1) CCP: see the first group.

65 There are exceptions. In some instances, representation by a process server is allowed as a consequence of Article 438a(2) CCP. This has been done to enable the parties to save costs.

4.2. *Objections to enforcement as such and in cases not covered by specific provisions*

In addition to the specific actions discussed above, Article 438 of the CCP gives two general actions for all disputes that may arise in the course of the enforcement of an enforceable title.[66] These actions are open to anyone who claims that his rights in some way have been or will be violated. In both cases, the competent court is the court that would be competent according to the ordinary rules,[67] the court where the attachment occurred, the court where the objects in dispute are located and the court where enforcement will take place. The choice lies with the claimant. Both procedures start with a writ of summons. In his lawsuit, a third party claimant will have to include both the creditor and the debtor as defendants (Article 438(5) CCP). Against judgments given in these procedures the ordinary remedies of appeal, cassation and opposition apply.

The first procedure is the ordinary procedure before the first instance court. The court has the power to stop the execution, to lift attachments, to order specific measures, to rule on costs and to impose security on the creditor if the enforcement later turns out to be unlawful. Starting this procedure will not suspend enforcement as of right, unless there is a specific provision to that purpose. These provisions are all related to the position of third parties and can be found in Articles 456,[68] 479e(2),[69] 538 and 539 of the CCP.[70] Challenging enforcement cannot be based on the ground that the enforceable title (judgment) is not based on a correct appraisal of the facts or law related to the case that was tried. That would introduce a sort of disguised remedy. Nevertheless, there are some possibilities to that extent; also, there is a special action that is open to the judicial officer only - both of these matters will be discussed below.

The first ground to challenge enforcement is that enforcement is unlawful. Obviously, there is a wide variety of possibilities, ranging from the absence of an

66 Currently, all procedures discussed in this section are decided by the non-cantonal judge or chamber. After enactment of the Attachment and Enforcement Modernisation Act, the cantonal judge will have jurisdiction in case of a dispute over a title issued by the cantonal judge. In summary enforcement proceedings under this Article, the cantonal judge will have jurisdiction on the same basis as in ordinary summary proceedings.

67 Articles 99-108 CCP. Apart from the general rule (the court where defendant is domiciled), there are some additional possibilities such as the court where the tort was committed and the court of the domicile of the claimant who is a consumer.

68 Opposition to the public sale of a non-registered movable by a third party who pretends to be the owner. The suspending force is obtained from the fact that the provision otherwise would be superfluous, but this is not undisputed.

69 Opposition of the garnishee who has a periodic debt to the debtor (such as the employer) against garnishment.

70 Opposition against the public sale of immovable property by a third party who pretends to be the owner or to have a right that is not being respected. The suspending force is to be found in the parliamentary history (Parliamentary History Changes to CCP (Introduction Books 3, 5 and 6), p. 246).

enforceable title and payment of the debt to the non-compliance with formal rules. The latter is applied in a strict way, which means either that a nullity is already foreseen in the law itself[71] or that the court will order to re-enact the formality concerned, mostly at the cost of the party enforcing the title.

The second ground is to allege abuse of the power of enforcement of a title that is enforceable but not final, such as a judgment against which an appeal is pending. This ground can be used when (*a*) after the judgment new circumstances created a case of emergency for the debtor to such a degree that it would be unacceptable to let the creditor continue enforcement; or (*b*) the judgment apparently is based on a major factual or legal error.[72] In exceptional circumstances, the (*b*)-ground can also be invoked if the judgment is final. This was accepted in a case in which it was clear that an order against the defendant to pay a certain sum clearly was in contradiction with the fact that both parties agreed that that sum had already been paid before the judgment.[73] The (*b*)-ground thus more or less introduces an extra remedy against judgments that are clearly mistaken, even though they are final and binding.

The third ground is the assertion that the way the title is enforced is vexatious towards the debtor. This ground can be invoked in the case of an imbalance between the amount enforced and the assets attached or when the means of enforcement chosen is particularly disadvantageous for the debtor.[74] This is the case when, for example, a creditor chooses to enforce his title on the trucks of a transport company (thus making it impossible for the business to continue operating) while other assets are available. A vexatious enforcement amounts to a tort and could therefore be the object of an injunction.

The second procedure is the procedure before the summary proceedings judge. This procedure is swift (the hearing can be arranged within a few hours if necessary) and has therefore to be followed in cases where an immediate ruling is needed. The grounds to be invoked by the claimant will be the same as in the procedure discussed above, but since here the judge has to decide on an interim measure these grounds will always be complemented by a balancing of the interests of the parties. The summary proceedings judge will not give a final decision on the merits, but will only order an interim measure based on a summary appraisal of the positions of the parties and their interests regarding that measure. The law specifies which measures can be taken in addition to the normal measures available to the summary proceedings judge. These measures are suspending enforcement for a certain period or until a decision has been taken in an ordinary procedure; allowing enforcement to continue but only against security; lifting attachments and garnishments (possibly under the obligation for the debtor to provide security); and deciding that formalities have to be re-enacted (possibly with a costs order regarding these formalities). The summary proceedings judge may also order that a

71 As in Articles 439, 440, 474c, 475, 479i, 479n, 502, 504, 505, 514, 565 and 584c CCP, all regarding the contents of the writs with which attachment is realised or with which attachment is notified to other interested parties.

72 HR 22 April 1983, ECLI:NL:HR:1983:AG4575, *NJ* 1984, 145 (*Ritzen/Hoekstra*).

73 HR 22 December 2006, ECLI:NL:HR:2006:AY9224, *NJ* 2007, 173 (*Schmidt/Thunissen*).

74 HR 24 November 1995, ECLI:NL:HR:1995:ZC1894, *NJ* 1996, 161 (*Tromp/Regency*).

third party, represented within the summary proceedings, will have to tolerate further enforcement and will have to cooperate (possibly under the obligation for the creditor to provide security).

The fourth section of Article 438 of the CCP opens a special, swift and informal action for a judicial officer who encounters difficulties in the process of enforcement. After describing these in an official report, he is allowed to apply to the summary proceedings judge for a decision on the difficulties. It is up to the summary proceedings judge to decide whether an *ex parte* decision should be given or whether the parties should be convoked first. The judicial officer in this procedure has an independent position and has the right to ask for a decision even without consulting the creditor. However, when the judicial officer acts without the consent of the creditor, he risks being ordered to pay the costs if he started this procedure needlessly. From the wording of Article 438(4) of the CCP, one can conclude that the decision has to be qualified as a judgment following a procedure that started with a writ of summons. Therefore, to decisions taken in this special procedure, the ordinary remedies of appeal, cassation and opposition apply.

4.3. *Objections to enforcement under BIR*

Under BIR, the possibility of enforcement of foreign judgments in the Netherlands is only subject to the provisions discussed in Section 3 above. As regards possible remedies, including the application for refusal, the following remarks can be made.

The application for refusal as meant in Article 47 of BIR has been implemented in Article 10 of IAB IA. This article merely designates the competent courts for the remedies of Articles 47, 49 and 50 of BIR. This implies that no other grounds can be invoked than those mentioned in Article 45 of BIR. On the other hand, all remedies available during and against enforcement as discussed above do apply, including the remedies mentioned.[75] Special circumstances may therefore always be taken into account. Obviously, as regards an appeal in the state of origin, the Dutch courts are restricted by Article 51 of BIR and the requirement that the power to stay proceedings should only be used in extraordinary circumstances.[76]

Article 10(1) of IAB IA specifies that the application for refusal has to be submitted by writ of summons to the court designated in Article 438 of the CCP.[77]

75 Parliamentary Proceedings II 2012/13, 33676, 3, p. 13.

76 As was the case in Rb Middelburg 5 July 2006, ECLI:NL:RBMID:2006:AY5728, where the court refused to stay the proceedings in the Netherlands because the appeal in the state of origin was based on arguments that had already been put forward in first instance.

77 The new system of BIR gave the Dutch legislator the opportunity to synchronise various related procedures. To challenge enforcement, the debtor has to follow the approach indicated by Article 438 CCP (see Sections 1.9.5 and 4.3.1). For this procedure, an application by means of a writ of summons is prescribed. Under Brussels I, the application for an exequatur (recognition and permission of enforcement) had to be submitted by means of a petition (as stated in the then applicable Article 2 Implementation Act of 2 July 2003, DBAOD 2003, 290). Now, an application for refusal of enforcement as meant in Article 47 BIR has to be submitted by means of a writ of summons to the court that has jurisdiction according to the rules of Article 438 CCP. Thus, all claims and actions regarding enforcement (and implicitly, →

This is the court discussed earlier. The ordinary procedural rules apply, supplemented by the rules of Article 47 of BIR. Consequently, there are no specifics regarding documents.

Service of the writ of summons follows the ordinary rules and the same applies to legal representation. This means that in cases representing a value of less than €25,000 the rules for procedures before the cantonal judge apply, which implies that legal representation is not mandatory.

The object of the application for refusal can only be the refusal of enforcement of the foreign title. There is no separate procedure foreseen in which recognition can be rejected other than as a ground for the decision to refuse enforcement. However, an applicant who wishes to obtain a declaration to that effect from the court could always request such a declaration as part of the procedure based on Article 438 of the CCP, as can be understood from Article 302 of Book 3 of the Civil Code.

The remedies for both parties are appeal (Article 10(2) IAB IA) and cassation (Article 10(3) IAB IA), as discussed in Section 1.7. The ordinary rules apply.

The application for refusal is regulated by Article 10 of IAB IA, and this article simply refers to Article 47 of BIR. During parliamentary proceedings, no issue was raised regarding the identity of the party who has the possibility to submit this application. That is understandable, since Dutch law gives access to justice to everyone whose rights may be violated by enforcement. There is no reason to limit this to the parties mentioned in the title or in any other way as long as there is an interest recognised by the law (Article 303 of Book 3 of the Civil Code).

All the protective measures mentioned earlier are available to the parties against whom enforcement is sought. This explains why specific implementation of Articles 40 and 44 of BIR was not needed.[78]

When enforcement is disputed, protective measures prior to enforcement may become relevant. The system of protective measures available for the creditor has been discussed in Section 1 above. In short, the holder of a title will have the possibility to attach any assets owned by the debtor or other assets that are subject to enforcement. When the title is enforceable under BIR, no prior permission has to be requested. This system meets the requirements of Article 40 of BIR. In addition to the sections mentioned, some remarks about the freezing effect of protective measures under Dutch law seem appropriate.

Protective measures do freeze the assets of the debtor, but not in such a way that his powers to transfer or mortgage his property are affected.[79] For instance, when the car of a debtor has been attached the debtor still has the power to sell and transfer the car to a buyer. The freezing effect is to be found in Articles 453a, 505(2), 475h(1), 566(2), 567 and 584e of the CCP, to be summarised in the rule that all types of transfer and mortgage undertaken by the debtor can be ignored by the creditor

recognition) may be submitted to the same court in the same procedure. In this way, the intention of Recital 30 of the regulation, stating that parties should be able to invoke national and international grounds to challenge enforcement to the extent possible in the same procedure, has been fully implemented.

78 Parliamentary Proceedings II 2012/13, 33676, 3, p. 16 (table).

79 HR 20 February 2009, ECLI:NL:HR:2009:BG7729, *NJ* 2009, 376 (*Ontvanger/de Jong qq*).

but have otherwise full effect. In the example of the car, the creditor will still have the right to sell the car to the public in order to recover his claim, and the buyer will not be able to do anything about it, although the purchase and the transfer made the car his property.

There are some exceptions. The first is that – in the case of non-registered movables – rights obtained by third parties in good faith and against payment of a reasonable sum will have to be respected (Article 453a(2) CCP). After garnishment of a claim, the garnishee is freed of his obligations to the debtor when payment cannot be prevented despite all efforts (Article 475h(1), second sentence, CCP). After attachment of an aircraft, the third party is protected when the debtor did not know about the attachment (Article 584e, last part, CCP). The protection of third parties in the case of attachment of immovable property is complicated. When the notarial deed of conveyance has been passed before the writ of attachment is registered, but is registered itself the first day on which the public registry is opened after the day of registration of the writ, the creditor will lose his rights (Article 505(3) CCP).

The grounds for refusal of enforcement as stated in Article 45 of BIR do not differ much from the grounds already mentioned in Brussels I.[80] Where in the past an issue has risen regarding the question of whether an assessment of the grounds for refusal of enforcement could be combined with national grounds for challenging enforceability,[81] this problem has been solved by the integration of the procedure of Article 47 of BIR into the procedure of Article 438 of the CCP. From the case law under Brussels I, the following can be understood regarding the national interpretation of each of the grounds for refusal.

The public policy ground has always been interpreted in a restricted way in accordance with the intention of this clause as already expressed in the Jenard report.[82] This has been expressed in the rule that foreign judgments are only contrary to Dutch public policy when there is a manifest violation of the principles of a fair procedure that are recognised as fundamental in the Dutch legal order.[83] When, for instance, the foreign title does not state its grounds, this may be considered to be manifestly contrary to public policy in the Netherlands, but not in cases where the defendant did recognise the claim.[84]

A real problem arose only when enforceability was requested in respect of a Bulgarian decision that was unmistakably deliberately contrary to EU law. The Dutch Supreme Court submitted preliminary questions to the European Court of

80 Only the protection of weak parties as foreseen in Article 45(1)(e)(i) has been extended to employees.

81 In HR 12 March 2010, ECLI:NL:HR:2010:BK4932, *NJ* 2010, 156, the Supreme Court had to answer the question of whether the fact that the debtor had already complied with the title could be included in the public policy ground of Article 34 Brussels I. A preliminary ruling of the ECJ was requested, and the answer was that the grounds of Articles 34 and 35 Brussels I are not to be extended beyond their intended scope (ECJ 13 October 2011, C-139/10, ECLI:EU:C:2011:653).

82 *Dutch Gazette of Treaties* 1969, 101, p. 122.

83 HR 2 May 1986, ECLI:NL:HR:1986:AB7998, *NJ* 1987, 481. This is in line with ECJ 28 March 2000, C-7/98, ECLI:EU:C:2000:164, *NJ* 2003, 626.

84 Among other decisions HR 18 March 2011, ECLI:NL:HR:2011:BP0002.

Justice (ECJ),[85] but the answer was that even in that case enforceability should be granted.[86] Being faithful to EU law, the Supreme Court followed this preliminary ruling, but from its wording it was evident that the Dutch justices did not agree.[87] Since the ECJ only allowed an exception in cases where the error on EU law constitutes a manifest breach of a rule of law regarded as essential in the EU legal order, the question is when such a breach occurs. The apparent lack of loyalty to EU law might lead to national judges deliberately disregarding the jurisdiction clauses of BIR and thus awarding claims against the nationals of other countries outside the scope of their jurisdiction. It would be hard to accept that these decisions were enforceable against these parties in their own state.

Another issue relating to public policy rose out of the concurrent applicability of Article 31(2) of CMR (Convention on the Contract for the International Carriage of Goods by Road), which provides for a test of jurisdiction which is incompatible with Article 35(3) of Brussels I. The question of priority under Article 71(2) of Brussels I was submitted to the ECJ, which stated a rule that gives priority to Brussels I in cases where the principle of *favor executionis* would otherwise be violated.[88]

The default of appearance ground did not provoke any particular issues. The Supreme Court clarified that the rule does not state that the document which institutes proceedings actually reached the defendant.[89] Since the exception at the end of the clause almost always applies, applications for refusal of enforceability based on this ground are hardly ever successful.[90]

The grounds regarding related actions and irreconcilable judgments have not been problematic either. Whether the same parties are involved is decided in accordance with the criteria given by the ECJ.[91] These criteria are sufficiently clear to deal with issues such as transfer of rights and other types of legal succession. Moreover, the nature of the decisions have to be taken into account. For instance, interim rulings in one country are not irreconcilable with a ruling on the merits in another country because of their provisional character.[92]

Establishing whether the jurisdiction clauses of Article 35 of Brussels I (which has the same contents as Article 45(1)(e) BIR) were violated has not led to specific decisions.

85 HR 20 December 2013, ECLI:NL:HR:2013:2062, *NJ* 2014, 37.
86 ECJ 16 July 2015, C-681/13, ECLI:EU:C:2015:471.
87 HR 8 July 2016, ECLI:NL:HR:2016:1431, *NJ* 2017, 33.
88 ECJ 4 May 2010, C-533/08, ECLI:EU:C:2010:243.
89 HR 11 October 1996, ECLI:NL:HR:1996:ZC2170, *NJ* 1998, 95.
90 As in Rb Rotterdam 30 September 2009, ECLI:NL:RBROT:2009:BJ9135, in which case the available procedure in Romania had not been followed. Rb Rotterdam 2 December 2015, ECLI:NL:RBROT:2015:8701, is one of the rare cases in which the application for refusal was granted, but this was due to the fact that the creditor did not raise any objections to the statements of the debtor. Another decision granting the refusal on this ground (Rb Haarlem 25 April 2008, ECLI:NL:RBHAA:2008:BD0602) was later quashed by the Supreme Court (HR 11 September 2009, ECLI:NL:HR:2009:BI3436).
91 ECJ 19 May 1998, C-351/96 (*Drouot/Protea*), *NJ* 2000, 155.
92 Rb The Hague 25 August 2011, ECLI:NL:RBSGR:2011:BT2370.

5. Final remarks

The Dutch system is flexible, fast and relatively cheap. Once the creditor has a right to his claim (proven by an enforceable title) he will have no real difficulties recovering the debt when indeed the debtor's assets are sufficient. Protective measures can be obtained easily. BIR simplified the enforcement of foreign titles falling under the scope of that instrument even more, since no court procedure is needed to start enforcement and an application for refusal has been integrated into existing procedures.

What remains is the general problem that debtors sometimes do not have sufficient assets or succeed in hiding them, despite their obligation to provide all necessary information.[93] This is a problem that is not easily solved.

Another drawback of the Dutch system can be found in the numerous provisions prescribing writs and notifications by writs. Judicial officers are not cheap and writs are certainly more expensive than a registered letter or an email (varying from €80 to €200). Cheaper means of communication should be explored.

Lastly, the rules governing enforcement are notoriously complicated. They were already enacted in the code of 1838 and have been heavily amended since. That created an intricate web of cross-references that are very hard to decipher, into which Section 4 above provided modest insight. An entire revision is desirable.

93 This obligation can be found in Article 475g(1) CCP, supplemented by rules given in HR 20 September 1991, ECLI:NL:HR:1991:ZC0338, *NJ* 1992, 552 (*Tripels/Masson*). The same article provides the process server with many possibilities to obtain information about the debtor from (semi-)government agencies and private employers.

T. Ivanc

THE INTERPLAY BETWEEN BRUSSELS I RECAST AND THE SLOVENIAN RULES ON REMEDIES UNDER THE NEW SYSTEM OF DIRECT ENFORCEMENT OF FOREIGN JUDICIAL DECISIONS

1. Introduction

One of the most important objectives when adopting Brussels I Recast (hereinafter BIR or Recast)[1] was to simplify and expedite the circulation of judgments given within the territory of the European Union. BIR preserves the previous provisions concerning recognition of judgments under the Brussels I Regulation,[2] while at the same time abolishing the exequatur procedure, thereby harmonising the core of the mechanism of the recognition and enforcement of foreign judgments. Consequently, a judgment given in the EU automatically becomes an enforcement title in the territory of Slovenia (or any other EU Member State), that is, it can be immediately enforced without an enforceable clause (declaration of enforceability) from a Slovenian court. The only items required now to initiate enforcement proceedings are a copy of the judgment along with the certificate of enforceability issued by the court of origin. Theoretically, it is not even necessary to include a translation of these documents although the authorities or the debtor might request so.

This 'simplification' of rules[3] on the cross-border recognition and enforcement of judgments is based on the principle of mutual trust as one of the cornerstones of cooperation in the field of European Union private international law. Both the Recitals contained in BIR and the case law of the Court of Justice of the European

1 Regulation (EU) No. 1215/2012 of the European Parliament and of the Council of 12 December 2012 on jurisdiction and the recognition and enforcement of judgments in civil and commercial matters, OJ L 351, 20 December 2012, p. 1-32.

2 Regulation (EC) No. 44/2001 of 22 December 2000 on jurisdiction and the recognition and enforcement of judgments in civil and commercial matters, OJ L 012, 16 January 2001, p. 0001-0023.

3 Exequatur has also been abolished in two other European instruments, namely the European Payment Order and the Regulation on Small Claims.

Union (CJEU)[4] confirm the important roles that mutual trust and the guarantee of procedural efficiency play in facilitating the free circulation of judgments throughout the European Union. Mutual trust rests upon the principle of reciprocal faith among the national judicial systems of the Member States.[5]

Recital 26 of BIR explains that:

> Mutual trust in the administration of justice [with]in [the European] Union justifies the principle that judgments given in a Member State should be recognised in all Member States without the need for any special procedure. In addition, the aim of making cross-border litigation less time-consuming and costly justifies the abolition of the declaration of enforceability prior to enforcement in the Member State addressed.

Eliminating the need for a separate declaration of enforceability in the new system of BIR certainly helps to reinforce the notion of mutual recognition of judgments. Judgments rendered by the courts of other Member States now are treated equally as domestic judgments, subject only to enumerated grounds for refusal of recognition to be examined later in this contribution (Article 45 BIR) and no longer in a separate exequatur proceeding, but rather directly within the respective national enforcement proceeding.

Adverse consequences stemming from automatic mutual recognition may be ameliorated by applying the refusal grounds, which, when taken together, represent a system of predictable safeguards for the refusal of recognition and enforcement of foreign judgments in specific circumstances delineated under BIR. Additionally, the abolition of the exequatur procedure has given rise to new defences for the judgment debtor, who now may resist (invoking the grounds for refusal or suspension of the enforcement) enforcement of the judgment on the grounds provided by national law, to the extent that these defences are not 'incompatible with' the specific grounds available under BIR (Article 41(2) BIR).

However, legal critics have noted that a significant adverse consequence stemming from the otherwise laudable principle of mutual recognition is 'that it requires mutual trust and [a] principle of recognition … requires in its extreme … that a domestic legal system allows for enforcement of judgments based on procedural rules and ideological values over which the Member State has no influence and very little knowledge.'[6] Some level of trust among Member States is

4 Case 120/78 – *REWE-Zentral AG v. Bundesmonopolverwaltung für Branntwein – Cassis de Dijon* [1979]. According to the *Cassis de Dijon* case, mutual recognition has become the vital mechanism for removing barriers to the fundamental freedoms. The CJEU has interpreted fundamental provisions on mutual recognition by using the principle of mutual trust in the following case law: Case C-116/02 – *Erich Gasser GmbH v. Misat Srl.* [2003] ECR I-14693; Case C-185/07 – *Allianz SpA et al. v. West Tankers Inc* [2009] ECR I-663; Case C-157/12 – *Salzgitter Mannesmann Handel GmbH v. SC Laminorul SA;* Case C-456/11 – *Gothaer Versicherung et al. v. Samskip GmbH,* ECLI:EU:C:2012:719; Case C-452/12 – *Nipponkoa Insurance Co. (Europe) Ltd v. Interzuid Transport BV,* ECLI:EU:C:2013; Case C-619/10 – *Trade Agency Ltd v. Seramico Investments Ltd,* ECLI:EU:C:2012:531.

5 See, for a discussion of the role of the principle of mutual trust, Pontier & Burg 2004; Weller 2015, p. 64-102.

6 Andersson 2005, p. 247.

crucial for the effective implementation of procedural safeguards. The European Parliament in its report[7] concluded that, 'A Member State before which proceedings are brought is entitled to preserve its fundamental values; therefore, equally, it must be the case for a Member State in which the enforcement of a judgment is sought.'[8]

The quickest way for the legal title to be effective is if the judgment debtor voluntarily complies with the judgment.[9] However, irrespective of whether there is possible voluntary or eventually forced compliance with the condemnatory decision, it is imperative that the parties' legal protection be both predictable and efficient.[10] From the judgment creditor's standpoint, a paramount issue is whether he or she will be able to actually enforce the judgment. After all, a paper judgment that cannot be enforced and collected upon is, at the end of the day, of no practical value. In a similar vein, a fair legal system must promote certainty and efficiency and therefore it is important that the rules allow for enforcement of judgments in ways that are both speedy and streamlined.

In the first part of the contribution, we shall consider how the new rules impact the interests of both the creditor and the debtor, including how changes in the rules could cause delays in the enforcement proceedings. Furthermore, it is paradoxical that despite the fact that the exequatur proceeding has been abolished, some of the safeguards that remain may actually delay and in some cases even prevent the achievement of a swift, unhindered free movement of judicial decisions within the EU.

Some aspects of BIR are designed to protect the interests of the debtor. Examples of this include the requirement of service of the certificate on the debtor and allowing the debtor to request translation of the foreign judgment. The judgment creditor can take no measures of enforcement against the judgment debtor, other than protective measures, until a requested translation has been provided to the person against whom enforcement is sought (Article 43(2) BIR). Compared to the other EU instruments, namely, the European Payment Order[11] and the Regulation on Small Claims,[12] BIR has retained the refusal grounds, although there is a reversed procedure for refusal of recognition (Article 45 BIR) or for a declaration that there are no grounds for refusal (Article 36(2) BIR) possible, however with no *ex officio* examination of grounds by the court in the Member State of enforcement. The abolition of exequatur and the fact that there is no intermediate

7 Report on the proposal for a regulation of the European Parliament and of the Council on jurisdiction and the recognition and enforcement of judgments in civil and commercial matters (recast), (COM (2010) 0748 – C7-0433/2010 – 2010/0383(COD)).

8 Hess, Bergström & Storskrubb 2016.

9 In his article 'Procedural fairness and compliance', Verkerk argues that promoting procedural fairness might contribute to voluntary compliance with a judgment; see Verkerk 2010, p. 253-267.

10 *Ibid.*, p. 266.

11 Regulation (EC) No. 1896/2006 of the European Parliament and of the Council of 12 December 2006 creating a European order for payment procedure, OJ L 399, 30 December 2006, p. 1-32.

12 Regulation (EC) No. 861/2007 of the European Parliament and of the Council of 11 July 2007 establishing a European Small Claims Procedure, OJ L 199, 31 July 2007, p. 1-22.

procedure for adopting the foreign title could also be seen as an advantage for the creditor.

However, the rules relating to the protection of the judgment debtor are necessary and important. In this connection, the possibility of exercising all of the objections (under BIR and national systems) against recognition and enforcement in one procedure is a practical and efficient way for the judgment debtor to secure 'instant' protection. Despite the salutary benefits these rules have in terms of the judgment debtor's legal interests, it nevertheless follows that the principle of mutual recognition and free movement of judgments is, to some extent at least, compromised by these provisions.

From the viewpoint of the creditor, one of the first considerations when initiating an action in a cross-border matter is the probability of ultimate success of recognition and enforcement of the judgment. However, the fact that national systems significantly differ among each other raises the important question of how the immediate enforcement of the judgment, following the abolishment of exequatur, will impact the national enforcement proceedings. BIR affects national enforcement laws because of the principle of supremacy of EU law. According to Article 41(2) of BIR, national laws regulating the grounds for refusal or for suspension of enforcement must be compatible with EU law (grounds referred to in Article 45 BIR). Accordingly, the abolition of exequatur in BIR required a 'new' system of remedies and recourses in the Member State of origin and the Member State of enforcement. BIR regulates this system in point a. of Article 38, and in Articles 49 and 50. On the other hand, a draft for BIR[13] proposed the system of splitting the remedies enabling the judgment debtor to prevent the judgment given in one Member State from taking effect in another Member State.[14]

This contribution examines the rules on the recognition and enforcement of civil and commercial judgments with an emphasis on the Slovenian enforcement system.

The first part provides an outline of the mechanisms of enforcing the foreign judgment according to the provisions of BIR and the manner in which those mechanisms have changed with respect to both the creditor and the debtor. The next part focuses on the procedural aspects of the application for refusal and the role of national law. As exequatur has been abolished, the focus is on the enforcement procedure and national autonomy, as adopted by Article 41 of BIR. The last part of the contribution explores both the rules on suspension of enforceability and the limitation to protective measures as provided by BIR. When the judgment debtor applies for refusal of enforcement, enforcement measures are not automatically excluded. However, upon the application of the judgment debtor, the court has discretion to limit enforcement to protective measures, make enforcement conditional on the provision of a security, or suspend enforcement

13 Proposal for a Regulation of the European Parliament and the Council on jurisdiction and the recognition and enforcement of judgments in civil and commercial matters (Recast), COM (2010) 748 final, Brussels, 14 December 2010.

14 Sladič 2013, p. 352.

either wholly or in part. The court will consider the likelihood of the judgment debtor's objections to the enforcement. If the enforceability of the judgment is suspended in the Member State of origin, the enforcement court or authority has no such discretion and must suspend the enforcement proceedings upon the application of the debtor.

2. Practical aspects concerning the relative positions of the creditor and debtor in the enforcement of foreign judgments

BIR provides that the judgments that fall under the scope of the Regulation are automatically enforceable in any other Member State without the need for a declaration of enforceability (Articles 36 and 39 BIR). By abolishing the exequatur requirement, there no longer is an intermediate procedure for adopting the foreign title to the *lex fori* of the addressed Member State. Rather, the enforcement of the foreign judgment is subject to the same conditions as would be the case for a judgment given in the Member State addressed (Article 41(1) BIR). However, upon the interested party`s initiative, the court may refuse recognition, while on the other hand the courts may issue a declaration that there are no grounds for refusal (Article 36(2) BIR). The direct transposition of refusal grounds into the enforcement stage is problematical, due to the differences among various enforcement systems.[15] As Dickinson has argued,[16] it could be 'advantageous for the import of judgments initially to be channelled through a court or courts designated for this purpose, rather than proceeding directly to measures of execution, which may take place in a local court with little or no experience of cross-border matters.' Without the declaration of enforceability, the competent enforcement authority is the first authority confronted with the foreign judgment in the addressed Member State (Article 42 BIR).

Once the judgments are in the hands of the enforcement authority, the enforcement is initiated against the debtor using ordinary enforcement procedure governed by national law.

In addition to the direct enforcement of a judgment given in another Member State, BIR provides for additional changes to both the creditor's rights and the debtor's rights. Under the previous Brussels I Regulation, the creditor had a right to initiate actual measures of enforcement immediately after the period for appealing the exequatur decision had lapsed or after the appeal had been dismissed (Article 47(3) BIR). Additionally, the creditor was able to initiate the actual enforcement procedure one month after the service of the exequatur decision or two months after the decision in cases where the debtor was domiciled outside the enforcement state (Article 43(5) BIR). In comparison with the Brussels I Regulation,[17] under BIR the

15 Rijavec 2014, p. 5-11.

16 Dickinson 2009.

17 The power to proceed to protective measures was enabled only after the exequatur proceeding (Article 47(3) Brussels I Regulation). During the time for lodging an appeal and, if an appeal is lodged, until judgment has been given, the creditor is only allowed to take protective measures as available under the law of the requested Member State.

advantageous change for the creditor is certainly the possibility, which derives from the effects of the enforceable judgment, to proceed to the protective measures available in the Member State of enforcement (Article 40 BIR). Furthermore, prior service of the certificate from Article 53 of BIR to the debtor (Article 43(3) BIR) is not a condition precedent for proceeding to protective measures.

BIR gives discretion to the Member States of enforcement to decide upon the competent enforcing body (court or agency) and further to determine how the procedure of adaptation of the foreign judgment is to be carried out (Recital 28 BIR). The existence of these variables necessarily will require the creditor to take some additional steps in the enforcement procedures in order to ascertain the competent enforcement body in the Member State addressed.[18] Also, the creditor is further burdened with determining whether a measure contained in the judgment is similarly recognised in the law of the Member State addressed. Article 54 of BIR requires that, 'If a judgment contains a measure or an order which is not known in the law of the Member State addressed, that measure or order shall, to the extent possible, be adapted to a measure or an order known in the law of that Member State which has equivalent effects attached to it and which pursues similar aims and interests.' A negative aspect of Article 54 of BIR is that if this adaptation duty is performed by the enforcement authority, and not by the courts, the enforcement procedure is likely to be prolonged.[19] Furthermore, a creditor is likely to have less motivation to initiate enforcement in a state other than the Member State of origin if delays in enforcement will become apparent only after the enforcement is actually sought, and not beforehand.[20]

BIR requires that the certificate issued pursuant to Article 53 be served on the debtor prior to the first enforcement measure (Article 43(1) BIR).[21] It is unclear why the 'surprise effect'[22] has not been considered, as is the case under the European

18 Under the past system, the exequatur procedure was entrusted to the competent courts. According to Article 74 of the Brussels I bis Regulation, the Member States shall provide a description of national rules and procedures concerning enforcement, including competent authorities, debtor protection rules and information on any limitations on enforcement. However, on the European Judicial Atlas website, there is no information on issues of national enforcement law.

19 Magnus & Mankowski 2016, p. 973-974.

20 It is clear that the amendment of Slovenian enforcement law does not include provisions for the adaptation procedure for unknown measures under Article 54 as is the case, for example, in Germany (see § 1114 ZPO).

21 However, the Commission first proposed that the moment when the debtor is first served with the foreign judgment could be 'the date of the first enforcement measure having the effect of making his property non-disposable in whole or in part.' According to Dickinson, this would mean that 'by the time that the respondent is able to react, that measure, or its effects, may be irreversible – the property (depending on local procedures in the place of enforcement) may have been sold or damaged and the respondent may have been unable to meet contractual or other obligations relating to that property' (Dickinson 2010, p. 267).

22 Therefore, if the creditor deems the surprise effect necessary to prevent the disappearance of the debtor's assets, the European account preservation order will in many cases constitute a more efficient instrument to reach this goal. See Anzenberger & Ivanc 2017, p. 57-70.

Account Preservation Regulation,[23] and the debtor still needs to be informed that the enforcement of the judgment will proceed in the addressed Member State.[24] According to Article 37 of BIR, the submission of the certificate when seeking recognition is required, whereas the former Regulation did not make this mandatory.

Welcomed simplifications for the creditor, on the other hand, are that, firstly, there is no longer a requirement for the creditor to have a postal address in the Member State of enforcement, and, secondly, the creditor is no longer required to appoint a legal representative *ad litem* (Article 41 para 3 BIR).

The Recast also provides quite a few changes impacting the debtor's rights. Further safeguards for the debtor lie in the fact that BIR requires the service of the certificate[25] and the foreign judgment before the first enforcement measure (Article 43 BIR). The direct enforcement of judgments in another Member State will not have a negative impact on the debtor's rights, as the debtor still has the right to apply for the refusal of recognition or enforcement of judgments, especially if the debtor believes that one of the refusal grounds under BIR and under the law of the Member State addressed exists. Since the intermediate exequatur procedure has been eliminated, the debtor needs to apply for refusal on his or her own motion after the certificate and judgment have been served.

Aside from the fact that the debtor may apply for preventive application for refusal of recognition (Article 45 BIR), the Regulation's procedure for recognition mostly remained unchanged.[26] Additionally, the debtor may still delay enforcement, in particular by requesting a translation of the judgment. The debtor is entitled to a translation of the judgment if he or she is domiciled in a Member State other than the state of origin, and if the judgment is written in a language that he or she does not understand and that is not an official language at the place of his or her domicile (Article 43(2) BIR). Until the debtor is provided with a translation of the judgment, no measures of enforcement may be taken, other than protective measures. Contrary to Article 43 of the Brussels I Regulation, the Recast no longer provides a time limit within which an appeal may be lodged against a decision on

23 Regulation (EU) No. 655/2014 of the European Parliament and of the Council of 15 May 2014 establishing a European Account Preservation Order procedure to facilitate cross-border debt recovery in civil and commercial matters, OJ L 189, 27 June 2014.

24 The one rationale for this obligation to serve the certificate is in the fundamental procedural right for the party to be informed of the issuance of any judicial document in the proceedings to which he is a party; Magnus & Mankowski 2016, p. 858.

25 According to the form set out in Annex I, the certificate (Article 53 Brussels I bis Regulation) is more detailed than the one foreseen under the former Brussels I Regulation. However, some information will not be included, such as whether the decision is final. Additionally, the data on the statutory interests will be indicated by way of a reference to the applicable foreign national law of the state of origin, which will certainly make it harder for the enforcement authority to determine the interests. Requejo Isidro 2017, p. 84.

26 A judgment can still be recognised incidentally without the special procedure for recognition (Article 36 Brussels I bis Regulation). The procedure for recognition, however, consists in a reversed application, meaning that any interested party may request the court to establish that there are no grounds for refusal of recognition.

the application for refusal of enforcement (Article 49 BIR). This means that national law will apply. According to Recital 31 of BIR, 'Pending a challenge to the enforcement of the judgment, it should be possible for the courts in the Member State addressed, during the entire proceedings relating to such a challenge, including any appeal, to allow the enforcement to proceed subject to a limitation of the enforcement or to the provision of security.' Depending on the national law of the Member State addressed, the differences in national systems could additionally mean not only a delay[27] in the cross-border enforcement but also potentially a decrease in the uniformity of the application of BIR.

In addition to the requirement of service of the certificate (with the judgment if not yet served) before the first enforcement measure is sought (Article 43(1) BIR), a translation of the judgment is needed under conditions set down in para 2 of Article 43 of BIR. In favour of safeguarding the debtors' rights, the following 'delays' of enforcement proceedings are possible:

- Proceeding for application for refusal of enforcement together with the remedies against the decision (Articles 49 and 50 BIR);
- Proceeding for suspension or limitation of enforcement (Articles 44 and 51 BIR);
- Proceeding for adaptation of unknown measures with the right to challenge the decision (Article 54 BIR).

3. Procedural aspects of the application for refusal of enforcement and the role of national law

The grounds for refusal of enforcement were much debated during the revision of the Brussels I Regulation. During the process of adopting the revision, the first idea was to eliminate the possibility of raising any grounds for refusal in the addressed country.[28] The rationale behind this proposal was that for all judgments rendered in a Member State, the enforcement could be requested in another Member State without any specific procedure.[29] The Proposal in 2010[30] provided for three possibilities of opposing recognition or enforcement. According to the first refusal ground, the debtor would be able to contest the judgment in the Member State of origin if he or she was not properly informed about the proceedings in that state.

27 The delays will even more influence the efficiency of the cross-border enforcement of judgments, where the debtor applies for refusal of enforcement and the national procedural laws prohibit the enforcement during the time of appeal; Je Timmer 2013, p. 140.

28 Magnus & Mankowski 2016, p. 868.

29 Oberhammer suggested that, even though there is no practical need for abolishing the grounds for refusal of recognition and enforcement, it would be possible to refer all of the grounds under the former Articles 34 and 35 of the Brussels I Regulation to review proceedings in the state of origin. He furthermore elaborated that public policy should be replaced by a uniform European extraordinary review of gross violations of procedural fairness. See Oberhammer 2010, p. 197-203.

30 Proposal for a Regulation of the European Parliament and the Council on jurisdiction and the recognition and enforcement of judgments in civil and commercial matters (Recast), COM (2010) 748 final, Brussels, 14 December 2010.

The second possibility was the proposal for an extraordinary remedy in the Member State of enforcement that would enable the defendant to contest any other procedural defects which might have arisen during the proceedings before the court of origin and which have infringed his right to a fair trial. The third ground envisaged that the defendant could move to stop the enforcement of the judgment in a situation where it was irreconcilable with another judgment which had been issued in the Member State of enforcement or - provided that certain conditions were fulfilled - in another country.[31]

In the end, the Parliament accepted the abolition of exequatur, but reintroduced the possibility to contest the enforcement in a Member State addressed under the grounds previously listed in Article 34 of the Brussels I Regulation.[32] One can conclude that the refusal grounds set forth in Article 45 of BIR are designed to advance the same goals as the previous Brussels I Regulation did, which is to substantiate the correctness of the foreign judgment. However, the grounds of refusal contained in Article 45 of BIR will influence the enforcement stage despite the fact that exequatur has been abolished.

In addition to the provisions regarding the grounds for refusal of enforcement (Article 45 BIR), BIR also regulates the effect of the application on the enforceability of foreign judgments (Article 44 BIR), the documents which are to be provided (Article 47(3) BIR), the right not to have a postal address or an authorised representative in the Member State of enforcement (Article 47(4) BIR), the length of the procedure (Article 48 BIR) and provides an appeal procedure against the decision on the application (Articles 49 and 50 BIR). All other issues are governed by the law of the Member State of enforcement. The previous Brussels I Regulation provided rules on the time frame within which a declaration of enforceability could be challenged.[33] There is no similar provision in BIR, which means that *lex fori* rules will apply.

Recital 30 of the Preamble encourages Member States to enable applicants 'to invoke, in the same procedure, in addition to the grounds for refusal provided for in this Regulation, the grounds for refusal available under national law and within the time-limits laid down in that law.' This means that the debtor may also invoke

31 Commission proposal, COM (2010) 748 final, under point 3.1.

32 The Commission's proposal introduced the idea of abolishing substantive public policy as a refusal ground. This decision had its basis also in a survey that demonstrated that the application of substantive public policy does not play any considerable role in the case law of the Member States. Hess & Pfeiffer 2011, p. 30 *et seq*. Furthermore, scholars are of the opinion that it would be wise to 'allow the defendant also to invoke substantive public policy issues via a legal remedy available in the state of enforcement. The cases where substantive public policy is at question are very rare, and this additional option would not represent a notable obstacle to the free circulation of judgments' (Kramberger Škerl 2011, p. 489).

33 An appeal against the declaration of enforceability is to be lodged within one month of service thereof. If the party against whom enforcement is sought is domiciled in a Member State other than that in which the declaration of enforceability was given, the time for appealing shall be two months and shall run from the date of service, either on him in person or at his residence. No extension of time may be granted on account of distance (Article 43(5) Brussels I).

national refusal grounds of both a procedural and a substantive nature against the claim for enforcement in a special procedure, which eventually need to be compatible with the refusal grounds referred to in Article 45 of BIR.

In addition, the question regarding how the Member States will adapt to the possibility of the debtor having the right to invoke grounds for refusal under national law (whether these grounds will be considered in the same proceedings as grounds under BIR or only in enforcement proceedings)[34] will have practical importance on the efficiency of the enforcement proceedings. According to the precepts contained in Recital 30 of the Preamble to the Recast, it would be reasonable for the debtor to invoke grounds for refusal of enforcement, together with the objection against the enforcement order under national law, which means that the proceedings would be carried out before the local enforcement court. Legal theory[35] compels the same conclusion that Article 41 of BIR does not mandate that all grounds for refusal of enforcement (either pursuant to Article 45 BIR or under domestic law) must be available in the same procedure. This in turn means that Member States are free to establish either separate procedures for the purpose of allowing debtors to resist enforcement on each series of grounds (under both BIR and national law) or a unified procedure for both.[36]

The following findings are based on the national reports prepared for the project "Remedies concerning Enforcement of Foreign Judgments according to Brussels I Recast.[37] When analysing these reports, it becomes clear that the French[38], Italian[39], Dutch[40] and Czech[41] reporters provide that the national law permits parallel application of opposition grounds in refusal proceedings. This result stems in large measure from combining the refusal proceedings with the actual enforcement proceedings, rather than establishing a separate (fast) track procedure. The one-track system in the above-mentioned Member States relies on the coincidental raising of the objections. It is therefore up to the Member States either to establish one single procedure to resist enforcement on both series of grounds simultaneously or to establish separate procedures enabling debtors to resist enforcement on each series of grounds in special procedures.

In Slovenia, it has been established that district courts (*okrožno sodišče*) are competent to decide on the refusal grounds against the declaration of enforceability under Brussels I and they will have the same competence according to BIR. The

34 On three different possibilities, see Kramberger Škerl 2016, p. 134.

35 Magnus & Mankowski 2016, p. 848.

36 *Ibid.*

37 The national reports were prepared as one of the results of the research project 'Remedies concerning Enforcement of Foreign Judgements according to Brussels I Recast' supported by the EU under the Specific Programme Civil Justice of the European Commission. See the official website of the project at <https://www.pf.um.si/en/acj/projects/pr04/>, last accessed 10 June 2019.

38 Bošković Pillet 2017.

39 Giussani 2018.

40 Fernhout 2018.

41 Valdhans & Kyselovská 2018.

enforcement proceedings are conducted by local enforcement courts (*okrajno sodišča*), which are competent to decide on the refusal grounds under the domestic law. Another point to mention is that under BIR, which allows for domestic grounds to be invoked as a basis to refuse recognition, the enforcement court (in Slovenia, local courts) will need to evaluate whether the domestic grounds asserted for refusal are not incompatible with the grounds in Article 45 of BIR.[42] At the end of the proceedings, the enforcement court will need to test the grounds for compatibility with the refusal grounds under Article 45.

Article 41 of the Recast provides that the procedure for the enforcement of a foreign judgment is governed by the law of the Member State addressed. The rule goes on to state that, 'A judgment given in a Member State, which is enforceable in the Member State addressed, shall be enforced there under the same conditions as a judgment given in the Member State addressed.' Remedies against the decision on enforcement are governed by national law. According to Slovenian enforcement law, permission of the local court for enforcement of the judgment is needed in the form of a writ of execution. The judgment debtor's only legal remedy against the enforcement order (Article 53 Enforcement and Securing of Civil Claims Act (ESCCA) (*Zakon o izvršbi in zavarovanju* – ZIZ))[43] is an objection which represents an ordinary, bilateral remedy, decided by the first instance enforcement court that issued the enforcement order (a local court). Upon the objection, the first instance court is obliged to reconsider the correctness of its previous decision. An objection does not suspend the enforcement procedure (Article 9(6) ESCCA).[44] However, the judgment debtor may lodge a motion for suspension of the enforcement according to the grounds provided by the law.[45]

Against a warrant of execution, an appeal is possible for both the judgment debtor[46] (or third person) and the judgment creditor.[47] Article 55 of ESCCA provides for three categories of grounds for opposing the writ of execution, namely: defences concerning the conditions of admissibility of enforcement proceedings; defences stating that the enforcement is not allowed, because the creditor's claims are extinguished, even though a valid title exists; and, defences concerning the enforcement proceedings linked to the maturity and enforceability of the claim.[48] [49]

42 An example is the objection that the debt has been satisfied after the judgment was issued; Von Hein 2013, p. 110.

43 Enforcement and Securing of Civil Claims Act, Official Gazette RS, No. 3/07 – uradno prečiščeno besedilo, 93/07, 37/08 – ZST-1, 45/08 – ZArbit, 28/09, 51/10, 26/11, 17/13 – odl. US, 45/14 – odl. US, 53/14, 58/14 – odl. US, 54/15 in 76/15 – odl. US.

44 The creditor may not be repaid until the enforcement order has become irrevocable. Only in exceptional cases may the creditor receive repayment of his debt before the enforcement order issued upon the enforceable title becomes final. This is possible only in the case where the creditor applies for the attachment of a sum of money in the debtor's bank account (Article 46(3) ESCCA).

45 Additionally, the debtor has the right to lodge an objection as an extraordinary remedy.

46 If the debtor's objection against the warrant of execution is dismissed.

47 If the creditor's motion for getting the warrant of execution is dismissed.

48 For example, if the deadline for submitting a motion to enforce has expired.

49 Rijavec 2014, p. 11.

If new facts that relate to the claim have arisen after the decision became enforceable, the judgment debtor may file the objection at any time after the warrant of execution has become final up until the end of the enforcement procedure, if the judgment debtor was involuntarily unable to invoke this fact in the course of filing the objection (Article 56 ESCCA).

According to Article 57 of ESCCA, the judgment creditor has a right to respond to the judgment debtor's objection within eight days from the service of the debtor's objection. If the judgment creditor does not respond, the court will decide upon the objection. In this situation, the court will accept the judgment debtor's arguments included in the objection as true. If the judgment creditor makes timely objection to the judgment debtor's objection, stating the facts in support thereof and submitting evidence, the court will, according to the circumstances of the case, schedule the main hearing or issue a decision without the main hearing.[50]

In the communication submitted to the Commission according to Article 75 of BIR, Slovenia has determined that applications for refusal of enforcement need to be submitted to the district courts (*okrožno sodišča*) pursuant to Article 47(1) of BIR; and any further appeal is to be lodged to the Supreme Court pursuant to Article 50 of BIR.

Para 4, Article 45 of BIR states that the application for refusal of recognition shall be made in accordance with the procedures foreseen for the refusal of enforcement. The Slovenian legislator has decided that, since the district courts (*okrožno sodišče*)[51] were already competent for deciding in the principal proceedings on the recognition and enforcement of foreign judgments under the previous Brussels I Regulation, it would not be appropriate to authorise local enforcement courts (*okrajna sodišča*), competent for enforcement proceedings, to decide on refusal according to the BIR system. The new Slovenian provision (Article a42.b(1) ESCCA-L) provides the rules for the procedure for recognition and enforcement according to BIR. In this procedure, the debtor or interested party may submit an application for refusal of recognition, an application for a decision that there are no grounds for refusal of recognition or an application for refusal of enforcement of the foreign judgment before Slovenian district courts (Article 42.b(1) ESCCA-L). The interested party is obliged to state the facts with which the application is substantiated and thereof submit the evidence, otherwise the application will be considered to be unfounded, and rejected (Article a42.b(3) ESCCA-L).

Unlike under the previous Brussels I Regulation, the deliberation proceeding under BIR is adversarial from the beginning. The court is obliged to serve the application for refusal of recognition; the proposal for the decision that there are no grounds for refusal or recognition; or the proposal for refusal of enforcement of the

50 Upon the objection, the court may issue the following decisions: reject the objection as late, incomplete or submitted by an unauthorised person; dismiss the objection and confirm the enforcement order; grant the objection and repeal the enforcement order and reject the proposal; grant the objection and repeal the enforcement order; grant the objection and amend the enforcement order; decline its territorial jurisdiction and transfer the matter to the competent court that will decide on the objection; Rijavec 2003, p. 204.

51 The amended ESCCA foresees that a panel composed of three judges delivers the decision.

foreign judgment upon the opposite party for him or her to answer to the claims within thirty days. The court decides on the basis of the facts and evidence provided by the parties. If the party claims that the default judgment was issued but the defendant was not served with the document which instituted the proceedings in sufficient time and in such a way as to enable him to arrange for his defence (Article 45 (1)(b) BIR), the party may use all available evidence to prove that the grounds for refusal exist. As already mentioned, the court will serve the application on the opposing party (which will be invited to substantiate the answer to the application and provide opposing evidence), and in the event that the ultimate decision of the court depends on the resolution of disputed facts between the parties, the court may, according to Slovenian law, conduct an oral hearing (Article a42.b(6) ESCCA-L).

As already explained, according to the Slovenian law, the request for refusal of enforcement under BIR will need to be brought in separate proceedings, since local courts are only competent for enforcement and district courts are competent for proceedings for refusal of enforcement. The application for the decision on the refusal of recognition, the request for the decision that there are no grounds for refusal or recognition, and/or the request for refusal of enforcement of the foreign judgment each will need to be supported by the facts and evidence that substantiate the application.[52]

Encouraging the option of combining the refusal grounds under BIR and national defences in the same procedure is an improvement established by BIR. Since the wording of BIR encourages Member States to enable the parties to invoke both sets of grounds in one special procedure, Member States will decide what will be allowed in their national procedural law. This choice in Recital 30 and Article 41 of BIR was introduced because of the disagreement of some Member States with the decision in *Prism Invest*.[53] According to the Recital, this means that the judgment debtor may invoke the grounds for refusal of the enforcement or non-enforcement of a foreign judgment under Article 47 of BIR with the submission of his objection against the warrant of execution under Article 53 or 55 of ESCCA before local enforcement courts. It is common practice that the judgment debtor will invoke the grounds concerning the claim (e.g. partial payment of the judgment debtor, compensation, agreement on the repayment by instalments or suspension of the payment – under Article 55 of ESCCA) as justifications in support of the non-

52 On other issues in relation to the principal proceeding, which are not regulated in the enforcement law, the private international law (Private International Law and Procedure Act – PILPA (*Zakon o mednarodnem zasebnem pravu in postopku* – ZMZPP)) rules on the proceeding for recognition and enforcement apply; especially rules on exclusion of revision which is not permitted against a decision of the Supreme Court on appeal against the order (Article 111 ESCCA); and rules on the costs of the proceedings (Article 110 PILPA).

53 In the case *Prism Investments BV v. Jaap Anne van der Meer*, 2011 I-09511, the CJEU ruled that the court, with which the appeal in accordance with Articles 43 and 44 of the Brussels I Regulation is lodged, is precluded from refusing or revoking a declaration of enforceability of a judgment on a ground other than those set out in Articles 34 and 35 thereof, such as compliance with that judgment in the Member State of origin. See also the Proposal for amendment ESCCA-L, EVA 2016-2030-0008.

enforcement of a foreign judgment (the grounds under Article 45 BIR). However, it would be illogical for the Slovenian legislator to opt in favour of this solution, as Article 45(4) of BIR explicitly foresees that the application for refusal of recognition of the foreign judgment shall be made in accordance with the procedures for refusal of enforcement or enforcement of the foreign judgment. Furthermore, the Slovenian district courts already have specialised expertise for making decisions in proceedings on recognition and enforcement under the Brussels I Regulation, and so Slovenia has decided that the district courts will retain their competency to consider refusal of enforcement.

According to Articles 49 and 50 of BIR, remedies are foreseen only as remedies in the proceedings against the decision on the application for refusal of enforcement according to the grounds set forth in Article 45.[54] Article 49 provides for appeal against the first instance decision on the application for refusal of enforcement. However, since the provision does not offer a complete set of rules, the national rules of the forum will apply.[55] Nevertheless the question remains as to which reasons may be argued with the appeal provided in Article 49 of BIR. In legal writing it is stated that only the grounds of Article 45 of BIR may be adduced.[56] The issue of the time limit for lodging the appeal is left to the national laws of the Member States.

Second appeal against the decision issued on the basis of Article 49 of BIR is foreseen in Article 50. This 'second appeal' is possible where the respective Member State has communicated to the Commission the courts where it is to be lodged. By virtue of the wording of the said article, a further appeal is optional,[57] providing that Member States failing to notify the competent courts have decided not to make a final appeal available to the parties.[58] This means that BIR provides for at least two instances (Articles 47 and 49 BIR), but the Member States may have an additional remedy as a third instance (Article 50 BIR).

Slovenia implemented only a single appeal to the Supreme Court against a court's decision on recognition and enforcement (Article a42.b(7) ESCCA-L). The appeal must be lodged within thirty days of service of the order of the first instance court. The deadline for responding to the appeal is thirty days after the appeal has been served.[59]

54 Rijavec 2014, p. 8.
55 Cuniberti & Rueda 2016, p. 958.
56 *Ibid.*
57 Kramer *et al.* 2015, p. 491.
58 Cuniberti & Rueda 2016, p. 959.
59 Under the previous Brussels I Regulation, there were two possible remedies in the proceeding for a declaration of enforceability. The courts with which appeals referred to in Article 43(2) of Brussels I were lodged were the district courts (*okrožno sodišče*), and the judgment given on the appeal could then be contested by the appeal referred to in Article 44 at the Supreme Court of Slovenia.

3.1. *Slovenian case law regarding grounds for refusal*

Since the intermediate exequatur procedure no longer exists, the judgment debtor needs to apply for refusal of recognition and enforcement on his or her own motion after the certificate, according to Article 53 of BIR, and the judgment have been served. Article 45 of BIR contains an exhaustive list of refusal grounds for non-enforcement. Since Articles 34, 35 and 36 of the Brussels I Regulation were included in Article 45 of BIR, and because the refusal grounds maintained the same function for recognition and enforcement, the CJEU case law on refusal grounds according to the previous Brussels I Regulation will continue to apply also for Article 45.[60] Here, we will consider important Slovenian case law regarding the grounds for refusal according to BIR.[61]

By far the most common ground of refusal was based on public order; however, the courts are very restrictive in their decisions regarding this matter. The Supreme Court stated that, according to the case law of the CJEU,[62] national courts have jurisdiction in cases where the defendant brings an action contesting the validity of the declaration of enforceability of a judgment given in default of appearance in the Member State of origin, which is accompanied by the certificate claiming that he or she has not been served with the document instituting the proceedings.[63] The court of the Member State in which enforcement is sought hearing the action then must take steps to verify that the information contained in that certificate is consistent with the evidence. In the case at hand, the judgment debtor claimed that the enforcement order issued in Germany was not delivered in Slovenian, but rather in the German language, which represents grounds for refusal of the declaration of enforceability on the basis that such recognition is contrary to Slovenian public order. However, the court held that the judgment debtor had not claimed that he or she had not been served with the enforcement order, but instead only that he or she had problems with understanding the German language. In such circumstances, according to the court, the judgment debtor could not prevail, at

60 See Gascon Inchausati, cited in Requejo Isidro 2017, p. 92. However, another author highlights that Brussels I Recast deals with the prior Brussels I Regulation case law in four different ways: 1. Some CJEU case law has simply been left untouched and unaffected by the new BIR (Cases: C-261/90 – *Reichert and Kockler v. Dresdner Bank*; parts of Van Uden C-391/95 – *Van Uden Maritime v. Kommanditgesellschaft in Firma Deco-Line and Others*; and C-144/86 – *Gubisch Maschinenfabrik v. Palumbo*); 2. Some case law has been adopted into the text of BIR in a modified way (Cases: C-125/79 – *Denilauler v. Couchet*; C-104/03 – *St. Paul Dairy*; and, in part, C-39/02 – *Mærsk Olie & Gas*; 145/86 – *Hoffmann v. Krieg*); 3. A new provision has been inserted in order to dispel doubts in the wake of the case C-281/02 – *Owusu*; 4. Some case law has been abandoned: Case C-116/02 – *Gasser*, and *Van Uden* (C-391/95 – *Van Uden Maritime v. Kommanditgesellschaft in Firma Deco-Line and Others*). See Wilke 2015, p. 128-142.

61 There are also a number of decisions of higher Slovenian courts in which the procedure for recognition has been confused with the procedure for declaration of enforceability; Betetto 2010, p. 108-109.

62 Case C-619/10 – *Trade Agency Ltd v. Seramico Investments Ltd*, 6 September 2012.

63 Decision of the Supreme Court of the Republic of Slovenia, Sklep Cpg 10/2015.

least as long as the notification of the conditions for exercising the right for a refusal of documents in German was in the Slovenian language.

In the assessment of the judgment debtor's arguments regarding public order, the court needs to determine the factual possibilities of the judgment debtor to obtain a timely notice in order to prepare a defence, so that his or her rights to a fair trial are not violated. After all, the judgment debtor must have been aware of the contents of the decision, which presupposes that it was served on him or her.[64]

However, in another case[65] the Slovenian Supreme Court held that there had been a violation of Slovenian public order in the situation where, according to the law of the other Member State, there was no mandatory obligation for the foreign judgment debtor to be notified concerning the proper method of complying with the legal remedy granted to the judgment creditor, whereby the remedy submitted incorrectly had not been taken into account by the competent court. The Italian court failed to consider the judgment debtor's objection,[66] despite the fact that the judgment debtor had lodged timely objections to the payment order, on the grounds that the objection was submitted in a fashion that failed to comport with Italian law. In this case, the judgment debtor had received the payment order (*decreto ingiuntivo*) of the Italian court without any legal instructions on the method of lodging objections (especially the right to be represented by a lawyer and that the legal response must be submitted solely through the court's delivery service and not directly to the competent court by the judgment debtor). The Supreme Court pointed out that the right to be heard is one of the fundamental constitutional rights, acknowledged by most of the EU Member States, and that this right therefore must be guaranteed to every party, and thus constitutes an integral part of international public order. The document which instituted the proceedings had to be in compliance with the second point of Article 34 of the Brussels I Regulation and must be served upon the defendant and contain sufficient information to enable the defendant to arrange for a proper defence.[67]

As previously pointed out, the adversarial principle was one of the common grounds invoked by judgment debtors in the stage of the exequatur. For example, an Austrian court delivered a default judgment, which was submitted to a Slovenian court for a declaration of enforceability. After the dismissal of the debtor's objection by the court of first instance in the appellate proceeding before the Supreme Court, the judgment debtor argued that the documents which instituted the proceedings had not been served to the judgment debtor's permanent address and that the certificate on the return of service was not signed by him in person. The Supreme Court decided that the appeal was unfounded for the following reasons. Namely, the court in the Member State addressed is not bound to

64 C-283/05, *ASML Netherlands BV v. Semiconductor Industry Services GmbH* [2006] ECR I-12041.

65 Decision of the Supreme Court of the Republic of Slovenia, Sklep CPG 2/2008, 5 October 2010.

66 There was no decision on the dismissal or rejection of the objection issued by the Italian court, and the judgment debtor was not informed of the result of the objection.

67 The same reasoning was delivered by the Supreme Court of the Republic of Slovenia in a similar case. Decision of the Supreme Court of the Republic of Slovenia, Sklep Cpg 6/2014.

the formal rules of service, but instead needs to establish whether the defendant was timely informed on the commencement of the proceedings and in such a way as to enable him to arrange for his defence. In making this assessment, the court must strike a balance between protecting the judgment debtor's right to present a proper defence, on the one hand, while, on the other hand, preventing the situation in which the debtor is simply acting in bad faith to avoid the proceeding. In the case where the defendant was familiar with the Austrian decision and had been afforded the opportunity to challenge the decision, the debtor could no longer bring forward the objection in the exequatur proceedings if the available remedy was not pursued against the judgment before the court in the Member State of origin.[68]

In analysing Slovenian court practice, the primary questions that courts are confronted with pertain to public policy[69] and the adversarial principle, especially the lack of correct service as a reason for vacating default judgments.

3.2. *Suspension of enforceability and limitation to protective measures as possible delays of the enforcement proceedings according to Brussels I Recast*

The enforceability of a foreign title in a Member State of origin is an essential prerequisite (Article 39 BIR) for its enforcement in the Member State of enforcement. While exequatur and the possibility of appealing the declaration of enforceability have been abolished, thereby promoting the goal of minimising delay, the judgment debtor nevertheless still has the right to apply for the refusal of enforcement according to the grounds provided in Article 45 of BIR. However, the initiation of the procedure on refusal of enforcement does not automatically stay the enforceability of the foreign judgment. Under the previous Brussels I Regulation there was an automatic protection of the judgment debtor provided by operation of law.[70] Article 44 of BIR, however, allows the judgment debtor to apply for measures for limitation (or making enforcement conditional) or a suspension of the enforcement of the judgment, which means that merely applying for refusal of enforcement is not sufficient grounds to trigger protection.

In the event of an application for refusal of enforcement, the court may, on the application of a person against whom enforcement is sought, limit the enforcement proceedings to protective measures; make enforcement conditional on the provision of such security as it shall determine; and/or suspend, either wholly or in part, the enforcement proceedings (Article 44 BIR). There is no guidance provided in BIR relating to the conditions on which the court addressed may suspend enforcement. Furthermore, the word 'may' denotes the discretionary nature of the court's power

68 Same also: Decision of the Supreme Court of the Republic of Slovenia, Sklep Cpg 11/2016.

69 Compared to the old system in Brussels I, BIR does not contribute to the problem of defining public policy, which means that the old case law on the basis of the Brussels Convention and Brussels I is still applicable; Kresteš 2016, p. 89.

70 According to the previous Brussels I Regulation, enforcement was suspended during the time specified for an appeal against the declaration of enforceability and until such appeal had been determined (Article 47(3) Brussels I).

to suspend enforcement of the judgment and Article 44 does not establish any hierarchy among the three remedies. BIR in Article 47(2) provides that, 'The procedure for refusal of enforcement shall, in so far as it is not covered by this Regulation, be governed by the law of the Member State addressed.' This means that the court would apply the law of the *lex fori*. This option would mean, in the case of an appeal, that the court addressed would apply national rules on suspension of enforceability. However, one possibility could be that an autonomous interpretation is needed and that, when asked for, the conditions are determined by the CJEU.

The autonomous test for the conditions of granting limitation or suspension should be based on the requirement that the judgment debtor make an adequate showing that there is a risk of suffering special harm if he is to pay immediately. This special harm could be seen as a situation in which the financial situation of the judgment debtor would be jeopardised.[71] Besides the conditions for granting limitation or suspension, the court addressed has the discretion to decide on the appropriate remedy.[72]

There was a recent amendment of the Slovenian enforcement law,[73] which provides for the same conditions for the suspension of the enforcement of a foreign judgment, much as in the case of domestic proceedings for granting limitation or suspension of enforcement. A foreign judgment should be treated as if it were issued in the Member State addressed and as a domestic enforcement title, which means that the court should evaluate the conditions set forth in national regulations. The judgment debtor will have to prove that he or she has lodged a legal remedy against enforcement of the foreign judgment and will have to show with probability that with the immediate enforcement he or she would suffer irreparable harm and that this harm is greater than the damage which could occur to the judgment creditor if the measure for suspension is granted (amended Article 71 ESCCA).[74] However, Slovenian enforcement law does not allow the judgment debtor to propose limitations to the protective measures, although the judgment creditor may do so. Article 44(1)(b) of BIR allows the court to make enforcement conditional on the basis of such security as it shall determine. However, the payment of the security, as foreseen in BIR, is not regulated as an individual measure by Slovenian enforcement law. In the event that national law is not adapted to BIR, the court may directly rely on the provisions of BIR.

If Slovenia is an enforcement state, the judgment debtor may file a proposal for suspension of the enforcement at the enforcement court and the suspension will

[71] Cuniberti & Rueda 2016, p. 861.

[72] The decision that the creditor should provide security is regarded as the most preferred decision since it is less intrusive than the other two remedies; Cuniberti & Rueda 2016, p. 863.

[73] Official Gazette RS, No. 11/18.

[74] The judgment debtor may propose a postponement of enforcement in this context, for example, if the judgment debtor filed an extraordinary remedy against the judgment, which serves as a basis for enforcement; or, if the judgment debtor filed an application to repeal a certificate of enforceability, etc. (Article 71 ESCCA).

be granted, as long as the proceedings on the refusal of enforcement are not completed (Article 74 ESCCA).

In comparison to the remedies provided by Article 44(1) of BIR, the 'competent authority in the Member State addressed shall, on the application of the person against whom enforcement is sought, suspend the enforcement proceedings where the enforceability of the judgment is suspended in the Member State of origin' (Article 44(2) BIR). This means that in the event that in the Member State of origin the enforceability is lacking, the judgment debtor has the right to propose a suspension of the enforcement in the Member State addressed (Article 44(2) BIR).

In Slovenia, the competent authority for enforcing the rights provided in Article 44 of BIR is the local court before which the enforcement proceedings were initiated. The identity of the competent authority for deciding on the suspension will depend on the enforcement system established in the Member State addressed. In Europe, there are three basic systems: administrative (Sweden and Finland); independent and liberal (e.g. France, the Netherlands, Belgium, Estonia, the Czech Republic and Lithuania); and, court-based (e.g. Austria and Slovenia). In France, the court (*greffier*) issuing an enforceable title is responsible for certifying the enforceability of the title by stamping the *formule exécutoire* on the judgment. The judgment creditor is then able to submit such a judgment to the judicial officer, who is responsible for all enforcement measures (except for enforcement proceedings relating to immovable property and attachment of earnings).

In Austria and Slovenia, where a court-based system[75] applies, preliminary steps must be taken before enforcement may begin. Similar to the system in France, in the system in Austria and Slovenia, the court deciding on the merits confirms the enforceability of the judgment by verifying that the time for an appeal has expired, that no remedy with suspensory effect is available, and that the time for voluntary fulfilment of the obligation contained in the judgment has expired. To initiate commencement of the enforcement proceedings, the judgment creditor needs to obtain an enforcement order issued by the enforcement court with which the court permits the enforcement. The enforcement court needs to investigate whether the formal (procedural – jurisdiction; capacity of the party; existence of an enforceable title; content of the application to obtain the order, etc.) and substantive prerequisites are met. If all prerequisites are found to be present, then the court allows the enforcement to be undertaken, and the enforcement proceedings enter the next phase of the procedure. The court thus issues a 'decision' or 'order' permitting the enforcement. The described phase, in other words, is a precursor to further enforcement action for carrying out the enforcement. In this initial phase the court can 'import title' where it concerns foreign judgments, which means that Member States utilising this kind of procedural approach as part of their national law[76] will not be as greatly affected by the abolition of exequatur as those lacking it.

75 However, the agents are competent for several enforcement measures, such as the seizure and sale of tangible movables, or eviction.

76 The Slovenian enforcement procedure is divided into two stages, namely, permitting enforcement and proceeding with the enforcement itself. The issuing of an order authorising enforcement does not yet constitute a direct enforcement activity. An enforcement court may, →

According to the German Code of Civil Procedure (§ 1116 ZPO (*Zivilprocessordnung* (German Code of Civil Procedure)), the judgment debtor is required to provide to the German court deciding on the suspension of enforcement the decision of the court of origin on the unenforceability or limitation of the enforceability of a foreign enforcement title. In comparison to the wording of Article 44 (2) of BIR, the German law added an option of limitation of enforceability. In Germany, the application for suspension or limitation of enforcement and the proposal for the enforcement to be continued, subject to the condition of providing security (Article 44(1) BIR), shall be decided through the issuance of an interim order.

Austrian legislators have not, as of yet, amended their national rules to adapt to the requirements of Article 44 of BIR. However, Article 44 of BIR may be implemented in Austrian law on the basis of the application of the provisions on suspension of enforcement (§ 42-45 EO *Exekutionsordnung* (Austrian Enforcement Code)).

Under Article 51 of BIR:

> The court to which an application for refusal of enforcement is submitted or the court which hears an appeal lodged under Article 49 or Article 50 may stay the proceedings if an ordinary appeal has been lodged against the judgment in the Member State of origin or if the time for such an appeal has not yet expired. In the latter case, the court may specify the time within which such an appeal is to be lodged.

This remedy enables the judgment debtor to apply for a stay of proceedings in the Member State addressed until the proceedings in the state of origin are concluded.

Courts, or the appropriate enforcement authority in the Member State addressed, may stay proceedings in the event that the foreign judgment to be enforced in that Member State has been challenged in the state of origin. However, the court, or the appropriate enforcement authority, has the discretionary power to decide on whether to grant the stay, and if it does, its duration. For the judgment debtor, the rule has a protective nature, defending him from further enforcement of the foreign judgment until the proceedings on the ordinary appeal in the Member State of origin are decided and until he can determine whether the judgment will gain *res judicata* effect. According to the case *Van Dalfsen c.s. v. Van Loon and Berendsen* (C-183/90),[77] the power to stay the enforcement proceedings is an exception to the principle that a judgment given in a Contracting State and enforceable in that State may be enforced in another Contracting State even if it has not yet become *res judicata*. This case also endorses the proposition that this exception should be strictly interpreted (points 29 and 30 of the judgment). The aim of this exceptional measure is to protect the party against whom enforcement is sought against any damage which might result from the enforcement of a judgment

as soon as the creditor submits a complete application for enforcement, issue a resolution authorising enforcement, which may not be served on those who must carry out enforcement until after service of the certificate on the debtor.

77 [1991] ECRI-4743.

which has not yet become *res judicata* and might be amended (point 29 of the judgment). According to the ruling of the Supreme Court of Slovenia,[78] the term 'any damage' means only damage which exceeds the inconveniences which normally exist in enforcement. Under BIR the foreign judgment could be recognised and enforced even though it is still rebuttable in the proceedings with legal remedies. However, the provisions relating to staying the proceedings enable the court to consider the possibility of amendment of the foreign judgment with remedies in the Member State of origin.[79]

The wording of the rule in Article 51 of BIR has been left the same as in both the previous Brussels I Regulation and the Brussels Convention, and it does not provide more precise answers concerning the grounds or conditions that the court should consider in exercising its discretionary[80] power. Further, it fails to define 'ordinary appeal'.

The factors that the court, in exercising its sound discretion, may take into consideration when deciding on whether to grant a stay of proceedings have already been explained by the CJEU in *Van Dalfsen*. In that case, the CJEU ruled that the substance of a foreign judgment may not, under any circumstances, be reviewed by the courts of the Member State in which enforcement is sought. This means that the arguments previously submitted to the court of the Member State of origin may not be taken into consideration by the court in the Member State in which enforcement is sought. The CJEU also ruled that the court deciding on the stay may not assess the probability of success of an ordinary appeal lodged or to be lodged in the state in which the judgment was given. Relying on the reasoning from the decision in Case 145/86 (*Hoffmann v. Krieg* [1988] ECR 645), the CJEU explained that arguments undisclosed to the foreign court at the time of its judgment, because the appellant had failed to advance them, should not be taken into account, and that a party who had not appealed was precluded at a later stage in the proceedings from relying on a ground which he or she could have pleaded in such an appeal.

As a result, according to the *Van Dalfsen* case, the principal consideration that should inform the ultimate decision on whether to grant a stay of the enforcement proceeding is whether the court expects that the foreign judgment in the Member State of origin will be repealed or amended. Only arguments related to the facts or events that occur subsequent to the pronouncement of the foreign judgment, and which the judgment debtor could not have previously submitted to the court of the Member State of origin,[81] can be taken into account. However, according to the critics,[82] the rule in *Van Dalfsen* is too harsh. According to some legal experts, the

78 Supreme Court decision, VSRS Sklep Cp 9/2016, 19 May 2016.

79 Supreme Court decision, Sklep Cpg 5/2009, 9 March 2010; ECLI:SI:VSRS:2010:CPG.5.2009.

80 The word 'may' in Article 51 indicates that the court has discretionary authority to decide whether the enforcement proceedings should be stayed.

81 The breach of the adversarial principle will not constitute a sufficient ground for the refusal of recognition of a foreign judgment or for a declaration of its enforceability if the defendant in the Member State of origin failed to advance these arguments in support of a legal remedy claiming that breach; Supreme Court decision, VSRS Sklep Cpg 11/2016, 30 August 2016.

82 Magnus & Mankowski 2016, p. 962.

court of enforcement, when considering whether to issue a stay, should endeavour to predict the ultimate outcome of the proceedings in the Member State of origin, including whether there is a likelihood for the foreign court to annul or amend the foreign judgment. This assessment of the outcome of appellate proceedings in the Member State of origin will only be undertaken as a means of explaining the reasoning behind the exercise of its discretionary powers and not to review the proceedings in the Member State of origin. According to the advocates of this position, the court in the Member State addressed should allow as admissible all of the arguments that would be admissible before the foreign court.

As previously discussed, Article 51 of the Recast leaves the words 'ordinary appeal' undefined. However, the concept of 'ordinary appeal' was defined by the CJEU (C-43/77, 22. 11. 1977) in *Industrial Diamond Supplies v. Luigi Riva*. According to this decision, which through extrapolative reasoning we might use to supply a definition for the term 'ordinary appeal' used in Article 51 of the Recast, the rationale of the provision is 'a sufficiently broad interpretation of the concept of "ordinary appeal" to enable the court to stay the proceedings whenever reasonable doubt arises with regard to the fate of the decision in the State in which it was given.' The concept of ordinary appeal needs an autonomous definition, which means that it is not dependent on the characterisation of the appeal in its legal order of origin. The term 'ordinary appeal' should be interpreted within the context of BIR as a whole and regardless of the classification of remedies by any given national system in which the judgment was rendered.[83] If the meaning of 'ordinary appeal', as used in Article 51 of BIR, is to be defined by looking to the individual national legal system, whether that be (in a particular case) the legal system of the Member State of origin or that of the Member State in which enforcement is sought, this case-by-case (*ad hoc*) approach would certainly lead to uncertainty and unpredictability, thereby undermining the very purpose of BIR. National systems, as we know, take very different approaches towards the systematisation of appeals, with some acknowledging a distinction between ordinary and extraordinary appeals based on the law, while in others, classifications are made based on the works of leading authors, while in yet other states such distinctions are completely unknown. Even in the Member States where the distinction between ordinary and extraordinary appeals is acknowledged, this distinction gives rise to various classifications.[84]

The Slovenian system provides two instances of civil litigation and typically acknowledges the distinction between ordinary and extraordinary remedies. An ordinary remedy is called an appeal (*pritožba*) and is meant to challenge a non-*res judicata* judgment. Judgments with *res judicata* effect, on the other hand, can only be challenged by extraordinary remedies (revision).

The Austrian judicial system, on the other hand, recognises three instances, which means that a court decision could – theoretically – be revised twice.[85] The first instance judgment may be challenged by an appeal, while the legal remedy sought

83 *Industrial Diamond Supplies*, para 21.
84 *Ibid.*, paras 23, 24.
85 Nunner-Krautgasser & Anzenberger 2018.

to challenge a second instance judgment is called revision. Any other decision, order or disposal is called a resolution (§ 425 para 1 ZPO).[86]

Because of the differences in the national systems, we must look to BIR itself to try to define the term 'ordinary appeal'. The term 'ordinary appeal' must be interpreted within the context of BIR, regardless of the classification of appeals by the national law of the state in which the judgment is given. A sufficiently broad interpretation of the concept of 'ordinary appeal' means that a court may stay the proceedings whenever a reasonable doubt arises with regard to the fate of the decision in the state in which it was given.[87]

Besides the criteria of reasonable doubt with regard to the fate of the appellate proceedings in the Member State of origin, the CJEU has established further requirements:

- that the appeal 'may lead to the annulment or amendment of the judgment in question' (point 34), and
- 'forms part of the normal course of an action and which, as such, constitutes a procedural development which any party must reasonably expect' (point 37), and
- is 'bound by the law to a specific period of time which starts to run by virtue of the actual decision whose enforcement is sought' (point 38).

According to the Slovenian enforcement law, the judgment debtor may propose a postponement of the enforcement in this context, for example: if the judgment debtor filed an extraordinary remedy against the judgment, which serves as a basis for enforcement; or, if the judgment debtor filed an application to repeal a certificate of enforceability (Article 71 ESCCA). If the enforceable title is repealed, abolished, amended or declared void, or the certificate of enforceability is repealed, the court shall cease enforcement *ex officio* (Article 76 ESCCA).

4. Conclusion

The principle of national procedural autonomy provides that if EU law does not have its own procedural rules, national procedural law is applicable.[88] BIR allows the Members States to decide how they will adopt procedures for requests for refusal of enforcement. According to the relevant Recitals two options are possible. Either the Member States will allow the submission of the application within the enforcement proceedings or they will implement a separate, independent procedure of a declaratory nature with the same courts competent under the previous Brussels I Regulation for the exequatur procedure.

The previous Brussels I Regulation provided clear rules on the division between the exequatur and enforcement stages, meaning that no material objections

86 *Ibid.*

87 Case 43-77, *Industrial Diamond Supplies v. Luigi Riva*, ECLI:EU:C:1977:188.

88 Case 33/76, *Rewe*, [1976] ECR 1989.

arising after the closing of the hearing in the Member State of origin could be invoked in the exequatur stage.[89] The new system was adopted after the well-known case *Prism Invest*.[90] In this case, the CJEU decided that compliance with a judicial decision does not deprive that decision of its enforceable nature, or lead to its being given, at the time of its enforcement in another Member State, legal effects it would not have in the Member State of origin.

> Such a ground may, by contrast, be brought before the court or tribunal responsible for enforcement in the Member State in which enforcement is sought. In accordance with settled case-law, once that judgment is incorporated into the legal order of the Member State in which enforcement is sought, national legislation of that Member State relating to enforcement applies in the same way as to judgments delivered by national courts.[91]

In this context, BIR in para 2 of Article 41 provides for the possibility of invoking additional refusal grounds according to the national law of the Member State addressed if those additional grounds are compatible with the grounds set forth in Article 45 of BIR.

Until now, the Slovenian legislators have done very little to adopt national law.[92] However, the amendment of enforcement law ESCCA-L foresees some adaptations for the implementation of BIR. Nevertheless, there are some important procedural questions which Slovenian legislators will leave open, for example: the time period within which an application for refusal of enforcement may be made; and, the proceedings and the competent court for deciding on the adaptation of the unknown measures under Article 54 of BIR.

The Recast has added many provisions that favour the judgment debtor. For instance, BIR now has a number of provisions that enable the judgment debtor to delay the enforcement stage. Furthermore, and significantly, eliminating the surprise effect that the judgment creditor previously enjoyed severely prejudices the right of the judgment creditor and undermines or diminishes the value of the creditor's judgment (even making it worthless in some cases) since the judgment debtor now is in a better position to be able to hide assets, thereby making it more difficult (or sometimes even impossible) for the judgment creditor to satisfy his or her judgment. In order to inform the person against whom enforcement is sought of the enforcement of a judgment given in another Member State, the certificate established under BIR, if necessary accompanied by the judgment, should be served on that person in reasonable time before the first enforcement measure (Recital 32 BIR). The service of the certificate is the first obligatory stage, to be executed prior to any enforcement measure by the competent enforcing body (court or agent). The next stage consists of the right of the judgment debtor to request a translation of the foreign judgment if he or she is not domiciled in the Member State of origin. The main difference between the old system and the Recast is that now the control of the

89 *Eric Coursier v. Fortis Bank and Martine Coursier, née Bellami*, Case C 267/97, EU:C:1999:213.

90 *Prism Investments BV v. Jaap Anne van der Meer*, Case C-139/10, ECLI:EU:C:2011:653.

91 Nos. 39 and 40 in Case C-139/10.

92 The Slovenian legislator has failed to adopt the provisions under Brussels I.

foreign judgment before enforcement is executed is shifted to the judgment debtor with the option to oppose enforcement on the basis of initiating the procedure for refusal of enforcement on the refusal grounds provided for under Article 45 of the Recast.

BIR has come under heavy criticism owing to the fact that it has failed to eliminate the possibility that the Member States can control the 'regularity of the foreign decisions' in comparison with other European instruments without the exequatur proceedings.[93] Furthermore, some scholars advocate the use of a European enforcement order.[94] European enforcement orders may be issued only after a creditor obtains a judgment against the debtor and the court, upon application, certifies the judgment as a European enforcement order. However, the European enforcement order may only be issued if the claims are uncontested. The enforcement is then executed under the enforcement rules of the Member State addressed. The only reason that enforcement in another Member State may be refused is if it is irreconcilable with another judgment in the other Member State between the same parties. However, this ground may be invoked with remedies in the enforcement procedure only if the irreconcilability was not and could not have been raised as an objection in the court proceedings in the Member State of origin (Article 21 European Enforcement Order). In Slovenia, the court is obliged to consider the existence of *res judicata* on its own motion throughout the procedure.[95]

The trend of abolishing exequatur was applied also to the new BIR, thereby providing the basis for the direct enforceability of foreign decisions. While abolishing exequatur, and with many issues still left to national laws, the Recast, regrettably in this author's view, does not provide unified solutions for Member States as to the different enforcement procedures and remedies throughout the EU.[96] For example, the Recast fails to provide any EU-wide remedies against decisions on enforcement, since such remedies are covered only by national procedural law. These omissions are regrettable, because through unartful drafting, and lack of clarity and definition, BIR has unnecessarily caused uncertainty and confusion, which the law should try to avoid, not to create. Irrespective of the level of ambition, it would be helpful if there were minimum harmonisation[97] of the enforcement procedures so that national and international grounds for non-enforcement could be considered in the same set of proceedings.

93 Hess, cited in Requejo Isidro 2017, p. 93.
94 *Ibid.*
95 Rijavec 2007, št. 5, str. 791-814.
96 Sladič 2013, p. 354.
97 The European Parliament has already recognised the need for more harmonisation of the rules of national civil procedure in its working document on establishing common minimum standards for civil procedure in the European Union – the legal basis (Committee on Legal Affairs, 21 December 2015, PE572.853v01-00).

References

Andersson 2005
Andersson, T., 'Harmonization and Mutual Recognition: How to Handle Mutual Distrust', in: M. Andenas, B. Hess & P. Oberhammer (eds.), *Enforcement Agency Practice in Europe,* London: British Institute of International and Comparative Law, 2005, p. 245-251.

Anzenberger & Ivanc 2017
Anzenberger, P. & Ivanc, T., 'Provisional Account Preservation Measures in European Civil Procedure Law - A Comparison between Brussels Ia and the Regulation on the European Account Preservation Order from an Austrian and a Slovenian Perspective', *Austrian Law Journal,* 2017, p. 57-70.

Betetto 2010
Betetto, N., 'Implementation of European Civil Procedural Regulations in the Case Law of Slovenian Courts', in: C.H. Van Rhee & A. Uzelac (eds.), *Enforcement and Enforceability: Tradition and Reform,* Antwerp/Oxford/Portland: Intersentia, 2010, p. 103-112.

Bošković Pillet 2017
Bošković Pillet, O., *National Report-France,* 2017, available at: <https://www.pf.um.si/site/assets/files/3539/national_report_france.pdf>.

Cuniberti & Rueda 2016
Cuniberti, G. & Rueda, I., 'Article 44, Article 49 and Article 50', in: U. Magnus & P. Mankowski (eds.), *ECPIL European Commentaries on Private International Law, Commentary* (Vol. 1, Brussels Ibis Regulation), Cologne: Verlag Dr Otto Schmidt, 2016, p. 861-863, 958-959.

Dickinson 2009
Dickinson, A., 'Brussels I Review - The Abolition of Exequatur?', *Conflict of Laws.Net,* 2009, available at: <http://conflictoflaws.net/2009/brussels-i-review-the-abolition-of-exequatur/>.

Dickinson 2010
Dickinson, A., 'The Revision of the Brussels I Regulation: Surveying the Proposed Brussels Ibis Regulation - Solid Foundations but Renovation Needed', *Yearbook of Private Int'l Law,* 2010, p. 247-309.

Fernhout 2018
Fernhout, F., *National Report The Netherlands*, 2018, available at: <https://pf.um.si/site/assets/files/3539/national_report_the_netherlands.pdf>.

Giussani 2018
Giussani, A., *National Report Italy*, 2018, available at: <https://pf.um.si/site/assets/files/3539/national_report_italy.pdf>.

Hess & Pfeiffer 2011
Hess, B. & Pfeiffer, T., *Study on the Interpretation of the Public Policy Exception as referred to in EU Instruments of Private International and Procedural Law*, 2011, available at: <http://www.europarl.europa.eu/thinktank/en/document.html?reference=-IPOL-JURI_ET%282011%29453189>.

Hess, Bergström & Storskrubb 2016
Hess, B., Bergström, M. & Storskrubb, E. (eds.), *EU Civil Justice: Current Issues and Future Outlook, Swedish Studies in European Law*, Vol. 7, Oxford: Hart Publishing, 2016.

Je Timmer 2013
Je Timmer, L., 'Abolition of *Exequatur* under the Brussels I Regulation, ILL Conceived and Premature?', *Journal of Private International Law*, 2013, p. 129-147.

Keresteš 2016
Keresteš, T., 'Public Policy in Brussels Regulation I: Yesterday, Today and Tomorrow', *LeXonomica*, 2016, Vol. 8(2), p. 77-91.

Kramberger Škerl 2011
Kramberger Škerl, J., 'European Public Policy (with an emphasis on the *Exequatur* proceedings)', *Journal of Private International Law*, 2011, Vol. 7(3), p. 461-490.

Kramberger Škerl 2016
Kramberger Škerl, J., 'Certain open Issues Regarding the Refusal of Enforcement under the Brussels I Regulation in Slovenia', in: V. Rijavec (ed.), *24th Conference Corporate Entities at the Market and European Dimensions (May 19th-21st 2016, Portorož, Slovenia, Conference Proceedings)*, Maribor: University of Maribor Press, 2016, p. 131-144.

Kramer *et al.* 2015
Kramer, A. *et al.*, *The Brussels I Regulation Recast*, Oxford: Oxford University Press, 2015.

Magnus & Mankowski 2016
Magnus, U. & Mankowski, P. (eds.), *ECPIL European Commentaries on Private International Law, Commentary* (Vol. 1, Brussels Ibis Regulation), Cologne: Verlag Dr Otto Schmidt, 2016.

Nunner-Krautgasser & Anzenberger 2018
Nunner-Krautgasser, B. & Anzenberger, P., *National Report Austria*, 2018, available at: <http://www.pf.um.si/site/assets/files/3539/national_report_austria.pdf>.

Oberhammer 2010
Oberhammer, P., 'The Abolition of Exequatur', *IPRax*, 2010, Vol. 30(3), p. 197-203.

Pontier & Burg 2004
Pontier, J.A. & Burg, J.H.M., *E.U. Principles on Jurisdiction and Recognition and Enforcement of Judgments in Civil and Commercial Matters, According to the Case Law of the European Court of Justice*, The Hague: TMC Asser Press, 2004.

Requejo Isidro 2017
Requejo Isidro, M., 'The Enforcement of Monetary Final Judgments under the Brussels Ibis Regulation (A Critical Assessment)', in: V. Lazić & S. Stuij (eds.), *Brussels Ibis Regulation, Changes and Challenges of the Renewed Procedural Scheme*, The Hague: T.M.C. Asser Press, Springer, 2017, p. 71-95.

Rijavec 2003
Rijavec, V., *Civilno izvršilno pravo*, Ljubljana: GV založba, 2003.

Rijavec 2007
Rijavec, V., 'Postopek potrditve Evropskega izvršilnega naslova', *Podjetje in delo*, 2007, Vol. 33(5), p. 791-814.

Rijavec 2014
Rijavec, V., 'Introductory chapter', in: V. Rijavec, T. Keresteš & T. Ivanc (eds.), *Simplification of debt collection in the EU*, Alphen aan den Rijn: Kluwer Law International BV, 2014, p. 5-11.

Sladič 2013
Sladič, J., 'The Remedies and Recourses in European Civil Procedure after the Intended Abolition of the *Exequatur*', *Zeitschrift für Europarechtliche Studien*, 2013, Vol. 3, p. 329-358.

Valdhans & Kyselovská,
Valdhans, J. & Kyselovská, T., *National Report Czech Republic*, 2018, available at: <https://pf.um.si/site/assets/files/3539/national_report_czech_republic.pdf>.

Verkerk 2010
Verkerk, R., 'Procedural Fairness and Compliance', in: C.H. Van Rhee & A. Uzelac (eds.), *Enforcement and Enforceability – Tradition and Reform*, Antwerp/Oxford/Portland: Intersentia, 2010, p. 253-267.

Von Hein 2013
Von Hein, J., 'Die Neufassung der Europäischen Gerichtsstandsund Vollstreckungsverordnung (EuGVVO)', *RIW*, 2013, p. 97-111.

Weller 2015
Weller, M., 'Mutual Trust: In Search of the Future of European Union Private International Law', *Journal of Private International Law*, 2015, Vol. 11(1), p. 64-102.

Wilke 2015
Wilke, F.M., 'The Impact of the Brussels I Recast on Important "Brussels" Case Law', *Journal of Private International Law*, 2015, Vol. 11(1), p. 128-142.

V. Rijavec
T. Keresteš

INTERNATIONAL MUTUAL LEGAL ASSISTANCE IN CIVIL MATTERS FROM A SLOVENIAN PERSPECTIVE

1. Concept

International legal assistance is cooperation between courts (*auxilium iuris*), where official acts for the purposes of civil litigation are carried out in the territory of a court of another state. In addition to courts acting in matters within their jurisdiction, other state bodies also play a role in international legal assistance. In the broadest sense, international legal assistance is any legal assistance that states offer between one another through their judiciary and other bodies in various procedures: civil, criminal and administrative. In matters governed by administrative law, legal assistance is regulated separately, even if the outcome serves judicial proceedings (e.g. sending documents regarding personal status: birth, marriage, death, etc.).[1]

Even though the above-mentioned definition fits the purpose of this contribution, certain terminological issues must be addressed for reasons of caution. International legal assistance is often coupled with the terms of (mutual) 'judicial assistance' and 'judicial cooperation'. While legal assistance is, in the majority of cases, more or less synonymous[2] with judicial assistance, the same is doubtful to be true of judicial cooperation. The latter is generally a broader term,[3] encompassing legal (judicial) assistance and also covering the creation of international law, promoting the compatibility of the rules applicable in the Member States.[4] Legal

1 Kitić 2017, p. 299-304; see also Bordaš, Kneževič & Varadi 2005, p. 516-520.

2 Providing information about laws and judicial systems (foreign law) at the request of another state may fall outside the scope of the term judicial assistance, however it still may be applicable to the term 'legal assistance'.

3 Joks 1999, p. 80.

4 In this regard, see also the definition provided by the Max Planck online Encyclopaedia of Public International Law which provides that: 'Mutual legal assistance in civil and commercial matters belongs to the field of international [cooperation]. The overall purpose of this co-operation is to establish a functional legal network which ensures effective access to administration of justice and legal assistance in international cases...', available at: →

assistance must also be distinguished from the notion of 'legal aid', which covers legal assistance to individuals who may not have access to justice due to their socio-economic status.[5]

Questions of state sovereignty restrict the courts to exercising acts of authority only in the territory of their own country. For official acts in another country, cooperation with the authorities of that country is indispensable. Therefore, the courts are obliged to initiate international legal assistance in order to guarantee a rational and effective procedure.[6] This is because private interests that lead to civil proceedings are not tied to a single country; on the contrary, in today's world they are increasingly transnational, but national borders may hinder them. For this reason, the law is providing new paths for better cross-border cooperation between competent authorities.

In contrast to cases involving mere conflicts of laws and conflicts of jurisdiction, in matters of judicial assistance a country must perform an act which is not needed for performing its own national tasks. Only certain theories advanced in private international law, such as comity, universalist theories and reciprocity, can explain international judicial assistance. Other theories such as *res judicata* and vested rights theory are applicable only to the enforcement of foreign judgments but not to service of documents or the taking of evidence.[7] International treaties can provide a more tangible legal ground, creating an 'obligation' for the country in the field of (public) international law (*pacta sunt servanda*), especially where compulsory measures are required (e.g. compulsory service to an unwilling addressee).

International legal assistance may be considered a necessity, in contrast to domestic cases of legal assistance which presents itself more as a prudency (appropriate measure). In an international setting, it is necessary to request legal assistance for the simple reason that domestic courts cannot undertake certain measures abroad. However, domestic cases of legal assistance among sister courts are usually grounded on the requirements stemming from the principle of procedural economy ((cost) efficiency).[8]

The official act for the introduction of legal assistance is called a request (*la demande, der Antrag*).

2. Subject and scope of international legal assistance

The international legal assistance framework includes:

- service of documents relating to court proceedings to parties, witnesses and other persons from the state of origin, to addressees in another state;

<http://opil.ouplaw.com/abstract/10.1093/law:epil/9780199231690/law-9780199231690-e965?rskey=SRrnZY&result=3&prd=EPIL>, last accessed June 2019.

5 Salma 2013, p. 195.

6 Schack 1996, p. 68.

7 Joks 1999, p. 81.

8 Salma 2013, p. 195.

- assistance in obtaining evidence in the requested state, such as hearing parties, witnesses or experts, examination, transferring objects, providing an inventory of assets and obtaining various official and informal data;
- assistance in establishing foreign substantive law, including the validity of the law and the effects of case-law;
- recognition and enforcement of foreign judicial decisions, which is legal assistance in the widest sense. It creates a special field of international procedural law, governed in Slovenia by EU regulations and a number of international legal acts and the Private International Law and Procedure Act (hereinafter PILPA).[9]

Legal assistance is merely an official act that the requested court is supposed to perform. The request is rejected if the requested action is inadmissible, but it cannot be rejected merely because the requested action would be meaningless. The requesting court decides whether the action makes sense, not the requested court. The requested court is not obliged to examine the whole file in order to ascertain what actions need to be taken or how they should be performed. Therefore, the request must be sufficiently detailed. Among other things, it should include a description of the background of the case with specific explanations as to the circumstances that need to be taken into consideration when obtaining the requested evidence. When the request is made, the requested court is autonomous and is not subject to the control of the court that provided the request. At the request of a party, the requested judge may also obtain other evidence if the judge thinks that this is practical and if the party's new allegations of facts and evidence are not late through his own fault, or the new proposal for evidence would not lead to a delay in the procedure; for example, Article 218 of the Slovenian Civil Procedure Act (hereinafter CPA).[10] At the hearing, the requested judge follows the substantive law and procedural guidance principle to clarify the requested matters.

3. Legal bases of international legal assistance

3.1. *General*

There are no uniform rules of international public law in relation to the existence of a duty of cooperation between sovereign states. Fortunately, at present legal assistance is the subject of a number of international legal instruments. In particular, among the countries that are bound by significant economic cooperation, international legal assistance is regulated by bilateral or multilateral acts.

9 *Zakon o mednarodnem zasebnem pravu*, Official Gazette of the RS, No. 56/99.

10 *Zakon o pravdnem postopku*, Official Gazette of the RS, No. 26/99.

3.2. *EU law*

Judicial cooperation between EU Member States is subject to several regulations. This will be discussed below.

The EU provides support and information to authorities dealing with cross-border cases through a specific network – the European Judicial Network (EJN). The Network brings together the national authorities responsible for assisting local courts; it was established to facilitate judicial and legal cooperation between Member States. EJN-civil was established by Council Decision 2001/470/EC of 28 May 2001. All Member States except Denmark participate in EJN-civil.[11]

3.3. *International legal acts*

In the field of international legal assistance in civil matters, countries are usually bound by a number of international conventions. After independence, Slovenia adopted the principle of universal succession in respect of international treaties and agreements concluded by the Socialist Federal Republic of Yugoslavia (SFRY) as well as a number of the treaties that have been ratified since 1991. Among the multilateral acts, the so-called Hague Conventions on Legal Assistance are the most important. These include the Hague Conventions on: Civil Procedure, dated 1 March 1954; Service Abroad of Judicial and Extrajudicial Documents in Civil and Commercial Matters, dated 15 November 1965; Taking of Evidence Abroad in Civil or Commercial Matters, dated 18 March 1970; Abolishing the Requirement of Legalisation for Foreign Public Documents, dated 5 October 1961; and International Access to Justice, dated 25 October 1980. They apply only to civil and commercial matters, and the need for the autonomous interpretation of this concept under the Hague Conventions has been stressed. In particular, the common acquis concerns civil matters, not penal or fiscal matters. Consequently, the border areas of conventions between civil and public law matters, such as bankruptcy, labour law and insurance matters, are dominated by their civil law character, while tax matters concern administrative law. Nevertheless, one can use the Hague Conventions by mutual consent with the other party for a purely public law issue as well.[12]

3.4. *Legal assistance not based on international treaties or EU rules*

Slovenian courts also offer legal assistance to foreign courts outside of the obligations imposed by international treaties or EU regulations. Although there is no public duty to do so, courts provide legal assistance on the grounds of international comity (*courtoisie internationale*). The requested state (*état requis*), on the basis of a request, offers legal assistance to the requesting state (*état requérant*) in the expectation that it will also receive legal assistance if necessary. Within the

11 See <https://e-justice.europa.eu/content_about_the_network-431-en.do>, last accessed 4 January 2019.

12 Walter & Domej 2012, p. 369.

framework of the expectation of reciprocity, which is the basis for international comity, the requirements for effective reciprocity are not a matter of strict law.

One state cannot force cooperation on another state. Any default is only to the detriment of the parties.[13] Therefore, if there is no binding legal basis for the act to be performed, reciprocity is required for legal assistance (first paragraph of Article 175 CPA), which may be factual or formal. The existence of reciprocity is presumed in the absence of evidence to the contrary. Where questions on the existence of reciprocity arise, the Ministry of Justice will provide a 'clarification', which is not a formal decision.

Many countries regulate all areas of international legal assistance in one special act. In Slovenia, regulation of the provision of international legal assistance is found within different acts. General matters of procedure are regulated in the CPA (Articles 175-178) and the procedure for recognition and enforcement of foreign judgments in PILPA. Both are further linked to certain administrative rules. However, the domestic provisions are of subsidiary significance in comparison to the existing EU rules or the rules of binding international legal acts.

4. Jurisdiction to carry out international legal assistance

Whatever the source of the applicable rules on international legal assistance, the case is ultimately linked to a national legal system. For example, national rules regulate subject matter jurisdiction. The Slovenian CPA determines that the district courts have jurisdiction in matters of international legal assistance, including deciding on the recognition of foreign court decisions (Article 32(2) CPA). In cases of legal assistance, a single judge decides.

Territorial jurisdiction to execute the request is conferred on the court in the area in which the requested action is to be carried out. A dispute over jurisdiction between requested courts is resolved by a directly higher court. By analogy, the directly higher court also resolves any disputes between the requesting court and the requested court related to exercising legal assistance. If the request is rejected, a supervisory complaint to the president of the court is possible. The procedural acts carried out by the requested court are judicial acts, not acts of the administrative authorities.[14] The German legal order takes the opposite position, according to which, for example, the service of foreign documents represents an administrative act, and the same applies to a decision on whether legal assistance is allowed or not.[15]

However, in Slovenia, the Ministry of Justice has a significant supportive role in matters of judicial administration regarding international legal assistance, i.e. Article 74 of the Courts Act (hereinafter CA)[16] and Article 37 of the State Administration Act.[17] In such cases, the Ministry of Justice and the courts cooperate

13 Geimer 2001, p. 1056.
14 Rijavec 2006, p. 101.
15 Geimer 2001, p. 1058.
16 *Zakon o sodiščih*, Official Gazette of the RS, No. 19/94.
17 *Zakon o državni upravi*, Official Gazette of the RS, No. 113/05.

through the presidents of the courts. Collaboration can also be established directly with a judge (Article 76 CA).

The Slovenian judicial authorities (in particular the courts) communicate with foreign bodies, and vice versa, through the Department for International Legal Assistance of the Ministry of Justice. The autonomous tasks of this department include confirmation of the authenticity of the signatures of judges and court interpreters in the process of authentication of public documents for use abroad, in accordance with the Verification of Documents in International Transport Act[18] and the Hague Convention Abolishing the Requirement of Legalisation for Foreign Public Documents of 5 October 1961.[19]

5. The format and content of the requests

The request for international legal assistance must always follow the prescribed content and format and meet the language requirements. The Slovenian CPA contains no specific provision regarding the form of the request. Conventions, as a rule, require that the request be in writing. The Slovenian courts, when drawing up requests, must take into account the provisions of the Rules of Court.[20] The accompanying letter sent by the court, together with the request to the Ministry of Justice, must include the following information: the kind of writing, basic data concerning the parties and the address of the recipient. In relation to service, the court sends a letter to the Ministry of Justice with all of the above-mentioned information, but it is not necessary to write a request for service to a foreign authority, unless a special method of service is required.

The content of the requests may be specifically determined by EU regulations. Regulation 1393/2007[21] and Regulation 1206/2001[22] introduce special forms. In general, we can conclude that the scope of legal assistance must be reflected in each request. As a rule, it must include information on the subject matter of the dispute, and information about the requesting court, the parties and their representatives. The request shall indicate the acts that should be undertaken by the requested court and the manner in which they should be performed. For example, it is necessary to indicate who should be served by the court, who should be heard as a witness and the questions that should be asked.

In the case of requests for legal assistance, care must be taken to ensure that all documents, including translations, are adequately prepared for their use abroad. In the case of Slovenian documents, the Act on the Certification of Documents in

18 *Zakon o overitvi listin v mednarodnem prometu*, Official Gazette of the RS, No. 9/17.

19 Official Gazette of the FPRY, No. 10/62-Appendix.

20 *Sodni red*, Official Gazette of the RS, No. 87/16.

21 Regulation (EC) No. 1393/2007 of the European Parliament and of the Council of 13 November 2007 on the service in the Member States of judicial and extrajudicial documents in civil or commercial matters (service of documents), and repealing Council Regulation (EC) No. 1348/2000.

22 Council Regulation (EC) No. 1206/2001 of 28 May 2001 on cooperation between the courts of the Member States in the taking of evidence in civil or commercial matters.

International Transactions or the Hague Convention Abolishing the Requirement of Legalisation for Foreign Public Documents of 5 October 1961, or the provisions of any bilateral acts on this issue, should be taken into account.

6. Language restrictions

Language differences can significantly hinder any stage of the process. Especially from the point of view of the participants in the procedure, language is often the main obstacle, causing delays in the procedure, leading to higher costs, lack of trust and, consequently, less effective legal protection. Language barriers cannot be easily removed, but international private law recognises certain simplifications. The treaties on international legal assistance do not all deal with the question of the language that should be used in the documents to be sent abroad, but bilateral agreements often summarise the solution contained in the Hague Convention on Civil Procedure of 1954, and some of them specifically allow for service in the applicant's language if the addressee is ready to accept the shipment. In such a case, the court shall effect service only if the addressee wishes to accept the document, as the addressee has the right to refuse to accept the document without translation even if the language of the document is understood. It is therefore appropriate to enclose a translation in sensitive cases.[23] The Hague Convention of 1970 also allows the use of English and French in the taking of evidence. EU Regulation 1206/2001 introduces standardised forms and the possibility for countries to indicate, in addition to their language, an additional language for mutual communication. But some Member States did not provide for the use of additional languages. This is a step backwards compared to the Hague Convention of 1970, which requires Member States to at least receive applications in English and French.

Regulation 1393/2007 provides that the document to be served must be accompanied by a pre-printed form which must be completed in the language of the place where service is to be effected or in another language agreed by the Member State concerned (Article 4(3) Regulation 1393/2012). This ensures the correctness of service. The addressee may refuse to accept the document if it is not in one of the foreseen languages (Article 5 Regulation 1393/2012).[24] Regarding this rule, a Slovenian court decided not to prescribe mandatory translation of the document to be served. However, the rule defines the right of the addressee to refuse service of the document - either at the time of service or by returning the document to the receiving agency within one week - if it is not in one of the following languages or is not accompanied by a translation into one of the following languages: (*a*) the

23 Badovinac Bjelič 1994, p. 91.

24 'The question whether or not a person understands a foreign language ultimately depends on his own judgment.' Opinion of Advocate General Trstenjak in Case C-14/07, *Ingenieurbüro Weiss* [2008]. The literature stresses that it is not only difficult to prove that the defendant definitely has certain language skills, but plaintiffs and courts are also often not able to test these skills before the service of documents instituting the proceedings takes place. It could be argued that objective criteria are required that might indicate or even give a presumption of certain language skills. Stadler 2013, p. 157.

language understood by the addressee; or (*b*) the official language of the requested Member State or, where there are several official languages in that Member State, the official language or one of the official languages of the place where the service is to be effected.[25]

In Slovenia, the CPA, in Article 177, stipulates that the request and the annexes must be drawn up in the Slovenian language or a certified translation in the Slovenian language must be attached. If the condition is not fulfilled, the court does not accept the application. Such an approach, which was already present in the CPA in 1977, does not explain what the court should do if it does not accept the application. Even the doctrine is in discord on this issue. On the one hand it is argued that the request should be rejected, while on the other hand it is argued that the applicant should be required to supplement the request. The second position is more appropriate in terms of good and effective cooperation between countries in legal transactions, which is in the common interest of all countries.[26]

Under Article 178 of the CPA a Slovenian court that makes a request for legal assistance abroad is also ordered to take into account the language of that country. It is understood, however, that the CPA cannot determine the consequences of non-compliance with this requirement, because that is a matter for the foreign legal order.

7. Execution of the request

As to the legal assistance procedure itself, the national law of the requested court shall apply. In Slovenia, the CPA rules are linked to administrative rules. According to the Courts Act, certain aspects of international legal assistance fall within the competence of the judicial administration (Article 74 CA). Specific legal assistance is provided to the court that is making the decisions.

It is necessary to distinguish between refusal of the request and inability to act. If the request is rejected, the same request cannot be lodged again.[27] On the other hand, a court is unable to act if the necessary information does not appear in the request. In such a case, the requested court shall return the request to the applicant and indicate the defects. Also, if service within one month of receipt of notification was not possible, the receiving authority shall immediately notify the transmitting agency by means of a certificate on a standard form.

Slovenian law also allows the court to carry out the requested act by applying the rules of a foreign court if there is no contradiction with public policy. For example, domestic public policy conflicts with a request from a foreign court to interfere with the physical integrity of a party (e.g. drawing a blood sample) to identify paternity using coercive means. Although there is a public duty or obligation based on reciprocity to provide legal assistance, the courts are entitled to refuse a requested act that contravenes Slovenian public policy.

25 Judgment of the Ljubljana Court of Appeals No. II Cpg 1251/2016 of 17 November 2016.
26 Vuković 1982, p. 97.
27 Rijavec 2006, p. 107.

Public policy (*ordre public*) or the reservation of public policy has evolved as an institution of private international law. In the broader sense, public policy serves as a safeguard against the application of foreign law or its effects in another legal order, where this would lead to an unacceptable violation of fundamental values. In theory and practice, public policy is defined very loosely. A basic characteristic is its relativity: the content and scope depend on how an individual country values its own interests.[28] Slovenian theory, however, is fairly united about the principles that form part of Slovene public policy. These principles are: constitutional principles, fundamental principles derived from law and moral principles. The interests of the state shall also be taken into account and are normally referred to as constitutional principles. For example, it would not be possible to execute a request for an act that would constitute racial or other discrimination against persons or which would jeopardise the security of the requested state. Any rule that is part of public policy is of a compulsory legal nature, but the opposite does not always hold true. Generally, the notion of public policy does not include all moral rules, but only those which in a given legal order represent values of such significance that the Slovenian legal order cannot deviate from their protection under any circumstances.[29]

A refusal to execute a request because it contravenes public policy shall be sent by the requested court of its own motion to the Supreme Court for a final decision. If the Supreme Court issues a final decision on refusal, it shall inform the foreign court about this (Article 175(2) CPA).

The issue of public policy is often considered when recognizing and enforcing foreign judgments. An illustration is a Ukrainian judgment concerning a method of determining a maintenance allowance as a percentage of the salary of the maintenance debtor and limiting the minimum maintenance amount, based on a Ukrainian regulation fixing the amount of guaranteed maintenance for the child. It was decided by the Slovenian court that this was not in contradiction to the provisions of the Slovenian Family Act and therefore met the conditions for recognition in Slovenia.[30]

Parties cannot claim legal assistance directly. A party, a witness or an expert cannot object to a decision on legal assistance. Even under international legal instruments, the obligation to provide legal assistance exists only between countries. International legal assistance is given or requested by courts and other state authorities. The requested act may also be carried out against the will of the person concerned, in which case coercive means may be used.

Legal assistance is provided in connection with a specific case. Article 1(2) of Regulation 1206/2001 even contains an explicit prohibition against the request being made with the intention of obtaining evidence which is not intended for use in judicial proceedings, 'commenced or contemplated'. A violation of the prohibition is also, under national law, the reason for refusing the request.

28 Ilešič, Polajnar-Pavčnik & Wedam Lukič 1992, p. 25.

29 Rijavec 2006, p. 106.

30 Judgment of the Supreme Court of Slovenia No. Cp 7/2017 of 18 June 2015.

8. Method of cooperation between courts

The requested authority acts according to the rules for a particular type of legal assistance. Cooperation between courts can take place directly or indirectly.

The direct route for carrying out legal assistance, which is the simplest and cheapest method, can only be used if it is specifically foreseen, or if the requested state does not oppose such a method. In that event, direct contact may be made between the court of the requesting state and the court or other authority, or even directly with the addressee, in the requested state. It may be possible to send a request directly to the court of the requested state for the performance of certain acts or directly request clarification of the content of foreign law. Requests (documents) shall be sent to the addressee in the requested state in an informal manner such as by way of social media or by mail. The premise of the direct method of implementing legal assistance is good relations between states.[31] The Hague Convention on Civil Procedure (1954) provides for the sending of requests (documents) from one state to another directly to the addressee by post if this is not contrary to any bilateral agreements between the two countries, and if this mode is not opposed by the state in whose territory service is effected. The state cannot oppose a method of service which does not require coercive measures.

Indirect cooperation can take place through a central authority if one is specified in the act on legal assistance that binds the state, otherwise the diplomatic route is used, which is the oldest method of cooperation.[32] The indirect method also includes communication via consular or sectoral channels between ministries or by means of specially authorised persons. Consular procedure means that the Slovenian court sends a request to the Ministry of Justice, which it transmits to the Slovenian consular post in the requested state. This is permissible where allowed by an international treaty. The consular path is defined in the Hague Convention on Civil Procedure of 1954. Consular service is available for service on Slovenian citizens abroad, but without coercion.

9. Costs and free legal aid in cross-border disputes

Various legal instruments regulating legal assistance also contain solutions that make it easier for people of limited means to obtain legal assistance in a country other than their own country of residence. Council Directive 2003/8 of 27 January 2003 on improving access to justice in cross-border disputes introduced minimum common rules on legal assistance in cross-border disputes[33] and set minimum standards, not only as regards the procedure, but also as regards the very scope of

31 Vuković 1982, p. 92.
32 Kežmah 2016, p. 234.
33 OJ L 26, 31.1.2003, p. 41-47.

legal assistance in the EU.[34] In Slovenia, the directive was incorporated into the Legal Aid Act.[35]

All persons involved in a civil or commercial dispute referred to in this directive should be able to exercise their rights in the courts even if their personal financial situation prevents them from bearing the cost of the proceedings. Legal assistance is considered appropriate if the recipient provides effective access to justice under the conditions of assistance in the directive. Legal assistance should cover: pre-litigation advice with a view to reaching a settlement before the legal proceedings are initiated; legal assistance in bringing the case to court; representation in court; and assistance in covering or exempting payment of costs.

10. Cross-border service

An important step towards simplifying cross-border service was the adoption of the Hague Convention in 1965 regarding the service abroad of judicial and extra-judicial documents in civil or commercial matters.[36] Under the convention, service cannot be undertaken if the address of the person served is unknown (Article 2(2) 1965 Hague Convention). The convention also provides for a system of sending documents through the central authority[37] designated by each state party. It enables service via diplomatic channels for direct service abroad. The requested state shall refuse service if it considers that the fulfilment of the request would constitute an infringement of its sovereignty or security.[38] Thus the Hague Convention of 1965 still allows states to place national sovereignty before the procedural rights of the parties (effective service for the exercise of the right to be heard). A request cannot be dismissed by the court merely because, under its domestic law, it has exclusive jurisdiction over the case, or its internal law does not permit the procedure on which the request is based (Article 13 1965 Hague Convention). Problems arising in connection with the sending of judicial documents for service are settled through diplomatic channels (Article 14 1965 Hague Convention). In the event of a refusal, the central authority shall immediately inform the applicant of the reasons for the refusal.[39] If the requested state has no reservations on the way service is undertaken, it may be carried out in two ways. The first is service under the law of the requested

34 See more in Dolžan 2015, p. 55.

35 Legal Aid Act, Official Gazette of the RS, No. 96/04 – official consolidated version, 23/08, 15/14.

36 Official Gazette of the RS - IT, No. 19/2000. The Hague Convention on service does not define the concept of civil and commercial matters, therefore the concept is defined by national law; Adolphsen 2015, p. 241.

37 'Each Contracting State may designate other authorities in addition to the Central Authority and shall determine the extent of their competence. The applicant shall, however, in all cases, have the right to address a request directly to the Central Authority. Federal States shall be free to designate more than one Central Authority' (Article 18 of the 1965 Hague Convention).

38 So-called public policy – *ordre public* – reservation.

39 Refusal is possible if the document is not in the official language of the country where service is to be effected; Adolphsen 2015, p. 243.

state that applies to the service of documents to persons residing in its territory. In this case, the central authority may require the document to be written in the official language or one of the official languages of the requested state or translated into such language. The second is service effected in the specific manner required by the applicant, provided that it is not contrary to the law of the requested state. Here the document can always be served on the addressee if it is voluntarily accepted (Article 5(2) 1965 Hague Convention).

For EU Member States (except Denmark), the Hague Convention was replaced by Regulation 1348/2000,[40] which in turn was replaced by Regulation 1393/2007. The Regulation on service also applies to Denmark, which has already acceded to Regulation 1348/2000[41] by a special parallel agreement, and, by means of a notification[42] on the basis of that parallel agreement, also to Regulation 1393/2007. There are still various valid bilateral agreements between EU Member States and non-EU countries.[43]

Regulation 1393/2007 provides for different service systems:

- service through transmission and reception agencies;
- service by means of a central authority;
- service by post and other direct service;
- service by consular and diplomatic channels.

In addition to the primary system of communication via the competent authorities, the regulation also takes into account the right of Member States to serve persons residing in another Member State directly through their diplomatic or consular agents, but without any coercion, and only if the state does not object to such service in its territory, unless the documents are served on nationals of the Member State from which the documents originate (Article 13 Regulation 1393/2007).

Each Member State has the right to effect service directly via the post office (Article 14 of the Regulation on service) on persons residing in another Member State. In addition, the regulation does not prejudice the right of any person having an interest in judicial proceedings to serve judicial documents directly through judicial officials, other officials or other competent persons of the requested Member State. A Member State may make a reservation against such a method of service within its territory (Article 15 of Regulation 1393/2007).

40 Council Regulation (EC) No. 1348/2000 of 29 May 2000 on the service in the Member States of judicial and extrajudicial documents in civil or commercial matters.

41 Agreement between the European Community and the Kingdom of Denmark on the service of judicial and extrajudicial documents in civil or commercial matters, OJ L 300, 17 November 2005, p. 55–60.

42 Agreement between the European Community and the Kingdom of Denmark on the service of judicial and extrajudicial documents in civil or commercial matters, OJ L 331, 10 December 2008, p. 21.

43 Therefore, the agreements are published on the Ministry of Justice website, e.g. bilateral agreements concluded by the Republic of Slovenia or its legal predecessor SRFY, available at: <http://www.mp.gov.si/si/zakonodaja_in_dokumenti/mednarodne_pogodbe_s_podrocja_pravosodja/bilateralni_sporazumi/>, last accessed 25 March 2019.

For the effectiveness of service, the biggest problem in fact is the lack of an address[44] of the person or entity to be served. As is the case with service under the Hague Convention, even under Regulation 1393/2007 service is not possible if the address of the person served is unknown. The disadvantage of the regulation is also the absence of specific provisions governing modern forms of service by the use of information and communication technology.

Under Regulation 1393/2007, Article 8, the grounds for rejection of the request are very limited, and the regulation does not impose a public policy reservation; therefore, requests for the service of a judicial document cannot be rejected for reasons of national sovereignty.[45]

The Slovenian court carries out the requested act in accordance with its own rules, but it may also take into account foreign rules, if possible, as doing so will mean that the relevant acts are valid in the legal order where the results of the request are to be used. For example, under German law service is not valid when the documents are delivered to an available employee. It is only valid when they are delivered to a legal representative of the legal entity, since a public limited company has no procedural capacity itself (§§ 170 and 178 of the German Code of Civil Procedure (*Zivilprocessordnung* – ZPO)). Under Slovenian law, legal entities are served in such a way that the document is properly handed over to the person authorised to receive the mail, or to an employee in the office, on the business premises, or at the head office (Article 133 CPA). Under German law, service would be invalid if made to an employee found at the headquarters of the company, yet according to Slovenian law it would be appropriate. Therefore, a Slovenian court might follow the explicit request of the applicant for service under German law, so as not to risk the invalidity of service because it took place under Slovenian more lenient Slovenian rules, as this is not contrary to Slovenian public policy. Where foreign law is involved, the court acts only on an explicit request, not on its own initiative, even though the problem at issue might have been known to it.

For cases of service in which none of the simplifications presented applies, the more difficult path has to be taken: otherwise there is a risk that service will be found invalid. In a concrete case, a Slovenian court ruled that a decision that was

44 An important question concerning service abroad is also the role of fictitious methods of service. Numerous legal systems have methods of avoiding service abroad by providing for different fictitious methods of service within their own jurisdiction. In the *Alder* case (C-325/11, *Krystyna Alder and Ewald Alder v. Sabina Orlowska* [2012]) the Court of Justice of the European Union (CJEU) concluded that the regulation foresees two circumstances in which the service of a judicial document between Member States falls outside its scope: first, where the permanent or habitual residence of the addressee is unknown; and second, where that person has appointed an authorised representative in the Member State where the judicial proceedings are taking place. The theory emphasises that the CJEU in the *Alder* case was right in holding that methods of fictitious service jeopardise the fundamental right to be heard. Therefore, they may only be implemented as a last resort, when absolutely necessary. See Galič 2013, p. 69-73.

45 See also Sladič 2005, p. 1142; Hess 2010, p. 452.

not properly served personally (abroad - Bosnia and Herzegovina - through diplomatic channels, as there are no bilateral agreements) cannot become final.[46]

11. Cross-border acquisition of evidence

The cross-border acquisition of evidence via judicial assistance was also simplified through the existence of a central authority introduced by the Hague Convention of 1970.[47] The Hague Conference developed the Hague Evidence Convention specifically to provide methods of taking evidence that would 'be "tolerable" to the authorities of the State where it is taken.'[48]

The Evidence Convention requires judicial cooperation from both the requesting authority and the addressed authority. A judicial authority in the requesting jurisdiction must send a Letter of Request[49] to the judicial authorities in the jurisdiction in which the evidence is located. The requested authority determines whether to execute the Letter of Request and compel evidence production applying its own law as to the methods and procedures. However, the requested authority may follow a request of the requesting authority that a special method or procedure be followed, unless this is incompatible with the internal law of the state of execution or is impossible to perform by reason of its internal practice and procedure or by reason of practical difficulties (Article 9 Evidence Convention).[50]

Regulation 1206/2001 also establishes a central authority, but this authority acts only as an auxiliary body when the courts face problems in obtaining evidence. The general rule of the regulation instead requires direct communication between the courts without the need for an indirect phase of transferring the request to the central authority. Each EU Member State was required to draw up a list of the courts responsible for the cross-border taking of evidence. The list specifies the local and, where appropriate, special jurisdiction of these courts. However, information

46 Judgment of the Higher Labour and Social Court of Slovenia No. Psp 104/2012 of 29 March 2012.

47 Convention of 18 March 1970 on the Taking of Evidence Abroad in Civil or Commercial Matters, Official Gazette of the RS, No. 19/2000.

48 Von Mehren 1994, p. 23.

49 The Evidence Convention foresees three methods of the taking of evidence: by a diplomatic officer or consular agent, by a private commissioner, and through Letters of Request.

50 There are proposals for modernising the Evidence Convention, especially Article 23. Evidence Convention procedures rely on judicial cooperation; however, many signatory countries consider the extraterritorial reach of the United States of America a threat to national sovereignty. The result is the option for the signatory countries to exercise their Article 23 power under the Evidence Convention to declare that they will not execute Letters of Request seeking to obtain electronically stored information for pre-trial discovery in common law jurisdictions. Caylor 2010, p. 344-345. However, the American courts have rejected this argument, holding that sovereignty is no bar to discovery since private litigation is not a public matter. In the famous case *Société Nationale v. District Court*, 482 U.S. 522 (1987), the Supreme Court of the United States held that use of Evidence Convention procedures instead of the Federal Rules of Civil Procedure to obtain extraterritorial evidence during discovery in US courts is not mandatory. See Buxbaum 2003.

technology makes it possible to obtain evidence directly. Direct transmission of a request to the requested court nevertheless requires service of documents in a foreign country under Regulation 1393/2007. Courts are obliged to use the swiftest and most appropriate means (Preamble paras 8 and 9 Regulation 1206/2001). Requested states are obliged to assist by using the appropriate means that the requesting Member State has declared acceptable (Article 6 Regulation 1206/2001). According to the European Judicial Atlas, most Member States use mail, fax or email as the preferred means of receiving documents, but do not specify additional conditions for each of the listed methods. Only Slovakia has stated that when using email, the application must be authenticated by an electronic signature. But authentication of documents is still necessary.[51] In general, when information and communication technology is used for communication in court proceedings, Member States mainly regulate the electronic transmission of documents using electronic signature procedures (e.g. § 130a, 130b German Code of Civil Procedure and the German law on electronic signatures (*Signaturgesetz*)).[52]

12. Cross-border use of public documents

A document issued in the prescribed form by a state authority or another person with public authorisation within the limits of its competence shall constitute a public document, to which the law connects two assumptions:

- that the issuer is a person who issues a public document, and
- that the content of the document is true.

Examples of public documents include: administrative documents (diplomas and patents), notarial documents (a notary's records on the sale of real estate), documents of personal status (an extract from the registrar's register of births) and judicial documents (a decision or a document issued by a court).

For the use of public documents outside the country in which they are issued, additional administrative formalities are usually required for authentication. The traditional method of authentication of public documents for purposes of use abroad is legalisation. Legalisation means a chain of individual document authorisations. The regular legalisation procedure (i.e. full legalisation) provides for the legalisation of the document first by the competent authorities of the issuing state, followed by the embassy or consulate of the country in which it is to be used.[53]

In order to avoid the procedure of diplomatic or consular confirmation of foreign documents (the so-called 'long authentication'), some countries signed the Hague Convention Abolishing the Requirement of Legalisation for Foreign Public Documents of 5 October 1961 and replaced it with the apostille stamp. Documents

51 Mason 2010, p. 88.
52 Inchausti 2012, p. 154.
53 Dolžan 2012, p. 338.

which are provided with this stamp in the signatory countries of the Hague Convention need not be further certified.

The apostille stamp confirms the authenticity of the signature. It is provided by the competent authority of the country of origin of the document that is used in another country and does not relate to the content of the document itself. The apostille may only be issued by the competent authority of the issuing state for use in another Member State of the Hague Convention Abolishing the Requirement of Legalisation for Foreign Public Documents of 5 October 1961.

The legal acts governing the use of foreign documents in Slovenia are the Act on the Certification of Documents in International Transactions, PILPA, the above-mentioned Hague Convention of 1961, directly applicable EU acts and bilateral agreements concluded by the Republic of Slovenia itself or notifying succession to the agreements concluded by the former SFRY.

Within the EU, legalisation of documents is eliminated. Thus, Regulation 1215/2012,[54] in Article 61, provides that no documentary or similar formalities, not even an apostille, are required for documents issued in a Member State. Regulation 2201/2003[55] also dispenses with the need for legalisation (Article 52).

13. Protection of personal data for cross-border use

The safeguarding of personal data is a particular problem. This data should only be transmitted if there is an appropriate legal basis for it.[56] According to the CA, courts may transpose personal data from files, registers, directories, auxiliary documents, registers and public documents within the jurisdiction of the courts to the competent judicial authorities of other EU Member States, third countries and international organisations only if so provided by statute, international treaty or directly applicable legal act, or by decision of an international organisation to which Slovenia has transferred the exercise of part of its sovereign rights. When providing information, the courts should, in light of the content of the data or the request, indicate separately the extent of their accuracy, completeness, promptness and reliability. In processing data received from other countries or international organisations, courts are bound by restrictions imposed by the data forwarding authority (12.a(4) CA).

[54] Regulation (EU) No. 1215/2012 of the European Parliament and of the Council of 12 December 2012 on jurisdiction and the recognition and enforcement of judgments in civil and commercial matters.

[55] Council Regulation (EC) No. 2201/2003 of 27 November 2003 concerning jurisdiction and the recognition and enforcement of judgments in matrimonial matters and the matters of parental responsibility, repealing Regulation (EC) No. 1347/2000.

[56] Some states have laws that specifically provide protection of their citizens against the scope of discovery in US courts. Parties located in France may be subject to a French Blocking Statute that foresees criminal liability of individuals or entities transferring personal data for use in US courts. Namely, France's Blocking Statute prohibits requests for or production of any information in any form for the purpose of foreign judicial or administrative proceedings. Caylor 2010, p. 370-371.

In the case of cross-border exchanges, personal data are transmitted only to judicial authorities or other similar authorities of other countries or international organisations. Third-country authorities may only request information on the basis of an international treaty or in accordance with a decision of the national supervisory authority for the protection of personal data in accordance with the provisions of the act governing the protection of personal data.[57] Data processing restrictions on the transmission of personal data imposed by the Court of Justice, must be respected, in particular for the protection of procedural interests, the confidentiality of proceedings, the privacy of persons or the protection of the presumption of innocence and the right to a fair trial. A court may also mark these restrictions with the accompanying notes relating to the description of the state of affairs or the stage of the judicial proceedings or the importance of the official record in the legal order of the Republic of Slovenia (12.a(5) CA).

14. Recognition and enforcement of foreign judgments

14.1. Concept

The decisions of courts and other state bodies that decide on substantive rights and obligations create primary effects only in the legal order to which they belong. Legal effects in foreign jurisdictions do not occur automatically, but only on the basis of a procedure of 'adoption' of such a decision. No state recognises all foreign judicial decisions, rather restrictions on recognition are determined on the basis of various criteria, such as the type of legal relationship that is directly the subject of the decision, the type of procedure and the nature of the court decision. According to the first criterion mentioned above (the type of legal relationship), recognition is limited to foreign judgments governing civil relations. The concept of civil law relations for this purpose is determined by EU regulations, international conventions and national regulations. When applying national rules, the assessment of whether a relationship is civil is a matter that must be determined based on the law of the state of recognition, since the foreign court decision, on recognition, is incorporated into its legal order.[58]

In private international law, traditionally the notion of recognition is joined with the notion of enforcement, which does not mean deciding on execution, but is a part of the decision on the effects of the judgment, which also includes the issue of enforceability.[59] Foreign declaratory and constitutive judgments directly develop their effects in the other legal order immediately after recognition. Enforcement is only necessary to carry out the costs part of such decisions. For condemnatory judgments, both recognition and enforcement are necessary. PILPA thus regulates two ways in which a foreign decision may be integrated into the Slovenian legal

57 *Zakon o varstvu osebnih podatkov*, Official Gazette of the RS, No. 86/04.

58 Judgment of the Supreme Court of Slovenia No. 15/2014 of 14 May 2015.

59 Brussels I Regulation Recast also distinguishes between recognition (Articles 33 to 37) and enforcement (Articles 38 to 52).

order – by recognition and by enforcement. PILPA does not use the term 'exequatur' to mean the grant of enforceability, it only speaks of enforcement as an aspect of the integration of a foreign judgment.[60] This corresponds to the view that a court decision on enforcement of a foreign judgment has no constitutive but rather a declaratory nature. The conditions for achieving the enforcement aspect of integration are the same as for recognition except for the enforceability effect, which has to be obtained in the country of origin.[61] The older theory therefore states that it would be more appropriate to talk of 'recognising the effects of foreign judicial decisions', including recognising the effect of enforceability, rather than splitting it into 'recognition and enforcement'.[62] This divergence is classic and more closely aligned to systems that require the grant of 'exequatur', which is a constitutive act. This is also the position under Regulation 44/2001. In contrast, Regulation 1215/2012 now explicitly eliminates the grant of 'exequatur' and provides for the automatic recognition of a foreign enforceability effect in the state of enforcement.

According to PILPA, a decision on recognition and enforcement need not be initiated in a special procedure, which leads to a decree with the effect of *res judicata*. The court may decide on the recognition and enforcement of a foreign judgment as a preliminary issue in the enforcement procedure itself. Nevertheless, a special non-contentious civil procedure, governed by PILPA, is offered, which is often more appropriate for the assessment of a foreign title.[63] In this special procedure the court first issues an *ex parte* decision on recognition and enforcement, which the opposing participant has the right to challenge in the same court (objection). An appeal against the decision deciding the challenge can be lodged with the Supreme Court. In this procedure, there is no provision to lodge an application for revision.[64]

14.2. Legal sources

With regard to legal sources, it can be concluded that three legal regimes for the recognition and enforcement of foreign court decisions are relevant to Slovenia:

- EU law;
- International treaties;
- PILPA.

60 It should be noted that in the procedure for recognition and enforcement the court does not decide on leave for enforcement. Leave for enforcement can be obtained in an enforcement procedure according to national rules.

61 Cigoj 1984, p. 190.

62 Vuković & Kunštek 2005, p. 419.

63 In Italy, the special procedure for recognition and enforcement of foreign judicial decisions is called *giudizio di delibazione*. See also Vuković 1982, p. 144.

64 In the recognition procedure for a foreign judicial decision, an application for revision is not allowed.

14.3. Determination of foreign law

When conflict of laws rules determine that foreign substantive law should be applied, the Slovenian court must apply this law of its own motion, according to the principle *iura novit curia* (Article 12(1) PILPA). The court may request a statement on the content of foreign law from the Ministry of Justice or satisfy itself of its contents in another appropriate manner (Article 12(2) PILPA).

Very often a court requests assistance from the parties, who may submit a public or other document from the competent foreign authority or institution containing an explanation of foreign law (Article 12 PILPA). The parties may also participate in the identification of relevant sources of foreign law. However, there is no burden of proof on a party to prove foreign law. If a party does not respond to the court's request in relation to the content of the foreign law, this does not affect the claim. If a court fails to gain a proper insight into the foreign law, it is entitled to use Slovenian law instead (Article 12 PILPA). However, for the purpose of establishing foreign law, the court shall use all possible appropriate sources such as:

- journals, textbooks, monographs, collections of legislation, comments, databases;
- legal opinions from experts;
- notices of foreign law, where the European Convention on Information on Foreign Law of 1968 applies;[65] the court may contact the central authority of the country whose law is at stake in order to provide the relevant legal information.[66]

The court applies foreign law in the same way as it would have been applied by the judge in the country of origin. The parties are obliged to pay an advance to obtain information on foreign law. Both parties are also allowed to provide expertise on foreign law.

15. Comparative outlook with the United States of America

The rules of international legal assistance are pertinent to each country, either through domestic or international instruments of law. Since this contribution provides insight into the mechanisms of (international) legal assistance in Slovenia (and the EU at large), a brief comparison with a 'foreign' legal order such as that of the United States might be appropriate. In 1964, the United States enacted a rather straightforward regulation[67] on international legal assistance, liberalising the previously rigid regulation in an attempt to advance international cooperation in

65 *Zakon o ratifikaciji Evropske konvencije o obvestilih o tujem pravu*, Official Gazette of the RS - IT, No. 4/98.

66 Walter & Domej 2012, p. 337.

67 28 U.S. Code § 1782.

civil litigation.[68] By improving the US statutory scheme of international judicial assistance, the US legislator hoped to bring the country to the forefront of nations, adjusting their procedures to those of sister nations, and that its initiative would encourage other countries similarly to adjust their procedures.[69]

The statutory law, as it stands, provides that:

> [A d]istrict court of the district in which a person resides or is found may order him to give his testimony or statement or to produce a document or other thing for use in a proceeding in a foreign or international tribunal, ... The order may be made pursuant to a letter rogatory issued, or request made, by a foreign or international tribunal or upon the application of any interested person[70] and may direct that the testimony or statement be given, or the document or other thing be produced, before a person appointed by the court. ... The order may prescribe the practice and procedure, which may be in whole or part the practice and procedure of the foreign country or the international tribunal, for taking the testimony or statement or producing the document or other thing. To the extent that the order does not prescribe otherwise, the testimony or statement shall be taken, and the document or other thing produced, in accordance with the Federal Rules of Civil Procedure.

The cited procedures apply only when an individual possessing the relevant evidence is uncooperative.[71] This statutory ground may be applicable where evidence is sought, regardless whether a request is made under concurrent international treaties (e.g. the Hague Convention on the Taking of Evidence Abroad in Civil or Commercial Matters).[72]

As evidenced at first sight, the provision is indeed very general in its wording and may cover international legal assistance to arbitral tribunals and other adjudicating bodies.[73] Furthermore, it pertains to both civil and criminal matters. The actual measures undertaken after a request is made follow domestic rules. The understanding of the law is expanded in an abundance of case law, which cannot, however, be covered within this contribution.

68 Smit 1998, p. 1-2.

69 See Deutsch 1982, p. 177.

70 The term 'interested person' refers both to the persons designated under foreign law to seek evidence and to the parties to foreign or international litigation. *Ibid.*, p. 178.

71 28 U.S. Code § 1782(b).

72 Deutsch 1982, p. 180.

73 The previous regulation addressed only a foreign 'court'. The substitution of the word was deliberate, for the drafters wanted to make the assistance provided for available to all bodies with adjudicatory functions; see Smit 1998, p. 5. Whether judicial assistance can be used by arbitral tribunals is not a settled matter though. The main problem is that the US regulation allows 'any interested person' (therefore parties) to make the request to the court (without the arbitrator's approval), which is contrary to one of the fundamental rules of arbitration, that the arbitrator decides procedural questions. Furthermore, in the US regulation the court can grant the full range of discovery under the Federal Rules of Civil Procedure, whereas disclosure in international arbitration is much narrower; see Rothstein 2009.

16. Conclusion

Mutual legal assistance is a method of cooperation between states for obtaining assistance in civil litigation in cases with a cross-border dimension, where some official act in another state is required. Traditional forms of legal assistance include service of documents, taking of evidence and requests for information on foreign law. In a broader sense, the recognition and enforcement of foreign judgments is included as well. These cases may cover businesses, consumers or employment disputes, divorces, child custody or succession issues. Nowadays, there is an increasing level of cooperation between judicial authorities in cross-border family law matters.

Most often, requests for legal assistance and the provision of legal assistance are based on international instruments. Key institutions in the field of judicial cooperation are the Hague Conference on Private International Law, the European Union, the Council of Europe and the United Nations. International instruments may be multilateral treaties, regional agreements or bilateral agreements. Cooperation between the EU Member States is usually based on EU regulations. These instruments oblige the contracting states to provide legal assistance to the requesting state authorities under certain agreed conditions. The agreements and regulations also establish uniform procedures for drawing up and submitting requests for legal assistance, which means that the parties can receive assistance more easily and swiftly. At the same time, the provisions of the agreements and regulations enhance the legal protection of the parties in court proceedings.

In many cases legal assistance may be provided by virtue of national legislation or mere international comity. It is difficult to force cooperation on sovereign states, but in the modern world full of mutual interests and basic comity, this may be justified. One of the objectives is respect for universal human and civil rights as an essential prerequisite for stability and civil peace. A further aim is to provide legal advisory services oriented towards the market economy.

Finally, an enormous advance in more efficient and flexible conduct of cross-border court proceedings arises from progress in digitalisation and the application of new technologies in litigation. In cross-border cases, communication between judicial authorities of different Member States is crucial. Video-conferencing is one possible way of simplifying and encouraging such communication.

References

Adolphsen 2015
Adolphsen, J., *Europäisches Zivilverfahrensrecht*, Heidelberg: Springer, 2015.

Badovinac Bjelič 1994
Badovinac Bjelič, I., 'Mednarodna pravna pomoč', *Pravosodni bilten*, 1994, p. 84-129.

Bordaš, Knežević & Varadi 2005
Bordaš, B., Knežević, G. & Varadi, T., *Međunarodno privatno parvo*, Novi Sad: Forum, 2005.

Buxbaum 2003
Buxbaum, H., 'Assessing Sovereign Interests in Cross-Border Discovery Disputes: Lessons from Aérospatiale', *Texas Internationall Law Journal*, 2003, p. 87-102.

Caylor 2010
Caylor, M.L.P., 'Modernizing the Hague Evidence Convention: A Proposed Solution to Cross-Border Discovery Conflicts during Civil and Commercial Litigation', *Boston University International Law Journal*, 2010, p. 341-387.

Cigoj 1984
Cigoj, S., Mednarodno pravo osebnih in premoženjskih razmerij, Ljubljana: ČZ Ur. l. SRS, 1984.

Deutsch 1982
Deutsch, H.M., 'Judicial Assistance: Obtaining Evidence in the United States, under 28 U.S.C. 1782, for Use in a Foreign or International Tribunal', *Boston College International and Comparative Law Review*, 1982, p. 175-193.

Dolžan 2012
Dolžan, J., 'Tuje javne listine in njihova veljava v republiki Sloveniji', *Podjetje in delo*, 2012, p. 332-344.

Dolžan 2015
Dolžan, J., 'Brezplačna pravna pomoč v mednarodnih in čezmejnih civilnih sporih', *Pravosodni bilten*, 2015, p. 35-57.

Galič 2013
Galič, A., 'Service Abroad in Civil and Commercial Matters - From the Hague Conventions to the EU 1393/2007 Regulation', Collection of Papers, Faculty of Law, Nis, 2013, p. 59-77.

Geimer 2001
Geimer, R., *Internationales Zivilprozessrecht*, Cologne: Otto Schmidt, 2001.

Hess 2010
Hess, B., *Europäisches Zivilprozessrecht: ein Lehrbuch*, Heidelberg: C.F. Müller, 2010.

Ilešič, Polajnar-Pavčnik & Wedam Lukič 1992
Ilešič, M., Polajnar-Pavčnik, A. & Wedam Lukić, D., *Mednarodno zasebno pravo: komentar zakona*, Ljubljana: Uradni list RS, 1992.

Inchausti 2012
Inchausti, F.G., 'Electronic Service of Documents: National and International Aspects', in: M. Kengyel & Z. Nemessányi (eds.), *Electronic technology and civil procedure: new paths to justice from around the world*, Dordrecht, New York: Springer, 2012, p. 137-180.

Joks 1999
Joks, E., 'Some Problems of International Judicial Assistance from an Estonian Perspective', *Juridica International*, 1999, p. 80-85.

Kežmah 2016
Kežmah, U., *Vročanje in pravica do sodnega varstva v sodnih postopkih*, PhD thesis, Maribor, 2016.

Kitić 2017
Kitić, D., *Međunarodno privatno pravo*, Belgrade: Službeni glasnik, Pravni fakultet Univerziteta u Beogradu, 2017.

Mason 2010
Mason, S. (ed.), *Electronic evidence*, London: LexisNexis, Butterworths, 2010.

Rijavec 2006
Rijavec, V., 'Pravna pomoč', in: Ude, L. & Galič, A. (eds.), *Pravdni postopek - zakon s komentarjem*, part II, Ljubljana: Uradni list and GV Založba, 2006, p. 99-114.

Rothstein 2009
Rothstein, D.J., 'A Proposal to Clarify U.S. Law on Judicial Assistance in Taking Evidence for International Arbitration', *The American Review of International Arbitration*, 2009, p. 61-89.

Salma 2013
Salma, M., 'Mutual Legal Assistance in Civil Proceedings', *Zbornik radova*, 2013, p. 195-208.

Schack 1996
Schack, H., *Internationales Zivilverfahrensrecht*, Munich: Beck, 1996.

Sladič 2005
Sladič, J., 'Vročanje v civilnih in gospodarskih zadevah', *Podjetje in delo*, 2005, p. 1131-1150.

Smit 1998
Smit, H., 'American Assistance to Litigation in Foreign and International Tribunals: Section 1782 of Title 28 of the U.S.C. Revisited', *Syracuse Journal of International Law & Commerce*, 1998, p. 1-20.

Stadler 2013
Stadler, A., 'Practical Obstacles in Cross-Border Litigation and Communication between (EU) Courts', *Erasmus Law Review*, 2013, p. 151-168.

Von Mehren 1994
Von Mehren, R., 'International Control of Civil Procedure: Who Benefits?', *Law and Contemporary Problems*, 1994, p. 13-24.

Vuković 1982
Vuković, Đ., *Međunarodno građansko procesno pravo*, Zagreb: Informator, 1982.

Vuković & Kunštek 2005
Vuković, Đ. & Kunštek, E., *Međunarodno građansko postupovno pravo*, Zagreb: Zgombić i partneri, 2005.

Walter & Domej 2012
Walter, G. & Domej, T., *Internationales Zivilprozessrecht der Schweiz*, Bern/Stuttgart/Vienna: Haupt Verlag, 2012.

T. Zoroska-Kamilovska

CHALLENGES FACING MACEDONIAN LAWMAKERS IN THE FUTURE IMPLEMENTATION OF BRUSSELS I RECAST REGARDING ENFORCEMENT – AN ATTEMPT AT ASSESSMENT

1. Introduction

The accession of Macedonia to the European Union (EU) has loomed on the horizon for over a decade. Although many legislative and administrative measures have been undertaken and implemented, some of which have been successful in achieving their specific goals, it seems that Macedonia's progress towards meeting EU standards will be on the agenda of the European Commission for the foreseeable future.

Undoubtedly, the system of civil enforcement has been changed substantially over the last decade. In 2005, leaving behind a long-lasting tradition of a court-oriented system of civil enforcement, the Macedonian legislator opted for a completely new judicial officer (bailiff)-oriented system, thus completely restructuring the enforcement system, both in an institutional and in a functional sense.[1] It is inaccurate to claim that today Macedonia has a flawless system of civil enforcement, yet it is obvious that the new system is much more functional and effective and less time-consuming than the previous one.

The enforcement procedure, as designed by the national lawmakers in the Macedonian Enforcement Act (EA),[2] is viewed from a domestic standpoint and generally does not touch on cross-border relations. Still, in certain cases Macedonian judicial officers enforce civil judgments rendered by foreign courts. Enforcement of foreign judgments in Macedonia has traditionally been subject to compliance with the typical requirements which are examined in exequatur proceedings. Currently, this regime also applies to judgments taken in the EU Member States, since the

1 See Zoroska-Kamilovska 2012, p. 315-343; Zoroska-Kamilovska 2014, p. 27-31; Zoroska-Kamilovska & Rakočević 2016, p. 29-49.

2 Enforcement Act (Official Gazette of RM, No. 72/2016), hereinafter EA.

system created by Brussels I Recast (hereafter BIR)[3] does not apply yet. By the same token, the liberalisation of recognition and enforcement does not benefit third-country judgments, and this includes Macedonian judgments.[4] Nevertheless, having in mind the highest strategic priority for Macedonia – EU membership – we may pose the challenging questions: Is there a need to adapt and modify the national legislation for the application of BIR? And, what should the reaction of the Macedonian lawmakers be? Although at the moment it is an anticipated situation, this paper constitutes a starting point for a long-running effort to make a substantial contribution in this domain. In the contribution we will discuss the future implementation of BIR in the Macedonian legal order, placing emphasis on some salient issues from the Macedonian perspective. The goal is to open the debate about the inevitable modifications of Macedonian legislation in order to support and implement a smooth transition towards the future of cross-border enforcement without exequatur. The goal will be achieved if we succeed, at least partially, in answering these and other questions, while at the same time being aware of the need for a far more extensive analysis.

2. Enforcement of domestic and foreign court judgments and other enforceable instruments in Macedonia

In respect of the effect of judgments and the possibilities of their forced execution, Macedonian law initially distinguishes between judgments of Macedonian courts and foreign judgments.

It is well known that even in an internal national legal system in most cases judgments are not 'self-executing' and a certain procedure for their enforcement is necessary.[5] Enforcement entails making the judgment effective. This applies to the Macedonian legal system as well. Enforcement is conceived of as a separate procedure[6] that the judgment-holder is supposed to start before the competent judicial officer. There is no need of court interference before embarking on

3 Regulation (EU) 1215/2012 of the European Parliament and of the Council of 12 December 2012 on jurisdiction and the recognition and enforcement of judgments in civil and commercial matters (recast) [*2012*] OJ L 351/1.

4 The recognition and enforcement of judgments in civil and commercial matters of the Macedonian courts in the European Union continues to be subject to the legal regimes of the 28 Member States. Even if recognised in one Member State, the judgment does not enjoy the benefit of mutual trust in other Member States. The judgment has to pass through the recognition and enforcement procedure in each particular State where it needs to take effect.

5 Joint Response to the Green Paper on the Review of the Brussels I Regulation by Ulrich Magnus and Peter Mankowski, available at: <http://ec.europa.eu/justice/news/-consulting_public/0002/contributions/civil_society_ngo_academics_others/prof_magnus_and_prof_mankowski_university_of_hamburg_en.pdf>, last accessed 3 June 2019.

6 Within the new system of enforcement, there was debate about whether enforcement is regarded as civil procedure or a matter of administration. The principal position is that enforcement is conceived of as an autonomous procedure aiming to provide final legal protection. By the same token, requests addressed to judicial officers and each act of enforcement are considered to be procedural acts.

enforcement in purely domestic cases, meaning that it is not necessary to obtain a 'decision' or 'order' by a court permitting the enforcement. By virtue of the principle *nulla executio sine titulo,* the only hurdle for the creditor seeking enforcement is possession of an enforceable title or instrument.[7] An enforceable title means not simply a right or a basis to start enforcement proceedings,[8] it also refers to the totality of the substantive and procedural legal consequences originating from the legal relationship, which affect the rights and obligations of the parties and participants to the enforcement proceedings.[9]

In the Macedonian legal system all enforceable titles must be identified by the law. The EA sets forth an extensive list of enforceable titles which is comprised of: enforceable court decisions and court settlements, enforceable decisions and settlements in an administrative procedure on money claims, enforceable notarial deeds, conclusions of the judicial officers determining the enforcement expenses and notarial payment orders. Yet, it does not contain an exhaustive list of enforcement titles: the Act leaves the possibility to have enforcement titles provided by special law.[10] Furthermore, the EA defines the assumptions for enforceability of each type of enforcement title separately.[11]

In order to perform the enforcement, the judicial officer must be sure that the judgment or other title can be enforced; he/she needs sufficient confirmation of enforceability. Each of the aforementioned titles can be enforced only if the creditor obtains a special certification authorising the enforcement *(confirmation of enforceability, enforceability clause)*. As a procedural prerequisite for the enforcement proceeding, the enforceability clause is given by the court or authority which decided on the claim at first instance, or by the notary public.[12] The confirmation of enforceability serves as a certification that the enforcement title is (formally) enforceable, which means that the enforceable title has come into effect and that no legal remedy with a suspensive effect is available. The confirmation of enforceability also provides proof of the fact that the time limit for complying with the title (which is usually set in it) has expired.[13] The confirmation of enforceability of a judgment or other title which has not yet acquired this effect can be repealed (in the form of a decision) by the same court or authority *ex officio* or on application of

7 The request for enforcement shall be written by a lawyer in cases where the value of the main claim is over €10,000.

8 Article 2 EA.

9 Janevski & Zoroska-Kamilovska 2011, p. 42 *et seq.*

10 Article 12(1) EA.

11 Articles 14-16 EA. As an example, judgments rendered by the court of first instance cannot be enforced while they are still subject to appeal or the appellate proceeding is pending, unless otherwise prescribed by law.

12 Article 12(2) EA. In practice, the original or the authenticated copy of the title in question is usually stamped, stating that the title has acquired enforceability as of a certain date. Notarial deeds are subject to a special regime. By virtue of Article 53(5) of the Notary Public Act (Official Gazette of RM, No. 72/2016), upon written request of the debtor, the notaries themselves issue the confirmation of enforceability regarding documents they draw up or certify (notarial confirmation of enforceability).

13 Janevski & Zoroska-Kamilovska 2011, p. 51.

any person involved.[14] If the confirmation of enforceability is repealed, the judicial officer shall stop the enforcement *ex officio*.[15]

In addition to the enforceability clause, the enforcement title needs to be suitable for enforcement. Suitability derives from the content of the document; essentially, it has to be explicit enough to identify the creditor, the debtor, the type, and the extent and time for performance of the obligation. In the case of a decision that orders certain performance, it has to contain the period of time for voluntary performance, which, if missing, is provided by the judicial officer.[16]

The enforcement procedure itself is designed to enable the creditor to obtain the same result that he would have obtained if the debtor had complied with the title voluntarily. There are various kinds of enforcement proceedings, which are determined by the obligation the debtor is expected to discharge. Different procedures empower the creditor to recover a certain sum of money, to obtain the delivery of specified assets or to enforce orders compelling (or enjoining) the debtor to do something.[17]

As mentioned above, in the Macedonian system of civil enforcement, there is no need to obtain leave from the court to enforce enforceable titles. Yet, this does not mean that the courts are not involved in enforcement proceedings; courts can become involved upon a complaint (objection) of the parties (creditor and debtor) or third persons participating in enforcement. Parties and third persons are entitled to challenge the validity of the enforcement acts carried out by judicial officers. The remedy is called a complaint (objection) against enforcement irregularities and, it is filed at the first instance court located on the territory where the enforcement or part of it has been carried out.[18] The complaint shall be submitted within three days after learning of illegality or failure to take action, but no later than three months after taking action or failing to take action. The procedure upon complaint is adversarial and speedy.[19] If the court finds that the complaint is well founded, it determines that there are irregularities and declares void the undertaken enforcement actions or determines that certain enforcement actions have not been performed. However, the court cannot stop enforcement, nor order the judicial officer to take enforcement actions. Furthermore, the objection does not suspend the enforcement automatically. The parties or third persons may request that the court suspend the enforcement for a certain period of time, but no longer than ninety

14 Article12(3) EA. In this regard, the Supreme Court of Macedonia held that it is not admissible to conduct a lawsuit for repealing the confirmation of enforceability, because the authority that made the certification is entitled to repeal it, either on request or *ex officio*. See Decision of the Supreme Court, GZZ No. 55/94 of 27 September1999.

15 Article 93 EA.

16 Article 17 EA.

17 See Part three 'Enforcement for Collection of Monetary Claims' and Part four 'Enforcement for Realization of Non-Monetary Claims' of the EA.

18 Article 86 EA. The complaint shall be written by a lawyer in cases where the value of the main claim is over €10,000.

19 Under Article 86(4) of the EA, the court decides on the complaint within 72 hours after the deadline for responding by the judicial officer.

days.[20] It is noteworthy that a subsequent appeal to the appellate court is possible against the court decision upon the complaint.[21]

Traditionally, foreign judgments are not automatically enforceable in Macedonia. Instead, a national intermediary procedure - exequatur[22] - is required. A foreign judgment can only be enforced after having been declared enforceable in a separate procedure for recognition and enforcement.[23] The purpose of this procedure is to vest the foreign judgment with the same effect provided for national judgments, after reviewing the foreign judgment and verifying that certain requirements are met.[24]

The source of law affecting the requirements of exequatur is the Private International Law Act (PILA),[25] as well as several international treaties. Unless a treaty provides otherwise, exequatur is granted if a foreign court decision[26] meets several specific conditions. Some of them are set forth as grounds of approval, while others as grounds of refusal of the recognition of the foreign judgment, and they are considered by the court at the different stages of the procedure. Together, they embrace the two functions that are conventionally attributed to exequatur: the 'title import function' and the 'title inspection function',[27] as will be explained below.

PILA provides for a *contrôle limité* as far as the extent of review of a foreign decision is concerned. It lays down the procedural and substantive grounds of approval/refusal of recognition that function as safeguards in Macedonia as the addressed state, such as: the production of the judgment that satisfied the conditions to establish its authenticity,[28] confirmation of its finality (and enforceability, if required[29]), proper service and observance of the right to be heard in the foreign procedure, existence of international jurisdiction of the foreign court,

20 Article 91(3) EA.

21 Article 87 EA.

22 In the glossary of the European Judicial Network, exequatur is defined as 'a concept specific to the private international law and refers to the decision by a court authorising the enforcement in that country of a judgment, arbitral award, authentic instruments or court settlement given abroad.'

23 Article 8 of the EA explicitly states that the enforcement of decisions of a foreign court may be conducted in the Republic of Macedonia if the decision fulfils the prerequisites (conditions) of recognition established by law or international treaties ratified in accordance with the Constitution of the Republic of Macedonia.

24 On the essence and function of exequatur in general, see García 2010, p. 351, 354-357.

25 Private International Law Act (Official Gazette of RM, No. 87/2007 and No. 156/2010).

26 According to Article 99 of PILA, the term 'foreign court decision' comprises: a decision of a court of a foreign country, a court settlement and a decision of another authority which in the state where it is taken is equal to a court decision or a court settlement if it regulates relations envisaged in Article 1 of this law.

27 See Oberhammer 2010, p. 197, 197-199.

28 According to Article 101(2) of PILA, the applicant normally produces a translation of the foreign decision.

29 If the request for recognition of a foreign judgment requires the recognition of its enforceability as well, the applicant for recognition of the foreign court decision, despite confirmation of finality, must submit a certificate of enforceability under the law of the state in which the decision is taken (Article 102 PILA).

irreconcilability with a judgment given or recognised earlier by the Macedonian court (as long as the earlier judgment was between the same parties and concerned the same cause of action) and the public policy requirement. The major novelty regarding the substantial grounds is the abolishment of the reciprocity requirement by PILA.[30] Furthermore, there is no possibility for Macedonian courts to review the merits of the case.

Under PILA, the creditor has to commence a special procedure at the first instance court[31] in view of obtaining a decision for recognition of a foreign judgment as a prerequisite for its enforcement. The procedure in the first instance is characterised by simplicity: the creditor can access the competent court without representation by a lawyer, the procedure is unilateral and the defendant (debtor) is only notified of its results – granting the exequatur. In this respect, during the first stage the court will focus on examining the grounds for non-recognition *ex officio*, relating to the judgment, confirmation of its finality and enforceability, violation of designated exclusive jurisdiction rules of Macedonian courts, irreconcilability of judgments, and the public policy requirement. If the court finds that all requirements are met, it will grant exequatur, which is served on the defendant. Although PILA provides for grounds for refusal of exequatur, they are only relevant upon the debtor's complaint against the decision for recognition. Namely, the defendant can file a complaint against the decision for recognition on the grounds of being improperly served or because of other due process violations. The complaint is decided upon by the same first instance court. If the decision on the complaint depends on controversial facts, the case is discussed *inter partes* at a separate hearing. Besides the complaint, an appeal to the appellate court[32] is possible against the decision for refusal of recognition, as well as against the decision on the complaint.[33] To summarise, the Macedonian PILA establishes a separate non-contentious civil procedure especially tailored for recognition and enforcement (exequatur) of foreign judgments with a first *ex parte* stage, a second adversarial stage before the same court and a third adversarial stage at the appellate court.

The issue of recognition of a foreign judgment may also arise as a preliminary question in any civil procedure. The court may decide on such a preliminary question if there is no prior decision on recognition. The decision will have effect only in the proceeding in which it was made.[34] It is noteworthy that this incidental proceeding is not available in the enforcement procedure, since Macedonia has autonomous private judicial officers who are competent only to perform enforcement on the basis of an enforceable title, but not to decide on preliminary issues.

30 Articles 101-107 PILA. For the recognition and enforcement of foreign judgments in Macedonia, see Deskoski 2008, p. 456-458.

31 Each of the 27 first instance courts has jurisdiction for recognition and enforcement of foreign judgments.

32 There are 4 appellate courts in Macedonia (in Skopje, Bitola, Stip and Gostivar).

33 Article 113 PILA.

34 Article 112(3) PILA.

When exequatur is granted, the foreign judgment becomes effective, and a request for enforcement of that judgment can be filed. The exequatur decision provides for the enforceability of the foreign judgment, and authorises any judicial officer to start enforcement and attach assets. Both decisions - the foreign judgment and the exequatur decision - are required when a creditor seeks to effect the foreign judgment in Macedonia. However, the exequatur decision - rather than the foreign judgment - is the basis for enforcement. The decision for granting exequatur 'imports' the foreign judgment into the Macedonian legal order.

Once a foreign judgment has become enforceable in Macedonia, the enforcement proceeding is identical to the procedure purely for domestic cases.

3. Cross-border enforcement in the European Union under BIR

In contrast to the Macedonian national framework, recognition and enforcement of foreign judgments in civil and commercial matters in the EU context is experiencing dramatic changes. Having been initially formed upon negotiation of the 1968 Brussels Convention, it has been subsequently updated and renewed by the Brussels I Regulation, alongside other instruments addressing specific matters or specific proceedings,[35] and lately revised by BIR.[36] The legislative process itself has been marked by the gradual abolition of exequatur in order to enhance the free movement of judgments as a policy objective in the EU judicial area of justice. Although the abolition of exequatur was not a straightforward decision devoid of concerns and criticism,[37] the view that the level of trust among Member States has reached a degree of maturity that permits a move towards an automatic system of circulation of judgments prevailed.[38] The current legislative state of affairs clearly embodies the principles of mutual recognition and mutual trust as the cornerstones of judicial cooperation in civil and commercial matters with cross-border implications.

For the purposes of subsequent discussions on implementing provisions in the Macedonian Enforcement Act, we shall highlight some key features of the BIR regime.

While the Brussels I Regulation requires a declaration of enforceability (exequatur) before enforcement measures can proceed,[39] BIR provides for automatic enforceability. A judgment given in a Member State which is enforceable in that

35 The Brussels I Regulation was complemented by a number of instruments that have altered the original scope of its application, such as: Regulation (EC) No. 805/2004 of 21 April 2004 creating a European Enforcement Order for Uncontested Claims [2004] OJ L 143/15, Regulation (EC) No. 1896/2006 of 12 December 2006 creating a European Order for Payment Procedure [2006] OJ L 399/1, Regulation (EC) No. 861/2007 of 11 July 2007 establishing a European Small Claims Procedure [2007], OJ L 199/1.

36 See Dickinson & Lein 2015, p. 4-16; Alavi & Khamichonak 2015, p. 159-181; Kramer 2011, p. 633-641; Baumgartner 2014, p. 188-195.

37 Cuniberti & Rueda 2010. See also Schlosser 2010, p. 101-104; Oberhammer 2010, p. 197-203.

38 On the rationale (economic and political) for the abolition of exequatur, see Cuniberti & Rueda 2010, p. 5-6.

39 Article 38(1) Brussels I Regulation.

Member State shall be enforceable in the other Member States without any declaration of enforceability being required.[40] BIR promotes a system of direct implementation of the judgment in all Member States[41] upon submission of two documents to the competent enforcement authority of the Member State addressed: a copy of the judgment that satisfies the conditions necessary to establish its authenticity and a certificate issued by the court of origin in accordance with the form set out in Annex I to the regulation,[42] confirming the enforceability of the judgment and containing an extract of the judgment.[43] This means that enforceability is no longer granted *de novo* in each country in which the creditor intends to initiate the execution individually, but it is obtained at the same time across the EU.[44] The same rule concerns authentic instruments and court settlements, which also fall within the scope of BIR.[45] However, no enforcement measures will be taken before the debtor is informed of the request for enforcement. Namely, the certificate of enforceability, if necessary accompanied by the judgment, shall be served on the person against whom enforcement is sought prior to the first enforcement measure,[46] and thus prior to any forced execution. Nevertheless, protective measures are available as soon as the judgment is enforceable in the state of origin, and there is no need to serve the certificate and the foreign judgment on the judgment debtor prior to obtaining such measures.[47]

As to the enforcement procedure itself, BIR clearly states that enforcement remains to be governed by the national law of the Member State where the enforcement is to take place. National enforcement rules apply in the same way as to judgments delivered by national courts.[48] Since exequatur is abolished, national enforcement law has become more important.[49] However, since national enforcement laws are very different among Member States, one might argue that BIR creates problems when enforcing foreign judgments, as its adoption in the enforcing state with an equivalent effect will be almost impossible.

40 Article 39 BIR.

41 Judgments from other Member States lost the status of 'foreign judgments' as is clearly indicated by cancellation of the word 'foreign' from the relevant articles of BIR.

42 Although very important, the question of the legal nature of the certificate according to Article 53 of BIR remains unclear. Still, it seems that the prevailing opinion is that it is not a court decision and thus it has no binding effect. It is a mere certification, or public document with evidentiary value.

43 Article 42(1) BIR. Only when the enforcement authority deems it necessary, may a translation of the judgment or a translation or a transliteration of the contents of the certificate be required (Article 42(2) and (3) BIR).

44 Gottwald 1991, p. 285.

45 See Articles 58-60 BIR.

46 Article 43 BIR. See also Recital 32, which says 'in reasonable time before the first enforcement measure', but does not indicate how long 'prior' this must be. It will be for the courts (including the European Court of Justice) to determine what constitutes a reasonable time period.

47 Article 40 BIR.

48 Article 41 BIR.

49 Kramer 2011, p. 641.

Under the Brussels I Regulation, recognition was not a condition for taking into account the application for a declaration of enforceability. It is not a condition for automatic enforceability under BIR, either. It is clear that automatic enforceability goes further than recognition, because it means the consent to conduct enforcement on the basis of a foreign judgment which does not have to be recognised in the state of enforcement.[50] As a result, the territory of the Member State addressed should also be subject to other effects of the judgment, besides enforceability.

The replacement of the exequatur procedure by the system of automatic import of foreign judgments does not mean the complete elimination of the grounds for non-recognition/enforcement.[51] Recital 29 of BIR says, 'The direct enforcement in the Member State addressed of a judgment given in another Member State without a declaration of enforceability should not jeopardise respect for the rights of the defence.' Therefore, the possibility of verification of the grounds for refusal of enforcement in the state of enforcement remains under BIR, but the burden to successfully resist enforcement is reversed and transferred from the creditor to the debtor. In other words, the so-called second function of the exequatur procedure has not been entirely suppressed, but moved to another stage of the debt recovery process, namely the enforcement stage.[52] The verification of whether the foreign judgment would meet the requirements for producing its effect in the forum could be conducted in parallel with enforcement, and impacts on it only if the authority of the forum conducting such verification were to find that the said requirements were not met.[53]

Under BIR, the person against whom enforcement is sought (debtor) is entitled to apply for refusal of enforcement (and recognition) of a judgment if one considers one or more of the following grounds for refusal of recognition[54] to be present: a manifest contradiction with the public policy of the Member State addressed; absence of service of the document instituting the proceedings in sufficient time when the judgment was rendered by default; the irreconcilability of judgments; and a violation of the most important rules on jurisdiction by the court of the state of origin.[55] Moreover, a debtor should, to the extent possible and in accordance with the legal system of the Member State addressed, be able to invoke, in the same procedure, in addition to the grounds for refusal provided for in the regulation, the grounds for refusal available under national law and within the time limits laid down in that law.[56] The grounds for refusal or suspension of enforcement under the

50 See Oberhammer 2010, p. 199.

51 As J. Kramberger Škerl states, 'Exequatur was abolished in the narrow sense of the word, i.e. only the granting of declaration of enforceability.' See Kramberger Škerl 2016, p. 133.

52 Cuniberti & Rueda 2010, p. 15. In that direction, J. Sladič writes about 'Functional equivalence between the exequatur and recourses in the enforcement stage.' See Sladič 2013, p. 329, 354.

53 Cuniberti & Rueda 2010, p. 16.

54 The grounds for refusal of enforcement are the same as foreseen in Article 45 for non-recognition.

55 Article 45 BIR.

56 Recital 30 BIR.

law of the Member State addressed shall apply in so far as they are not incompatible with the grounds referred to in Article 45.[57] One can argue that it is not yet clear which grounds of national non-enforcement would not be compatible with the EU grounds. What is clear is that the national grounds for non-enforcement would have to be applied in a non-discriminatory way and should not be viewed as a means of widening the public policy exception.[58] However, under no circumstances may a judgment given in a Member State be reviewed as to its substance in the Member State addressed.[59]

It must be noted that according to BIR, the application for refusal of enforcement shall be submitted to the court which the Member State concerned has communicated to the Commission pursuant to point (a) of Article 75 as being the court to which the application is to be submitted.[60] The procedure for refusal of enforcement shall, in so far as it is not covered by BIR, be governed by the law of the Member State addressed.[61] Except for the principle of deciding without delay,[62] BIR does not give any answers as to the manner in which the courts verify the grounds for refusal under BIR (but also under national law), nor does it provide an answer to the question of whether the procedure for deciding on an application for refusal of enforcement is a unilateral or an adversarial procedure.[63] Nevertheless, it is quite clear that the design of this procedure is crucial to the practical effectiveness of BIR.

Academics and commentators argue over the different manners in which the courts verify the grounds for refusal under BIR. Generally, three avenues seem possible: (1) to decide on the grounds for enforcement as a preliminary (incidental) question within the enforcement proceeding, (2) to decide on these grounds together with the objections to enforcement under the national law, and (3) to have a separate procedure independent of the enforcement proceeding.[64] In Isidro's opinion, from a procedural point of view, the simplest solution would be to allow for the grounds of refusal provided for in Article 45 to be argued within the enforcement proceeding itself. However, this possibility may not be compatible with the provisions of the regulation itself, as it would imply that the enforcement proceedings would be different in the same Member State according to whether the enforceable title is a national or a foreign one. That is why a different, new procedure seems necessary.[65] By contrast, in Mankowski's opinion, the fact that the court cannot confirm the grounds for refusal *ex officio* does not eliminate the possibility of the Member States regulating the procedure for the refusal of

57 Article 41(2) BIR.
58 Beaumont & Walker 2015, p. 38.
59 Article 52 BIR.
60 Article 47(1) BIR. The information on the courts that have jurisdiction to decide on an application for refusal of enforcement, as well as on legal remedies against the decision on such application, are available on the European E-Justice Portal <https://e-justice.europa.eu/content_brussels_i_regulation_recast-350-en.do>, last accessed 3 June 2019.
61 Article 47(2) BIR.
62 Article 49 BIR.
63 Kramberger Škerl 2016, p. 136.
64 See Kramberger Škerl 2016, p. 134. See also Requejo Isidro 2016, p. 77 *et seq*.
65 Requejo Isidro 2014.

enforcement as an incidental procedure within the enforcement proceeding. No obligation ensues from BIR for the states to create a specific remedy only for the refusal of enforcement. Furthermore, it would be contrary to procedural economy if the debtor were compelled to initiate two proceedings if one wanted to invoke grounds for refusal of different origin, i.e. under the Regulation and under the national law.[66] It should be noted that even the creation of an autonomous European verification procedure has been mentioned.[67]

Regarding the question of whether the procedure for refusal of enforcement should be unilateral or adversarial, there is no explicit provision, so it seems that BIR is in favour of an adversarial procedure. According to BIR, the court may dispense with the production of the documents by the applicant (a copy of the judgment and, where necessary, a translation or transliteration of it) if it already possesses them or if it considers it unreasonable to require the applicant to provide them. In the latter case, the court may require the other party to provide those documents,[68] which suggests the participation of the creditor at this stage of the proceeding, giving an opportunity for *inter partes* arguments about the enforcement of the judgment.[69]

Conversely, BIR clearly states that both parties can lodge an appeal against the decision on the application for refusal of enforcement. The appeal is to be lodged with the court which the Member State concerned has communicated to the Commission pursuant to point (b) of Article 75 as the court at which such an appeal is to be lodged.[70] BIR gives the opportunity for a second appeal, but it is up to the Member State to decide whether to have it or not. Namely, the decision given on the appeal may only be contested by an appeal where the courts at which any further appeal is to be lodged have been communicated by the Member State concerned to the Commission pursuant to point (c) of Article 75.[71]

Under BIR, the application for refusal of enforcement may impact the actual enforcement of the foreign judgment. Upon the request of the debtor, the court of the Member State addressed is given the following options: to limit the enforcement to protective measures, to make enforcement conditional on the provision of such security as it shall determine or to suspend the enforcement proceedings. By the same token, suspension of enforceability in the Member State of origin entails the suspension of enforcement proceedings in the Member State addressed.[72] As a result, the enforcement of the foreign decision, even if it is a final one, may become provisional.[73]

Finally, the last element that has to be mentioned in this short overview is the possibility to adapt a measure or order unknown in the state of enforcement.

66 Mankowski 2015, p. 1117, 1119.
67 Cuniberti & Rueda 2010, p. 21.
68 Article 47(3) BIR.
69 For such interpretation, see Briggs 2015, p. 687.
70 Article 49 BIR.
71 Article 50 BIR.
72 Article 49 BIR.
73 Requejo Isidro 2016, p. 75.

Considering the variety of means of enforcement in the national laws of the Member States, and for the purposes of a 'functional equivalence',[74] BIR states that if a judgment contains a measure or an order which is not known in the law of the Member State addressed, that measure or order shall, to the extent possible, be adapted to a measure or an order known in the law of that Member State which has equivalent effects attached to it and which pursues similar aims and interests. However, such adaptation shall not result in effects going beyond those provided for in the law of the Member State of origin. The adaptation of a measure or order can be challenged before a court by either party.[75] Apart from these provisions, BIR does not clear up the manner of adapting foreign measures, nor does it specify by whom it should be done, which is an aggravating factor in the application of BIR. The manner of adapting measures or orders unknown in the state of enforcement itself has already been identified as 'a very complex legal question demanding a good knowledge of comparative law and often of a foreign language.'[76] It has raised many sub-questions that the national laws have to deal with, such as: Is there a need for a specialised authority for that purpose (especially for the purpose of unified case law)? Who will have to take the initiative for the adaptation? What would be the interplay between the adaptation procedure and the enforcement procedure? and many other procedural issues.

4. The implementation of BIR in Macedonian law

Undoubtedly, EU membership implies simplification in mutual civil and commercial relationships. Hence, immediately after EU accession, the existing regime of cross-border enforcement in civil and commercial matters in Macedonia will experience substantial changes. BIR will be directly applicable, which entails a good knowledge of its provisions, objectives and background. However, it should not be overlooked that BIR considerably relies on the implementation of provisions of the national law which it requires on many issues. The text of BIR suggests that most of the activities which have to be undertaken at the national level affect the Member States as the states of enforcement, even though some of them are addressed to the Member States of origin. Relevant legislative activities on the national level are needed.[77] By the same token, the application of BIR in Macedonia as a future Member State requires further actions by Macedonian lawmakers.

Before we begin with the elaboration of these actions, we would like to point out the following assumptions. In light of the above analysis, the application of BIR

[74] Requejo Isidro 2014.
[75] Article 54(1) and (2) BIR.
[76] Kramberger Škerl 2016, p. 138.
[77] The experiences of the Member States are quite different. The most attentive States made the necessary changes in their national laws even before BIR came into effect on 10 January 2015. For instance, the implementing provisions applicable in Germany were set forth in the new Sections 1110-1117 of the German Code of Civil Procedure of 2014, in Poland in the new addition to the third part of the Code of Civil Procedure, Volume four (Article 1153[13]-1153[24]) of 2014, in the Netherlands in the Dutch Act of 2 July 2003, as amended on 22 January 2014.

in Macedonia will evidently result in judicial officers being directly contacted, skipping the national courts for the purpose of recognition and obtaining a declaration of enforceability. Still, the relevance of enforcement proceedings in the context of the application of BIR cannot be considered separately from the system of judicial control of enforcement and is largely determined by it.

To begin with, the first intervention that has to be made in the Enforcement Act is in Article 8 of the EA, which states that enforcement of a foreign court decision or administrative decision or decision of another foreign authority or enforcement of foreign public instruments may be carried out in Macedonia provided that such decision or instrument fulfils the recognition and enforcement requirements established by law or international treaties ratified in accordance with the Constitution of the Republic of Macedonia or a directly applicable EU legal instrument.[78]

A further set of amendments will affect the enforcement titles. Court judgments from EU Member States, court settlements and public documents falling within the scope of BIR shall be included in the list of enforceable titles set forth in Article 12 of the EA, provided that the title coming from a Member State has already been granted a certificate of enforceability in that state. Hence, the granting of an additional confirmation of enforceability in Macedonia will not be required.

A decision has to be made on the competent authority to issue the certificate, according to Article 53 of BIR, accompanying the decision to be enforced abroad if Macedonia is the Member State of origin. But let us first clear up some important issues.

Article 53 of BIR refers to 'the court of origin', but it does not specify who within that court is competent to carry out the certification. Furthermore, the wording 'the court of origin' also raises the question as to whether it can be interpreted extensively. The Court of Justice of the EU has already had the opportunity to decide on a similar question (regarding Article 6(1) of Regulation (EC) No. 805/2004 of 21 April 2004 creating a European Enforcement Order for Uncontested Claims) and ruled that, 'Article 6 of Regulation No. 805/2004 must be interpreted as meaning that the certification of a judgment as a European Enforcement Order, which may be applied for at any time, can be carried out only by a judge.'[79] The ECJ held that

> in view of the scheme of Regulation No. 805/2004, it is possible to distinguish between the certification, as such, of a judgment as a European Enforcement Order, and the formal act of issuing the certificate, referred to in Article 9 of that regulation. ... that formal act, after the decision regarding certification as a European Enforcement Order has been taken, is not necessarily an act that has to be carried out by the judge, and

78 Cf. with the existing text of Article 8 EA, *supra* n. 23.

79 Case C-300/14, *Imtech Marine Belgium NV v. Radio Hellenic SA* [2015], para 50.

> may therefore be left to the registrar. By contrast, the actual certification itself requires a judicial examination of the conditions laid down by Regulation No. 805/2004.[80]

However, in the context of BIR control has been preserved in the state of enforcement and no review as to the substance is imposed in the state of origin (in particular in regard to the rights of the defence). Therefore, it seems that there would be no problem if the competence to carry out the certification is given to a judicial officer or a notary. Some EU Member States clearly support this view in light of the implementation of these rules. For example, in France, the application for certification of a judgment has to be addressed to the chief registrar of the court of origin,[81] but when authentic instruments are in question, the President of the Chamber of Notaries is competent.[82] In Germany, the notary and the judicial officer, who are functionally competent to issue an enforceable copy, also have the authority to draw up the certificate of enforceability.[83]

The above considerations lead us to the conclusion that, regarding the competent authority to issue the certificate according to Article 53 of BIR, extensive changes to the EA need not be carried out. It will be sufficient to stipulate that the same rules for issuing the confirmation of enforceability of a domestic title will apply for issuing the certificate according to Article 53 of BIR.[84] The competent authority (court or other authority that decides on the claim in first instance procedure) will examine the conditions of enforceability under the national law. Given that in line with Article 43, para 1 of BIR the service of the certificate of enforcement is executed by the Member State of enforcement, there is no need to foresee a provision in the EA on this issue if Macedonia is the state of origin. However, when Macedonia is the Member State addressed, it should be foreseen that the judicial officer to whom a judgment from another Member State is presented for enforcement shall serve the debtor a certificate issued according to Article 53 in the Member State of origin, along with a translation, if the debtor so requests.[85]

Another crucial issue concerning the certificate of enforceability is connected with the possibilities of its repeal or withdrawal. The lack of any provision on this issue in BIR should not be understood as an exclusion of these possibilities. Actually, the national legal systems of the Member States do envisage these possibilities, and usually the same mechanism as for domestic titles is applied, either by express statutory provision or analogously.[86] In regard to this, in order to remove the uncertainties it should be foreseen by the Macedonian lawmakers that the provision of the previously mentioned Article 12(3) of the EA shall apply also to the certificate according to Article 53 of BIR. As in the domestic debt recovery

80 *Ibid.*, paras 45-46.
81 Article 509(1) French Code of Civil Procedure.
82 Article 509(3) French Code of Civil Procedure.
83 Section 1110 German Code of Civil Procedure.
84 See, e.g., Article 42a Slovenian Enforcement and Security Act.
85 See, e.g., Article 1153[17] Polish Code of Civil Procedure.
86 See, e.g., Article 42c Slovenian Enforcement and Security Act.

process, it should be foreseen that if the certificate of enforceability is repealed in the Member State of origin, this shall represent a ground for cessation of the enforcement.

As discussed above, a non-mandatory procedure for review of the foreign judgment is established by BIR: it would be up to the person against whom enforcement is sought to apply for such a review. According to BIR, the verification of the grounds for refusal of enforcement in the state of enforcement relies highly on national procedural rules. As a future EU Member State, Macedonia has to communicate to the European Commission the court to which an application for refusal is to be submitted, but also has to determine the whole mechanism on how to invoke the grounds for refusal of enforcement and what the procedure will be upon such an application.[87]

Since enforcement in Macedonia is entrusted to a non-court authority and there is no stage of permitting enforcement by the court, indisputably the verification of the grounds for refusal of enforcement shall not be possible as an incidental question within the enforcement proceedings. Therefore, a separate court procedure should be created, parallel to the enforcement proceeding. This means that the debtor should be given the possibility to file an application (request) for the refusal of enforcement independently from a pending enforcement proceeding. It further implies that this request can only be lodged if there is an actual enforcement proceeding being carried out.

In regard to jurisdiction, it seems that it would be consistent with the Macedonian legal system to vest the first instance courts with powers to deal with the applications (requests) for refusal of enforcement.[88] Two main reasons go in favour of this solution: first, the first instance courts have jurisdiction to deal with recognition and enforcement of foreign judgments under PILA, and, secondly, they also have jurisdiction to control the validity of all enforcement acts carried out by judicial officers. As stated above, they decide on complaints regarding irregularities in enforcement, which is currently the only legal remedy for judicial control over enforcement (without taking into account the subsequent appeal). A territorially competent court should be determined on the basis of the criterion where the enforcement is carried out. Thus, all claims and applications regarding enforcement (including refusal of enforcement) should be submitted to the same court.[89]

As to the characteristics of the procedure for deciding on an application for refusal of enforcement, several issues should be mentioned. BIR clearly indicates

87 In addition to the application for refusal of enforcement, the debtor shall have an opportunity to use other remedies of protection provided for in the EA.

88 This is also the case in the majority of EU Member States. Namely, according to the E-Justice Portal of the EU, the majority of Member States notify the Commission of the jurisdiction of first instance national courts for deciding on the application for refusal of enforcement.

89 See Cuniberti & Rueda 2010, p. 21, who explain that in a model of enforcement proceedings where judicial involvement is not mandatory, but depends on the debtor, one could envisage assigning such verification to the court having general jurisdiction to control the validity of all enforcements acts in the relevant jurisdiction, pointing out not only some EU Member States, but also the example of Switzerland.

that the procedure for verification of the grounds for refusal of enforcement has a non-suspensive nature.[90] An application for refusal of enforcement would not impact immediate enforceability of the judgment. Thus, notwithstanding the application for refusal of enforcement being lodged, the enforcement proceedings should, in principle, be executed by the judicial officer. This is also the case with the current complaint (objection) against enforcement irregularities in purely domestic cases. On the application of the debtor, the court may limit the enforcement to protective measures, make enforcement conditional on the payment of a security, or suspend the enforcement, either wholly or in part. However, the procedure for deciding on the refusal of enforcement should not lead to automatic suspension of enforcement. In addition, as mentioned before, even though BIR does not expressly provide for it, it somehow indicates the adversarial nature of this procedure. In our opinion, it would be reasonable if Macedonian lawmakers were to provide adversarial proceedings for deciding on requests for refusal of enforcement. Since the aim of this procedure will be to verify the grounds for refusal of enforcement asserted by the debtor, both parties (creditor and debtor) should be given the opportunity to participate and share their perspectives, and the court will have a chance to decide on the basis of the allegations and evidence provided by both of them.[91]

Under Article 49 of BIR, both parties can lodge an appeal against the decision on the application for refusal of enforcement. Macedonia will have to notify the Commission of which court will have jurisdiction to decide on such an appeal. Consistent with the opinion that the first instance court should deal with the application for refusal of enforcement and the adversarial character of this procedure, the appellate courts in Macedonia, as second instance courts, should have jurisdiction on the appeals against the decisions upon the application for refusal of enforcement. Although BIR provides for a second appeal, within the Macedonian system of civil enforcement, it is difficult to find arguments for such an expanded possibility of review in the course of enforcement proceedings. Namely, the system of legal remedies in Macedonian enforcement proceedings is quite simple and it comprises only the complaint against enforcement irregularities and subsequent appeal. No further means of recourse are allowed.[92] The same situation exists under PILA for the procedure for recognition and enforcement of foreign court decisions. Therefore, in our opinion there is no need to provide for one more appeal in regard to the procedure for refusal of enforcement.

Having in mind the aforementioned, one can argue that the existing mechanism of review of the validity of enforcement acts in Macedonia can be used for the purpose of controlling the conditions for enforcement of foreign judgments.[93] This might be true in terms of having the same scheme for seeking verification of the requirements of enforcement, whether it is a domestic case or a cross-border

90 Article 44 BIR and also Recital 31.

91 For instance, the procedure for refusal of enforcement is adversarial in Germany. See Section 1115(4) German Code of Civil Procedure.

92 Article 87(8) EA.

93 See Cuniberti & Rueda 2010, p. 21.

case. This somehow seems to be in line with the suggestion that it is reasonable to decide on the grounds for refusal of enforcement under BIR together with the complaints against enforcement under the national law. The justification for merging these two remedies and procedures seems strong, but only at first sight. Seen against the background of the existing model of judicial control over enforcement, the merging of these two remedies and procedures may entail considerable changes to the actual procedural practice in Macedonian courts and go beyond the present scope of judicial control. And the most important change is whether from the substantial point of view the verification of the grounds for refusal of enforcement under BIR can match with verifying the validity of enforcement acts carried out by judicial officers. It seems that some of the grounds can be envisaged as compatible, such as the ground that the debtor has already paid the amount required in the judgment or the debtor is too poor to be able to satisfy the full amount of the judgment without his or his family being made destitute.[94] A deeper analysis will show whether the debtor will be able to invoke national grounds for non-enforcement in the same procedure with EU grounds, as Recital 30 of BIR strongly encourages.

It seems that the adaptation of unknown foreign measures will be the most problematic issue to deal with while implementing BIR. Although the judicial officers are established as a separate legal profession with the highest standards in terms of legal and professional background and appropriate process of selection, we are not very optimistic about the solution to give the authority for adapting unknown enforcement measures to the judicial officers. So far the judicial officers perform enforcement only by virtue of national law. Hence, the lack of expertise on such a complicated issue, which involves knowledge of foreign laws, is more than evident. It can be assumed that the judicial officers might proceed with the necessary adaptations directly only in cases where such adaptation does not raise any paramount questions. Otherwise it seems that court intervention will be needed. Furthermore, the enforcement proceeding, as it is designed now, is not suitable for dealing with such a question.

However, we are also not fully confident that the first instance courts and their judges, who carry out the control over the enforcement, will be ready for such a task. Dealing with enforcement in a European context, and especially with the adaptation of unknown enforcement measures, requires knowledge of comparative law, and the ability to compare different legal systems and apply their provisions accordingly. Macedonian judges do not dispose of much experience in this field. Knowledge of foreign languages is another crucial issue, for both judges and judicial officers. In regard to this, even if it is foreseen that the procedure for adaptation will be entrusted to the first instance courts (on whose territory the enforcement is carried out), much effort should be undertaken in order to gain adequate expertise on this issue.

[94] Article 5 EA.

5. Final remarks

A natural sense of patriotism motivates the author of this contribution to firmly believe that the application of BIR in Macedonia will happen soon. One of the paramount questions that will affect the success of the process of EU accession is whether Macedonia can inspire the trust of the European Commission as to the quality of the Macedonian judiciary and the procedures applied by the judges to deliver judgments. An adequate level of enforcement proceedings for providing effective and reasonably swift implementation of court judgments and the quality of the national judicial officers is also crucial. In this respect, although the country has achieved some level of preparation for applying the *acquis* and EU standards in the areas of the judiciary and human rights, and legal and institutional frameworks are largely in place,[95] it seems that Macedonia still has serious issues regarding judicial reform at the domestic level. Additional efforts have to be made in order to adjust to the rules with respect to protecting and effecting rights in the European judicial area, including the provisions of BIR.

The above discussion clearly and optimistically shows that in regard to the implementation of BIR, no extensive changes to Macedonian enforcement proceedings need to be carried out. Generally speaking, the changes will be more subtle adjustments to the Brussels regime. Of course, as was indicated in the Introduction, this contribution does not intend to give the final word on the subject matter. On the contrary, the proposals in this contribution are worded in an open way so as to leave room for different opinions, better alternatives or answers to a number of unresolved questions. As it always happens, the devil is in the details, and therefore this contribution calls for a more dynamic analysis. Let us be encouraged by the fact that even some older Member States are still working on coherently implementing provisions in their national laws.

On the other hand, in spite of the work on the statutory framework, much more effort has to be made in the field of training and expertise of Macedonian judges and judicial officers. At the moment, their level of expertise for cross-border enforcement is fairly low. Certainly, over the years the level of maturity in dealing with cross-border cases and application of EU instruments will grow. Still, since this is a long-running process, there is no time for hesitation and delay in starting systematic training comprising 'best practices' in the Member States related to the application of BIR as well as the complementing regulations.

95 See 2016 Progress Report on the former Yugoslav Republic of Macedonia, COM (2016) 715 final, available at: <https://ec.europa.eu/neighbourhood-enlargement/sites/near/files/-pdf/key_documents/2016/20161109_report_the_former_yugoslav_republic_of_macedonia.pdf>, last accessed 3 June 2019.

References

Alavi & Khamichonak 2015
Alavi, H. & Khamichonak, T., 'A Step Forward in the Harmonization of European Jurisdiction: Regulation Brussels I Recast', *Baltic Journal of Law & Politics*, 2015, Vol. 8(2), p. 159-181.

Baumgartner 2014
Baumgartner, S.P., 'Recent Reforms in EU Law: Recognition and Enforcement of Foreign Judgments', *Judicature*, 2014, Vol. 97, p. 188-195.

Beaumont & Walker 2015
Beaumont, P. & Walker, L., , 'Recognition and Enforcement of Judgments in Civil and Commercial Matters in Brussels I Recast and some Lessons from it and the Recent Hague Conventions for the Hague Judgments Project', *Journal of Private International Law*, 2015, Vol. 11(1), p. 31-63.

Briggs 2015
Briggs, A., *Civil Jurisdiction and Judgments*, Abingdon Oxon, New York: Informa Law from Routledge, 2015.

Cuniberti & Rueda 2010
Cuniberti, G. & Rueda, I., 'Abolition of Exequatur. Addressing the Commission's Concerns', *University of Luxembourg Law Working Paper* No. 2010-03, 2010, available at: <http://ssrn.com/abstract=1691001>.

Deskoski 2008
Deskoski, T., 'The New Macedonian Private International Law Act of 2007', *Yearbook of Private International Law*, 2010, Vol. 10, p. 441-458.

Dickinson & Lein 2015
Dickinson, A. & Lein, E., *The Brussels I Regulation Recast*, Oxford: Oxford University Press, 2015.

García 2010
García, R.A., 'Abolition of Exequatur: Problems and Solutions. Mutual Recognition, Mutual Trust and Recognition of Foreign Judgments: Too Many Words in the Sea', *Yearbook of Private International Law*, 2010, Vol. 12, p. 351-375.

Gottwald 1991
Gottwald, P., 'Internationale Zwangsvollstreckung', *IPRax*, 1991, p. 285-292.

Janevski & Zoroska-Kamilovska 2011
Janevski, A. & Zoroska-Kamilovska, T., *Gradjansko prosesno pravo, kniga treta, izvrshno pravo*, Skopje: Faculty of law 'Iustinianus Primus', 2011.

Kramberger Škerl 2016
Kramberger Škerl, J., 'Certain Open Issues Regarding the Refusal of Enforcement Under the Brussels I Regulation in Slovenia', in: V. Rijavec (ed.), *24th Conference Corporate Entities at the Market and European Dimensions (May 19th-21st 2016, Portorož, Slovenia, Conference Proceedings)*, Maribor: University of Maribor Press, 2016, p. 131-144.

Kramer 2011
Kramer, X.E., 'Abolition of Exequatur under the Brussels I Regulation: Effecting and Protecting Rights in the European Judicial Area', *Nederlands Internationaal Privaatrecht*, 2011, p. 633-641.

Mankowski 2015
Mankowski, P., in: T. Rauscher (ed.), *Europäisches Zivilprozess- und Kollisionsrecht, Kommentar, Brüssel Ia-VO, Band I, EuZPR – EuIPR*, Cologne: Sellier, Verlag Dr Otto Schmidt, 2015.

Oberhammer 2010
Oberhammer, P., 'The Abolition of Exequatur', *IPRax*, 2010, p. 197-203.

Requejo Isidro 2014
Requejo Isidro, M., *Recognition and Enforcement in the new Brussels I Regulation (Regulation 1215/2012, Brussels I Recast): The Abolition of Exequatur*, 2014, available at: <http://www.ejtn.eu/PageFiles/6333/Requejo_Doc.pdf>.

Requejo Isidro 2016
Requejo Isidro, M., 'The Enforcement of Monetary Foreign Final Judgments under the Brussels Ibis Regulation (A Critical Assessment)', in: V. Lazić & S. Stuij (eds.), *Brussels Ibis Regulation – Changes and Challenges of the Renewed Procedural Scheme – Short Studies in Private International Law*, The Hague: TMC, Asser Press, 2016, p. 71-95.

Schlosser 2010
Schlosser, P., 'The Abolition of Exequatur Proceedings – Including Public Policy Review?', *IPRax*, 2010, p. 101-104.

Sladič 2013
Sladič, J., 'The Remedies and Recourses in European Civil Procedure after the Intended Abolition of the Exequatur', *ZeuS*, 2013, p. 329-358.

Zoroska-Kamilovska 2012
Zoroska-Kamilovska, T., 'Reforms of Civil Enforcement Systems in the Countries of Southeastern Europe: From common tradition to different concepts', *ZZPInt*, 2012, p. 315-343.

Zoroska-Kamilovska 2014
Zoroska-Kamilovska, T., 'Dutch Influence on the Reform of the Macedonian System of Civil Enforcement', *Tijdschrift voor Civiele Rechtspleging*, 2014, p. 27-31.

Zoroska-Kamilovska & Rakočević 2016
Zoroska-Kamilovska, T. & Rakočević, M., 'A General Overview of Enforcement in Civil and Commercial Matters in Macedonia', *LeXonomica*, 2016, Vol. 8(1), p. 29-49.

www.ingramcontent.com/pod-product-compliance
Ingram Content Group UK Ltd.
Pitfield, Milton Keynes, MK11 3LW, UK
UKHW051921100926
8556IPUK00021B/1310

9 781780 687773